1987

Logical Introduction to Databases

John Grant
Towson State University

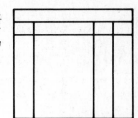

Harcourt Brace Jovanovich, Publishers
and its subsidiary, Academic Press

San Diego   New York   Chicago   Austin   Washington, D.C.
London   Sydney   Tokyo   Toronto

to my
teachers

Cover Photo: NASA

ISBN: 0-15-551175-0
Library of Congress Catalog Card Number: 86-80765

Printed in the United States of America

Preface

Logical Introduction to Databases began out of a desire to teach my students some important topics not covered in existing textbooks. I wanted my students to learn about some of the exciting new developments concerning database systems. These included the emergence of database systems on microcomputers for people who are not computer professionals, the beginning of the Fifth Generation Computer Systems Project in Japan, the applications of logic to database systems, the increasing popularity of fourth-generation languages, the use of databases in nontraditional areas, and the increased attention given to such issues as time and incomplete information for database systems.

I cover the major standard topics for database systems: database models, design, components, and implementation in the first seven chapters. Chapters 8–10 show the wide range of the applications of logic to databases. Some additional topics of interest are covered in Chapter 11; Chapter 12 deals with a number of specific database systems. The book contains more material than can be covered comfortably in one semester, giving the instructor considerable leeway in picking the topics to be studied. The minimum prerequisite is experience with a high-level programming language, such as COBOL or Pascal, and some knowledge of fundamental data structures.

Numerous exercises, many with several parts, are included at the end of each chapter so that students can practice the concepts and methods introduced in the chapter. An Instructor's Manual, containing answers to many of the exercises, is available. In addition to the exercises, some instructors may wish to assign longer projects, such as a more complex design problem or the implementation of a small database system.

The book contains a large number of examples which illustrate the uses of various languages and concepts. In fact, it should be possible in most cases just to work through the examples without studying the formal rules or definitions. These rules and definitions are included to make the book useful for reference. In particular, many of the formal syntax rules for NDL (Network Database Language) and SQL (Structured Query Language) are included using BNF notation.

iii

The word "logical" in the title of the book can be interpreted in several ways. The conceptual aspects of databases are usually called the "logical" aspects, as opposed to the file handling aspects, which are considered "physical." This book emphasizes the logical rather than the physical aspects of databases. Another meaning for "logical" refers to the fact that applications of logic to databases are emphasized. Finally, "logical" may be used in the ordinary sense of doing something in a logical manner. I believe that this book provides a truly logical introduction to databases.

Each chapter contains several references for additional reading. I have kept the number of references small and have included primarily books and survey articles, which contain additional references. My teaching practice is to place several books on the reserve list in the library, and at various times I suggest that students read certain chapters or sections from those books.

Synopsis

Chapter 1, although important, can be covered rapidly. Chapter 2 deals with the network database model. An important recent development for the network model is the 1986 standardization of NDL (Network Database Language). A large portion of the formal syntax for NDL is included in this chapter. It is not necessary, however, to study the formal definitions; most of the important topics are illustrated in the examples. Chapter 3 presents the hierarchic model, stressing the concepts in the IMS system. An instructor could restrict the course to the relational model by skipping Chapters 2 and 3 and some portions of later chapters.

The coverage of the relational database model begins in Chapter 4, which covers the relational algebra and SQL. Many books present the relational algebra using subscripts and Greek symbols, making the expressions look formidable; the presentation here uses English words for the operations. For SQL I did not completely follow the new ANSI syntax because it is oriented towards the embedded language.

Chapter 5 contains database design theory for the relational model and introduces the entity-relationship model. Algorithms are given for a lossless join decomposition to Boyce-Codd Normal Form as well as a lossless join and dependency preserving decomposition to Third Normal Form. I have also included a discussion of multivalued and inclusion dependencies as well as Fourth Normal Form and Domain-Key Normal Form. The second part of the chapter deals with the entity-relationship model, which has been found very useful for database design. Section 5.5 may be omitted; it shows how direct manipulation may be possible within the entity-relationship model.

Chapter 6 covers standard material on database components, while Chapter 7 contains topics that are important for database implementation. The first seven chapters can form the basis of a one-semester course on databases. Various topics can then be covered from the last five chapters as time permits. (Chapter 5 is not a prerequisite for studying Chapter 6 and Chapter 7; also, Sections 7.1 and 7.5 can be studied earlier in the course.)

The next three chapters form the logic unit, showing the applications of logic to databases. Chapter 8 begins with introductory material on first-order logic. Then the relational calculus is presented as the language based on first-order logic. The first two sections should be covered before going on to additional material on logic, even if the rest of Chapter 8 is not covered. In fact, the rest of Chapters 8–10 is not required for the remainder of the book, except for Section 11.4.

Except for the last section, Chapter 9 is mainly a continuation of the applications of logic to relational databases. Deductive databases extend the expressive power of relational databases by allowing implicitly defined relations. The notion of deductive database is formalized in logic. The bulk of Chapter 9 concerns Prolog, a language based on first-order logic, within which deductive databases can be defined. Prolog has been gaining prominence, partly because it was chosen as the foundational language for the Fifth Generation Computer Systems Project. It is not necessary to cover all of sections 9.1 and 9.2; the material on theorem proving can be skipped for those who did not go over Section 8.4. The last section of this chapter considers the problem of natural language interfaces to databases. This section is not dependent on logic and can be read independently of the material on logic.

First-order logic is useful for the formalization of many aspects of databases, as shown in Chapters 8 and 9. In fact, first-order logic can be used as a database definition language and a database query language for relational and deductive databases. In Chapter 10, an extension of first-order logic, called database logic, is shown to provide such a language for hierarchic and network databases. The other topic of Chapter 10 concerns database transformations. Such transformations include database normalization, the construction of external views, and database conversion. Database transformations can also be expressed in logic: first-order logic for relational databases and database logic if a hierarchic or network database is involved. In fact, logic provides a universal language for expressing database concepts.

Finally, Chapter 11 discusses some database issues, while Chapter 12 deals with specific database systems and languages. All of this material is optional and can be read in any order.

BNF Notation

BNF (Backus-Naur Form) is a notation used for describing the syntax of a programming language. In this book, much of the syntax of several database languages is given in an extended version of BNF. The following material provides an introduction to the symbols of BNF, using some examples from Figure 2.2.1 for illustration. The objects enclosed in angle brackets are the names of nonterminal symbols; these objects are the ones defined by the syntax rules. Terminal symbols are defined as themselves; they are the primitive objects and so do not require definitions. Keywords such as SCHEMA and RECORD as well as other symbols such as the period (in the definition of the nonterminal symbol "component identifier") are terminal symbols.

The terminal and nonterminal symbols are symbols in the language. BNF also contains meta-symbols: symbols that describe the syntax rules. The meaning of the meta-symbol "::=" is "is defined as." Each BNF definition starts with the nonterminal symbol to be defined. This symbol is followed by "::=". The part of the definition after "::=" provides the actual syntax rule for the construction of the nonterminal symbol. Alternatives are listed by separating them with a vertical bar, "|". For example, the nonterminal symbol "relation" is defined as being "<" or "<=" or "=" or ">=" or ">" or "<>".

Frequently it is convenient to use additional meta-symbols. The following are used in this book. Objects in square brackets, "[ ]", indicate optional elements. For example, a "component identifier" may have a qualifier followed by a period, but that is not required. Braces, "{ }", are used for grouping. For example, in the definition of "sorted order," SORTED must be followed by DUPLICATES. These two keywords are then followed by one of four possible keywords. Finally, the three dots, "...", stand for elements that may be repeated. For example, in the definition of "condition," the optional phrase "OR <alternative>" may be repeated.

Guide to the Database Literature

The purpose of this section is to inform the reader about those publications which are devoted to the subject of databases. In particular, the *ACM Computing Surveys* periodically contains interesting survey articles on databases. The *ACM TODS (Transactions on Database Systems)* and *Information Systems,* the latter published by Pergamon Press, are two important journals for database research. *Data Based Advisor* is a monthly magazine which contains information about microcomputer-based database systems. Members of the ACM SIGMOD (Special Interest Group on Management of Data) receive the *SIGMOD Record,* while members of the IEEE Computer Society Technical Committee on Database Engineering receive the *Database Engineering Bulletin.* Both of these publications appear on a quarterly basis and contain announcements and articles.

There are several ongoing, regularly held database conferences at which papers are presented describing database research. The proceedings of these conferences present a valuable guide to research directions.

The main conferences are the ACM-SIGMOD International Conference on Management of Data and the International Conference on Very Large Data Bases (VLDB), both of which have been held annually since the mid-1970s. The proceedings of the latter are now available through Morgan Kaufmann Publishing Corp. Since the early 1980s, two new conference series, the ACM SIGACT-SIGMOD Symposium on Principles of Database Systems, and the International Conference on Data Engineering, the latter sponsored by the IEEE Computer Society, have been held on an annual basis.

Several fairly recently established journals and conferences also deal with logic programming and Fifth Generation Computer Systems. *The Journal of Logic Programming* and *Future Generations Computer Systems* are published by North-Holland; *New Generation Computing* is published by Springer-Verlag. Another recent journal on databases is *Data & Knowledge Engineering*, published by North-Holland. *Expert Systems*, published by Learned Information, and *IEEE Expert* are both devoted to the expert systems area. During the last several years the Symposium on Logic Programming and the International Conference on Logic Programming have become yearly events. Several international conferences have also been held in recent years on the Entity-Relationship Database Model, Fifth Generation Computer Systems, and Expert Database Systems.

Acknowledgments

I want to express my thanks to all those individuals who helped me, directly or indirectly, in the preparation of this book. I am particularly grateful to the following reviewers for their many excellent comments and suggestions: Carl Cagan, California State University at Fullerton; Jesse H. Ruder Jr., Austin Community College; Glenn N. Thomas, Kent State University; and Maria Zemankova, Department of Computer Science, University of Tennessee, Knoxville. I greatly appreciate the important assistance given to me by some of my students in connection with the exercises. The comments and questions from many of my students were helpful in a general way. I must certainly thank all those people who sent me material: research papers, product information, and standardization drafts. Family members, colleagues, and friends encouraged me in my efforts. Many people at Harcourt Brace Jovanovich gave my project strong support and skillfully transformed my manuscript into a book: the acquiring editor, Richard J. Bonacci; the manuscript editor, Bill Teague; the production editor, Christopher B. Nelson; the designer, Cheryl A. Solheid; the production manager, Sharon Weldy; and others. Also, I could not have done this work without the insight I gained about databases by discussing the subject with experts, reading books and articles, listening to lectures, and conducting research into this fascinating subject.

For twenty years, starting out as a boy studying to read and write in first grade and ending up as a Ph.D. candidate completing a dissertation in graduate school, I had the privilege of learning from a diverse group of fair, kind, and caring individuals. During this time I missed the opportunities to express my appreciation for their influence on my life. Therefore, it is quite fitting for me to dedicate my work on this book to my teachers.

John Grant

Contents

Chapter 1

Basic Database Concepts

1.1 Introduction

It is only in recent years that the great impact of information on organizations and individuals has been recognized. Previously, people used to deal primarily with tangible assets whose value could be appraised with reasonable precision. Money in the bank is an example of such assets. But also, the value of real estate, furniture, machinery, and so on can be figured out without too much difficulty. The value of information is harder to pin down exactly, but nonetheless can be enormously important. It's hard to place an exact figure on the value of a potential customer list for a real estate company, but such a list could be worth a great deal. Information on rock formations and previous oil drillings in a certain area of potential oil wells could be highly useful. Information about an individual's credit history may be very important to a bank considering the extension of a personal loan. The list of possibilities seems endless.

Computers process data to derive information, and data is stored in many cases in databases. Complex software called **database systems** or **database management systems** (abbreviated as **DBMS**) have been written which *allow for the convenient storage and retrieval of data in order to provide information*. The topics of this book are the concepts and techniques involved in database systems. We will look at some of the historical developments, the main problems, and some proposed solutions in an attempt to discover where we are today and what we can expect in the future. Over the last decade, and even within the last several years, great progress has been made. It seems that more and more people are using database systems every day. Until a few years ago, database systems were used almost exclusively in large organizations on mainframes and mini-computers. Today, many people interact with database systems on micro-computers for personal and business applications.

It is necessary to understand many basic concepts involving computer systems before a serious study of database systems can be attempted. Although it is assumed that the reader understands these concepts, we will review some of them here. We start by considering files because they are the basic components of database systems. We do this through an example. Consider the EMPLOYEE file of Figure 1.1.1. This file contains data that represents information about the employees of a company. Our examples will be unrealistic in that a real employee file might contain thousands of entries, while our examples will have only a few, but they will be used to illustrate various ideas.

Files *contain data or information.* Sometimes a distinction is made between the words "data" and "information," with the former meaning the raw data while the latter referring to data that is used or interpreted in some context. We will not necessarily make such a distinction in the use of these words. There are many ways to think of the data in a file. Files are usually stored on an external device such as a disk or tape. One way to describe a file is through its bit pattern. Although that is a true representation of the actual file, the pattern of bits by itself is not meaningful to people. The way that data is encoded and organized is usually considered the *physical aspect* of data representation. In contrast to this, the meaning of the data in a format like the one shown in Figure 1.1.1 is called the *logical aspect* of the data. In this book we will emphasize the logical aspects of data as opposed to the physical aspects.

Note in Figure 1.1.1 that there is a special row on top, (ID, NAME, ADDRESS, TELNO, SALARY, SEX), which gives information about the types of objects present in the file. The elements in this top row are called

FIGURE 1.1.1
An EMPLOYEE File (Table)

ID	NAME	ADDRESS	TELNO	SALARY	SEX
111111111	Smith J	160 York Rd	123-4567	22500	M
222333444	Jones B	2100 North St	256-1178	24750	F
778866555	Roberts K	278 South Ave	779-0500	31005	M
555555555	Ford L	5308 Peach Ave	555-5555	27594	M
234567890	Cramer T	666 First St	444-8822	30575	F

attributes or **field names.** The actual data is given in the rest of the rows. Each row contains related information about a particular entity, in this case about an employee. Each column contains values for the attribute associated with that column. Thus the value "M" is meaningful for the attribute SEX, but would not be meaningful for the attribute SALARY.

Since we visualize files as two-dimensional objects with rows and columns, we will often refer to them as **tables,** but will continue to use the term "file" in some cases where that is standard terminology. We note that sometimes *file* is used to refer to data in external storage, while *table* is used to refer to storage in memory. We will not make such a distinction. We wish to point out that we will not be dealing with text files, such as files containing computer programs. We would not think of such a file as a table because there is not necessarily any relationship between the objects in the same column, and the rows may be incomparable. Thus for our purposes, files are data files presented in a tabular format.

We now come to the distinction between schema and instance. The **schema** *describes the structure of the tables,* namely the *attributes,* the *types of values* allowed for each attribute, and the *relationships* between the tables in the database. For example, meaningful values for the SALARY attribute are numbers, not letters. An **instance** of the database *describes the contents of the files (tables).* Figure 1.1.1 represents an instance of the EMPLOYEE file. So does Figure 1.1.2. These two database instances, each consisting of a single table, have the same schema. Sometimes when the word "database" or "file" or "table" is used by itself, we may wonder if the schema or the instance is meant. We will generally use the word for the instance rather than the schema.

Database systems usually require a **type declaration** for each attribute in the schema. For example, the type for ADDRESS may be all character strings of length 20. In our tables for the instances, we will not show the padded blanks at the end of the strings; these are often compressed by the database system anyway.

FIGURE 1.1.2
Another EMPLOYEE File (Table)

ID	NAME	ADDRESS	TELNO	SALARY	SEX
345234123	Byron B	258 Second Ave	333-4444	30085	F
543876098	Wolf C	3578 Bright Rd	654-3210	28950	M
667788990	Turner W	555 Fifth Ave	333-4100	25005	M
234567890	Cramer T	666 First St	444-8822	30575	F

Next we indicate some additional terminology involving files. Each row in a file is called a **record.** So, for example,

```
<111111111 | Smith J | 160 York Rd | 123-4567 | 22500 | M>
```

is a record. Each individual item within a record is called a **field** or **field value.** Thus, "Smith J" is a field value, and so is 22500. Recall that the pictures in Figures 1.1.1 and 1.1.2 are simply a convenient (logical) representation of the information in the file. As with files, sometimes there is confusion between the *description* of a record (or field) and an *instance* or *occurrence*. We will mainly use these terms to signify the instance. We will not consider in any detail the questions of where exactly the records and fields are located and what kinds of encodings are used. These are file implementation problems which we will briefly consider in Chapter 7. Our approach is to concentrate on the logical aspects.

Files have been in use for a long time for storing information. Manual files continue to be in wide use, while electronic files have been around since the beginning of the development of computer technology. Modern computer operating systems contain various routines for file management. Commonly used programming languages like BASIC, COBOL, FORTRAN, Pascal, and PL/I all have built-in routines for managing files. That is, a programmer writing a program in such a language can create, modify, and manipulate files by using specific statements in the language.

Let's see now what problems come up as application programs are developed using different files in an organization. We will take the following example of a university database given in Figure 1.1.3 to illustrate the situation. The Payroll Office uses an EMPLOYEE file for the payroll system which contains data needed for payroll processing. The Registrar has a grade-reporting system which uses a STUDENT file and a GRADE file to send the students their grades at the end of each semester. The Scheduling Office has a course-scheduling system which uses a student REQUEST file and a COURSE file. The Office of Academic Affairs uses an INSTRUCTOR file for its merit-awards system to pick possible candidates for merit pay.

Let us assume that all of these systems are working fine individually. But suppose that at the time of course scheduling we would like to know the previous grades or the grade point average (GPA) of students requesting a particular class. All of the information is available. The previous grades are in the STUDENT file owned by the Registrar for the grade-reporting system, while the course-scheduling system deals with the requests and courses. However, it may not be easy at all to put together the information from these files. One reason is that different programs may have been written in different languages using different file structures. Perhaps the grade-reporting system was written in COBOL using indexed sequential files, while the course-scheduling system was written

FIGURE 1.1.3
Application Programs and Files

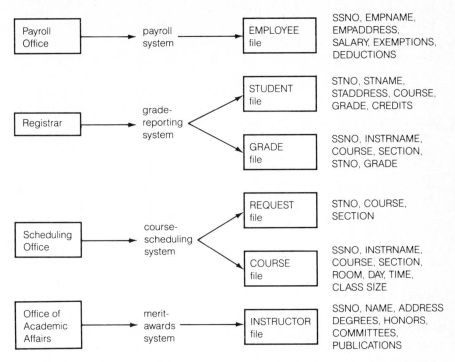

in PL/I using a regional file structure. Even the individual items may have been encoded differently, perhaps one using ASCII code and the other one using EBCDIC code.

This leads to a situation where all the data necessary to answer a question is available, scattered in various files; yet it is difficult to actually get the answer. If the answer is needed immediately, but substantial programming effort must be exerted to provide the answer, we have an information extraction problem. Another possible problem is data duplication, which can lead to data inconsistency. Note that both the Payroll Office and Academic Affairs have files which contain information about instructors. What happens when an instructor moves? Perhaps the Payroll Office is notified about the change of address. But that does not necessarily mean that Academic Affairs is also automatically notified. So for an instructor we may get two different addresses, depending on which file we search. Such data inconsistencies can lead to errors at worst and contradictions at best.

Now let's review how the university manages its data. Various individuals own related data in files accessed by their programs. This can lead to data duplication, with its consequent inconsistencies, as well as great difficulty in putting together information from different files accessed by different programs. We would really prefer to separate the data and the programs. This would allow us to have a consistent format for the data, a format on which any and all programs can operate.

Database (management) systems were introduced to do exactly this. Consider Figure 1.1.4. All the data is handled by a DBMS. The programs must interface with the DBMS to get to the data. The DBMS enforces a separation of programs and data alleviating the problems mentioned above. Since the DBMS handles all the data, it can integrate it in some convenient format. It should be considerably easier now to share information between different offices because in some sense all the information (outside of security concerns) can be made available to everyone. As a matter of fact, the integration of the data can lead to *increased* security because security standards can be centrally enforced. Data consistency and integrity become easier to attain when the information exists in one place without (or with minimal) duplication. Finally, the users need not concern themselves with the physical aspects of storage structures; they can view files as we did in Figures 1.1.1 and 1.1.2 and concentrate on the information itself rather than encodings and storage manipulations.

There may be several different categories of users for a database system. **End-users** *are people who use the information that is in the database,* typically without having to write programs. Many times programmers prepare specific programs for such end-users which they can use to generate reports or get information on the screen of a terminal. Also, many systems have user-friendly query languages that can be used without the need for writing complex programs. Some systems, particularly ones on microcomputers, prepare menus or forms for users to guide them through an application. In the last several years, many companies have established an Information Center to help their employees retrieve and use information. While an Information Center may make different types of software (including spreadsheet and word processing systems) available to people, database systems typically form an important component.

It is usually necessary to have application programmers available for database systems, particularly ones on large computers. In many cases, the **application programmers** *prepare complex requests for end-users.* Large organizations often set up an office for a **database administrator (DBA)** who then *administers the database system.* Application programmers are often on the staff of the DBA. The DBA must set up the storage structures for the files, authorize people to use (perhaps portions of) the system, help them by writing programs, set priorities, enforce procedures in the case of system failures, monitor database use, and, in general, take care of the problems that come up in managing the database system. It is a complex job. Since, as we mentioned above, data is extremely valuable, the position of DBA is one of high importance and responsibility.

FIGURE 1.1.4
Applications Handling Files by a DBMS

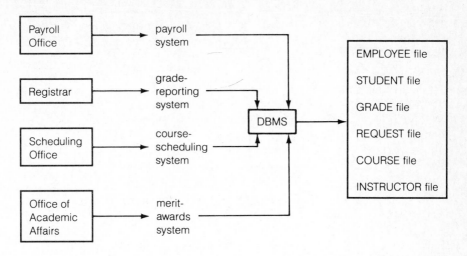

In the rest of this chapter, we introduce the basic concepts involved in database systems. In Section 1.2 we discuss a standard database architecture. In Section 1.3 we classify database systems by how they handle relationships between files. In Section 1.4 we discuss the languages used to communicate with a database system. Section 1.5 contains some remarks concerning historical developments and prospects for the future. Finally, in Section 1.6 we consider various important issues concerning database systems.

1.2 The Three-Level Architecture

In this section, we introduce an architecture for database systems that is based on the one proposed by the ANSI/SPARC Study Group on Data Base Management Systems in 1975. (This group was set up by the American National Standards Institute in the early 1970s to consider standardization activity for database systems.) Not all database systems actually conform to this architecture; nevertheless, it provides a useful framework for investigating such systems. The basic idea of this architecture is illustrated in Figure 1.2.1. (A mapping is a transformation; here it is used between different levels in the database architecture.) There are three levels: external, conceptual, and internal.

The **conceptual view** *contains the structure of the entire database without concern for the physical implementation aspects.* Thus, the conceptual view

FIGURE 1.2.1
The Three-Level Database Architecture

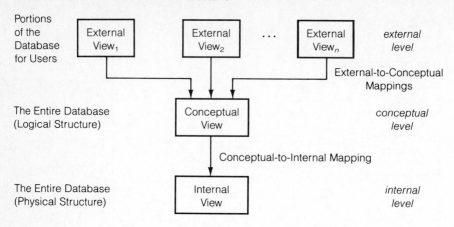

must contain all the relevant tables in the database and represent the relationships between them. Sometimes the conceptual view is called the community user view. The conceptual view is at the conceptual level. The description of the conceptual view in a database language is called the **conceptual schema.** Because the term "view" is often used for such a description, that is, the schema, we use "view" in that way also.

Now let's go back to our example of a database system handling several files for a university database (as illustrated in Figure 1.1.4) and construct a conceptual view based on it. As we will see later, there are various methods for representing the relationships between files and there are different languages for describing a conceptual view. For now, we describe the conceptual view in an informal manner in Figure 1.2.2. We first write down the six files with the corresponding attributes. For example, we have a STUDENT file where each record occurrence contains a value for STNO, STNAME, STADDRESS, COURSE, GRADE, and CREDITS. We also indicate the types of the attributes. In this case there are only two types, string and numeric.

Finally, we write the constraints. These **constraints** *deal with data integrity and with relationships between files.* For example, Constraint 2 indicates that STNO uniquely determines the attributes STNAME and STADDRESS in the STUDENT file. The database system should enforce such a constraint and so should not allow conflicting data, such as two different names or addresses to be entered about a student. Note that the second part of this constraint indicates that no matter how many times a particular COURSE value appears in the file, the number of

FIGURE 1.2.2
A Conceptual View

```
VIEW   UNIVERSITY

FILES              ATTRIBUTES
  EMPLOYEE           SSNO,EMPNAME,EMPADDRESS,SALARY,
                     EXEMPTIONS,DEDUCTIONS
  STUDENT            STNO,STNAME,STADDRESS,COURSE,GRADE,
                     CREDITS
  GRADE              SSNO,INSTRNAME,COURSE,SECTION,STNO,
                     GRADE
  REQUEST            STNO,COURSE,SECTION
  COURSE             SSNO,INSTRNAME,COURSE,SECTION,ROOM,
                     DAY,TIME,CLASSSIZE
  INSTRUCTOR         SSNO,NAME,ADDRESS,DEGREES,HONORS,
                     COMMITTEES,PUBLICATIONS
TYPES
  STRING             SSNO,EMPNAME,EMPADDRESS,STNO,STNAME,
                     STADDRESS,COURSE,GRADE,INSTRNAME,
                     SECTION,ROOM,DAY,TIME,DEGREES,HONORS,
                     COMMITTEES,PUBLICATIONS
  NUMERIC            SALARY,EXEMPTIONS,DEDUCTIONS,CREDITS,
                     CLASSSIZE
```

Constraints

1. In the EMPLOYEE file each SSNO value uniquely determines the EMPNAME, EMPADDRESS, SALARY, EXEMPTIONS, and DEDUCTIONS values. Also, each pair of SALARY and EXEMPTIONS values uniquely determines the DEDUCTIONS value.
2. In the STUDENT file each STNO value uniquely determines the STNAME and STADDRESS values. Also, each COURSE value uniquely determines the CREDITS value. Also, each pair of STNO and COURSE values uniquely determines the GRADE value.
3. In the GRADE file each SSNO value uniquely determines the INSTRNAME value. Also, each pair of COURSE and SECTION values uniquely determines the SSNO value. Also, each pair of COURSE and STNO values uniquely determines the SECTION and GRADE values.
4. In the REQUEST file each pair of STNO and COURSE values uniquely determines the SECTION value.
5. In the COURSE file each SSNO value uniquely determines the INSTRNAME value. Also, each pair of COURSE and SECTION values uniquely determines the CLASSSIZE value.
6. In the INSTRUCTOR file each SSNO value uniquely determines the INSTRNAME, DEGREES, HONORS, COMMITTEES, and PUBLICATIONS values.
7. Each SSNO in the COURSE file and in the INSTRUCTOR file must appear in the EMPLOYEE file, and the corresponding NAME, EMPNAME, and INSTRNAME values, as well as the corresponding ADDRESS and EMPADDRESS values, must be identical.
8. Each STNO in the GRADE file and in the REQUEST file must appear in the STUDENT file.

CREDITS associated with it should always be the same. The enforcement of Constraint 7 assures us that the INSTRUCTOR and EMPLOYEE files cannot have inconsistent data concerning a faculty member's name or address. Such a constraint also indicates a relationship between these two files.

The conceptual view is a logical representation of the database. A database system must also be given information about the physical structure of the files. Files may be organized in different ways; depending on these organizations the database must use specific routines in order to access and manipulate the files. We will briefly discuss file organization in Chapter 7. *The structure of the entire database at the physical level is the* **internal view.** In this book we will concentrate on the logical level and will therefore not deal much with the internal view.

Going in the other direction from the conceptual level we come to the external level, which is the level of the users of the database system: the end-users and application programmers. In general, most users are interested in only a portion of the database. An **external view** *is the structure of the database as seen by a user and is described by an* **external schema.** We will describe three possible external views (write the external schemas, that is) for the example conceptual view given above. We will use the same notation as for the conceptual view.

The first view is given in Figure 1.2.3(a). This may be the view needed by the Payroll Office to process payroll. This external view is simply a subview of the conceptual view. Namely, it contains one of the files, EMPLOYEE, with all the attributes it had in the conceptual view. The types are the same as before for the conceptual view. There are two constraints: the determination of the various attributes based on the SSNO value and the determination of deductions based on SALARY and EXEMPTIONS. The constraints are inherited from the conceptual view.

The second view is given in Figure 1.2.3(b). This may be a view needed by the Registrar to process grade reports. This view is not a simple subview of the conceptual view, because the STUDENT and GRADE files do not contain all the attributes from the conceptual view. In particular, the GRADE file does not contain the STNO attribute. This apparent omission is taken care of by the second constraint, which states that each GRADE record is uniquely associated with a STUDENT record. The first constraint again is one inherited from the conceptual view. Note also that some attributes have been renamed: STNAME to NAME and STADDRESS to ADDRESS.

The third view is given in Figure 1.2.3(c). This view contains primarily the REQUEST file of the conceptual view. However, it has an additional attribute, GPA, not present in the conceptual view. The grade point average must be computed from data in the conceptual view; however, to the user, GPA appears as just another attribute. Also, the order

FIGURE 1.2.3
External Views

(a) The Payroll Office

```
VIEW   PAYROLL

FILES              ATTRIBUTES
  EMPLOYEE         SSNO,EMPNAME,EMPADDRESS,SALARY,
                   EXEMPTIONS,DEDUCTIONS
TYPES
  STRING           SSNO,EMPNAME,EMPADDRESS
  NUMERIC          SALARY,EXEMPTIONS,DEDUCTIONS
```

Constraints
In the EMPLOYEE file each SSNO value uniquely determines the EMPNAME, EMP-ADDRESS, SALARY, EXEMPTIONS, and DEDUCTIONS values. Also, each pair of SALARY and EXEMPTIONS values uniquely determines the DEDUCTIONS value.

(b) The Registrar

```
VIEW   GRADE-REPORTS

FILES              ATTRIBUTES
  STUDENT          STNO,NAME,ADDRESS
  GRADE            COURSE,SECTION,GRADE
TYPES
  STRING           STNO,NAME,ADDRESS,COURSE,SECTION,GRADE
```

Constraints
1. In the STUDENT file each STNO value uniquely determines the NAME and ADDRESS values.
2. Each record in the GRADE file is uniquely associated with a record in the STUDENT file.

(c) The Scheduling Office

```
VIEW   REQUEST

FILES              ATTRIBUTES
  STUDENTREQUEST   COURSE,SECTION,STNO,GPA
TYPES
  STRING           COURSE
  NUMERIC          SECTION,STNO,GPA
```

Constraints
In the STUDENTREQUEST file each STNO value uniquely determines the GPA value.

of the attributes in STUDENTREQUEST is different from their order in the original REQUEST file. The constraint for this external view involves the attribute GPA.

From these examples we can see that the files of an external view are obtained from the files of the conceptual view, but that the attributes may be rearranged and even additional attributes can be introduced as shown in the last example. In practice, some database systems which follow the three-level architecture may have restrictions on the methods of view construction and may not allow some of the changes we made to the conceptual view. Assuming that users work with external views, a number of steps must be taken by the database system to serve the users. These steps are illustrated in Figure 1.2.4. A query or a command (such as an update) is written by a user on the external view. This must be translated to queries or commands on the conceptual view which in turn must be translated to the internal view.

We now describe informally the external-to-conceptual mappings for the three views that we created above. The first mapping is just the identity mapping from the Payroll view to the University view for the EMPLOYEE file. In the second case, some attributes must be renamed, but the major change is the change in the association of the STUDENT and GRADE files. In the third case, the order of the attributes of the STUDENTREQUEST and REQUEST files are not the same and so must be changed, and a procedure needs to be given for the computation of the GPA on the external view. These three cases are illustrated in Figure 1.2.5. We will discuss such external-to-conceptual mappings in greater detail in Chapter 10.

Let us consider the advantages of the three-level architecture. *The separation of the conceptual view from the internal view means that we can give a logical description of the database without the need to be involved with storage structures.* This leads to what is called **physical data independence.** Let's suppose that the database administrator wishes to change the structure of certain files for the sake of efficiency. Perhaps an indexing is to be

FIGURE 1.2.4
The Transformation of User Requests

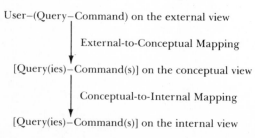

User–(Query–Command) on the external view

        External-to-Conceptual Mapping

[Query(ies)–Command(s)] on the conceptual view

        Conceptual-to-Internal Mapping

[Query(ies)–Command(s)] on the internal view

FIGURE 1.2.5
External-to-Conceptual Mappings

(a) External View: Payroll
     Conceptual View: University
     Mapping: Map an EMPLOYEE record for Payroll to the corresponding EMPLOYEE
              record for University.

(b) External View: Grade-reports
     Conceptual View: University
     Mapping: Map a STUDENT record for Grade-reports to the corresponding STU-
              DENT record for University after renaming STNAME to NAME, and
              STADDRESS to ADDRESS.
              Map a GRADE record (associated with a STUDENT record) to the corre-
              sponding GRADE record for University by including the STNO value from
              the STUDENT record.

(c) External View: Request
     Conceptual View: University
     Mapping: Map a STUDENTREQUEST record for Request to a REQUEST record for
              University by a proper permutation of the attributes and map the GPA
              attribute to a procedure in University which computes the GPA of a student
              using his or her grades in all courses taken.

added. The conceptual view need not be changed. Only the internal view
is changed as well as the conceptual-to-internal mapping. Programs that
have been written for use on the conceptual view (or which have been
translated by the external-to-conceptual mapping) need not be changed.
Let's contrast this situation with the situation using file management.
Since the file management programs are written using specific commands that depend on the file structure, any change in the file structure
requires that all the programs written for that file must be rewritten.
This work may take a great deal of time and introduce errors in a previously bug-free program.

The advantage of separating the external view from the conceptual
view is called **logical data independence.** This *refers to the fact that it is
possible to change the conceptual view without having to make changes to programs
written for external views.* In many cases, it becomes necessary to add new
files or to add new attributes to existing files as the database system
becomes more widely used and additional data is entered into the database. Fortunately, the only change needed is in the external-to-conceptual mappings. Of course, if a user who has a particular external view
wishes to use new attributes or files, he or she must either set up a new
external view or modify the old external view. If the first option is taken,
then no changes need to be made to the programs on the old external view.

1.3 The Three Major Database Models

We now examine in more detail the conceptual and external views. Such views consist of a group of interrelated files. The primary difference between the three major database models is in the way that the relationships between the files are expressed. These relationships are usually represented as graphs or trees, and so we start by reviewing some basic definitions and concepts involving these objects.

A **graph** *consists of a set of nodes (or vertices) and a set of edges.* Figure 1.3.1(a) is an example of a directed graph. The nodes are marked as *A, B, C, D*. The edges are indicated by lines between the nodes. In a directed graph, each edge, indicated by a line, has an arrow at one end, indicating the direction of the edge. (Since all of our graphs and trees will be directed, we will use "tree" or "graph" when we mean "directed tree" or "directed graph," respectively.) Often the node where the line originates is called the **parent node** while the node near the arrow is called the **child node.** In this case, there are edges from *A* to *B*, from *D* to *B*, from *B* to *C*, and from *D* to *C*. A **cycle** in a graph is a sequence of edges following the arrows that starts and ends at the same node. The graph in Figure 1.3.1(a) has no cycles, but if we added an edge from *C* to *A* we would get a cycle: *A* to *B*, *B* to *C*, *C* to *A*. A **tree** *is a special type of graph: it has no cycles, and no node has more than one parent* (edge leading into it). Thus, the graph in Figure 1.3.1(a) is not a tree because *B* has two parents (the same is true for *C*). Figure 1.3.1(b) is a tree. Note that for a tree a node may have more than one child, like *A*, but at most one parent.

Graphs and trees are very useful in representing relationships between objects. They are used a great deal in computer science. We use graphs and trees in this section to represent relationships between files. Typically, there are three types of relationships between two files (that is, between records in the two files): one-to-one, one-to-many (the reverse of which is many-to-one), and many-to-many. In Figure 1.3.2, we give an example of each such relationship.

FIGURE 1.3.1
A Graph and a Tree

(a) A graph

(b) A tree

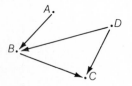

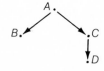

Figure 1.3.2(a) illustrates a one-to-one relationship. The two files are called STUDENTCOLLEGEINFO and STUDENTHIGH-SCHOOLINFO. They contain information about college students, with the second file containing information about the high schools from which the students graduated. Thus one record from one file is associated with a unique record from the other file if the two records contain the identical STNO value.

Part *(i)* of Figure 1.3.2(b) illustrates a one-to-many relationship. The two files are called EMPLOYEE and JOBHISTORY. An employee may have worked for zero, or one, or more companies previously. So possibly many records of the second file are associated with one record of the first file. We say that the relationship is one-to-many from EMPLOYEE to JOBHISTORY and represent it by the picture given in part *(ii)* of Figure 1.3.2(b). We can think of this picture as a graph (tree in this case) with the file names marking the nodes and the edge representing the

FIGURE 1.3.2
Relationships between Files

(a) One-to-one

```
FILES                          ATTRIBUTES
  STUDENTCOLLEGEINFO             STNO,SNAME,SADDRESS,GPA
  STUDENTHIGHSCHOOLINFO          STNO,HIGHSCHOOLNAME,
                                 HSAVERAGE,SATSCORE
```

(b) *(i)* One-to-many

```
FILES                          ATTRIBUTES
  EMPLOYEE                       E#,NAME,ADDRESS,SALARY,AGE
  JOBHISTORY                     COMPANY,DATES-OF-
                                 EMPLOYMENT,JOBTITLE
```

(ii) Data structure diagram

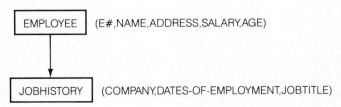

(c) Many-to-many

```
FILES                          ATTRIBUTES
  TEACHER                        SS#,TNAME,POSITION,DEPT
  STUDENT                        SSNO,SNAME,ADDRESS,TELNO,
                                 CLASSIFICATION
```

one-to-many relationship. This picture is a modified version of what is called a **Bachman diagram** (named after C. W. Bachman, who initiated the use of this type of diagram). We will call this type of picture a **data structure diagram.** If there are more files with additional one-to-many relationships, the data structure diagram may become a complex graph.

Figure 1.3.2(c) illustrates a many-to-many relationship. The two files are called TEACHER and STUDENT. A relationship exists between a teacher record and a student record if the teacher teaches that student. Because a teacher may have many students and a student may have several teachers, we obtain the many-to-many relationship.

The three major data models—network, hierarchic, and relational—differ in the way that relationships are represented between files. The network and hierarchic models allow the direct representation of one-to-many relationships in the form of a data structure diagram as explained above. The difference between these two models is in the structure of the data structure diagram. For the **network model** *the data structure diagram can be any graph.* The **hierarchic model** *restricts the data structure diagram to be a tree.* We will see later how a graph can be transformed to a tree for the hierarchic model, as well as how to deal with many-to-many relationships, which cannot be directly represented in either model. Note that the words "hierarchic" and "hierarchical" are used interchangeably; we will use the former.

In Figure 1.3.3(a), we give the data structure diagram for a hierarchic database view for an insurance company. A state record contains only the name of the state. There may be many offices in any one state. Each office may have many staff members and agents. Each agent has a list of clients. A slight modification of this diagram is given in Figure 1.3.3(b). Each staff member has a personal physician whose name, address, and telephone number are stored in the PHYSICIAN file. Several staff members may have the same physician, so there is a one-to-many relationship between the PHYSICIAN and STAFF files. This diagram is no longer a tree because two edges lead to the STAFF node. Thus it represents a network database view.

The hierarchic and network data models are alike in that they allow two types of objects: the files which are represented as nodes of a graph (tree) and the one-to-many relationships which are represented as the edges of a graph (tree). **Relational databases,** on the other hand, *allow only one type of object: files* (also called relations or tables). Thus, for relational databases there are no separate links between files. One may wonder how it is possible to represent one-to-many relationships in a relational database. The answer is that such relationships are represented implicitly by the attributes of the files.

Let's reconsider part *(ii)* of Figure 1.3.2(b), which represents a one-to-many relationship between an EMPLOYEE file and a JOBHISTORY file. The downward arrow representing the relationship means that, if this is part of a hierarchic or network database, the database system itself

FIGURE 1.3.3
Hierarchic, Network, and Relational Representation

(a) Data structure diagram for a hierarchic database view

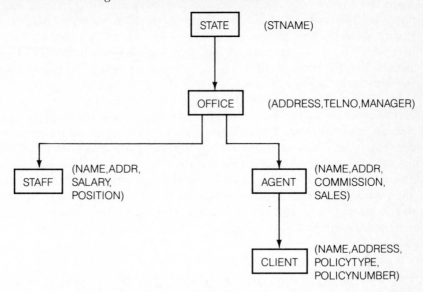

(b) Data structure diagram for a network database view

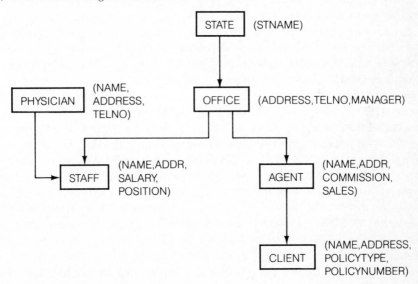

(c) Relational representation of a one-to-many relationship

```
FILES                ATTRIBUTES
   EMPLOYEE          E#,NAME,ADDRESS,SALARY,AGE
   JOBHISTORY        E#,COMPANY,DATES-OF-
                     EMPLOYMENT,JOBTITLE
```

stores this relationship. Therefore it is possible to query the system for the JOBHISTORY records associated with a particular EMPLOYEE record or for the EMPLOYEE record associated with a particular JOB-HISTORY record. In Figure 1.3.3(c), we indicate the relational representation. We assume that an E# value uniquely determines an EMPLOYEE record. Note that we placed the E# value into every JOBHISTORY record. Thus now we can find the relationship between EMPLOYEE and JOBHISTORY records, even in the absence of explicit links, by looking for the identical E# values.

We end this section by pointing out that over the years many different database models have been proposed. In this book, we will emphasize the relational model because it is the predominant model at the present time. However, the hierarchic and network models are also important because several important database systems use them. We will discuss these three major database models in Chapters 2, 3, and 4. In Chapter 5, we will also take a look at the entity-relationship model, one that is particularly useful for database design, and which is the model for some recent database systems.

1.4 Communication with Database Systems

In this section, we discuss and classify the types of languages that are used to communicate with database systems. An understanding of these classifications will help us to distinguish among the different types of database systems themselves. A database language often has two components: the **data definition language (DDL)** and the **data manipulation language (DML).** The DDL is used to declare the files for the conceptual view—that is, to write the conceptual schema. Later, a programmer can write database programs (in the DML) that work *on* the files without having to declare them. Let's consider briefly what type of information needs to be expressed in the DDL (as part of the schema). In a sense, we already considered the DDL in Section 1.2 when we discussed the three-level architecture and gave examples of views. We described these views in an informal, ad hoc language which also illustrates what is needed for the DDL. Referring back to Figure 1.2.2, we see that the DDL must allow the naming of files, their attributes, and the types of these attributes. In addition, the DDL should provide facilities for expressing constraints. In particular, for a hierarchic or network database the DDL should allow some description of the data structure diagram for indicating the relationships between files.

In general, users of database systems use their own external views rather than the conceptual view. Thus the DDL must allow for the definition of external views (the external schema) as well. This is not really a problem since external views contain the same kinds of objects as a conceptual view: files, attributes, types, and constraints. However, associated with each external view there must be a mapping of the external view to the conceptual view. We illustrated such mappings in Figure 1.2.5. Sometimes the definition of the external view along with the mapping is written in a language called the subschema DDL. If there is only one DDL, then it can be used both by the database administrator to describe the conceptual view and by users for describing their external views.

The conceptual view is a logical description of the database, while the internal view is a physical description of the database. A language is needed for the database administrator to describe the internal view (the internal schema). This may be the same as the DDL mentioned above, or it may be a different DDL. In any case, it must allow for the definition of the conceptual-to-internal mapping. Once the internal view and the conceptual-to-internal mapping are defined, they are not affected by users creating or modifying external views.

In addition to the data definition language, we need a language for manipulating the database. If each user has an external view then we may assume that a DML needs to be defined for the manipulation of external views only. There are several different ways in which DMLs may be classified. (Note that we have already classified database languages one way: DDL and DML.)

First we distinguish between queries and updates. This is not really a language classification because DMLs usually contain both query and update statements. However, it is a useful distinction to make. A **query** *is a question for the database.* For example, for the Payroll view of Figure 1.2.3, a query may ask for the name and address of an employee given an SSNO value. This is illustrated in Figure 1.4.1(a). Updates themselves can be classified in three ways. An **update** *may be an insertion, a deletion, or a modification.* (In the database literature the term "update" is often used to refer to modification only.)

In Figure 1.4.1(b), we give an example of an insertion, a deletion, and a modification for the same view. In the case of the deletion, we list only the SSNO value, meaning that all rows for the employee with that social security number are to be removed. It is important to observe that an update usually changes the database (unless, for example, we try to insert something that is already there), while a query does not. In many cases, some users are restricted to querying a database and are not allowed to change it or may be allowed only one type of update, such as insertion, but not another, such as deletion.

Next we distinguish database languages (both DDL and DML) in the way that they are or are not tied to a host programming language. There are two possibilities. A database language may be a **stand-alone language** not related to any programming language, or it may be tied to a programming language in some way. First we consider those which are stand-alone languages. In some cases a stand-alone language is primarily

FIGURE 1.4.1
Query vs. Update

(a) A query

```
GET EMPNAME AND EMPADDRESS FOR SSNO='123456789' IN
  EMPLOYEE
```

(b) Updates

(*i*) An insertion

```
INSERT INTO EMPLOYEE
  <123456789,Smith H,250 York Road,27650,4,288>
```

(*ii*) A deletion

```
DELETE FROM EMPLOYEE
  <123456789,...>
```

(*iii*) A modification

```
MODIFY IN EMPLOYEE
  FROM
  <123456789,Smith H,250 York Road,27650,4,288>
  TO
  <123456789,Smith H,250 York Road,28550,4,305>
```

a query language for users who wish to quickly query their database view. However, a stand-alone language for a database system may itself incorporate both data definition facilities and programming language constructs, such as loops and selection statements, thus allowing use of a single language for all interactions with the database system. Stand-alone languages for database manipulation are relatively recent and are predominant among database systems used for microcomputers.

Most database languages used for mainframe database systems interface in some way with **standard (host) programming languages.** COBOL, FORTRAN, PL/I, and Assembler interfaces are most common. These interfaces are primarily for users who are application programmers. The host programming language interface can be achieved in three ways: explicit procedure calls, implicit procedure calls, and native syntax.

The **explicit procedure calls interface** *refers to the calling of special database procedures from a program in the programming language.* Such database procedures are written separately from the program and are processed by the database system. In an **implicit procedure calls interface,** *database statements are written within the programming language using some convention to allow a precompiler to distinguish the database statements from the programming language statements.* Finally, in a **native syntax interface,** *the database facil-*

ities are embedded in the programming language itself. This is actually the situation in stand-alone languages; however, here we are dealing with standard programming languages rather than ones created specifically for database applications. The main example of this case is the proposal to add facilities for database definition and manipulation to the COBOL language.

One topic that we did not mention is the assistance given to the user by the database system in the writing of database programs. All systems that use a specific syntax give error messages if some syntax rule is violated. This is not too important for some recent database systems that use a natural language interface, but even there the system may not be able to handle some statements. Database systems, like language compilers, differ widely in the facilities that they provide for the identification and correction of errors. The technique of providing menus for users can help them avoid many mistakes; however, it may also restrict users to specific, predefined actions. Menus are provided mostly for database systems on microcomputers, which are often used by nonprogrammers.

In the previous section, we discussed the three main data models. The DMLs used for one type of model tend to be quite different from the DMLs used for another type of model. We will deal with such languages in more detail in the next several chapters. Here we just mention that languages which are used with the network and hierarchic models usually take advantage of the associated graph (or tree) structure. So, for example, to find the clients of a particular insurance agent in the database view of Figure 1.3.3(b), one would usually start by finding the specific state, then follow the arrow to find the specific office, again follow the arrow to find the agent, and finally follow the arrow from the agent to obtain the clients.

When a database system uses the relational model, there are no arrows to follow. File relationships are represented in a different way in the relational model. For example, for the database view of Figure 1.3.3(c), if we wish to find the job history of a particular employee, once knowing E#, it is not necessary to (we cannot in fact) follow the arrow in part *(ii)* of Figure 1.3.2(b); we just look in the JOBHISTORY file which now contains the attribute E#. In cases where it is not possible to find all the information in one file, relational database systems allow the use of the **join operation** which *combines the information in two files to create a new file.*

Our final classification is for query languages, and it is related to the dichotomy between the hierarchic and network models on one hand and the relational model on the other. Usually, in the query languages associated with the hierarchic and network models, each command deals with one record at a time. This is a natural extension of file processing in programming languages where a file manipulation statement deals with a single record, finds a record, or updates a record. If such a language is used for the insurance example discussed above, it is necessary to set up a loop, after finding the agent, to find all of the agent's clients. This is illustrated in Figure 1.4.2(a). We call such a query language, which fits into the framework of a high-level programming language, a **low-level query language.**

Relational databases are usually associated with query languages that deal with a *set* of records at a time. We give an example in Figure 1.4.2(b), where one FIND statement is used to find the set of all JOB-HISTORY records—see Figure 1.3.3(c)—given a particular E# value. We call a query language, which allows for the processing of a set of records at a time, a **high-level query language.** Relational database query languages are a level above programming languages. So, while low-level query languages correspond to high-level programming languages, high-level query languages correspond to *very* high-level programming languages. This distinction does not necessarily carry over to update statements, because even for the hierarchic and network models, the deletion of a single record may have a side effect causing the deletion of additional records. Again, for the insurance company example, the deletion of a single agent may cause the deletion of all the clients of that agent as well. This is not a genuine manipulation of a set of records at a time, but the effect is the same.

Traditionally, relational database systems have been associated with high-level query languages, while hierarchic and network database systems have been associated with low-level query languages. However, for interfacing a relational database system with a conventional high-level language, it has become necessary to set up low-level language alternatives. We will show in Chapter 10 that by using the formalism of database

FIGURE 1.4.2
Low-Level vs. High-Level Query Languages

(a) Low-level query language for the network model

```
FIND STATE RECORD (given an STNAME value)
FIND OFFICE RECORD (given an ADDRESS value)
FIND AGENT RECORD (given a NAME value)
FIND FIRST CLIENT RECORD
IF the record exists THEN SET FOUND TO TRUE
WHILE FOUND DO
   FIND NEXT CLIENT RECORD
   IF no such record exists THEN SET FOUND TO FALSE
                            ELSE PRINT CLIENT
   END WHILE
```

(b) High-level query language for the relational model

```
FIND JOBHISTORY RECORDS (given an E# value)
```

logic, it is also possible to extend the high-level query languages used for relational databases in a uniform way to apply to hierarchic and network databases.

1.5 Development of Database Systems

In this section, we consider some of the historical developments that have led to the database systems of today. The operating systems of the 1960s offered several useful file access methods: the three standard methods are sequential, random, and indexed sequential. We illustrate these file structures in Figure 1.5.1.

In a **sequential** file *the records are placed in consecutive locations and must be accessed in the given order.* Sequential files are particularly appropriate for a storage medium like tape or cartridge. But searching such a file tends to be slow since to reach, say, the 98th record, it is necessary to go through the first 97 records (if we start at the beginning). However, sequential files are usually ordered by a key value; thus it is easy to go through all the records of a file based on the key order.

FIGURE 1.5.1
Operating Systems File Access Methods

(a) Sequential

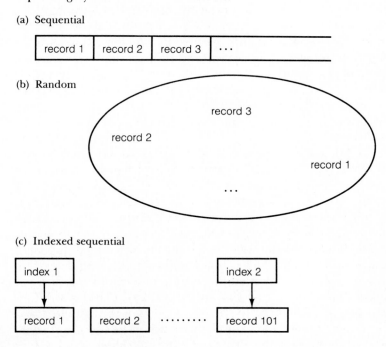

(b) Random

(c) Indexed sequential

Another type of access is **random.** This type of access is *appropriate for a storage medium such as disk or drum.* Random access is usually achieved by the use of a randomizing function that assigns a location to a record by using a key value. Using a random file usually speeds up retrieval relative to a sequential file. A third file structure, **indexed sequential,** *combines the sequential access of sequential files with indexes* (which we will discuss in Chapter 7) to give fast retrieval.

Programming languages like COBOL and PL/I use the file access methods of the operating system for file manipulation. In particular, they have statements for file manipulation using these types of files. During the 1960s a number of file management systems became available. Typically, a **file management system** *has some programming language capabilities and includes report writers, sorting programs, and file handling facilities.* The language used with a file management system may have powerful operators that allow easier programming, up to the capabilities of the file management system. In Figure 1.5.2(a), we show how high-level programming languages and file management systems interact with the file handling facilities of an operating system.

In the late 1960s, the need for database systems became great as the large number of files with relationships between them could not be conveniently handled within programming languages or file management systems. The three major database models were developed at this time. Figure 1.5.2(b) shows that a database system typically uses a more complex file organization put on top of the standard ones available on the operating system.

The hierarchic model was implemented in a database system called **IMS (Information Management System)** by IBM in 1969. IMS became a very important system because many organizations adopted it. IMS is a fairly difficult system to use; it was designed for programmers rather than casual users. However, a hierarchic structure is natural for many applications. (Actually, IMS is not purely hierarchic and can also handle some network structures.)

The network database model was investigated in detail by the **CODASYL (Conference on Data Systems Languages) group,** *a voluntary organization which represents manufacturers and user groups.* CODASYL had been previously responsible for the development of COBOL. CODASYL formed a group called **DBTG (Data Base Task Group),** which produced a report about database systems in 1969 and then a revised report in 1971. This report defined the notions of data manipulation language, schema definition language, and subschema definition language. The schema definition language allowed the writing of a combination of the conceptual view and the internal view. Although DBTG did not define a device/media control language for the description of the storage structures, one was to be defined by an implementation. The subschema definition language allowed for the writing of external views.

FIGURE 1.5.2
Interaction with Operating System File Access

(a) High-level language and file management system

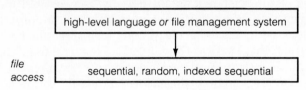

(b) Database system

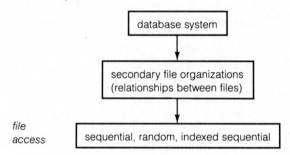

     In the early 1970s, CODASYL decided that the subschema defini-
tion language and the data manipulation language could be added to a
later version of COBOL. This way, a programmer could use COBOL as
a database system language. (Various proposed extensions to COBOL
contain such database features.) Then, in 1978, CODASYL decided that
the schema definition language would be used for defining the conceptual view and that a different language, called a data storage description
language, would be designed for defining the internal view. The data
storage description language replaced the previously mentioned device/
media control language. In fact, during the 1970s, CODASYL made
numerous changes, both major and minor, to the earlier versions.
     A major reason for the splitting of the conceptual and internal view
definitions in the CODASYL proposal was due to the recommendation
of the ANSI/SPARC Study Group in their interim report of 1975. This
report recommended the three-level architecture, suggesting a clear distinction between the internal and conceptual views (as discussed in Section 1.2).
     Several manufacturers and software houses implemented the
CODASYL database proposals in the 1970s. Consequently, a number of
database systems exist which follow these recommendations. Because these
systems were originally implemented in the early 1970s, they tend to
follow the earlier CODASYL proposals rather than the later ones. Toward
the mid- and late 1970s there were suggestions to standardize database

development based on the CODASYL proposals. These suggestions were not adopted, primarily because of the emergence of relational database systems.

The definition of the relational database model is associated with E. F. Codd. Although there were a number of early database attempts in the 1960s using essentially the relational ideas, Codd formalized the major database concepts in several papers starting in 1970. First he showed that the relational model has a theoretical background in the mathematical theory of relations. He also devised two major data manipulation languages to be used with the relational model: the relational algebra and the relational calculus. Additionally, he began the study of the theory of database design recommending the use of third normal form, which we will study in Chapter 5.

In the mid-1970s, several experimental relational database systems were implemented. Efficiency was the main problem in dealing with large databases. This should not be surprising since the languages used with such systems were high-level database languages as opposed to the low-level procedural languages associated with the hierarchic and network database systems. By the end of the 1970s, several efficient implementations of relational systems were available and their ease of use gained favor with database users.

Initially, database systems were implemented for mainframe computers. As minicomputers became more popular and powerful in the mid-1970s, several database systems were implemented for them. In fact, some relational systems were originally implemented for minicomputers. By the beginning of the 1980s, microcomputers became very popular. Since that time, numerous database systems have been implemented for microcomputers. Many people are using database systems directly or indirectly at the present time. Most microcomputer-based database systems use the relational model and are generally used with much smaller databases than the mainframe or minicomputer systems. Microcomputer-based systems tend to stress ease of use for nonprogrammers.

Another recent development has been the introduction of **natural language interfaces for database systems.** These *allow people to use a database system,* usually in a limited way, *without doing anything that resembles the writing of a computer program,* because the system "understands" questions posed to the database in English. Research has also been done in extending other ideas from artificial intelligence to databases to allow the construction of intelligent database systems. Database machines have been built which implement some of the database operations in hardware rather than software. Fourth-generation languages with many interesting and useful features have evolved primarily from database query languages. The aim of the Japanese **Fifth Generation Computer Systems Project** is *the development of knowledge information processing systems which*

FIGURE 1.5.3
Important Database Developments

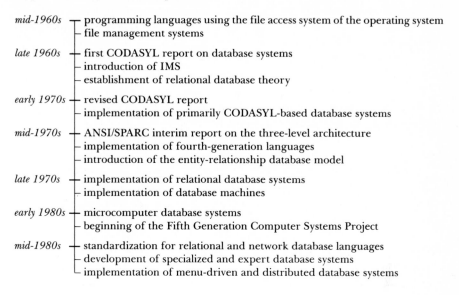

mid-1960s	programming languages using the file access system of the operating system
	file management systems
late 1960s	first CODASYL report on database systems
	introduction of IMS
	establishment of relational database theory
early 1970s	revised CODASYL report
	implementation of primarily CODASYL-based database systems
mid-1970s	ANSI/SPARC interim report on the three-level architecture
	implementation of fourth-generation languages
	introduction of the entity-relationship database model
late 1970s	implementation of relational database systems
	implementation of database machines
early 1980s	microcomputer database systems
	beginning of the Fifth Generation Computer Systems Project
mid-1980s	standardization for relational and network database languages
	development of specialized and expert database systems
	implementation of menu-driven and distributed database systems

involve large intelligent database systems. The database field is a quickly developing one at present. Some important developments in database technology are summarized in Figure 1.5.3.

1.6 Some Important Database Issues

In this section, we discuss some of the important issues dealing with database systems. Later on in the book we will deal with these topics in more detail. We start by considering some of the properties of database systems which fulfill a need not previously addressed and which gave rise to the introduction of database systems. We have already mentioned the elimination of redundancy and inconsistency as important goals. We have also discussed, in connection with the three-level architecture, the importance of data independence, both physical and logical. In this section we concentrate on some other important concepts.

Integrity *deals with the correctness of data.* Although we may not be able to make absolutely sure that all data in the database is correct, at least we can try to flag down incorrect data before it is entered into the database. In Chapter 5, we will consider integrity constraints in greater detail in association with database design. One example of an integrity

constraint is called a key constraint. Such a constraint specifies a particular attribute as a key and (if enforced) does not allow two rows to be
entered in a table with the same key. For example, if employee number
is the key, it would not allow the insertion of two different employees
with the same employee number.

Database **security** has several aspects. There may be confidential
information in a database which only certain individuals are allowed to
inspect. Also, some individuals who inspect the database may not be allowed
to make any changes. Perhaps an employee who has access to all the
salary values in an organization should not be allowed to modify any
salaries. Security aspects are often implemented using passwords and
authorizations.

Database integrity and security are high priorities for database systems. With a centralized database system, it should be easier to maintain
integrity and security than with the older file management systems. However, the recent proliferation of microcomputers has caused some problems in this area. Many individuals can now download data from a central
database system. This is good because it allows them to use this data and
to manipulate it without using up-system resources. Unfortunately, once
data is downloaded, it may be more difficult to keep it secure from unauthorized individuals. Also, since the downloaded data is frozen at the
time of downloading and does not reflect modifications, inconsistencies
may arise between the downloaded data and the real data in the centralized database, as well as between data downloaded at different times.

Although most of the microcomputer database systems at present
are used on an individual basis, for larger databases, particularly on
mainframes and minicomputers, it is necessary to allow many users **concurrent** or **simultaneous access** to the database. This presents a problem
if one user is reading from a portion of the database, while another user
is updating it at the same time. It is possible to obtain incorrect answers
to queries under such circumstances. Usually, the concurrency problem
is solved by locks that are placed on portions of the database, thus locking
out other users for some period of time.

Sometimes systems go down. Therefore it is necessary to have
recovery procedures available for database systems. **Recovery procedures** *usually consist of the creation of backup copies of the database and the
keeping of a log of database changes.* If backup copies are made periodically
and a log is kept, then even if during a system crash the database is lost,
it can be re-created by reloading the database and making the changes
to it from the log. Problems come up in this case, however, in connection
with those programs that are running at the time of the crash.

A database system usually comes with several **utilities.** A loading
utility allows for the loading of the database. A recovery utility is used
after a system crash as explained before. Occasionally, a database must

be reorganized. Often the reorganization is due to changes in the storage structure, but it may be done if the conceptual schema is greatly modified. A journaling utility allows the keeping of a log both for queries and updates to the database. Additionally, a utility may allow for statistical analysis concerning database usage and the use of various system resources.

Some database systems come with a data dictionary; in addition, there exist stand-alone dictionaries. Basically, a **data dictionary** *is a database about the database.* It contains information such as the names of files and their relationships, the names of attributes and domains, and the existence of keys. Thus the data dictionary can be used to look up to see what type of data is in the database. It may also contain synonyms. We will consider security, concurrency, recovery, database utilities, and data dictionaries in Chapter 6.

Originally, database systems were devised to bring together all of the data of an organization in a central facility. But in some cases it is more advantageous to have the data distributed in various computers in various locations without the users necessarily being aware of the distribution, in a **distributed database system.** A simple example is that of a bank with branches in different locations. It is reasonable to distribute the customer accounts according to the locations of the customers. All those problems which we have discussed, such as security, recovery, and integrity, become more complicated when the system is distributed.

The method of storage organization and the order of operations performed by a database system can significantly affect the speed with which the database system responds to user queries. For efficient performance, **query optimization** is an important aspect of database systems. Various computer architectures, called **database machines,** have also been proposed and constructed to facilitate database operations. A database system manages an extremely important resource, the data, in an organization. The administration of this software system is a complex task. We will discuss database implementation, including distributed databases, query optimization, database machines (including aspects of the Fifth Generation Computer Systems Project), and database administration in Chapter 7.

The Fifth Generation Computer Systems Project is a Japanese project which has as its goal the creation of powerful computer systems, ones that include a highly efficient and intelligent database system. We will cover the foundations of intelligent databases, which involve logic and deductions, in Chapter 8; we will then see how such capabilities can be applied to databases. A simple example can illustrate this point for now. If we are given a family relationship which includes the facts "John is the father of Mary" and "Paul is the father of John," then we can deduce that "Paul is a grandfather of Mary" (assuming unique names). We essentially follow a rule concerning the relationships "father" and "grandfather."

We would like a database system to be able to make such deductions. The rule that "the father of a father is a grandfather" should suffice for an intelligent database system without the need for any facts about grandfathers in the database. In Chapter 9, we will discuss properties and examples of intelligent database systems.

Another important topic is **database conversion.** In practice, converting from one database system to another is a complex task. This is particularly so if the database systems use different database models; for example, one may be a network system while the other one is a relational system. Some utilities exist for such a process, particularly from vendors who, having started with a particular type of system and then created a different system, want to provide continuity to their users—or who want to allow people using another system to convert to theirs. We will give a logical framework for unifying the network, hierarchic, and relational database models and a methodology for database conversion in Chapter 10.

In many cases, some data values are unknown. For example, in the EMPLOYEE file of Figure 1.1.1, we may wish to insert data about an employee whose telephone number is not known. Perhaps that individual does not (yet) have a telephone. This is an example of **incomplete information,** called a **null value.** Another aspect of data in a database has to do with time. Data does change over time; in the EMPLOYEE file, salaries change, employees leave, and new employees are hired. These events require database updates. In many cases, a user will want to know what the database looked like at various times—to analyze trends, for example. The handling of **time** for databases is therefore an important topic.

Throughout this book we will be dealing with the major concepts related to standard commercial databases. In recent years, new kinds of applications for **specialized database systems** have become important: statistical, scientific, geographical, textual, and design databases. These specialized databases need certain capabilities which standard database systems do not provide.

A complicated situation occurs when an organization has several database systems. Although, as we stated, the original idea was to integrate all the data in the database, it happens often enough that different groups in an organization consolidate their own data in their own database system. When companies merge, separate databases need to be integrated. The several database systems may contain overlapping data, so that some of the problems are similar in kind to those with the older file management systems discussed in Section 1.1. Recently, some work has been done in constructing a database system that can interconnect several systems and essentially make them into one (as far as the users are concerned). This process is called **database uniformization.** We will study incomplete information, time, specialized database systems, and database uniformization in Chapter 11.

There are many database systems available today for machines ranging from large mainframes to small microcomputers. Additionally, fourth-generation languages with significant database capabilities or in conjunction with existing database systems have become quite popular. In recent years spreadsheet systems have become ubiquitous in the microcomputer environment. We will survey some of the presently available database systems, fourth-generation languages, and spreadsheet systems in Chapter 12.

Until now we have considered only the advantages of database systems. We should, however, point out that database systems may also have **disadvantages.** For one thing, a mainframe or even a minicomputer database system may be quite expensive. Additional resources may be needed just to run a database system, whether of hardware (if an upgrade is required) or of people (such as the DBA). Conversions from existing file systems may also be costly. Sometimes, people who fear the loss of exclusive ownership of their data react negatively to the idea of an integrated database system. Database systems can introduce an additional complexity which does not exist with earlier systems. Finally, a database system is more vulnerable to failure because a problem in one component can stop the operation of the whole system. Although the possible disadvantages of database systems should be kept in mind, database systems have become popular and are in wide use today.

1.7 Exercises

1.1 (a) Describe a conceptual view for a criminal court. The files must contain data about judges, cases, lawyers, defendants, witnesses, evidence, and sentences.

  (b) Describe an external view and the corresponding transformation for the following:

  (*i*)   A view for the clerk that involves witnesses for cases.

  (*ii*) A view for reporting what types of sentences various judges impose.

  (*iii*) A view for identifying the types of cases handled by various lawyers.

  (*iv*) A view for the inventory of evidence.

1.2 For each of the graphs in Figure 1.7.1, find all of its cycles (if any) and indicate why it is or is not a tree.

1.3 For each of the relationships shown on the following page, indicate if it is one-to-one, one-to-many (in which direction?), or many-to-many (in the usual case).

FIGURE 1.7.1
Graphs

(a)

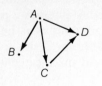

(b)

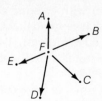

(c)

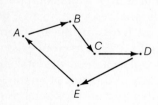

(d)

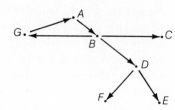

(e)

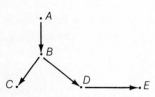

(f)

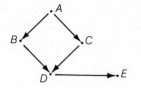

(a) equipment—serial number
(b) department store—customer
(c) house—contractor
(d) social security number—person
(e) teacher—principal
(f) judge—lawyer
(g) employee—employee number
(h) department—employee
(i) state—county

1.4 Draw data structure diagrams for the one-to-many relationships in Exercise 1.3. (Use appropriate attributes.)

1.5 Convert all data structure diagrams in Exercise 1.4 to the relational representation.

1.6 For the two data structure diagrams in Figure 1.7.2, which represents a hierarchic view and which represents a network view?

FIGURE 1.7.2
Data Structure Diagrams

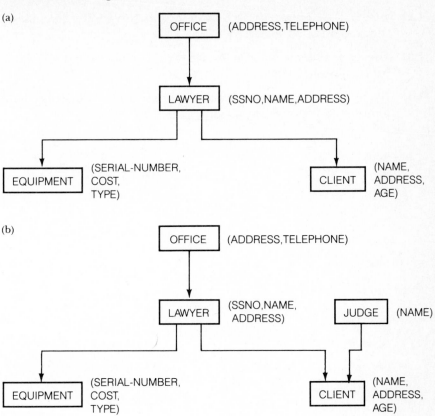

(a)

OFFICE   (ADDRESS,TELEPHONE)

LAWYER   (SSNO,NAME,ADDRESS)

EQUIPMENT   (SERIAL-NUMBER, COST, TYPE)

CLIENT   (NAME, ADDRESS, AGE)

(b)

OFFICE   (ADDRESS,TELEPHONE)

LAWYER   (SSNO,NAME, ADDRESS)

JUDGE   (NAME)

EQUIPMENT   (SERIAL-NUMBER, COST, TYPE)

CLIENT   (NAME, ADDRESS, AGE)

1.8 Guide to Further Reading

Of the many books available, we will mention here four which deal exclusively with database systems (as opposed to those books which include a detailed study of file structures). [1.1] gives a thorough discussion of many important database issues and describes some popular (primarily mainframe) database systems. [1.2] is the fourth edition of the first successful textbook on the subject. [1.3] contains the expanded treatment of various topics treated more briefly in [1.2]. [1.4] blends both theoretical and practical aspects of database systems in depth. All of these books list a large number of references to the database literature. We will refer to specific chapters from these books as we cover the corresponding material.

[1.1] Cardenas, F. *Data Base Management Systems.* 2d ed. Boston: Allyn and Bacon, 1985.

[1.2] Date, C. J. *An Introduction to Database Systems.* 4th ed. Reading, Mass.: Addison-Wesley, 1985.

[1.3] Date, C. J. *An Introduction to Database Systems.* Vol. 2. Reading, Mass.: Addison-Wesley, 1983.

[1.4] Ullman, J. D. *Principles of Database Systems.* 2d ed. Rockville, Md.: Computer Science Press, 1982.

Chapter 2

The Network Database Model

2.1 The Codasyl Set Concept

As we learned in Section 1.5, the network database model was investigated in detail by various CODASYL committees. But the CODASYL specifications have changed since the publication of DBTG's influential 1971 report. One major change has been the clearer separation of the conceptual and internal schema definitions, as suggested by the ANSI/SPARC Study Group's interim report of 1975. In this chapter we follow the latest language for network databases, the **ANSI (American National Standards Institute) NDL (Network Database Language).** This *became the national standard language for the network database model in 1986.* To familiarize ourselves with this language, we consider portions of the ANSI syntax rules in several figures. We note that ANSI syntax is somewhat different from those recommended years ago by the CODASYL committees; at present, most network implementations follow the older proposals.

In this section, we discuss the fundamental concept of **Codasyl set.** We begin with a notion we discussed in Section 1.3: the data structure diagram in the network model. In such a diagram the nodes represent files and the edges represent one-to-many relationships; the network model allows the data structure diagram to be a graph. In CODASYL terminology, two nodes connected by an edge form a "set." Since we wish to use the word "set" in the ordinary mathematical sense for a collection of objects, we use the term "Codasyl set" for the former construct (except

FIGURE 2.1.1
A Codasyl Set (Type)

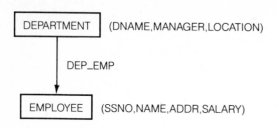

in those cases where the name of the Codasyl set already appears). We will continue to use the acronym CODASYL in our other references to this group.

Consider Figure 2.1.1, which illustrates a Codasyl set. The two nodes represent the DEPARTMENT file and the EMPLOYEE file. The name of the Codasyl set is DEP_EMP. The arrow going from DEPARTMENT to EMPLOYEE indicates that there is a one-to-many relationship between the DEPARTMENT file and the EMPLOYEE file. That is, each individual department record may have zero, one, or more employee records associated with it. But an employee record may not be associated with more than one department record. In CODASYL terminology, the parent file is the **owner** (DEPARTMENT in this case), and the child file is the **member** (EMPLOYEE in this case).

We need to distinguish between the notions of **type** and **occurrence.** *Type refers to a description, while occurrence refers to an instance.* A Codasyl record type, like EMPLOYEE, is the *description* of a file; a Codasyl set type, like DEP_EMP, indicates a *correspondence* between record types. A record occurrence is simply a record instance, while a Codasyl set occurrence refers to an owner record instance *and* its corresponding member record instances. We will not specify "occurrence" or "type" when it is clear from the context.

Although the conceptual model need not have much to do with the internal representation of the database, with the CODASYL model it is useful to think about the implementation that the designers of the model had in mind. A **linked list** *is a linear sequence of elements, all of the same type, joined by pointers.* Figure 2.1.2 illustrates a linked list of cities. There are actually several types of linked lists; these are usually discussed in detail in books on data structures. In particular, links go in both directions for a doubly linked list, and for a circularly linked list the last element points back to the first one. A linked list with a head node has an initial node which may be of different type than the other nodes.

Let's go back to the DEP_EMP set of Figure 2.1.1. A particular occurrence of this Codasyl set may be implemented as a set of circularly linked lists with head nodes, one for each department record. We show this representation in part (a) of Figure 2.1.3. Each record of the DEPARTMENT file is the head node for a linked list, all of whose elements are members of the EMPLOYEE file. If the structure is singly linked, then we can get quickly from one employee record to the next one for the same department. If the list is doubly linked, then it is also easy to go to the previous employee record as shown in part (b). If there also is a pointer to the head node from each element, then we can get quickly to the owner record for a particular member record, as illustrated in part (c). This method can also be combined with doubly linked lists, as in part (d). To keep later drawings simple, we continue to draw only singly linked lists as in part (a); however, for fast access to records in the database it is convenient to identify the implementation with the drawing in part (d).

FIGURE 2.1.2
A Linked List

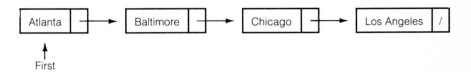

FIGURE 2.1.3
Linked List Representations of a Codasyl Set (Occurrence)

(a) Singly linked and circular

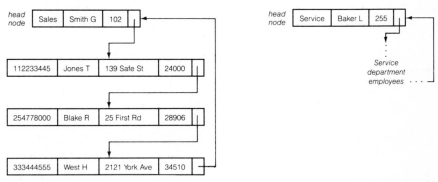

(continued)

FIGURE 2.1.3 *(continued)*

(b) Doubly linked and circular

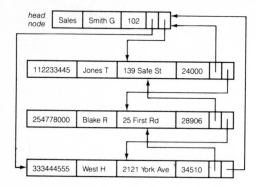

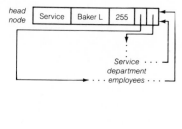

(c) Singly linked and circular with a pointer from each element to the head node

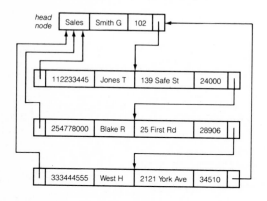

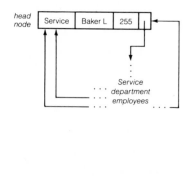

(d) Doubly linked and circular with a pointer from each element to the head node

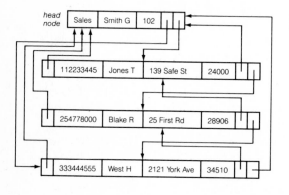

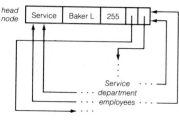

FIGURE 2.1.4
A Two-Level Hierarchy

(a) Data structure diagram

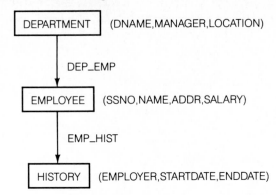

(b) Linked list representation

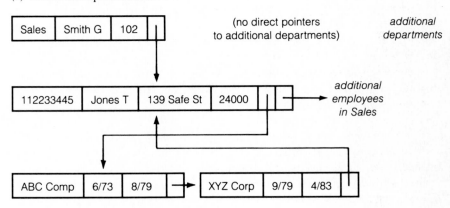

Now let's consider an example of a hierarchy with two levels. For example, suppose that to the Codasyl set example of Figure 2.1.1 we wish to add another file to contain employee histories, where each record of such a file contains the name of an employer and the start and end date for an individual who worked there. Now there is a one-to-many relationship between the EMPLOYEE file and the HISTORY file. The data structure diagram is shown in part (a) of Figure 2.1.4. In part (b), we show the (singly) linked list representation of part of such a database. Each employee record now has two pointers. One points to the next employee for the department in its DEP_EMP set and the other one points to the first history record of the employee. Assuming the singly linked circular structure, each record has as many pointers as the number of Codasyl sets in which it participates. When the record is an owner, it is a head node; when it is a member, it is an element of a linked list. Since each Codasyl set represents a one-to-many relationship, each specific record, which is either an owner or a member, may appear only once.

We can see from Figure 2.1.4(a) that while the employee and history records are ordered in some way, so we can easily go to the next one by following a pointer, this is not the case for department records, or in general when a file has no edges leading into it. The CODASYL approach allows the placement of such records in a list structure by a construct called the singular set. A **singular set** *has the database system as its owner,* in the form of a dummy file called SYSTEM; this way the records of a file, which would not be linked otherwise, are linked together. We show the data structure diagram with the singular set added in Figure 2.1.5(a) and the linked list representation in Figure 2.1.5(b).

All of our examples so far have been hierarchies. We have not yet considered the important case of a nonhierarchic structure, allowed by the network model. So, let's go back to the example of Figure 2.1.1 and suppose that we wish to add a file concerning health plans for employees. Each employee may be in only one health plan, but a health plan may have zero, one, or more employees in it. Thus we have a one-to-many relationship between the HEALTHPLAN and EMPLOYEE files. The data structure diagram is shown in part (a) of Figure 2.1.6. Note that this is not a hierarchy. A portion of the linked list representation for an instance is given in part (b). Each employee record is in two linked lists: one for its owner department record, and one for its owner health-plan record.

So far we have considered only one-to-many relationships between files. However, it is certainly possible to have many-to-many relationships between files. The last example suggests how we can represent such a relationship. Suppose that we consider the implicit relationship between the DEPARTMENT and HEALTHPLAN files as follows: a department record is related to a health-plan record if there is an employee who is in that department with that particular health plan. Since in any department there may be employees belonging to different health plans, and a health plan may have members from several departments, we do get a many-to-many relationship. Thus we see that a many-to-many relationship (implicit here) can be handled using two Codasyl sets and an additional file which forms the connection (EMPLOYEE in this case) between the two files.

In the previous example, the many-to-many relationship was somewhat forced, as the other relationships were the main ones. Let's consider a situation where the many-to-many relationship is the principal one. Suppose that we wish to represent the many-to-many relationship between the TEACHER file and the STUDENT file as shown in Figure 1.3.2(c). We need to construct a **connection file** (which is allowed to have no attributes). In our case the connection file (CLASS) contains course and

FIGURE 2.1.5
Two-Level Hierarchy with Added Singular Set

(a) Data structure diagram

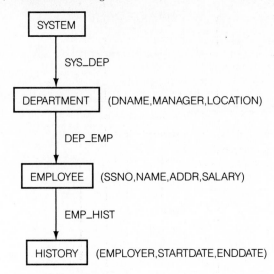

(b) Linked list representation

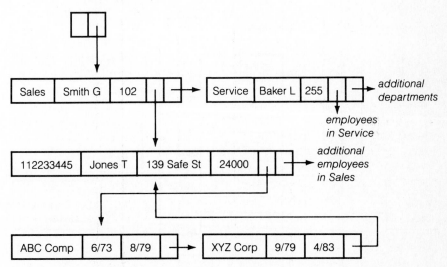

grade information. Such a situation is pictured in part (a) of Figure 2.1.7. A portion of the linked list representation is shown in part (b) for an occurrence. Note that there is a class record for each student for each course that the student has taken.

FIGURE 2.1.6
Nonhierarchic Database

(a) Data structure diagram

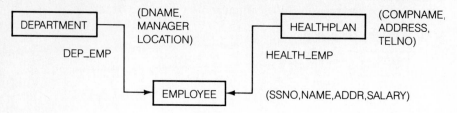

(b) Linked list representation

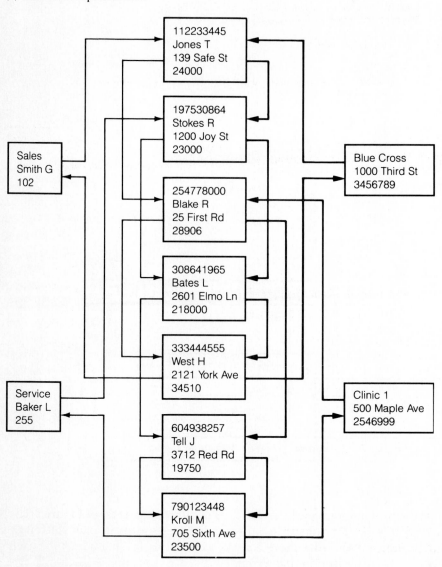

FIGURE 2.1.7
Representing Many-to-Many Relationships

(a) Data structure diagram

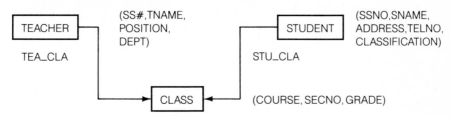

(b) Linked list representation

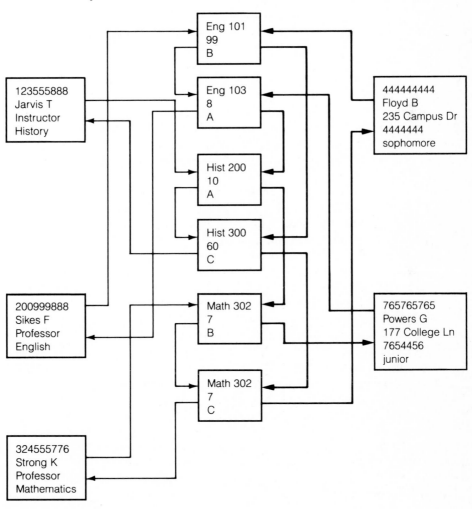

2.2 Data Definition Language

Network Database Language (NDL) is composed of four sublanguages: a Schema Definition Language, a Subschema Definition Language, a Module Language, and a Data Manipulation Language. The Schema Definition Language and the Subschema Definition Language compose, in effect, the Data Definition Language (DDL). In this section we deal primarily with the **Schema Definition Language,** which *is used to describe conceptual views.* We consider the Subschema Definition Language briefly at the end of this section and the Data Manipulation Language in the next two sections. (The Module Language, used primarily to write procedures, will not be covered here.) We discuss the languages by giving and explaining some examples.

In Figure 2.2.1, we show portions of the syntax for the Schema Definition Language. These syntax rules are written in standard BNF notation, which is explained in the Preface. The syntax rules are given for reference purposes only; the examples illustrate the main options.

Consider the data structure diagram given in Figure 2.2.2, which is a somewhat modified version of Figure 1.3.3 and which contains a singular set. In Figure 2.2.3, we present a sample schema definition for this example. We now go over this definition in detail to gain a general understanding of the Schema Definition Language.

Note that the schema definition starts by naming the schema. The general structure of the schema definition consists of defining the record types (files) first, followed by the Codasyl set types. Each file definition starts with naming the file. This is followed by the data types for the attributes of the file. These items may be arrays, but we use only single items in our examples. Optionally, in each file definition we may define one or more attributes or combinations of attributes, whose values cannot be duplicate. Any such attribute (or combination of attributes) is a key. Thus, for the OFFICE file, OFFICEADDRESS is a key; for the AGENT file, ANAME,ADDR is a key; and for the CLIENT file, both POLICY-NUMBER and the combination CNAME,CADDR are keys.

Complexity enters into the schema definition with the definition of the Codasyl sets. We cover the various options separately. Each Codasyl set must be given a name. Then the parent node, called the owner, must be identified. This is followed by the ORDER clause which defines the order in which new records of the child node, called the member, are inserted into the Codasyl set. For the OFFICE_AGENT set the records in the AGENT file (for any office record) are sorted according to the key, which is the combination ANAME,ADDR. The DUPLICATES PROHIBITED clause indicates that the attempted duplication of a key value for AGENT in a Codasyl set would cause an error. (This adds no information here because of the UNIQUE clause for AGENT.)

FIGURE 2.2.1
Syntax Rules for the Schema Definition Language

Notes: 1. Additional syntax rules for NDL are presented in Figures 2.2.5, 2.3.2, and 2.4.1.
2. All names are identifiers which must start with a letter and may contain letters, digits, and underscores.
3. Length, precision, and scale are positive integers.
4. A literal is either a character string in double quotes or a number in fixed or floating-point form.

```
<schema>   ::=   <schema name clause>
                     [ { <record type> | <set type> } ... ]
<schema name clause>   ::=   SCHEMA <schema name>
<record type>   ::=   <record name clause>
                         [ { <record uniqueness clause> |
                             <component type> | <record check clause> } ... ]
<record name clause>   ::=   RECORD <record name>
<record uniqueness clause>   ::=   UNIQUE <component identifier> ...
<component identifier>   ::=   [ <qualifier>. ] <component name>
<qualifier>   ::=   <record name> | OWNER | MEMBER
<component type>   ::=   ITEM <component name> <data type>
<data type>   ::=   CHARACTER  [ <length> ] | INTEGER
                    FIXED <precision> [ <scale> ] |
                    FLOAT <precision> | REAL
<record check clause>   ::=   CHECK <condition>
<condition>   ::=   <alternative> [ { OR <alternative> } ... ]
<alternative>   ::=   <simple condition> [ { AND <simple condition> } ... ]
<simple condition>   ::=   <subcondition> | <negated subcondition> |
                            <relation condition>
<subcondition>   ::=   ( <condition> )
<negated subcondition>   ::=   NOT ( <condition> )
<relation condition>   ::=   <operand> <relation> <operand>
<operand>   ::=   <component identifier> | <component view identifier> |
                   <parameter identifier> | <literal>
<relation>   ::=   < | <= | = | >= | >  | <>

<set type>   ::=   <set name clause> <owner clause>
                    <order clause> <member clause>
<set name clause>   ::=   SET <set name>
<owner clause>   ::=   OWNER { <record name> | SYSTEM }
<order clause>   ::=   ORDER <order option>
<order option>   ::=   FIRST | LAST | NEXT | PRIOR | DEFAULT |
                        <sorted order>
<sorted order>   ::=   SORTED DUPLICATES { PROHIBITED | FIRST |
                        LAST | DEFAULT }
```

(continued)

FIGURE 2.2.1 *(continued)*

Note: If sorted order is specified, then a key clause must be included in the member clause.

```
<member clause>   ::=   <member record name clause> <insertion clause>
                        <retention clause> [ <key clause> ]
<member record name clause>   ::=   MEMBER <record name>
<insertion clause>   ::=   INSERTION { AUTOMATIC | MANUAL|
                           STRUCTURAL <structural specification> }
<structural specification>   ::=   <component identifier match>
                                   [ { AND <component identifier match> }
                                   . . . ]
<component identifier match>   ::=   <component identifier> =
                                     <component identifier>
<retention clause>   ::=   RETENTION { FIXED | MANDATORY | OPTIONAL }
<key clause>   ::=   KEY { ASCENDING | DESCENDING }
                     { <component identifier> } . . .
```

FIGURE 2.2.2
Data Structure Diagram for the Insurance Company Example

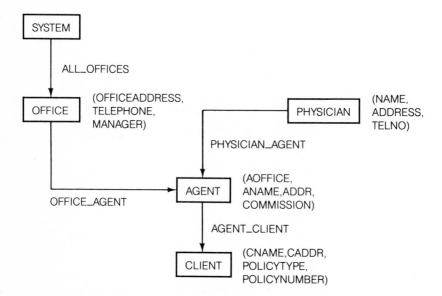

Consider Figure 2.2.4(a). In part *(i)* we represent a Codasyl set for the office located at 500 Maple St. The agent records are ordered by name and secondly by address. When Farmer is inserted, part *(ii)* shows that it is placed in the correct location according to the sorting. Next we look at the PHYSICIAN_AGENT set. Here the ORDER is DEFAULT,

FIGURE 2.2.3
The Insurance Company Schema

```
SCHEMA   INSURANCE_COMPANY
  RECORD   OFFICE
    UNIQUE   OFFICEADDRESS
    ITEM   OFFICEADDRESS   CHARACTER 20
    ITEM   TELEPHONE   CHARACTER 10
    ITEM   MANAGER   CHARACTER 15
  RECORD   AGENT
    UNIQUE   ANAME,ADDR
    ITEM   AOFFICE   CHARACTER 20
    ITEM   ANAME   CHARACTER 15
    ITEM   ADDR   CHARACTER 20
    ITEM   COMMISSION   FIXED 8 2
  RECORD   PHYSICIAN
    ITEM   NAME   CHARACTER 15
    ITEM   ADDRESS   CHARACTER 20
    ITEM   TELNO   CHARACTER 10
  RECORD   CLIENT
    UNIQUE   CNAME,CADDR
    UNIQUE   POLICYNUMBER
    ITEM   CNAME   CHARACTER 15
    ITEM   CADDR   CHARACTER 20
    ITEM   POLICYTYPE   CHARACTER 1
    ITEM   POLICYNUMBER   CHARACTER 13
  SET   OFFICE_AGENT
    OWNER   OFFICE
    ORDER SORTED   DUPLICATES PROHIBITED
    MEMBER   AGENT
    INSERTION STRUCTURAL   AGENT.AOFFICE=
                          OFFICE.OFFICEADDRESS
    RETENTION FIXED
    KEY   ASCENDING   ANAME,ADDR
  SET   PHYSICIAN_AGENT
    OWNER   PHYSICIAN
    ORDER DEFAULT
    MEMBER   AGENT
    INSERTION MANUAL
    RETENTION OPTIONAL
  SET   AGENT_CLIENT
    OWNER   AGENT
    ORDER FIRST
    MEMBER   CLIENT
    INSERTION AUTOMATIC
    RETENTION MANDATORY
  SET   ALL_OFFICES
    OWNER   SYSTEM
    ORDER LAST
    MEMBER   OFFICE
    INSERTION AUTOMATIC
    RETENTION FIXED
```

FIGURE 2.2.4
The Effect of the ORDER Clause

(a) Sorted

    (*i*) Before   (*ii*) After

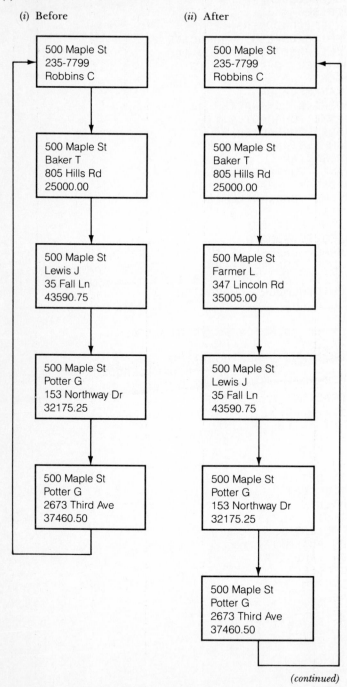

(continued)

(b) First

    (*i*) Before   (*ii*) After

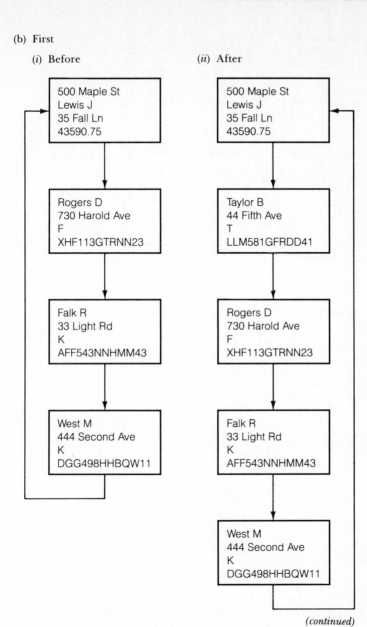

(continued)

FIGURE 2.2.4 *(continued)*

(c) Last

    (*i*) Before   (*ii*) After

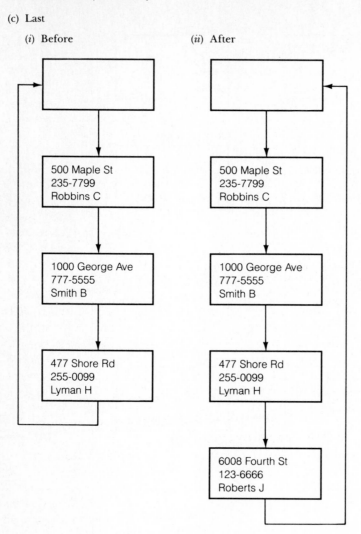

allowing the system to define an arbitrary order. For the set AGENT_
CLIENT, the ORDER is FIRST. This means that each time a new client
record is added it is placed into the first position for that Codasyl set.
Figure 2.2.4(b) illustrates this possibility with Taylor added as a new client
of Lewis. When the ORDER is LAST, a new child record is placed into
the last position in the list. This is illustrated in Figure 2.2.4(c), where a
new office record is placed in the last position for the singular set ALL_
OFFICES.

    Next we consider the INSERTION and RETENTION clauses. There
are three choices for insertion: STRUCTURAL, AUTOMATIC, and

MANUAL. For a STRUCTURAL and an AUTOMATIC insertion, a member record is inserted into its appropriate Codasyl set occurrence at the time it is inserted into the database. We start by considering the STRUCTURAL method and illustrate it for the OFFICE_AGENT set. The idea of **STRUCTURAL INSERTION** is that *the owner record is found by matching a field value in the inserted member record.* Suppose that a new agent record is inserted into the database. The owner record is selected by identifying the value of AOFFICE in the agent record with the value of OFFICEADDRESS in an office record. This way each new agent record is placed into the proper OFFICE_AGENT set occurrence.

     AUTOMATIC INSERTION *means that the owner record is the most recently accessed (owner) record for the Codasyl set.* We illustrate this method for the AGENT_CLIENT set. When a new client record is inserted, its owner becomes the most recently accessed agent record. Suppose that we wish to insert Rogers as the client of Lewis. At the time that Rogers is inserted we may not know which agent record was accessed most recently. We can make certain that the client record (Rogers) is inserted into the proper Codasyl set occurrence by first accessing (finding) the agent record (Lewis) which is to be its owner. (For the singular set ALL_OFFICES, there is no problem because the owner must be the SYSTEM itself.)

     The last case is MANUAL INSERTION. The **MANUAL INSERTION** clause *means that a new member record must specifically be inserted into its Codasyl set occurrence by a statement.* We will show in Section 2.4 how to use the CONNECT statement for this purpose. Our example for MANUAL INSERTION is the PHYSICIAN_AGENT set. Thus, whenever a new agent record is added to the database, at the time of insertion it is not placed into any PHYSICIAN_AGENT set occurrence.

     There are three choices for retention: FIXED, MANDATORY, and OPTIONAL. **FIXED RETENTION** *means that once a member record is placed into a particular Codasyl set, it is fixed there:* it cannot be taken out of that Codasyl set and placed somewhere else (unless it is deleted and reinserted). **MANDATORY RETENTION** *means that once a member record is placed into a particular Codasyl set, it is mandatory for its existence in the database* (unless it is deleted and reinserted) *to be a member record for some Codasyl set of that type.* Thus it is possible to move it from one owner record to another one. **OPTIONAL RETENTION** *means that the existence of a record as a member record in the Codasyl set is entirely optional.* It can be removed from its Codasyl set and still exist in the database.

     Let's consider for our example the OFFICE_AGENT set. In this case the retention is FIXED. This means that once an agent record is inserted into the database in a particular Codasyl set, done here by the value of OFFICEADDRESS, that record cannot be removed from the Codasyl set occurrence unless the record is entirely removed from the database. Thus an agent must be associated with the specific office into which he or she was placed initially. In the case of the PHYSICIAN_AGENT set, the retention is OPTIONAL. Therefore, an agent record can be removed from its Codasyl set and not placed into any other such Codasyl set, indicating perhaps that the agent is looking for a new physician. For the set AGENT_CLIENT, the retention is MANDATORY. Thus a client record may be moved from one occurrence of the AGENT_CLIENT set to another one; in other words, the client may change agents. However, a client record cannot exist without being in some AGENT_CLIENT set occurrence; that is, each client must always have an associated agent.

    Next we briefly consider the Subschema Definition Language. In Figure 2.2.5, we show portions of its syntax definitions. The idea is that the schema represents the conceptual view, while a subschema represents an external view in the three-level architecture. Essentially, a subschema is a portion of the schema. Some of the Codasyl sets, files, and attributes may be omitted. The restriction is that the subschema must be consistent: for example, it cannot have the definition of a Codasyl set type unless both record types associated with that Codasyl set type are also defined. Names of fields, files, and Codasyl sets, as well as the order of the attributes in a record type, may be changed. We give an example of a subschema definition for the schema of Figure 2.2.3 in Figure 2.2.6. This

FIGURE 2.2.5
Syntax Rules for the Subschema Definition Language

Note: Additional syntax rules are presented in Figures 2.2.1, 2.3.2, and 2.4.1.

```
<subschema>   ::=   <subschema name clause>
                    [ { <record view> | <set view> } . . . ]
<subschema name clause>   ::=   SUBSCHEMA <subschema name> OF
                    <schema name>
<record view>   ::=   RECORD [ <record name> RENAMED ] <record view name>
                    [<component list>]
<component list>   ::=   <component view> . . . | ALL
<component view>   ::=   ITEM [ <component name> RENAMED ]
                    <component view name>
<set view>   ::=   SET [ <set name> RENAMED ] <set view name>
```

FIGURE 2.2.6
The Subschema DOCTORS

```
SUBSCHEMA  DOCTORS OF INSURANCE_COMPANY
   RECORD  PHYSICIAN  ALL
   RECORD  AGENT
     ITEM  ANAME
     ITEM  ADDR
   SET  PHYSICIAN AGENT RENAMED_PATIENT
```

subschema contains only information concerning physicians and agents. We omit some of the items and rename the set PHYSICIAN_AGENT to PATIENT.

2.3 Database Navigation

In this section, we start our consideration of the Data Manipulation Language, or DML. The Codasyl sets form the links between the files. Typically, a database program goes through some records of a file and then uses the link provided by the Codasyl set construct to get to another file, continuing this process until the desired result is obtained. This movement through the records of a file and through the links connecting files is called **database navigation.** Since data manipulation is usually done on subschemas (external views), we illustrate the ideas through the subschema example of Figure 2.2.6. We show an instance of the DOCTORS subschema in Figure 2.3.1.

Before we get to the actual data manipulation statements, we need to have an understanding of the environment of a database program. In NDL a module specifies a high-level programming language (COBOL, FORTRAN, Pascal, or PL/I), a subschema, and a collection of database procedures. These procedures are much like procedures in a programming language: they include parameters and can be called from a high-level language program. A special STATUS parameter is used for error processing. An object called the **session state** is associated with each module execution. The session state consists primarily of **cursors,** also called **database keys,** which are addresses of various records.

A session cursor points to the most recently accessed record. For each record type there is a cursor to point to the most recently accessed record for it. Also, for each Codasyl set type there are two cursors to identify the most recently accessed parent and child records for it. In particular, suppose that in Figure 2.3.1 the last two actions accessed the records for Dr. D. Hall and agent L. Farmer. Then the session cursor would point to Farmer, the cursor for PHYSICIAN would point to Dr. Hall, the cursor for AGENT would point to Farmer, and the cursors for PHYSICIAN_AGENT would point to Dr. Hall and Farmer, respectively.

Now we are ready to discuss the major DML statements. In this section we deal with the crucial **FIND statement.** This statement *finds a particular record in the database and establishes it as the most recently accessed record* for the session cursor, the record cursor of its record type, and as the parent or child record of its Codasyl set types. It is useful to have in mind the linked list representation here, as almost every step in the navigation corresponds to following some pointer in a linked list. In Figure 2.3.2, we present the major syntax rules for the FIND statement.

The FIND statement can be used to find a physician's record given the physician's name. For example, we may want to find the record for

FIGURE 2.3.1
An Instance of the DOCTORS Subschema

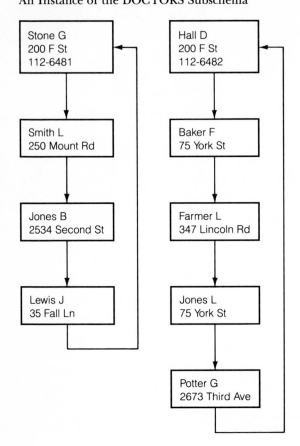

FIGURE 2.3.2
Syntax Rules for the FIND Statement of the Data Manipulation Language

Note: Additional syntax rules for NDL are presented in Figures 2.2.1, 2.2.5, and 2.4.1.

```
<find statement>   ::=   FIND <find specification>
                         [ <find intent> ] [ <find cursor disposition> ]
<find specification>   ::=   <database key identifier> | <search specification>
<database key identifier>   ::=   SESSION | <record view name> |
                                  { OWNER | MEMBER } <set view name>
<search specification>   ::=   <search orientation> <domain specification>
                               [ WHERE <condition> ]
<search orientation>   ::=   FIRST | LAST | NEXT | PRIOR
<domain specification>   ::=   <record view name> [ IN <set view name> ]
```

FIGURE 2.3.3
Examples of the FIND Statement

(a) Find the record for Dr. G. Stone.

```
FIND FIRST PHYSICIAN WHERE NAME = "Stone G"
                            ADDRESS = "200 F St"
                            TELNO = "112-6481"
```

(b) (*i*) Find the record of a physician whose address is 200 F St.

```
FIND FIRST PHYSICIAN WHERE ADDRESS = "200 F St"
```

(*ii*) Find the record of another physician whose address is 200 F St.

```
FIND NEXT PHYSICIAN WHERE ADDRESS = "200 F St"
```

(c) Assume that the current record is the one for agent B. Jones. Find the record of the physician for Jones.

```
FIND OWNER PATIENT
```

(d) (*i*) Assume that the current record is the one for Dr. D. Hall. Find the record of Dr. Hall's first patient.

```
FIND FIRST AGENT IN PATIENT
```

(*ii*) Find the record of Dr. Hall's next patient.

```
FIND NEXT AGENT IN PATIENT
```

(e) (*i*) Assume that the current record is the one for Dr. D. Hall. Find the record of Dr. Hall's first patient, whose address is 75 York St.

```
FIND FIRST AGENT IN PATIENT WHERE ADDR = "75 York
    St"
```

(*ii*) Find the record of Dr. Hall's next patient, whose address is 75 York St.

```
FIND NEXT AGENT IN PATIENT WHERE ADDR = "75 York
    St"
```

(f) Find the most recently accessed PHYSICIAN record.

```
FIND PHYSICIAN
```

Dr. G. Stone. This is done by issuing a FIND statement as in Figure 2.3.3(a). We give all the attribute values for the physician record since we are not assured otherwise that the right record would be found. Now suppose that we want to find a physician whose address is 200 F St. There may be several physicians with that address; in fact, in our database there are two. We can issue a FIND FIRST command using the address value in a condition. This locates the first physician record in the database with that address. To find another physician with the same address we use a FIND NEXT command. These are illustrated in Figure 2.3.3(b).

Next, we use the FIND statement to navigate between files. Basically there are two ways to do this. If a file is an *owner* in a Codasyl set, then for a record of that file we can find one of its member records. Going in the other direction, if a file is a *member* in a Codasyl set, then for a record of that file we can find its unique owner record. We start with the second case. Let's assume that the current record (the one pointed to by the session cursor) is the one for agent B. Jones. Because we wish to find Jones's physician, we need to find the owner record for Jones. This FIND is illustrated in Figure 2.3.3(c).

Now we consider the case where the current record is at an owner node in a Codasyl set and we want to find some member record of it. There are two ways of doing this. Either we have some attribute values for the member record or we have no attribute values. Again we start with the second case. Suppose that we wish to find the first patient of Dr. D. Hall and the current record is that of Dr. Hall. We use a FIND FIRST IN command. To find the next patient of Dr. Hall we use a FIND NEXT IN command. These are illustrated in Figure 2.3.3(d).

Next, suppose that we are interested only in those patients of Dr. Hall whose address is 75 York Street. Again we assume that the current record is that of Dr. Hall. But now we must also use a condition for the address value. Another such patient can be found by using a FIND NEXT IN command with the same condition. Both are illustrated in Figure 2.3.3(e).

We have covered the main versions of the FIND statement used for database navigation. FIND can also be used to locate a record which is the cursor for a record (type) or for a Codasyl set (type). Assume that we are working with the patients of Dr. Hall, but the last physician record accessed was that of Dr. G. Stone. We can go back to the record of Dr. Stone, as shown in Figure 2.3.3(f), since it is in the session state as the current record of the PHYSICIAN file. There is a related version of FIND which can be used to find a record given its database key (address). We will discuss this later in connection with the notion of temporary set, which is a list of database keys. Finally, we note that if a record which a FIND statement attempts to find in the database is not there, then an error occurs.

2.4 Database Updates and Programs

We will now consider the statements of the DML used for updating, and then write some program segments to illustrate various applications. NDL assumes the explicit procedure calls method, which was explained in

FIGURE 2.4.1

Syntax Rules for Update Statements of the Data Manipulation Language

Note: Additional syntax rules for NDL are presented in Figures 2.2.1, 2.2.5, and 2.3.2

<store statement>   ::=   STORE <to database move>

<to database move>   ::=   <record view name>
                                    [<to database move clause> . . .]

<to database move clause>   ::=   SET <component view name> TO <operand>

<erase statement>   ::=   ERASE <database key identifier>
                                    WITH <cascade specification>

<database key identifier>   ::=   SESSION | <record view name> |
                                    { OWNER | MEMBER } <set view name>

<cascade specification>   ::=   FULL CASCADE | PARTIAL CASCADE

<connect statement>   ::=   CONNECT <database key identifier>
                                    TO <set view name>

<reconnect statement>   ::=   RECONNECT <database key identifier>
                                    IN <set view name>

<disconnect statement>   ::=   DISCONNECT <database key identifier>
                                    FROM <set view name>

<get statement>   ::=   GET <to parameter move>

<to parameter move>   ::=   <record view name>
                                    <to parameter move clause> . . .

<to parameter move clause>   ::=   SET <parameter identifier> TO <operand>

<modify statement>   ::=   MODIFY <to database move>

Section 1.4, for interfacing with programming languages. This interfacing is accomplished by having the programmer write a module that contains database procedures and a program written in a high-level programming language that explicitly calls these procedures. Because we will use this method in Chapter 3 when we discuss the hierarchic model, in our presentation for this section we illustrate the implicit procedure calls method. We do so by writing NDL before each database statement in the embedded program segments. (However, we do not write NDL for program segments which contain only database statements.)

Recall from our discussion in Section 1.4 that there are three types of updates: insertion, deletion, and modification. The corresponding statements in NDL are STORE, ERASE, and MODIFY, respectively. In addition, we may want to make an update to Codasyl set membership, for example, by inserting a record into a particular Codasyl set. The statements for such updates are CONNECT, DISCONNECT, and RECONNECT. In Figure 2.4.1, we show the syntax rules for some of the update definitions. For our examples in this section we use the INSURANCE_COMPANY schema of Figure 2.2.3, which we treat as if it were a subschema.

FIGURE 2.4.2
Insertions

(a) Insert a physician record for Dr. B. Hughes.

```
STORE PHYSICIAN
  SET NAME TO "Hughes B"
  SET ADDRESS TO "6040 Raven Blvd"
  SET TELNO TO "789-1122"
```

(b) Insert B. Taylor as a client of J. Lewis.

```
FIND FIRST AGENT WHERE
  ANAME = "Lewis J"
  ADDR = "35 Fall Ln"
STORE CLIENT
  SET CNAME TO "Taylor B"
  SET CADDR TO "44 Fifth Ave"
  SET POLICYTYPE TO "T"
  SET POLICYNUMBER TO "LLM581GFRDD41"
```

(c) Insert agent R. Osler into the office at 200 North Dr.

```
(i) STORE AGENT
      SET AOFFICE TO "200 North Dr"
      SET ANAME TO "Osler R"
      SET ADDR TO "456 Pine St"
      SET COMMISSION TO 23500.00

(ii) FIND FIRST PHYSICIAN WHERE NAME = "Stone G"
                                ADDRESS = "200 F St"
                                TELNO = "112-6481"
      CONNECT AGENT TO PHYSICIAN AGENT
```

Suppose that we wish to insert a new physician record into the database. This can be done as in Figure 2.4.2(a). We indicate in the STORE statement the attribute values for the PHYSICIAN record. Note that PHYSICIAN is not a member file in any Codasyl set. However, when we insert a record into a file which is a member file in a Codasyl set, we usually want that record to be placed into a Codasyl set also. The insertion mode determines how to do this.

Consider the insertion of a client record. When we insert such a record we want it to be placed in the correct AGENT_CLIENT set. Here the insertion mode is AUTOMATIC. If we wish to store B. Taylor as a client of agent J. Lewis, we can do so as in Figure 2.4.2(b). First we find the agent's record. Observe that we also give the agent's address in case more than one agent has the same name. The STORE command then inserts the client record into the database and also places it into its

AGENT_CLIENT set using the cursor for the owner of AGENT_CLIENT, which, after the FIND statement, points to the agent J. Lewis.

Next, let's insert an agent record into the database. Note that AGENT is the member file in two Codasyl sets; it is also an owner file in a Codasyl set, although that is not important here. The agent record to be inserted should also be inserted into an OFFICE_AGENT set. This can be achieved as shown in part *(i)* of Figure 2.4.2(c). Recall that for OFFICE_AGENT the insertion is STRUCTURAL, based on the OFFICEADDRESS value. Therefore, the agent record is inserted into the OFFICE_AGENT set for which the OFFICEADDRESS value matches the AOFFICE value in the new record. (An error occurs if there is no matching OFFICE-ADDRESS value.)

At this point R. Osler does not have a physician in the database: that is, the record has not been placed into a PHYSICIAN_AGENT set. Since insertion is MANUAL in this case, Codasyl set placement must be done by using the CONNECT statement. Assume that Osler is to be a patient of Dr. G. Stone. Then we can continue the program segment as in part *(ii)* of Figure 2.4.2(c). The first step yields the cursor for the owner of the PHYSICIAN_AGENT set. Then the CONNECT statement is used to put Osler in as a patient of Dr. Stone.

Next we consider deletions. The command is ERASE. Let's delete a physician, Dr. G. Stone, from the database. This deletion is given in Figure 2.4.3(a). First we must find the record for Dr. Stone and then we delete it by using ERASE. There are two options for the cascade specification (which we discuss next). We may wonder what happens to the *agents* of the physician who is deleted from the database. This depends on the retention mode for the Codasyl set.

FIGURE 2.4.3
Deletions

(a) Delete the physician Dr. G. Stone from the database.

```
FIND FIRST PHYSICIAN WHERE NAME = "Stone G"
                           ADDRESS = "200 F St"
                           TELNO = "112-6481"
ERASE PHYSICIAN WITH PARTIAL CASCADE
```

(b) Delete the physician Dr. G. Stone from the database as well as all of the agents who are patients of Dr. Stone and all of the clients of these agents.

```
FIND FIRST PHYSICIAN WHERE NAME = "Stone G"
                           ADDRESS = "200 F St"
                           TELNO = "112-6481"
ERASE PHYSICIAN WITH FULL CASCADE
```

The ERASE statement WITH PARTIAL CASCADE deletes the member records in the Codasyl set occurrence if retention is FIXED and disconnects them if retention is OPTIONAL. ERASE WITH PARTIAL CASCADE is not allowed for the MANDATORY case. In this case, because the retention mode is OPTIONAL, the agent records for Dr. Stone are not deleted from the database. We repeat this example using WITH FULL CASCADE in Figure 2.4.3(b). This version deletes all the descendants of the record for Dr. Stone. In particular, all the agent records (patients) of Dr. Stone are deleted. But deletion *cascades;* hence, for each deleted agent all the client records of that agent are deleted also.

Suppose now that before deleting an agent we wish to transfer a client, M. West, first to another agent, say, T. Baker. This can be achieved as shown in Figure 2.4.4. First we find the client record and the new agent record. Then the RECONNECT statement deletes the record of West from its present Codasyl set, and places it into the Codasyl set for the current agent, namely, Baker.

So far we have shown an example of CONNECT and one of RECONNECT. Recall now that if for a Codasyl set the retention mode is OPTIONAL, then we can just remove a member record from a Codasyl set and not place it into any other Codasyl set. We illustrate this in Figure 2.4.5. We simply find the record for the agent and DISCONNECT it from the Codasyl set.

Finally, we consider a modification to a record. This is achieved by using MODIFY. Suppose that we wish to add $200 to the COMMISSION value for the agent R. Osler. This is illustrated in Figure 2.4.6 (using COBOL). The FIND command merely sets cursors; it is the GET command which actually fetches a value from the database record. We use here a GET after the FIND to SET a parameter Z to the COMMISSION value. We then change the value of the parameter (in the programming language) and use MODIFY to replace the present value of COMMIS-

FIGURE 2.4.4
Transfer the client M. West to the agent T. Baker.

```
FIND FIRST CLIENT WHERE CNAME = "West M"
                        CADDR = "444 Second Ave"
FIND FIRST AGENT WHERE ANAME = "Baker T"
                       ADDR = "805 Hills Rd"
RECONNECT CLIENT IN AGENT_CLIENT
```

FIGURE 2.4.5
Remove agent T. Baker from its PHYSICIAN_AGENT set.

```
FIND FIRST AGENT WHERE ANAME = "Baker T"
                       ADDR = "805 Hills Rd"
DISCONNECT AGENT FROM PHYSICIAN_AGENT
```

FIGURE 2.4.6
Add 200 to the COMMISSION value for agent R. Osler.

```
NDL-FIND FIRST AGENT WHERE ANAME = "Osler R"
                              ADDR = "456 Pine St".
NDL-GET AGENT   SET Z TO COMMISSION.
ADD 200 TO Z.
NDL-MODIFY AGENT  SET COMMISSION TO Z.
```

SION in the current agent record with the value of *Z*. We note that some MODIFY statements may lead to errors. For example, it is illegal to change a client's policy number to an already existing policy number since POLICYNUMBER is a key for CLIENT. A more subtle error occurs if we try to change the AOFFICE value for an agent. By STRUCTURAL INSERTION this would lead to changing the OFFICE_AGENT set occurrence for this agent, a change which is not allowed because the retention is FIXED.

This takes care of the update commands. Next we write a few program segments, primarily to illustrate some processing in the database. We continue to use COBOL as the programming language. The first program segment is given in Figure 2.4.7. The problem is to print the name of every agent in the office at 200 North Dr. We do not actually give all the COBOL details. In the loop, we find the next agent each time and print the agent's name. We assume that, initially, DB-STATUS equals "00000". Each time a database statement is executed, a value for DB-STATUS is returned by the system: for a successful operation the code is "00000"; a different code is returned for each type of unsuccessful operation.

FIGURE 2.4.7
Print the name of every agent in the office at 200 North Dr.

```
    .
    .
    PERFORM INITIALIZATION.
    PERFORM LOOP UNTIL DB-STATUS IS NOT EQUAL TO '00000'.
    .
    .
INITIALIZATION.
    NDL-FIND FIRST OFFICE WHERE OFFICEADDRESS =
                         "200 North Dr".
    NDL-FIND FIRST AGENT IN OFFICE_AGENT.
LOOP.
    NDL-GET AGENT   SET AGENT-NAME TO ANAME.
    WRITE AGENT-NAME.
    NDL-FIND NEXT AGENT IN OFFICE_AGENT.
    .
    .
```

FIGURE 2.4.8
Print the name of every physician who has a patient in the office at 200
North Dr.

```
    .
    .

     PERFORM INITIALIZATION.
     PERFORM LOOP UNTIL DB-STATUS IS NOT EQUAL TO '00000'.
    .
    .
INITIALIZATION.
     NDL-FIND FIRST OFFICE WHERE OFFICEADDRESS =
                              "200 North Dr".
     NDL-FIND FIRST AGENT IN OFFICE_AGENT.
LOOP.
     NDL-FIND OWNER PHYSICIAN_AGENT.
     IF DB-STATUS IS EQUAL TO '00000'
       NDL-GET PHYSICIAN  SET PHYSICIAN-NAME TO NAME
       WRITE PHYSICIAN-NAME.
     NDL-FIND NEXT AGENT IN OFFICE_AGENT.
    .
    .
```

FIGURE 2.4.9
For each office print the address of the office and the name of every physician
who has a patient at that office.

```
    .
    .

     NDL-FIND FIRST OFFICE IN ALL_OFFICES.
     PERFORM MAIN-LOOP UNTIL DB-STATUS IS NOT EQUAL TO
       '00000'.
    .
    .
MAIN-LOOP.
     NDL-GET OFFICE  SET OADDR TO OFFICEADDRESS.
     WRITE OADDR.
     NDL-FIND FIRST AGENT IN OFFICE_AGENT.
     PERFORM INNER-LOOP UNTIL DB-STATUS IS NOT EQUAL TO
       '00000'.
     NDL-FIND NEXT OFFICE IN ALL_OFFICES.
INNER-LOOP.
     NDL-FIND OWNER PHYSICIAN_AGENT.
     IF DB-STATUS IS EQUAL TO '00000'
       NDL-GET PHYSICIAN  SET PHYSICIAN-NAME TO NAME
       WRITE PHYSICIAN-NAME.
     NDL-FIND NEXT AGENT IN OFFICE_AGENT.
    .
    .
```

The next program segment, given in Figure 2.4.8, which is again a loop, prints the name of every physician who has a patient in the office at 200 North Dr. The loop takes care of the case where an agent does not have a physician by checking the DB-STATUS. Note the database navigation from the OFFICE file to the AGENT file and then to the PHYSICIAN file. (We do not delete duplicate names.) Then, in Figure 2.4.9, we do what we did in the previous example, for each office. We use a separate outer loop to traverse the singular set ALL_OFFICES. We assume that "200 North Dr" is the address of an office and that each office has at least one agent.

Our next example, Figure 2.4.10, is an extension of the one in Figure 2.4.4. But in this case we wish to transfer all the clients of J. Lewis to T. Baker and then remove J. Lewis from the database. We set up a loop where we go back and forth between Lewis and Baker and reconnect the clients one at a time. When there are no more clients left, we remove Lewis from the database. We use a construct here called a **temporary set** (the older term is **keep list** for a similar construct) *which is a singular set whose members are cursors.* We assume that the temporary set AGENTLIST has already been declared. We initialize AGENTLIST with two elements:

FIGURE 2.4.10
Transfer all the clients of J. Lewis to T. Baker and delete J. Lewis from the database.

```
        .
        .
    PERFORM INITIALIZATION.
    PERFORM LOOP UNTIL DB-STATUS IS NOT EQUAL TO
       '00000'.
    NDL-ERASE AGENT WITH FULL CASCADE.
        .
        .
INITIALIZATION.
    NDL-FIND FIRST AGENT WHERE ANAME = "Lewis J"
                              ADDR = "35 Fall Ln".
    NDL-CONNECT AGENT TO AGENTLIST.
    NDL-FIND FIRST CLIENT IN AGENT_CLIENT.
    NDL-FIND FIRST AGENT WHERE ANAME = "Baker T"
                              ADDR = "805 Hills Rd".
    NDL-CONNECT AGENT TO AGENTLIST.
LOOP.
    NDL-FIND LAST AGENT IN AGENTLIST.
    NDL-RECONNECT CLIENT IN AGENT_CLIENT.
    NDL-FIND FIRST AGENT IN AGENTLIST.
    NDL-FIND FIRST CLIENT IN AGENT_CLIENT.
        .
        .
```

FIGURE 2.4.11
Print the name and address of the agent with the largest commission value and
the name of this agent's manager.

```
    .
    .
      PERFORM INITIALIZATION.
      PERFORM MAIN-LOOP UNTIL DB-STATUS IS NOT EQUAL TO
        '00000'.
      PERFORM PRINT-NAME.
    .
    .
INITIALIZATION.
      MOVE 0 TO BEST_COMMISSION.
      NDL-FIND FIRST OFFICE IN ALL_OFFICES.
      NDL-GET OFFICE
        SET BEST-MANAGER TO MANAGER
MAIN-LOOP.
      NDL-FIND FIRST AGENT IN OFFICE_AGENT.
      PERFORM INNER-LOOP UNTIL DB-STATUS IS NOT EQUAL TO
        '00000'.
      NDL-FIND NEXT OFFICE IN ALL_OFFICES.
      NDL-GET OFFICE   SET NEW-MANAGER TO MANAGER.
INNER-LOOP.
      NDL-GET AGENT
        SET NEW-COMMISSION TO COMMISSION
        SET NEW-NAME TO ANAME
        SET NEW-ADDR TO ADDR.
      IF NEW-COMMISSION IS GREATER THAN BEST-COMMISSION
        MOVE NEW-NAME TO BEST-NAME
        MOVE NEW-ADDR TO BEST-ADDR
        MOVE NEW-MANAGER TO BEST-MANAGER.
      NDL-FIND NEXT AGENT IN OFFICE_AGENT.
PRINT-NAME.
      WRITE BEST-NAME.
      WRITE BEST-ADDR.
      WRITE BEST-MANAGER.
    .
    .
```

the cursor to Lewis's record is the first element and the cursor to Baker's
record is the second (last) element. The last example is given in Figure
2.4.11. The objective here is to find the agent with the largest commission
and the name of this agent's manager. Again we set up a double loop as
we go through all the agents in all the offices to get the answer. We note
that only the data about one agent is printed, even if there is a tie for
the largest commission value.

2.5 Exercises

2.1   (a) Represent a sample occurrence for the LAWYER_CLIENT set given in Figure 2.5.1(a) as a
   (*i*)   singly linked list.
   (*ii*)   circular singly linked list.
   (*iii*) circular doubly linked list.
   (*iv*)   circular singly linked list with a pointer from each element to the head node.
   (*v*)   circular doubly linked list with a pointer from each element to the head node.
   (b) Same as at (a) but for the PRINCIPAL_TEACHER set given in Figure 2.5.1(b).
   (c) Same as at (a) but for the data structure diagram in part (*ii*) of Figure 1.3.2(b).

2.2   Draw the linked list representation for a database represented by the data structure diagram of
   (a) Figure 1.3.3(a).   (c) Figure 1.7.2(a).
   (b) Figure 1.3.3(b).   (d) Figure 1.7.2(b).

2.3   Construct a connection file with attributes and draw a data structure diagram to represent the many-to-many relationship between
   (a) House and Contractor.   (b) Store and Supplier.

FIGURE 2.5.1
Codasyl Sets

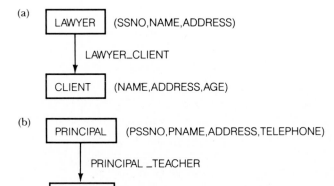

(a)

| LAWYER | (SSNO,NAME,ADDRESS) |

LAWYER_CLIENT

| CLIENT | (NAME,ADDRESS,AGE) |

(b)

| PRINCIPAL | (PSSNO,PNAME,ADDRESS,TELEPHONE) |

PRINCIPAL _TEACHER

| TEACHER | (TSSNO,TNAME,CLASS,RANK) |

FIGURE 2.5.2
Data Structure Diagram for a Department Store

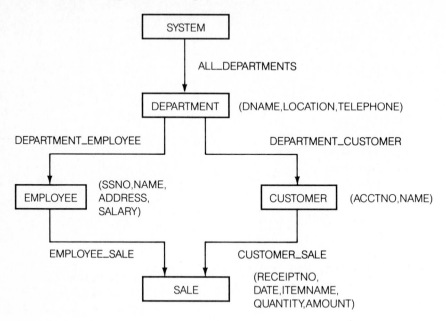

2.4 Write a schema for a department store given the data structure diagram of Figure 2.5.2.

2.5 Write a schema for a law firm given the data structure diagram of Figure 2.5.3.

2.6 Write a schema for a library given the data structure diagram of Figure 2.5.4.

2.7 Write a schema for a service department given the data structure diagram of Figure 2.5.5.

2.8 Using your answer to Exercise 2.5, write a subschema for the offices of the law firm which contains the files OFFICE and LAWYER and the set OFFICE_LAWYER. Rename OFFICE_LAWYER to ATTORNEY, TELNO to PHONE, and omit SSNO and STATUS.

2.9 Using your answer to Exercise 2.6, write a subschema for the borrowers of the library which contains the files BORROWER and OUT_MATERIAL and the set BORROWER_OUT. Rename BORROWER_OUT to RECORDS and omit BIRTHDATE, NUMBER, and PUBLISHER.

FIGURE 2.5.3
Data Structure Diagram for a Law Firm

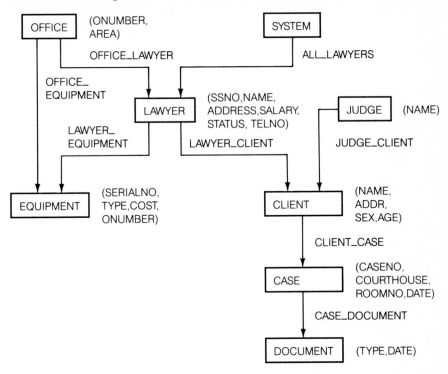

2.10 Using your answer to Exercise 2.7, write a subschema for the customers of the service department which contains the files TEAM, EMPLOYEE, and CUSTOMER and the sets TEAM_EMPLOYEE and EMPLOYEE_CUSTOMER. Rename TEAM to TEAM-MEMBER, ESSNO to SSNO, ENAME to NAME, and ESALARY to SALARY. Omit LOCATION and EADDR.

2.11 Using your answer to Exercise 2.8, use the FIND statement to write commands for the following:
   (a) Find the record for the office whose number is 103.
   (b) If the current record is the one for office number 103, find a record for a lawyer whose salary is greater than $30,000.
   (c) Find the record of a lawyer whose office number is 200.
   (d) If the current record is the one for lawyer T. Jones, find the record of the office of T. Jones.
   (e) Find the record of a lawyer whose office number is 225 and whose address is 123 Home St.

FIGURE 2.5.4
Data Structure Diagram for a Library

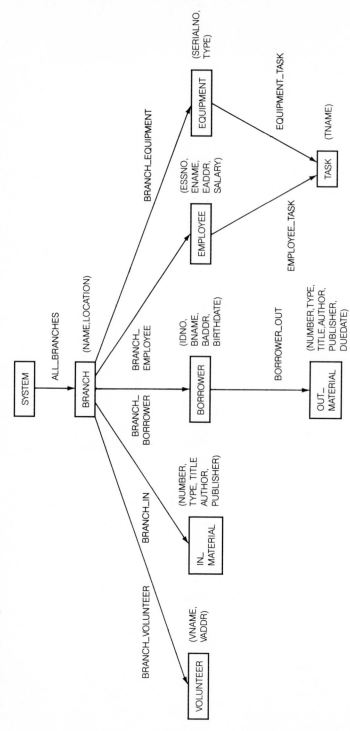

FIGURE 2.5.5
Data Structure Diagram for a Service Department

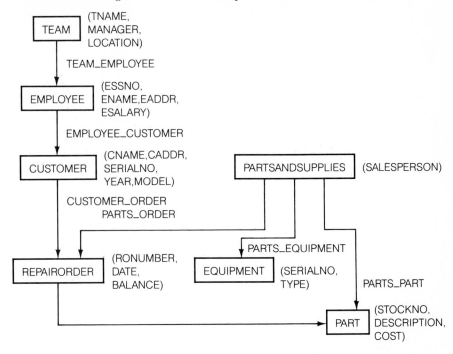

2.12 Using your answer to Exercise 2.9, use the FIND statement to write commands for the following:

(a) Find the record for a borrower named K. Smith.

(b) Find the record of another borrower named K. Smith.

(c) Find the record of the borrower L. Jones at 26 Brick Rd.

(d) If the current record is the one for K. Smith, find the record of some material that K. Smith has checked out.

(e) Find the most recently accessed borrower record.

2.13 Using your answer to Exercise 2.10, use the FIND statement to write commands for the following:

(a) Find the record of an employee whose salary is greater than $20,000.

(b) If the current record is the one for the employee with the social security number 123-45-6789, find the record for this employee's team.

(c) Under the same assumptions as in (b), find the record for a customer of the employee.

(d) Find the record of another customer of the employee found in (b).

(e) Find the record of a customer who owns a 1985 Corolla.

2.14 Using your answer to Exercise 2.4 and treating it as a subschema, write program segments for the following:
  (a) Print the total amount of all sales made by the employee with social security number 555-66-7777.
  (b) Print the name and salary of each employee in the Furniture department.
  (c) For each department, print its name and location and the name of each customer who has made a purchase for over $100.

2.15 Using your answer to Exercise 2.5 and treating it as a subschema, write program segments for the following:
  (a) Insert an office record for office number 301 whose area is 640.
  (b) Insert case number 671 as a case of client B. White, who lives at 2204 Branch Rd. The COURTHOUSE, ROOMNO, and DATE values are Central, 65, and 7/24/86, respectively.
  (c) Delete the lawyer with social security number 111-22-3333 from the database without deleting this lawyer's clients, if possible. If not possible, explain why not.
  (d) Transfer the equipment with serial number VAC37PQH9R from office number 200 to 307, if possible. If not possible, explain why not.
  (e) Change the age of D. Fisher, who is a client of the lawyer with social security number 221-13-3445, to 25.
  (f) Transfer D. Fisher (see [e]) to the lawyer with social security number 987-65-4321.
  (g) Print the name and address of each lawyer in office number 205.
  (h) Print the name of the oldest client in the database and the name of this client's lawyer and judge.
  (i) Print the list of all document data associated with each male client who is under the age of 25.

2.16 Using your answer to Exercise 2.6 and treating it as a subschema, write program segments for the following:
  (a) Print all data about the materials that are out with the borrower whose ID number is 266135.
  (b) Insert the book *Introduction to Logic Programming* by C. J. Hogger, published by Academic Press, number QA76.6.H624, as being checked out with a due date of January 3, 1988, by the borrower with ID number 266135.
  (c) Change the address of the volunteer K. Smith from 907 Hill St. to 43 Green Way.
  (d) Print the name of every author whose material is available at the library branch on South St.

(e) Delete the employee whose social security number is 234-56-7890.
(f) Transfer the employee with social security number 555-22-2333 from the Towson branch to the Tucson branch.
(g) Print the name and address of the employee with the lowest salary at the Parkville branch.
(h) Print the name and address of every volunteer at the Parkville branch.
(i) Print the names of all the tasks of the employee S. Johnson at the Parkville branch.

2.17 Using your answer to Exercise 2.7 and treating it as a subschema, write program segments for the following:
(a) Insert the customer S. Morgan, whose address is 6000 South Ave. and who owns a 1985 Celebrity with serial number AFT135GM6689, as a customer of the employee with social security number 455-35-5655.
(b) Print the name of each customer for the Blue team.
(c) Print the ID number for every part needed by the customer R. Davis, whose address is 445 Bird St.
(d) Print the address of customer F. Landers. (If there are several customers named F. Landers, print all the addresses.)
(e) Print the stock number values for all parts handled by the salesperson G. Jones as well as the serial number of each piece of equipment assigned to Jones.
(f) Delete the customer R. Davis, whose address is 445 Bird St., from the database. (This customer may have several cars.) Will this delete all of this customer's repair orders?

2.18 NDL allows the owner and member files to be the same. We show an example of such a Codasyl set in Figure 2.5.6 for courses that may have prerequisites, which may have their own prerequisites, and so on. Discuss the difficulties associated with the handling of

FIGURE 2.5.6
Data Structure Diagram with a Recursive Codasyl Set

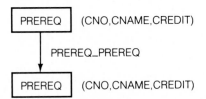

such recursive Codasyl sets. (In our syntax definitions we did not include some options of the FIND statement useful for the recursive case.)

2.6 Guide to Further Reading

The network database model is the subject of [2.3]. It is also discussed in [1.1] Chapter 5, [1.2] Chapter 23, [1.4] Chapter 3, and [2.4] Chapter 6. [1.2] gives IDMS as its example of a network database system. All of these books consider earlier versions of the network database model. Our discussion of NDL is based on the ANSI standard, [2.1]. [2.2] discusses the host language interface problem.

[2.1] Database Language NDL. New York: American National Standards Institute, 1986.

[2.2] Gallagher, L. J. "Procedure Language Access to Proposed American National Standard Database Management Systems," *Computer Networks* 8 (1984), pp. 31–42.

[2.3] Olle, T. W. *The Codasyl Approach to Data Base Management.* New York: John Wiley & Sons, 1978.

[2.4] Tsichritzis, D. C., and F. H. Lochovsky. *Data Models.* Englewood Cliffs, N.J.: Prentice-Hall, 1982.

Chapter 3

The Hierarchic Database Model

3.1 Hierarchic Representation

The great influence of the hierarchic database model is due to the widespread use of IBM's IMS (Information Management System) database system, whose early version dates from 1969. In this chapter, we discuss the hierarchic model based primarily in terms of IMS, without getting into highly specific details. IMS is not the only database system based on the hierarchic model: SYSTEM 2000 DBMS is also a popular hierarchic system, but it uses a different language. One important reason for the success of the hierarchic model is that data can often be placed in a natural way into hierarchies.

Consider the data structure diagrams in Figure 3.1.1. They are based on the diagrams of Figures 2.2.2 and 2.1.4(a), respectively. The pattern of the data is a sequence of one-to-many relationships in both cases. An office may have many agents, but each agent has only one office; an agent may have many clients, but each client has only one agent. A department may have many employees and pieces of equipment, but each employee and piece of equipment belongs to only one department; an employee may have many history records, but each such record is associated with only one employee.

When the data structure diagram is a tree, the diagram forms the basis for a hierarchic database schema. But problems occur when we try to represent many-to-many relationships. Recall that when we used two one-to-many relationships in the network model, the data structure diagram no longer retained the tree structure. Therefore, we cannot rep-

FIGURE 3.1.1
Hierarchic Data Structure Diagrams

(a) Insurance company example

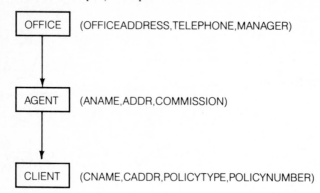

OFFICE (OFFICEADDRESS,TELEPHONE,MANAGER)

AGENT (ANAME,ADDR,COMMISSION)

CLIENT (CNAME,CADDR,POLICYTYPE,POLICYNUMBER)

(b) Department example

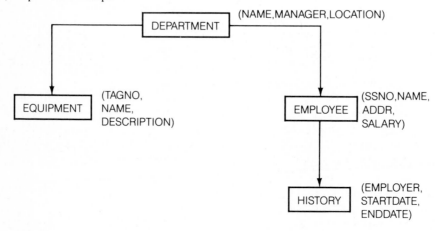

DEPARTMENT (NAME,MANAGER,LOCATION)

EQUIPMENT (TAGNO, NAME, DESCRIPTION)

EMPLOYEE (SSNO,NAME, ADDR, SALARY)

HISTORY (EMPLOYER, STARTDATE, ENDDATE)

resent many-to-many relationships in such a manner. Let's review the many-to-many relationship between **TEACHER** and **STUDENT** as shown in Figure 3.1.2(a), which we saw earlier in Figure 1.3.2(c). We give several methods for representing the relationship hierarchically.

Consider the representation in Figure 3.1.2(b). We picked a hierarchic order arbitrarily, placing **TEACHER** as the parent node and **STU-DENT** as the child node. With this representation, it is simple to find all the students of a teacher. But because **TEACHER-STUDENT** is a many-to-many relationship, each student record must be repeated for each teacher record where that teacher teaches the student. Therefore, we

FIGURE 3.1.2
Representing a Many-to-Many Relationship

(a) A many-to-many relationship

```
FILES          ATTRIBUTES
   TEACHER        SS#,TNAME,POSITION,DEPT
   STUDENT        SSNO,SNAME,ADDRESS,TELNO,
                  CLASSIFICATION
```

(b) An arbitrarily chosen hierarchic ordering

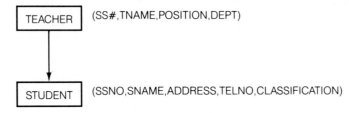

(c) Using two trees

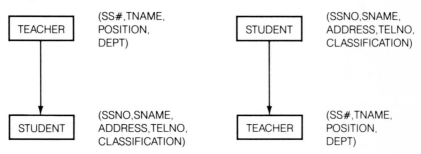

(d) Using virtual files

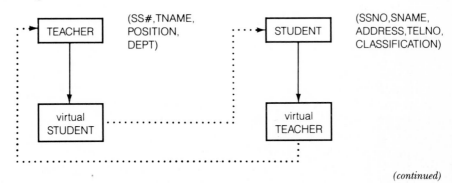

(continued)

FIGURE 3.1.2 *(continued)*

(e) Using virtual records and a connection record

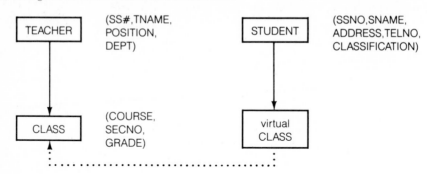

(f) A modification of part (e)

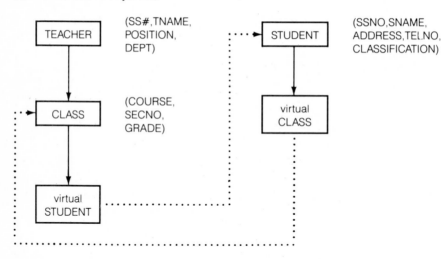

see two problems with this representation. First, there may be much duplication of data, which can lead to inconsistencies as discussed in Section 1.1. Second, to find all the teachers of a student is now a more complex process, because the whole database may have to be searched. Note that we have arbitrarily introduced asymmetry into a symmetric situation.

We next attempt to rectify the asymmetry problem introduced before. This attempt is shown in Figure 3.1.2(c). The idea is to use two trees: in one tree, TEACHER is the parent node and STUDENT is the child node, while in the other tree, STUDENT is the parent node and TEACHER is the child node. In this case, it is just as simple to find all the teachers of a student as it is to find all the students of a teacher—by using the

STUDENT-TEACHER tree in the first case and the TEACHER-STUDENT tree in the second case. But now the duplication problem becomes much worse. Not only is a student record duplicated for each teacher record where that teacher teaches the student as before, but also a teacher record is duplicated for every student record where again the teacher teaches the student.

The disadvantage of the previous representation is duplication of data; if we could solve that problem, we would have a better representation. Our third attempt uses a virtual file and is shown in Figure 3.1.2(d). A **virtual file** *contains virtual records.* Think of a **virtual record** as *a pointer to the actual record.* The dotted lines with arrowheads on them indicate these pointers. Because each student record appears only once (as a parent record in its tree) and each teacher record appears only once (as a parent record in its tree), the duplication problem is now solved. The symmetry of the original relationship is also retained.

Our final two methods for representation involve the use of a connection file. Recall from Chapter 2 that for network databases we introduced a connection file as the child of the two files in the many-to-many relationship. Figure 2.1.7(a) showed this approach for the TEACHER-STUDENT case. A hierarchic representation based on that earlier diagram appears in Figure 3.1.2(e). Note that more information is included here than for the previous three cases because of the connection file. But there is also an increase in complexity. For example, note how much more complicated it is to find all the students of a teacher. That process now requires finding children nodes in the TEACHER-CLASS tree, then scanning all the trees for STUDENT–virtual CLASS, and then following the virtual CLASS pointers to identify the students. Note also that the diagram is still not symmetric.

We can also modify this diagram while retaining its basic principles. For example, if finding all the students of a teacher is a frequent request, then we can place a virtual STUDENT file under CLASS as shown in Figure 3.1.2(f). In this case, each class record (as parent) has one virtual student record (as child) because we are really inverting the one-to-many STUDENT-CLASS relationship.

Suppose now that we are given a network data structure diagram which we wish to make into a hierarchy. Figure 3.1.3(a) illustrates a way of doing this for the simplest case of a network that is not a hierarchy. We just remove one parent, B in this case, and make a second tree with the virtual child file as the child of B. The result is given in Figure 3.1.3(b). In the general case, since a new tree is created every time a node has an additional parent, the number of trees at the end is $k + 1$ where k is obtained by summing $(p - 1)$ over all nodes with at least one parent, where p is the number of parents for a node.

We illustrate the effect of this method on a more complex network situation, such as the insurance company example of Figure 3.1.4(a) (which is based on Figure 2.2.2). We have made it more of a network by adding another parent node for CLIENT, called EMPLOYER, which represents the client's employer. This additional node may be useful if many employees of an employer have insurance through this particular insurance company. We have also added another node called STAFF, which gives information about other personnel in the insurance office. This node does not add any particular complications, in contrast to the EMPLOYER node.

Figure 3.1.4(b) shows the breakup of the network data structure diagram into a hierarchic diagram. In this case, because both AGENT

FIGURE 3.1.3
Transforming a Network Data Structure Diagram to a Hierarchic Data Structure Diagram

(a) Network data structure diagram   (b) Hierarchic data structure diagram

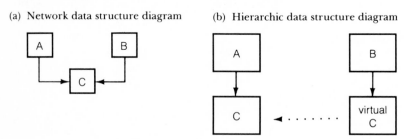

FIGURE 3.1.4
Transforming the Insurance Network Data Structure Diagram to a Hierarchic Data Structure Diagram

(a) Network data structure diagram

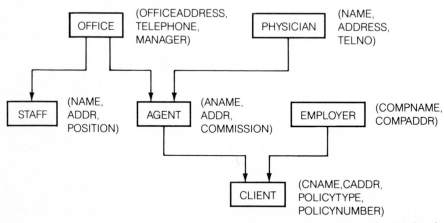

(continued)

(b) Hierarchic data structure diagram with three trees

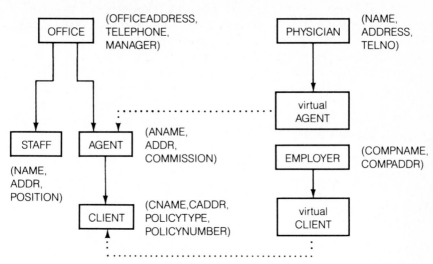

(c) Another hierarchic data structure diagram

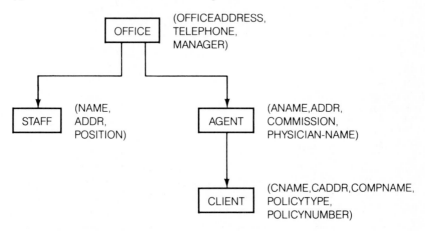

and **CLIENT** have two parents, $k = (2 - 1) + (2 - 1) = 2$, and so we obtain three trees. Because a virtual record requires an extra access by way of the pointers, it is a good idea to place the actual records in the place where they are accessed the most frequently. In this case, we assume that an agent is accessed more frequently through an office than through a physician, and a client is accessed more frequently through an agent than through an employer.

In the previous example, we were given a network data structure diagram which we converted into a hierarchic data structure diagram by constructing several trees. Another possibility is to include information about a parent record in a child record. We show one way of doing this in Figure 3.1.4(c). We place information about an agent's physician in the agent record and information about the employer of a client in the client record. We do not include all the information about the physician and the employer, but it would be possible to do so. This would be a reasonable representation to use also if we had originally started out designing a hierarchic structure.

3.2 Hierarchic Data Structures and IMS Concepts

In this section, we deal briefly with some implementation aspects for hierarchic database systems in general and for IMS in particular. Recall from our discussion in Section 2.1 (on the implementation of network databases) that it is convenient to implement each Codasyl set as a circularly linked list with head node. Because a hierarchy is a special kind of a network, the same implementation method can be used for a hierarchic database. However, it is not necessary to follow this procedure; there is a simpler method.

Let us consider again the portion of the insurance company example which is a two-level hierarchy—that is, OFFICE-AGENT-CLIENT. This means that there is a tree (occurrence) associated with each office. This tree contains all the agent records for that office and all the client records for each agent. The complete database then is a **forest,** which is just *an ordered collection of trees.* In Figure 3.2.1(a), we give an example of a possible tree in this forest. To keep the example simple we include only three agents each with only a few clients.

Trees may be traversed in various ways. In any such traversal, each node is visited exactly once. A particularly suitable traversal for a hierarchic database is the **preorder traversal.** The rule for preorder traversal is given recursively: *the root is visited first, then each subtree, from left to right, is traversed using the preorder method.* For the complete database the trees are traversed one by one in order from left to right. Thus the preorder traversal yields a straightforward and sequential implementation for the whole database. We illustrate it for the insurance company example in Figure 3.2.1(b). Thus the whole database can be represented as a sequential file. Note that this may not really be a good implementation, particularly if there are insertions to consider. In any case, conceptually we can think of the database as such a sequential file.

We mentioned in the previous section that IMS is a widely used hierarchic system, and it will be useful to discuss some of its aspects. We

FIGURE 3.2.1
Implementation for the Insurance Company Example

(a) The tree structure

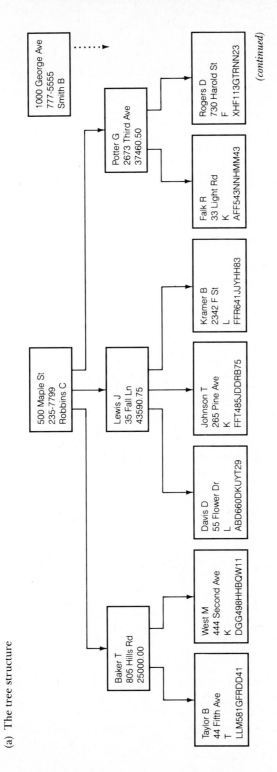

(continued)

FIGURE 3.2.1 (*continued*)

(b) Sequential implementation using preorder traversal

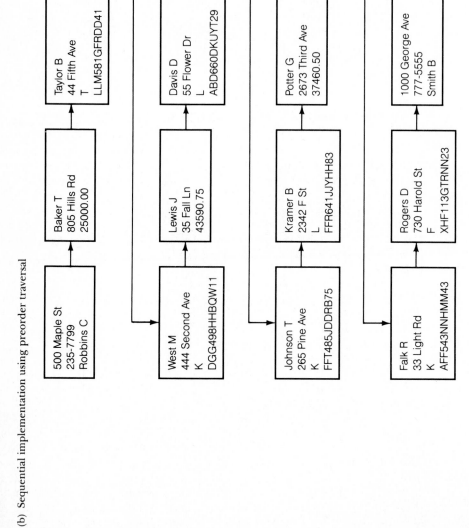

(c) Database description

```
DBD     NAME = INSPDBD
SEGM    NAME = OFFICE, BYTES = 43
FIELD   NAME = (OADDR,SEQ), BYTES = 20, START = 1
FIELD   NAME = TELNO, BYTES = 8, START = 21
FIELD   NAME = MANAGER, BYTES = 15, START = 29
SEGM    NAME = AGENT, PARENT = OFFICE, BYTES = 39
FIELD   NAME = (ANAME,SEQ), BYTES = 15, START = 1
FIELD   NAME = ADDR, BYTES = 20, START = 16
FIELD   NAME = COMMISS, BYTES = 4, START = 36
SEGM    NAME = CLIENT, PARENT = AGENT, BYTES = 49
FIELD   NAME = (CNAME,SEQ), BYTES = 15, START = 1
FIELD   NAME = CADDR, BYTES = 20, START = 16
FIELD   NAME = POLTYPE, BYTES = 1, START = 36
FIELD   NAME = POLICYNO, BYTES = 13, START = 37
```

start by considering database descriptions. In IMS, each tree has a name, called its DBD (database description). The storage in bytes is given for each record type and for each field type. Additionally, the starting position for each field within a record must be indicated. Each SEGM (segment) is the name of a node (or file) in the hierarchy. The parent node must be named for each node except the root. The field names (or attributes) of a file are given in order after the node name. The first field of a segment is sequenced, indicated by SEQ, meaning that the records are sorted on that field, and that the sequence field (unless specified otherwise by the letter M) is considered a key field for the segment. The segments are written using the preorder ordering of the data structure diagram. Identifiers are restricted to eight characters.

In Figure 3.2.1(c), we show the conceptual schema portion of the database description for the insurance company example. We choose the name INSPDBD as an abbreviation for Insurance Company Physical Database Description. In this example, there is only one DBD because there is only one tree. Because OADDR is a sequence field, the offices are stored in ascending order on office address, and office addresses are unique. Here, in contrast to Figure 2.2.3, ANAME is the key for AGENT and CNAME is the key for CLIENT. However, ANAME is the key for AGENT only within a specific OFFICE; thus, there may be several agents in the database with the same name, but not in the same office. Similarly, CNAME is the key for CLIENT within a specific OFFICE and AGENT hierarchy. If we want the combination ANAME,ADDR to be the key for AGENT, as in Figure 2.2.3, we can make the concatenation of ANAME and ADDR the sequence field. The same thing can be done for CLIENT with CNAME and CADDR.

The database description we just gave refers to the description of the conceptual view. But in IMS, users operate on external views that are defined by a **Program Communication Block (PCB).** Essentially, an external view is obtained from a conceptual view by omitting various items. We may omit a tree, for instance. If we omit a node of a tree, we must also omit the children of that node. Within each node we may omit any of the attributes and can reorder the attributes. In Figure 3.2.2(a), we give the database description for the more complex insurance company example of Figure 3.1.4(c).

In Figure 3.2.2(b), we give an external view that is essentially the database of Figure 3.2.1(c). Note that the nodes and fields which are included in the external view must be given. In IMS terminology, these items are called **sensitive.** Here we get the sensitive segments OFFICE, AGENT, and CLIENT. If all the attributes are included, then nothing further needs to be said. However, for AGENT and CLIENT we *exclude* one field. In this case, all the retained fields must be indicated. PROC-OPT is an abbreviation for processing options. G is used for get, I for insert, D for delete, and R for replace. Thus, this particular external view

FIGURE 3.2.2
IMS Descriptions for the More Complex Insurance Example

(a) Conceptual view

```
DBD      NAME = INSCPDBD
SEGM     NAME = OFFICE, BYTES = 43
FIELD    NAME = (OADDR,SEQ), BYTES = 20, START = 1
FIELD    NAME = TELNO, BYTES = 8, START = 21
FIELD    NAME = MANAGER, BYTES = 15, START = 29
SEGM     NAME = STAFF, PARENT = OFFICE, BYTES = 45
FIELD    NAME = (SNAME,SEQ), BYTES = 15, START = 1
FIELD    NAME = SADDR, BYTES = 20, START = 16
FIELD    NAME = POSITION, BYTES = 10, START = 36
SEGM     NAME = AGENT, PARENT = OFFICE, BYTES = 54
FIELD    NAME = (ANAME,SEQ), BYTES = 15, START = 1
FIELD    NAME = ADDR, BYTES = 20, START = 16
FIELD    NAME = COMMISS, BYTES = 4, START = 36
FIELD    NAME = DOCTOR, BYTES = 15, START = 40
SEGM     NAME = CLIENT, PARENT = AGENT, BYTES = 59
FIELD    NAME = (CNAME,SEQ), BYTES = 15, START = 1
FIELD    NAME = CADDR, BYTES = 20, START = 16
FIELD    NAME = COMPNAME, BYTES = 10, START = 36
FIELD    NAME = POLTYPE, BYTES = 1, START = 46
FIELD    NAME = POLICYNO, BYTES = 13, START = 47
```

(b) An external view

```
PCB      TYPE = DB, DBDNAME = INSCPDBD, KEYLEN = 50
SENSEG   NAME = OFFICE, PROCOPT = G
SENSEG   NAME = AGENT, PARENT = OFFICE, PROCOPT = G
SENFLD   NAME = ANAME, START = 1
SENFLD   NAME = ADDR, START = 16
SENFLD   NAME = COMMISS, START = 36
SENSEG   NAME = CLIENT, PARENT = AGENT, PROCOPT = G
SENFLD   NAME = CNAME, START = 1
SENFLD   NAME = CADDR, START = 16
SENFLD   NAME = POLTYPE, START = 36
SENFLD   NAME = POLICYNO, START = 37
```

is set up for retrieval only. Combinations of G, I, D, and R may be specified. The KEYLEN item indicates the maximum length of a sequence of keys in the hierarchic structure; in this case it is 50, which we obtain by adding 20 for OADDR, 15 for ANAME, and 15 for CNAME. Such a sequence identifies a record.

Recall now our discussion in the previous section concerning the representation of network structures in a hierarchic database. There we discussed the use of a virtual file to eliminate the duplication problem. We now examine the technique used in IMS to set up such a file. In

Figure 3.1.2(e), a virtual connection file CLASS represented the many-to-many relationship between TEACHER and STUDENT; we outline the database descriptions corresponding to this case in Figure 3.2.3.

There are three parts. The first part is given in Figure 3.2.3(a): it describes the TEACHER-CLASS hierarchy. The only new entry here is the LCHILD definition. In IMS terminology, virtual CLASS is considered a logical CHILD of CLASS. The LCHILD definition indicates that the segment CLASS has a logical child (that is, it appears in a virtual mode) in the hierarchy SVCPDBD.

The second part of the description is shown in Figure 3.2.3(b). This is the STUDENT–virtual CLASS hierarchy. Both this hierarchy and the previous one are considered to be physical. The physical-logical distinction refers to the difference between actual and virtual entries. (It is also used in another sense to distinguish between the conceptual and the external views.) For the segment VCLASS, there are no actual fields. (A record may also be partly actual and partly virtual.) We need to indicate that VCLASS has a pointer to a logical parent called CLASS which is actually in TCPDBD. (The TWIN pointer notion will be explained later.)

The third part of the description for the STUDENT-CLASS hierarchy describes the logical database—that is, what the user sees. This is shown in Figure 3.2.3(c). There are two files, STUDENT and VCLASS. The source for STUDENT is SVCPDBD. VCLASS is described in SVCPDBD but is in fact a virtual file whose actual value is CLASS in TCPDBD.

We continue our discussion of IMS by briefly describing some important concepts about IMS storage structures. In general, these structures illustrate various methods for storing a hierarchic database. IMS provides the following storage structures: **HSAM (Hierarchic Sequential Access Method), SHSAM (Simple Hierarchic Sequential Access Method), HISAM (Hierarchic Indexed Sequential Access Method), SHISAM (Simple Hierarchic Indexed Sequential Access Method), GSAM (Generalized Sequential Access Method), HDAM (Hierarchic Direct Access Method), and HIDAM (Hierarchic Indexed Direct Access Method).** In the sequential access methods, the records of a tree occurrence are physically placed in order, while in the direct access methods, the records are physically distributed and are connected by pointers. We consider here briefly some aspects of HSAM, HISAM, HDAM, and HIDAM.

Recall our discussion at the beginning of this section about the sequential implementation using preorder traversal. For an HSAM database, think of the elements as being on a tape in proper order. The difference between HSAM and HISAM reflects the distinction between sequential and indexed sequential files. Figure 3.2.4 illustrates this distinction for the first hierarchic insurance company example (see also Figures 3.1.1 and 3.2.1[b]). There are two offices: the first has three

FIGURE 3.2.3
Database Descriptions for TEACHER, STUDENT, CLASS

(a) Database description for the TEACHER-CLASS hierarchy

```
DBD       NAME = TCPDBD
SEGM      NAME = TEACHER, BYTES = 56
FIELD     NAME = (SS,SEQ), BYTES = 9, START = 1
FIELD     NAME = TNAME, BYTES = 20, START = 10
FIELD     NAME = POSITION, BYTES = 12, START = 30
FIELD     NAME = DEPT, BYTES = 15, START = 42
SEGM      NAME = CLASS, PARENT = TEACHER, BYTES = 7
LCHILD    NAME = (VCLASS,SVCPDBD)
FIELD     NAME = COURSE, BYTES = 3, START = 1
FIELD     NAME = SECNO, BYTES = 3, START = 4
FIELD     NAME = GRADE, BYTES = 1, START = 7
```

(b) Database description for the STUDENT–virtual CLASS hierarchy

```
DBD       NAME = SVCPDBD
SEGM      NAME = STUDENT, BYTES = 67
FIELD     NAME = (SSNO,SEQ), BYTES = 9, START = 1
FIELD     NAME = SNAME, BYTES = 20, START = 10
FIELD     NAME = ADDRESS, BYTES = 25, START = 30
FIELD     NAME = TELNO, BYTES = 10, START = 55
FIELD     NAME = CLASSIFY, BYTES = 3, START = 65
SEGM      NAME = VCLASS, POINTER = (LPARNT,TWIN),
          PARENT = ((STUDENT),(CLASS,VIRTUAL,TCPDBD))
```

(c) Database description for the STUDENT-CLASS hierarchy

```
DBD       NAME = SCLDBD, ACCESS = LOGICAL
DATASET LOGICAL
SEGM      NAME = STUDENT, SOURCE = ((STUDENT,,SVCPDBD))
SEGM      NAME = VCLASS, PARENT = STUDENT,
              SOURCE = ((VCLASS,,SVCPDBD),(CLASS,,TCPDBD))
```

agents, while the second has two agents. Each agent has one, two, or three clients. In this picture we do not indicate specific values for the attributes; we merely number each OFFICE, AGENT, and CLIENT record.

For HDAM and HIDAM, pointers are used to find the next element. There are basically two different ways used for setting up pointers: the hierarchic method and the sibling-child method. The IMS terminology is **HIER** for *the hierarchic method* and **TWIN** for *the sibling-child method*. We illustrate the difference in Figure 3.2.5. In the hierarchic method, we get a linked list of the entries using the preorder ordering. For the sibling-child method, there is a pointer from each record to its first child and to its next sibling. The second method involves more

FIGURE 3.2.4
HSAM and HISAM Structures for the Insurance Company Example

(a) HSAM

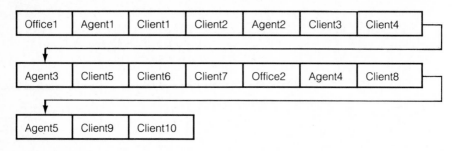

(b) HISAM

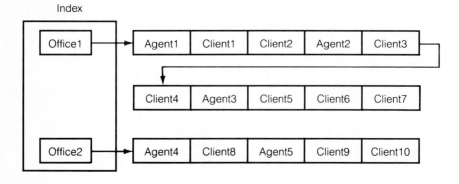

pointers, but it can lead to faster access for the database. Otherwise, the difference between HDAM and HIDAM is similar to the difference between HSAM and HISAM. In HDAM, direct access (by hashing) allows finding a particular root record very quickly. For HIDAM, the root records are indexed much like in HISAM. We do not go into any more details of these access methods here.

We end this section by mentioning some additional aspects of IMS. For one thing, IMS is a very complex system, and in our descriptions we omitted many details. One topic that we have not mentioned is **secondary indexing.** This method *can be used for indexing on a field which is not a key or sequence* and allows quick access to portions of the database based on certain values in an attribute. IMS is quite flexible in this regard, allowing not only a secondary index on any field of a file but also on any field in a node which is a descendant node in the tree structure. Take the insurance company example of Figure 3.1.1; with secondary indexing it is possible to index OFFICE on MANAGER and even on COMMISSION in AGENT. To be indexed secondarily, a node need not be a root node.

FIGURE 3.2.5
HIER vs. TWIN Pointers

(a) HIER

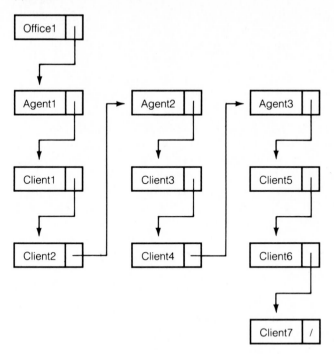

(b) TWIN

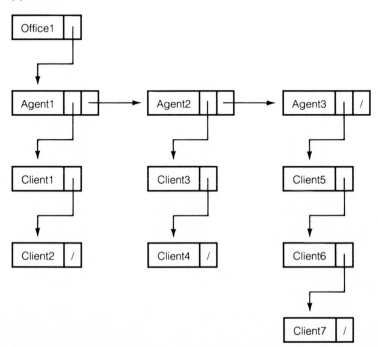

3.3 Hierarchic Database Retrieval

So far we have discussed hierarchic data structures in general and in IMS in particular. In this section, we discuss a procedural data manipulation language for hierarchic databases that is based on *the IMS data manipulation language,* **DL/I.** We find that the part of the language not involving storage structures is simpler than the network language that we discussed in Chapter 2, because there is not that much navigation that is done in a hierarchic database. A good way to begin is to recall that each occurrence of a tree, given in the database description, is a forest where the root of the first tree is just the first root occurrence in the tree. The elements are given using a preorder traversal.

DL/I is invoked from a host language which may be COBOL, PL/I, or IBM Assembler language. We use a PL/I orientation. IMS contains **a user working area (UWA)** to store various items such as templates for the files and a status indicator. Variables for these items are declared in the host language. We assume that these names are identical to the names used in the database. We also follow the convention that a successful DL/I operation leads to a STATUS value " " (2 blanks). IMS also maintains cursors to keep track of the current position in the database. The cursors are based on the notion of hierarchic sequence key value; this is a value which uniquely determines each record in the database.

The **hierarchic sequence key value** for an item *is obtained by concatenating the sequence (key) values for each node in the tree for that item starting at the root.* Additionally, a hierarchic order code, based on preorder traversal, is included for each segment. In the insurance company example at Figure 3.2.2(a), the hierarchic order codes are 1 for OFFICE, 2 for STAFF, 3 for AGENT, and 4 for CLIENT. The hierarchic sequence key for the office at 26 York Ave is

```
"126 York Ave          ";
```

for the staff member M. Smith, who works at that office, (using the codes 1 and 2) it is

```
"126 York Ave          2Smith M         ";
```

and for L. Rogers, who is a customer of T. Baker at the same office, we obtain

```
"126 York Ave          3Baker T          4Rogers L         ".
```

We note that not only does each segment have a hierarchic order code, but that the order (according to the preorder ordering of the tree)

of the segment occurrences is, in fact, identical to the ascending ordering of the hierarchic sequence keys. In our example, the keys are fairly long; it is customary to use shorter keys in order to avoid long hierarchic sequence keys.

The retrieval commands are **GU (Get Unique), GN (Get Next),** and **GNP (Get Next Within Parent).** The GU command is in fact a Get First command which finds the first record, of some type, in the database, starting at the beginning. All of the commands include one or more segment names in the preorder traversal, which can be qualified, so that we can retrieve, using a single command, the first record such that some condition holds. With the GN command we can retrieve the next record for which some condition holds. Finally, the GNP command allows the retrieval of a record if it is a descendant of some specified record in the tree. So, to be more precise, GNP really stands for "Get Next Within Ancestor." As in the case of the network model we discussed in Chapter 2, it is very important to keep track of where we are in the database.

We use the insurance company example of Figure 3.2.2(a) and treat it here as an external view. In part (a) of Figure 3.3.1, we write the retrieval to obtain the record for the office at 500 Maple St. This is a root segment. Next we consider the retrieval to find the record for the first staff member for the office at 500 Maple St. This is given in part (b). Here STAFF is not qualified as we are simply interested in the first staff member. Next we retrieve the record for a client named D. Rogers, as shown in part (c). If there are several clients in the database named D. Rogers, then the first such record is obtained.

Now we consider retrievals which involve loops. In each case, we print the requested data. Here we start using PL/I statements. We use a simplified version of DL/I where we indicate each call statement by start-

FIGURE 3.3.1
Retrieval Using GU

(a) Find the record for the office at 500 Maple St.

```
GU    OFFICE (OADDR = '500 Maple St')
```

(b) Find the record for the first staff member for the office at 500 Maple St.

```
GU    OFFICE (OADDR = '500 Maple St')
      STAFF
```

(c) Find the record for a client named D. Rogers.

```
GU    OFFICE
      AGENT
      CLIENT (CNAME = 'Rogers D')
```

FIGURE 3.3.2
Retrieval Using GN

(a) Print the address of every client named D. Rogers.

```
CALL DLITPLI( GU    OFFICE
                    AGENT
                    CLIENT (CNAME = 'Rogers D') );
DO WHILE (STATUS = '  ');
    PUT SKIP LIST (CLIENT.CADDR);
    CALL DLITPLI( GN   CLIENT (CNAME = 'Rogers D') );
    END;
```

(b) Print all client names and their policy numbers.

```
CALL DLITPLI(GU    OFFICE
                   AGENT
                   CLIENT );
DO WHILE (STATUS = '  ');
    PUT SKIP LIST (CLIENT.CNAME, CLIENT.POLICYNO);
    CALL DLITPLI( GN   CLIENT );
    END;
```

ing it with CALL DLITPLI. First, suppose that we wish to print a list of the addresses for every client named D. Rogers. This can be done as shown in Figure 3.3.2(a). The GU command finds the first record for a client named D. Rogers. In the DO WHILE loop, we print the address of the client and then apply the GN command to find the next client named D. Rogers in the database. It is not necessary with the GN command to indicate the complete hierarchy. Next, suppose that we want to print a list of all client names and their policy numbers. The program segment given in Figure 3.3.2(b) will go through all the clients in order.

Our first example using GNP asks for all the staff records for the office at 500 Maple St. The program segment is given in Figure 3.3.3(a). The GU statement finds the office. The GNP statement, first outside and then inside the loop, finds the next staff record. The GNP statement will not retrieve any more records after it has retrieved all the records which are descendants of the current parent, in this case the office record for which the address is 500 Maple St. The current parent is always the most recently found record by a GU or GN statement.

Let us now find the name and address for each client of agent J. Lewis. The program segment is given in Figure 3.3.3(b). First we find the record of agent J. Lewis by a GU command. Then we set up a loop to find all the clients of that agent using the GNP command. (If there are several agents named J. Lewis, this program segment will find the clients of only the first such agent in the database.) We mentioned before that GNP need not be limited to the immediate parent; it can refer to a parent further up in the tree. The example in Figure 3.3.3(c) illustrates

FIGURE 3.3.3
Retrieval Using GNP

(a) Print the staff records for the office at 500 Maple St.

```
CALL DLITPLI( GU    OFFICE (OADDR = '500 Maple St') );
CALL DLITPLI( GNP   STAFF );
DO WHILE (STATUS = '  ');
    PUT SKIP LIST (STAFF);
    CALL DLITPLI( GNP   STAFF );
    END;
```

(b) Print the name and address for each client of the agent J. Lewis.

```
CALL DLITPLI( GU    OFFICE
                    AGENT (ANAME = 'Lewis J') );
CALL DLITPLI( GNP   CLIENT );
DO WHILE (STATUS = '  ');
    PUT SKIP LIST (CLIENT.CNAME, CLIENT.CADDR);
    CALL DLITPLI( GNP CLIENT );
    END;
```

(c) Print the names of all the clients for the office at 500 Maple St.

```
CALL DLITPLI( GU    OFFICE (OADDR = '500 Maple St') );
CALL DLITPLI( GNP   CLIENT );
DO WHILE (STATUS = '  ');
    PUT SKIP LIST (CLIENT.CNAME);
    CALL DLITPLI( GNP CLIENT );
    END;
```

this ability: the GNP CLIENT in this example retrieves the next client record, which is a *grandchild* of the office record whose address is 500 Maple St.

In some cases, it is useful to obtain not only a particular record occurrence but also its parent. For example, we may know that there is a client, T. Johnson, whose policy number and policy type as well as whose agent's name are requested. Assume that we know that T. Johnson is a client in the office at 500 Maple St. The retrieval is shown in Figure 3.3.4(a): the command code D retrieves the agent record that is associated with (is the parent of) the retrieved client record. Note how a command code is placed after an asterisk following the appropriate segment name. A similar situation arises if we want to find the name, address, and manager of the agent with the largest commission value. This is the example used for NDL in Figure 2.4.11; the hierarchic version appears in Figure 3.3.4(b). Again, only data about one agent gets printed.

The GU, GN, and GNP commands ordinarily move forward in the database according to the hierarchic order. In some cases, however, it may be necessary to move backward. If we want to find the first staff

FIGURE 3.3.4
Retrieval Using Command Codes

(a) Print the name of the agent, the policy type, and policy number for T. Johnson, who is a client at the 500 Maple St., office.

```
CALL DLITPLI( GU    OFFICE (OADDR = '500 Maple St')
                    AGENT*D
                    CLIENT (CNAME = 'Johnson T') );
PUT SKIP LIST (AGENT.ANAME, CLIENT.POLTYPE,
              CLIENT.POLICYNO);
```

(b) Print the name and address of the agent with the largest commission value and the name of this agent's manager.

```
BESTCOMMISSION = 0;
CALL DLITPLI( GU    OFFICE*D
                    AGENT );
NEWMANAGER = OFFICE.MANAGER;
NEWNAME = AGENT.ANAME;
NEWADDRESS = AGENT.ADDR;
DO WHILE (STATUS = ' ');
   NEWCOMMISSION = AGENT.COMMIS;
   IF  NEWCOMMISSION > BESTCOMMISSION
       THEN  DO;
                   BESTCOMMISSION = NEWCOMMISSION;
                   BESTNAME = NEWNAME;
                   BESTADDRESS = NEWADDRESS;
                   BESTMANAGER = NEWMANAGER;
                   END;
   CALL DLITPLI( GN    OFFICE*D
                       AGENT );
   END;
```

(c) Print the name of the first staff member in the office where B. Miller is an agent.

```
NOTFOUND = '1'B;
CALL DLITPLI( GU    OFFICE );
CALL DLITPLI( GNP   AGENT (ANAME = 'Miller B' AND
                          ADDRESS = '1234 T St') );
IF STATUS ¬= ' ' THEN
   DO WHILE (NOTFOUND);
      CALL DLITPLI( GN OFFICE );
      CALL DLITPLI( GNP AGENT (ANAME = 'Miller B' AND
                              ADDRESS = '1234 T St') );
      IF STATUS = ' ' THEN
         NOTFOUND = '0'B;
      END;
CALL DLITPLI( GNP STAFF*F );
PUT SKIP LIST (STAFF.SNAME);
```

member in the office where B. Miller is an agent, then once we find B. Miller, because of the hierarchic structure we are past all the staff members. In such cases the command code F can be used to go back to another record occurrence within the same parent (in our example, the office where B. Miller is the agent). This command is illustrated in Figure 3.3.4(c). In PL/I, '1'B is true and '0'B is false. The method is to find the agent B. Miller and to set up the parent record office as Miller's office. Then, using the command code F, we can obtain the first staff member in that office.

3.4 Hierarchic Database Updates

As we explained in Section 1.4 and discussed in connection with the network database model, there are three types of updates: insertion, deletion, and modification. The corresponding IMS statements are **ISRT (Insert), DLET (Delete),** and **REPL (Replace).** We now give some examples using these update commands.

Let's insert a new agent, B. Roberts, into the database. In IMS the hierarchic sequence from the root is determined first; otherwise the most recently accessed path is followed. IMS does not allow the MANUAL type of NDL insertion, discussed in Section 2.2, where a record may exist in the database without a parent record in a Codasyl set. Thus, because OFFICE is the root of the tree to which AGENT belongs in the data structure diagram and is the parent of AGENT, we need to know to which office record the new agent record should belong. Let's suppose that B. Roberts is inserted into the office at 500 Maple St. We also need additional data about this agent to obtain values for the other fields. We build up the record in the user working area first. The program for this insertion is given in Figure 3.4.1(a). If we just wrote ISRT AGENT;, then this agent record would be inserted into the most recently accessed office record. If this were the one at 500 Maple St., then we would obtain the same result. In either case, because the agents within an office are ordered by the sequence field, this agent record will be placed in the appropriate position.

There is a special situation when a new root record is inserted, for in this case there is no hierarchic sequence to the root. IMS uses the command code D in this case and also when several records are inserted in a hierarchic manner. First, suppose that we wish to insert a new office record. Such an insertion is shown in Figure 3.4.1(b). Let's suppose that we wish to insert not only a new office record but also the record of a staff member at that office. An example is shown in Figure 3.4.1(c). We note here that a database is originally loaded by a sequence of insertions.

Next we consider deletions. Here we find the need for the Hold variation on the GET statement. The word "Hold" is used to indicate an

FIGURE 3.4.1
Hierarchic Insertions

(a) Insert the new agent B. Roberts into the office at 500 Maple St.

```
AGENT.ANAME = 'Roberts B';
AGENT.ADDRESS = '157 Second St';
AGENT.COMMISS = 54300.25;
AGENT.DOCTOR = 'Stone G';
CALL DLITPLI( ISRT  OFFICE (OADDR = '500 Maple St')
                    AGENT );
```

(b) Insert a new office at 260 Fine St.

```
OFFICE.OADDR = '260 Fine St';
OFFICE.TELNO = '357-1100';
OFFICE.MANAGER = 'Jones L';
CALL DLITPLI( ISRT   OFFICE*D );
```

(c) Insert a new office as in (b) and a staff member J. Williams into the office.

```
OFFICE.OADDR = '260 Fine St';
OFFICE.TELNO = '357-1100';
OFFICE.MANAGER = 'Jones L';
STAFF.SNAME = 'Williams J';
STAFF.SADDR = '3311 Pine Ave';
STAFF.POSITION = 'Secretary';
CALL DLITPLI( ISRT   OFFICE*D
                     STAFF );
```

impending update. The three statements are **GHU (Get Hold Unique),
GHN (Get Hold Next),** and **GHNP (Get Hold Next within Parent).**
Basically, what happens in a deletion is that a particular record occurrence is found which is then deleted. So let's suppose that we wish to
delete a client named B. Taylor, using the program segment given in part
(a) of Figure 3.4.2. Note that this program simply deletes the first client
named B. Taylor. That may not be the right person if there are several
individuals with the same name in the database! If we know the agent
and the office, then we can be certain that the right client is deleted. This
more specific request appears in part (b).

CLIENT is a leaf node in the tree. What happens if we delete a
nonleaf node, such as AGENT? Because each client record must be associated with an agent record, once the agent record is deleted then its
client records cannot exist either. Therefore, the deletion of a nonleaf
node results in the deletion of all of its descendants (like using the FULL
CASCADE phrase for NDL as discussed in Section 2.4). In Figure 3.4.2(c),
we give an example of deleting agent T. Baker at the above address and
all of this agent's clients. Here a deleted record for each record type

FIGURE 3.4.2
Hierarchic Deletions

(a) Delete the client B. Taylor from the database.

```
CALL DLITPLI( GHU    OFFICE
                     AGENT
                     CLIENT (CNAME = 'Taylor B') );
CALL DLITPLI( DLET   CLIENT );
```

(b) Delete the client B. Taylor from the database, where this client's agent is T. Baker, who
    is in the office at 500 Maple St.

```
CALL DLITPLI( GHU    OFFICE (OADDR = '500 Maple St')
                     AGENT  (ANAME = 'Baker T')
                     CLIENT (CNAME = 'Taylor B') );
CALL DLITPLI( DLET   CLIENT );
```

(c) Delete agent T. Baker, who is at the office on 500 Maple St., and all of T. Baker's clients.

```
CALL DLITPLI( GHU    OFFICE (OADDR = '500 Maple St')
                     AGENT (ANAME = 'Baker T') );
CALL DLITPLI( DLET   AGENT );
```

remains in the user working area. Thus we can put T. Baker back into the database, but not all the clients. In particular, in the previous example we could have put the client B. Taylor back into the database.

The last update operation is modification. With modification we retrieve a record, make the appropriate change in the user working area, and place the new record back in the database. Again, the GET HOLD retrieval statements must be used. Let's assume, for example, that the client B. Taylor moves. Assuming that we know this client's agent and the agent's office, we show the modification in Figure 3.4.3. We note that a record modified by REPL must stay in the same place in the database, hence REPL cannot be used to modify the key (sequence) field.

Let us reconsider the example where we deleted the agent T. Baker and all of this agent's clients. In Section 2.4 we had a similar example for NDL, and there we showed how to transfer all the clients to another agent before deleting them from the database. We now do the same thing in the hierarchic case, transferring the clients of T. Baker to the agent G. Potter. In the network case, we used a temporary set to keep track of the two positions in the database. In the hierarchic IMS version we use two external views (PCBs), both of which refer, in fact, to the same database. However, we can track our location separately in each view and so keep track of the two positions.

The program segment for this hierarchic modification appears in Figure 3.4.4. We assume the existence of two views called INSC1 and

FIGURE 3.4.3
Hierarchic Replacement

Change the address of the client B. Taylor to 200 East St. Taylor's agent is T. Baker, who is in the office at 500 Maple St.

```
CALL DLITPLI( GHU    OFFICE (OADDR = '500 Maple St')
                     AGENT (ANAME = 'Baker T')
                     CLIENT (CNAME = 'Taylor B') );
CLIENT.CADDR = '200 East St';
CALL DLITPLI( REPL  CLIENT );
```

FIGURE 3.4.4
Hierarchic Modification

Transfer all the clients of T. Baker to G. Potter, and delete T. Baker from the database.

```
CALL DLITPLI( GHU(INSC1)    OFFICE (OADDR = '500 Maple St')
                            AGENT (ANAME = 'Baker T') );
CALL DLITPLI( GNP(INSC1)    CLIENT );
DO WHILE (STATUS(INSC1) = '   ');
   CLIENT(INSC2) = CLIENT(INSC1);
   CALL DLITPLI( ISRT(INSC2)   OFFICE(OADDR = '500 Maple St')
                               AGENT (ANAME = 'Potter G')
                               CLIENT );
   CALL DLITPLI( GNP(INSC1)    CLIENT );
   END;
CALL DLITPLI( DLET(INSC1) AGENT );
```

INSC2. Now, to indicate the effect of the various statements, we write INSC1 and INSC2 after each. Thus we find the record of Baker to obtain the records of all of Baker's clients. Each client record is then inserted as a client of Potter. After all the clients have been inserted, we delete the original agent record for Baker along with all the client records associated with it.

We end this section by briefly considering how updates to an external view affect the conceptual view. We indicated previously that in IMS, processing options (PROCOPT) are given for the various record types. We are now considering the case where PROCOPT includes I, D, or R (standing for insert, delete, and replace, respectively) in addition to G (get). We do not give the IMS rules, which are complicated, but instead present a brief discussion of some problems with deletions.

Consider the three-level hierarchy with OFFICE, STAFF, AGENT, and CLIENT nodes, which we used in this chapter as the conceptual view. Suppose that an external view does *not* contain CLIENT. Now, if the user with that external view deletes an agent, as we mentioned before, all the clients are also automatically deleted—with little possibility of the user being aware of this deletion. Another problem concerns virtual records. Assume that we have the TEACHER-STUDENT relationship represented as in Figure 3.1.2(d). Suppose that we wish to delete a teacher in the TEACHER–virtual STUDENT tree. Would this mean that the actual students of that teacher are deleted also? After all, the virtual STUDENT records are deleted. And what about the virtual TEACHER records for that TEACHER in the STUDENT–virtual TEACHER tree? It is a complex situation, and IMS has complicated rules and options about the effects of these operations.

3.5 Exercises

3.1 (a) Consider the many-to-many relationship of Figure 3.5.1(a).
   (*i*) Represent it in a hierarchic manner without using a connection file.
   (*ii*) Represent it in a hierarchic manner using a connection file.
   (b) Same as (a) for the many-to-many relationship of Figure 3.5.1(b).

3.2 (a) Consider the network data structure diagram of Figure 2.5.2 for a department store. Omitting SYSTEM and the Codasyl set names, transform the figure to a hierarchic data structure diagram.
   (b) Same as (a) for the data structure diagram of a law firm in Figure 2.5.3.
   (c) Same as (a) for the data structure diagram of a library in Figure 2.5.4.
   (d) Same as (a) for the data structure diagram of a service department in Figure 2.5.5.

FIGURE 3.5.1
Many-to-Many Relationships

(a)

```
FILES               ATTRIBUTES
   JUDGE               NAME
   LAWYER              SSNO,NAME,ADDRESS,SALARY,STATUS,TELNO
```

(b)

```
FILES               ATTRIBUTES
   EMPLOYEE            ESSNO,ENAME,EADDR,SALARY
   EQUIPMENT           SERIALNO,TYPE
```

3.3 Write the DBD (conceptual view) for the hierarchic data structure diagram in

(a) Figure 3.5.2(a).
(b) Figure 3.5.2(b).
(c) Figure 3.5.2(c).

3.4 Using your answer to Exercise 3.3 in each of the following, write a PCB (external view) for retrieval:

(a) For the DBD of Exercise 3.3(a), omit SALARY from EMPLOYEE and LOCATION from DEPT.
(b) For the DBD of Exercise 3.3(b), omit CLIENT.
(c) For the DBD of Exercise 3.3(c), omit OUTMATERIAL and BIRTHDATE from BORROWER.

3.5 Write the DBD (conceptual view) for the hierarchic data structure diagram involving a virtual file in

(a) Figure 3.5.3(a).
(b) Figure 3.5.3(b).
(c) Figure 3.5.3(c).

3.6 For the conceptual view of Exercise 3.3(a), write program segments for the following database retrievals:

(a) Find the record of the employee whose social security number is 444-55-6666.
(b) Print the telephone number of the Toy department in store 1527.
(c) Print the name and salary of every employee in the Shoe department of store 1325.
(d) Print the name, address, and department of every employee whose salary is greater than $20,000.
(e) Print the telephone number of every department for the store at 1000 Wall St.

3.7 For the conceptual view of part (b) of Exercise 3.3, write program segments for the following database retrievals:

(a) Find the record of a lawyer whose office number is 200.
(b) Print the serial number and cost of every computer in the office of the lawyer with social security number 123-12-3123.
(c) Print the number of cases for the lawyer with social security number 123-12-3123 that involves female clients over the age of 64.
(d) Print the name, address, and telephone number of every lawyer at office number 200.
(e) Print the number for every office that has at least one lawyer whose salary is greater than $50,000.

FIGURE 3.5.2
Hierarchic Data Structure Diagrams

(a)
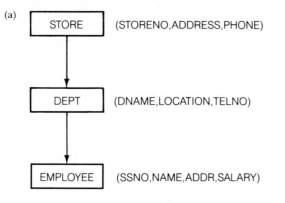

STORE (STORENO,ADDRESS,PHONE)

DEPT (DNAME,LOCATION,TELNO)

EMPLOYEE (SSNO,NAME,ADDR,SALARY)

(b)
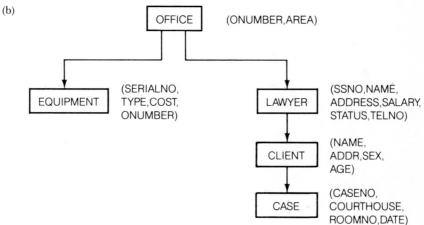

OFFICE (ONUMBER,AREA)

EQUIPMENT (SERIALNO, TYPE,COST, ONUMBER)

LAWYER (SSNO,NAME, ADDRESS,SALARY, STATUS,TELNO)

CLIENT (NAME, ADDR,SEX, AGE)

CASE (CASENO, COURTHOUSE, ROOMNO,DATE)

(c)
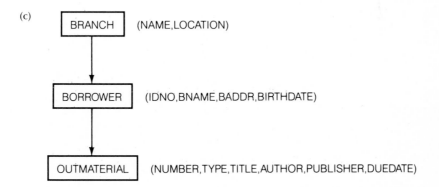

BRANCH (NAME,LOCATION)

BORROWER (IDNO,BNAME,BADDR,BIRTHDATE)

OUTMATERIAL (NUMBER,TYPE,TITLE,AUTHOR,PUBLISHER,DUEDATE)

FIGURE 3.5.3
Hierarchic Data Structure Diagrams with Virtual Files

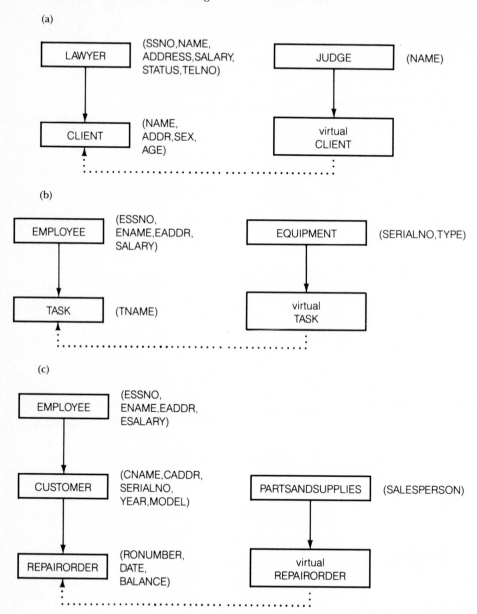

3.8 For the conceptual view of part (c) of Exercise 3.3, write program segments for the following database retrievals:

(a) Find the record of the Homeville branch.

(b) Print the name and address of the borrower with ID number 28197.

(c) Print the author and title of every item presently checked out by the borrower with ID number 28197.

(d) Print the name and address of every borrower at the Homeville branch.

(e) Print the number of books by W. Shakespeare presently checked out of the Homeville branch.

3.9 For the conceptual view of part (a) of Exercise 3.3, write program segments for the following database updates:

(a) Insert an employee with social security number 777-66-6888, whose name is S. Jones, at the address 800 King St., with salary $24,500, into the Hardware department at store number 1503.

(b) Insert a store with store number 1785, address 11101 Bank St., and phone number 555-0080.

(c) Delete the employee with social security number 888-99-9000 from the database.

(d) Delete the Furniture department and all of its employees at every store.

(e) Change the address of F. Smith from 445 Bird St., to 544 Canary Ave.

(f) Transfer the employee with social security number 111-22-2333 to the Shoe department.

3.10 For the conceptual view of part (b) of Exercise 3.3, write program segments for the following database updates:

(a) Insert an office with number 301 and area 640.

(b) For the lawyer with social security number 111-22-3333, insert client B. White, who lives at 2204 Branch Rd., is female, and is 45 years old, as well as her case, which has a number of 671 and is to be tried in Room 65 at the Central Courthouse on July 24, 1988.

(c) Delete the lawyer A. Green in office 250, and all of this lawyer's clients, from the database.

(d) Delete the equipment with serial number ABC11689 from the database.

(e) Change the age of D. Fisher, who is a client of the lawyer with social security number 221-13-3445, to 25.

(f) Transfer D. Fisher to the lawyer with social security number 987-65-4321.

3.11 For the conceptual view of part (c) of Exercise 3.3, write program segments for the following database updates:

(a) Insert a borrower at the Homeville branch whose name is P. Simon, who lives at 26 Wood Rd., who has ID number 123456, and who was born on February 5, 1960.

(b) Insert the book *Introduction to Logic Programming* by C. J. Hogger, published by Academic Press, number QA76.6H624, as being checked out with a due date of January 3, 1988, by the borrower with ID number 266135.

(c) The item with number AH279.6 has just been returned. Modify the database so it will no longer show the item as being out.

(d) Delete the borrower with ID number 446688 and count the number of items that this borrower has out.

(e) Change the due date for the book with number QA76.6H624 to January 17, 1988.

(f) Transfer all borrowers from the Towson branch to the Tucson branch and delete the Towson branch.

3.12 Discuss the relationship of the NDL insertion and retention modes considered in Chapter 2 to the hierarchic language discussed in this chapter.

3.6 Guide to Further Reading

The hierarchic database model, primarily as implemented in IMS, is discussed in [1.1] Chapter 7, [1.2] Chapter 22, [1.4] Chapter 4, and [2.4] Chapter 7. [1.1] also discusses System 2000 DBMS, which is marketed by SAS Institute and is another hierarchic database system, in Chapter 8. More information about IMS can be found in [3.1] and [3.2].

[3.1] IBM Corporation, IMS/VS Version 1, General Information Manual GH20-1260, 1982.

[3.2] Kapp, D., and J. F. Leben. *IMS Programming Techniques: A Guide to Using DL/I*. New York: Van Nostrand Reinhold, 1978.

Chapter 4

The Relational Database Model

4.1 Basic Definitions

In Section 1.3, we discussed briefly the three major database models: network, hierarchic, and relational. In the previous two chapters we dealt in detail with the network and hierarchic models. We now consider the relational model. E. F. Codd formalized this database model around 1970 and then was highly influential in relational database research and implementation. The relational database model has its foundations in two areas of mathematics: algebra and logic. In this chapter we emphasize the algebraic aspects; we will consider the logical aspects in Chapter 8.

In the relational model, there are no explicit pointers between tables as in the hierarchic and network models. In dealing with the relational model, we use the terminology "table" instead of "file" and "row" instead of "record." A database schema describes the structure of the database: for each table it gives the name of the table and the names of the columns (called attributes). We write an example database schema in Figure 4.1.1(a). In this case there are three tables: DEPARTMENT, ITEM, and EMPLOYEE. Each table has several attributes and each attribute has a type associated with it which indicates the domain of values allowed for that attribute. Figure 4.1.1(b) gives a small sample database (instance) which conforms to the schema.

Now let's see how a mathematical foundation can be given to the basic concepts of relational databases. A fundamental mathematical notion is that of **set** which stands for *a collection of elements*. Using sets $S_1, \ldots, S_n$, not necessarily distinct, it is possible to form the Cartesian product

FIGURE 4.1.1
Relational Database Schema and Instance

(a) Schema

```
TABLES              ATTRIBUTES
   DEPARTMENT          DNAME,LOCATION,MANAGER
   ITEM                INAME,PRICE,VOLUME
   EMPLOYEE            SSNO,ENAME,DNAME,SALARY

TYPES               ATTRIBUTES
   CHAR(2)             LOCATION
   CHAR(9)             SSNO
   CHAR(12)            DNAME
   CHAR(15)            MANAGER,ENAME
   CHAR(20)            INAME
   INTEGER             VOLUME,SALARY
   REAL                PRICE
```

(b) Instance

DEPARTMENT		
DNAME	LOCATION	MANAGER
Sales	15	Smith L
Delivery	07	Jones B
DP	29	Borden T

ITEM		
INAME	PRICE	VOLUME
Printer	455.69	23
TV Set	599.00	10
Camera	127.50	70

EMPLOYEE			
SSNO	ENAME	DNAME	SALARY
111111111	Smith J	Sales	22500
222333444	Jones B	Sales	24750
667788990	Turner W	Sales	25005
555555555	Ford L	Delivery	21004
234567890	Cramer T	DP	27790

of these sets, written as $S_1 \times \ldots \times S_n$. The Cartesian product is also a set; it contains all those n-tuples (an ordered sequence of n elements) where the ith element is in S_i for each i. The number of elements in $S_1 \times \ldots \times S_n$ is $|S_1| * \ldots * |S_n|$, where $|S_i|$ is the number of elements in S_i for each i. A **relation** (on $<S_1, \ldots, S_n>$) is a subset of $S_1 \times \ldots \times S_n$. In Figure 4.1.2(a) we give an example of three sets, S_1, S_2, S_3, and the Cartesian product, $S_1 \times S_2 \times S_3$. In Figure 4.1.2(b) we indicate a relation on $<S_1, S_2, S_3>$. Since each n-tuple may or may not be in a relation and each set of n-tuples is a relation, the number of possible relations on $S_1 \times \ldots \times S_n$ is 2^m where $m = |S_1| * \ldots * |S_n|$.

We obtain the connection between relations and tables by considering a table as a relation. Let's take the ITEM table as our example from Figure 4.1.1(a). In this case let S_1 be the set of all possible INAME (CHAR(20)) values, let S_2 be the set of all possible PRICE (REAL) values, and let S_3 be the set of all possible VOLUME (INTEGER) values. Now consider a row of the ITEM table, such as $<$Camera,127,50,70$>$. This can be considered a 3-tuple which is an element of $S_1 \times S_2 \times S_3$. But then the ITEM table itself, being a set of three 3-tuples, can be considered a relation on $<S_1, S_2, S_3>$. Thus we can identify each table with its corresponding relation.

We may wonder how this mathematical analysis helps. It turns out that treating tables as relations allows us to use the theory of relations, which has been studied in mathematics for many years. This theory not only provides a foundation for databases, it also allows the mathematical machinery for relations to be applied to tables and hence to databases. In particular, there is an important relational database language called the **relational algebra** which *is based on operations on relations*. We will study the relational algebra in the next section.

First, however, we consider the representation of relationships between tables within the context of relational databases. (Incidentally,

FIGURE 4.1.2
(Cartesian) Product and Relation

(a) A product

$S_1 = \{a_1, b_1\}$, $S_2 = \{a_2, b_2, c_2\}$, $S_3 = \{a_3, b_3\}$
$S_1 \times S_2 \times S_3 = \{<a_1, a_2, a_3>, <a_1, a_2, b_3>, <a_1, b_2, a_3>, <a_1, b_2, b_3>,$
$\quad\quad <a_1, c_2, a_3>, <a_1, c_2, b_3>, <b_1, a_2, a_3>, <b_1, a_2, b_3>,$
$\quad\quad <b_1, b_2, a_3>, <b_1, b_2, b_3>, <b_1, c_2, a_3>, <b_1, c_2, b_3>\}$

(b) A relation on $<S_1, S_2, S_3>$

$R = \{<a_1, a_2, a_3>, <a_1, b_2, b_3>, <a_1, c_2, a_3>, <b_1, b_2, a_3>\}$

the term "relational database" was originally introduced because of the identification of a table, or file, with a relation.) Recall that no two rows of a table (records of a file) may be identical on the key attribute(s). Section 1.3 indicated that in one-to-many relationships, the key attributes of the parent table are included as extra attributes in the child table. Thus, reconsidering Figure 1.3.2(b)—involving the one-to-many relationship between EMPLOYEE and JOBHISTORY—the relational representation contains the extra attribute E# from EMPLOYEE in JOBHISTORY, as shown in Figure 1.3.3(c).

Next, let's consider the many-to-many relationship between TEACHER and STUDENT, as given in Figure 1.3.2(c). There are several ways to represent the relationship using the relational approach. A direct method is indicated in Figure 4.1.3(a). Just as in the one-to-many relationship case, we put the key attribute(s) of one table into the other table. Here we place the SSNO attribute, which refers to a student's social security number, into the TEACHER table. Note that this creates an asymmetric situation, as when we tried to represent a many-to-many relationship in a hierarchic database in Figure 3.1.2(b).

In Chapter 2, we explained the method of using a connection file for representing a many-to-many relationship in a network database. In particular, for the TEACHER-STUDENT case we used the connection file (table) CLASS in Figure 2.1.7(a). We now apply this concept to the relational representation in Figure 4.1.3(b). The TEACHER and STUDENT tables are unchanged, but the connection table CLASS contains the keys from TEACHER and STUDENT, which are the parent tables for CLASS in the network structure.

We take now a more complex example, the network data structure diagram of Figure 2.2.2 (minus SYSTEM). We want to transform this diagram into a relational database description. We assume that OFFICEADDRESS is the key for OFFICE, and that NAME and ADDRESS

FIGURE 4.1.3
Representation for a Many-to-Many Relationship

(a) Direct method

```
TABLES          ATTRIBUTES
  TEACHER         SS#,TNAME,POSITION,DEPT,SSNO
  STUDENT         SSNO,SNAME,ADDRESS,TELNO,CLASSIFICATION
```

(b) Connection file method

```
TABLES          ATTRIBUTES
  TEACHER         SS#,TNAME,POSITION,DEPT
  STUDENT         SSNO,SNAME,ADDRESS,TELNO,CLASSIFICATION
  CLASS           SS#,SSNO,COURSE,SECNO,GRADE
```

FIGURE 4.1.4
Relational Representation for the Insurance Company Example

```
TABLES              ATTRIBUTES
   OFFICE              OFFICEADDRESS,TELEPHONE,MANAGER
   PHYSICIAN           NAME,ADDRESS,TELNO
   AGENT               OFFICEADDRESS,NAME,ADDRESS,ANAME,ADDR,
                          COMMISSION
   CLIENT              OFFICEADDRESS,ANAME,ADDR,CNAME,CADDR,
                          POLICYTYPE,POLICYNUMBER
```

form the key for PHYSICIAN. We present the result in Figure 4.1.4. Note that the OFFICE and PHYSICIAN tables are not changed because they do not have a parent in the network. For the AGENT table we include the keys from the two parents, OFFICE and PHYSICIAN (the key for OFFICE appears there already). Finally, for CLIENT we include the keys from its parent AGENT as well as OFFICE, which is the parent of AGENT. It is generally sufficient to include only the key(s) from the parent(s), but sometimes, as here, it is useful to include key(s) from additional ancestor nodes. There are many other ways to create a relational database structure from the given data structure diagram. For example, we may place some attributes from AGENT or CLIENT into the OFFICE or PHYSICIAN tables. We will deal with relational database design in more detail in Chapter 5.

In discussing both the network and hierarchic cases, we touched on several implementation issues. For network databases, we mentioned circularly linked lists, and for hierarchic databases we considered tree structures. A simple way of representing a relational database is to use a separate (physical) file for each table. It should be recognized, however, that we are dealing here with the conceptual and possibly the external views. But even if the conceptual view is relational, that does not mean that the internal view, which represents the storage structures, must also be relational. In particular, in the internal view there may be links between the files representing the tables, and the file structure may even be different from the table structure.

Recall that the network and hierarchic models were predominant early in the emergence of database technology. For years it seemed to many people that relational databases could not be made efficient enough to be practical. However, by the late 1970s, some of the efficiency problems were solved, and relational database systems became practical and came into wide use. Virtually all of the database systems implemented in the early 1980s, primarily on microcomputers, are relational. The great advantage of relational databases is their general ease of use over other types. In the rest of this chapter, we will consider two important languages for the relational database model.

4.2 Relational Algebra

In the previous section, we mentioned that treating tables as relations allows us to use the algebra of relations as a language for operations on relations. The **relational algebra** *is a fundamental language for relational databases,* and several implemented languages for relational databases are based on it. In this section we describe the operations of the relational algebra, with the proviso that the relational algebra has not been implemented in precisely the way we present it. In Figure 4.2.1 we list the operations of the relational algebra using our notation and give their definitions.

FIGURE 4.2.1
Operations of the Relational Algebra

Notes: 1. We use T and r (with subscripts) for tables and rows, respectively. A and B (with subscripts) are attributes; if A_i (respectively, B_i, C_i) is an attribute, then a_i (b_i, c_i) is a value appropriate for that attribute. A table is a set of rows. The result of each operation is a table; duplicates are omitted.
2. For UNION, INTERSECT, and DIFFERENCE, T_1 and T_2 must have the same sequence of attributes.
3. For SELECT, C is a condition involving attribute names, constants, and standard relational and Boolean operators.
4. The JOIN is performed on all the common attribute(s) of T_1 and T_2 unless specified otherwise.
5. For THETA-JOIN, either T_1 and T_2 have exactly one common attribute, or one common attribute must be specified. Theta is a relational operator ($<$, $<=$, $=$, $>$, $>=$, or $<>$).
6. For DIVIDE, the sequence of attributes in T_2 must be the same as the final sequence of attributes in T_1.
7. For each attribute A we write D(A) for the domain of the attribute—that is, the set of elements (data type) for A. EMPTY is the empty set. D(A) and EMPTY may be used as tables.

UNION(T_1,T_2)
    The set union of T_1 and T_2.
    r is a member of UNION(T_1,T_2) if r is a member of T_1 or of T_2.
INTERSECT(T_1,T_2)
    The set intersection of T_1 and T_2.
    r is a member of INTERSECT(T_1,T_2) if r is a member of T_1 and of T_2.
DIFFERENCE(T_1,T_2)
    The set difference of T_2 from T_1.
    r is a member of DIFFERENCE(T_1,T_2) if r is a member of T_1 but not of T_2.
PRODUCT(T_1,T_2)
    The Cartesian product of T_1 and T_2.
    Contains all rows "glued together" from T_1 and T_2.
    Let $A_1, \ldots, A_n$ be the attributes of T_1 and $B_1, \ldots, B_m$ be the attributes of T_2.
    $<a_1, \ldots, a_n, b_1, \ldots, b_m>$ is a member of PRODUCT(T_1,T_2) if
    $<a_1, \ldots, a_n>$ is a member of T_1 and
    $<b_1, \ldots, b_m>$ is a member of T_2.

(continued)

PROJECT(T; sequence of attributes)

    The vertical subtable of T containing only the columns for the attributes specified in the sequence in that order; the columns of a table may be reordered this way by specifying a new sequence.

    Let $A_1, \ldots, A_n$ be the attributes of T, and

        $A_{i1}, \ldots, A_{im}$ the attributes in the sequence.

    $<a_{i1}, \ldots, a_{im}>$ is a member of PROJECT$(T; A_{i1}, \ldots, A_{im})$ if there is a row

        $<a_1, \ldots, a_n>$ of T such that a_{ij} is the value for the attribute A_{ij} for each j, $1 <= j <= m$.

SELECT(T: C)

    The horizontal subtable of T containing those rows of T for which the condition is true.

    r is a member of SELECT(T: C) if C(r) is true, where C(r) is obtained from C by substituting for each attribute name in C the value for that attribute in r.

JOIN(T_1, T_2)

    Contains rows "glued" together from T_1 and T_2 where the values for the common attributes are equal.

    Let $A_1, \ldots, A_n, C_1, \ldots, C_k$ be the attributes of T_1 and

        $C_1, \ldots, C_k, B_1, \ldots, B_m$ be the attributes of T_2.

    $<a_1, \ldots, a_n, c_1, \ldots, c_k, b_1, \ldots, b_m>$ is a member of JOIN(T_1, T_2) if

        $<a_1, \ldots, a_n, c_1, \ldots, c_k>$ is a member of T_1 and

        $<c_1, \ldots, c_k, b_1, \ldots, b_m>$ is a member of T_2.

THETA-JOIN(T_1, T_2)

    Contains rows "glued" together from T_1 and T_2 where the value for the common attribute in T_1 is in the relation *theta* to the value for the common attribute in T_2.

    Let $A_1, \ldots, A_n, C$ be the attributes of T_1 and

        $C, B_1, \ldots, B_m$ be the attributes of T_2.

    $<a_1, \ldots, a_n, c_1, c_2, b_1, \ldots, b_m>$ is a member of THETA-JOIN(T_1, T_2) if

        $<a_1, \ldots, a_n, c_1>$ is a member of T_1,

        $<c_2, b_1, \ldots, b_m>$ is a member of T_2, and

        c_1 *theta* c_2 is true.

DIVIDE(T_1, T_2)

    The subtable of T_1, which contains all the columns for the attributes not in T_2 for those rows whose product with T_2 is a subtable of T_1.

    Let $A_1, \ldots, A_n, B_1, \ldots, B_m$ be the attributes of T_1 and

        $B_1, \ldots, B_m$ be the attributes of T_2.

    $<a_1, \ldots, a_n>$ is a member of DIVIDE(T_1, T_2) if for every

        $<b_1, \ldots, b_m>$ which is a member of T_2,

        $<a_1, \ldots, a_n, b_1, \ldots, b_m>$ is a member of T_1.

    We illustrate these operations by means of several examples. Consider first the WORKER and MANAGER tables in part (a) of Figure 4.2.2. Note that they have identical structures. Such tables are called **union-compatible.** A very basic operation on sets (and hence relations) is the operation of union. If two (or more) tables are union-compatible, then we can perform the union operation on them. The union of WORKER and MANAGER is shown in part (b). The other two important operations

FIGURE 4.2.2
Examples of Operations of the Relational Algebra

(a) The WORKER and MANAGER tables

WORKER				
E#	NAME	SALARY	AGE	DEPT
123	Jones	18000	25	1
462	Smith	25000	31	1
263	Brown	21000	30	2
068	Kramer	27000	45	2

MANAGER				
E#	NAME	SALARY	AGE	DEPT
068	Kramer	27000	45	2
059	Taylor	32000	51	1

(b) The union operation

UNION(WORKER,MANAGER)				
E#	NAME	SALARY	AGE	DEPT
123	Jones	18000	25	1
462	Smith	25000	31	1
263	Brown	21000	30	2
068	Kramer	27000	45	2
059	Taylor	32000	51	1

(c) The intersection operation

INTERSECT(WORKER,MANAGER)				
E#	NAME	SALARY	AGE	DEPT
068	Kramer	27000	45	2

(continued)

(d) The difference operation

DIFFERENCE(WORKER,MANAGER)				
E#	NAME	SALARY	AGE	DEPT
123	Jones	18000	25	1
462	Smith	25000	31	1
263	Brown	21000	30	2

DIFFERENCE(MANAGER,WORKER)				
E#	NAME	SALARY	AGE	DEPT
059	Taylor	32000	51	1

on union-compatible tables are intersection and difference. The intersection of WORKER and MANAGER appears in part (c). Union and intersection are commutative operations. The **union** table simply consists of all the rows from each table (with duplicates, if any, removed), while the **intersection** table consists of the common rows. Difference is not commutative, however. Both **differences** for the WORKER and MANAGER tables are shown in Figure 4.2.2(d). DIFFERENCE (WORKER,MANAGER) contains the rows for those workers who are not managers and DIFFERENCE(MANAGER,WORKER) contains the rows for those managers who are not workers.

There is one more traditional algebraic operation that is very useful for tables, the (Cartesian) product. We illustrate the product by introducing first another table, called DEPTINFO, in Figure 4.2.3(a). The product of MANAGER and DEPTINFO is given in Figure 4.2.3(b). Each row in the **product** is obtained by "gluing" together every row from the first table with every row from the second table. Thus, if the first table contains m rows and the second table contains n rows, then the product contains $m \cdot n$ rows. Sometimes, when a product of two tables is constructed, those tables contain identical attributes. Because a table cannot have two identical attributes, we have to distinguish between them in the product. In our example, we write M.DEPT for DEPT from MANAGER and D.DEPT for DEPT from DEPTINFO.

It turns out that for database operations, particularly for database querying, the standard set-theoretic operations we have considered so far—union, intersection, difference, and product—are not the most useful ones. We now introduce three relational operations that are particularly useful for database querying: projection, selection, and (natural) join. Projection and selection are operations on a single table, while join is applied to two tables. The idea of **projection** is to take a table and omit some of the columns; the idea of **selection** is to take a table and omit some of the rows.

Part (a) of Figure 4.2.4 illustrates a projection by taking the WORKER table and projecting on the attributes E# and AGE, thus omitting the columns for NAME, SALARY, and DEPT. In a projection we may also reorder the columns. Selection is illustrated in part (b), where those rows are picked where the SALARY value is greater than $22,000. For selection, a condition must be given, and the rows which satisfy the condition are selected. We allow the standard types of conditions that are allowed in programming languages using the usual relational and Boolean operations, such as $<$, $<=$, $>$, $>=$, $=$, $<>$, and $\&$, $\vee$, $-$. Thus, a selection may involve several columns. We illustrate this in part (c).

Very often when a database is queried, the required information is contained in several tables. One way to put together two tables is by taking

FIGURE 4.2.3
The Product Operation

(a) The DEPTINFO table

DEPTINFO		
DEPT	DNAME	DTASK
1	Operations	Transfer
1	Operations	Safety
2	Systems	System1

(b) A product

PRODUCT(MANAGER,DEPTINFO)							
E#	NAME	SALARY	AGE	M.DEPT	D.DEPT	DNAME	DTASK
068	Kramer	27000	45	2	1	Operations	Transfer
068	Kramer	27000	45	2	1	Operations	Safety
068	Kramer	27000	45	2	2	Systems	System1
059	Taylor	32000	51	1	1	Operations	Transfer
059	Taylor	32000	51	1	1	Operations	Safety
059	Taylor	32000	51	1	2	Systems	System1

FIGURE 4.2.4
Projection, Selection, and Join Examples

(a) A projection example

PROJECT(WORKER; E#,AGE)	
E#	AGE
123	25
462	31
263	30
068	45

(b) Selection example—simple condition

SELECT(WORKER: SALARY > 22000)				
E#	NAME	SALARY	AGE	DEPT
462	Smith	25000	31	1
068	Kramer	27000	45	2

(c) Selection example—complex condition

SELECT(WORKER: SALARY > 20000 & AGE <= 40)				
E#	NAME	SALARY	AGE	DEPT
462	Smith	25000	31	1
263	Brown	21000	30	2

(d) Natural join example

JOIN(MANAGER,DEPTINFO)						
E#	NAME	SALARY	AGE	DEPT	DNAME	PROJECT
068	Kramer	27000	45	2	Systems	System1
059	Taylor	32000	51	1	Operations	Transfer
059	Taylor	32000	51	1	Operations	Safety

their product. Consider the example in Figure 4.2.3(b) again. A row like the first row,

```
<068,Kramer,27000,45,2,1,Operations,Transfer>
```

is not a particularly meaningful piece of information. It provides data about an individual named Kramer, who is in Department 2, and data about Department 1. However, a row like the third row,

```
<068,Kramer,27000,45,2,2,Systems,System1>
```

is meaningful, because it indicates data about an individual named Kramer, as well as Kramer's department. That is, if we only take rows where M.DEPT = D.DEPT, then we get a new, meaningful table. But then it is not necessary to repeat the DEPT value. Such an operation, which is based on the product, but with only those rows where the identical attributes have identical values and where such attributes are not repeated, is called the **natural join.** It is illustrated in Figure 4.2.4(d).

Since the "natural join" is the most common type of join used, we just call it the "join." However, there are other types of joins, called **theta-joins.** The natural join is essentially an equi-join (with the extra columns removed), in that the requirement for an element to be in it is that the values on the joined (common) attributes be equal. But we could require another relational operation to hold between the values of the common attributes, such as $<$ or $<=$ or $>$ or $>=$ or $<>$, to get a different kind of join, such as a $<$-join, a $<=$-join, and so on. Theta is the general name given to a relational operation in this context. Such a join is not particularly appropriate in our example, so we illustrate it by using a different example.

Figure 4.2.5(a) presents two tables, EMP and ELIGIBILITY. EMP contains information about employees, including the number of years an employee has worked at the company. ELIGIBILITY contains information about benefit packages available after a certain number of years of service. We may want to find all the benefits that an employee is eligible to obtain. This can be done by using a $>=$-join, which is also shown in the figure. We list all those rows where the number of years worked for an employee is at least as great as the one necessary for a benefit package.

There is one additional operation in the relational algebra, and that is **division.** This is a binary operation where the attributes of the second table are the same as the last sequence of attributes of the first table. Consider the CLASS table of Figure 4.2.5(b), which indicates the grades given by teachers to students. Suppose that we would like to know the names of all the teachers who gave Baker a "B" and Adams a "C". We create a new table on the attributes STUDENT and GRADE called STU-

FIGURE 4.2.5
Other Relational Algebra Operations

(a) A >=-join example

EMP		
NAME	AGE	YRSWORKED
Smith	31	2
Jones	25	4
Brown	30	3
Kramer	45	9

ELIGIBILITY	
YRSWORKED	BENEFIT
1	A
3	B
5	C
10	D

>=-JOIN(EMP,ELIGIBILITY)				
NAME	AGE	EMP.YRSWORKED	ELIG.YRSWORKED	BENEFIT
Smith	31	2	1	A
Jones	25	4	1	A
Jones	25	4	3	B
Brown	30	3	1	A
Brown	30	3	3	B
Kramer	45	9	1	A
Kramer	45	9	3	B
Kramer	45	9	5	C

(b) A division example

CLASS		
TEACHER	STUDENT	GRADE
Porter	Jones	A
Smith	Baker	B
Carter	Adams	B
Porter	Baker	B
Smith	Adams	C
Porter	Adams	C
Carter	Baker	A

STUDENTGRADES	
STUDENT	GRADE
Baker	B
Adams	C

DIVIDE(CLASS,STUDENTGRADES)
TEACHER
Porter
Smith

DENTGRADES. Then, the division operation on CLASS and STU-
DENTGRADES yields exactly the list of those teachers who gave Baker
a "B" and Adams a "C", who in this case are Porter and Smith. Although
division is useful in some cases, it can be defined in terms of product,
subtraction, and projection, and so we do not deal with it further. (Actually,
we did not try to give a minimal set of operations for the relational
algebra. For example, intersection could have been defined in terms of
union and difference.)

  We end this section by writing some programs in the relational
algebra. We use as our example the database schema given in Figure
4.1.1. First, in part (*i*) of Figure 4.2.6(a), we write a program to print the
name of the manager of the Sales Department. We use an unofficial
syntax including : = for assignment. First we select the rows (single row
in this case) for which DNAME = "Sales" and then we project on the
attribute MANAGER. If we nest statements, we can write the whole program as a single statement—as shown in part (*ii*) of Figure 4.2.6(a). We
continue to use the first approach, rather than nesting, for the other
examples.

  Our second example is a program to print the name and salary of
every employee in the Sales department. This program is similar to the
one in the first example; however, while then we expected a single answer,
now we obtain a list. This second program is given in part (b) of Figure
4.2.6. It is very similar to the program in part (a). The relational algebra
is a powerful language in which it is unnecessary to set up a loop, although
a loop would be needed in a like situation for the hierarchic or network
languages we discussed in the previous chapters. The power of the relational algebra comes from the fact that we can deal with sets of rows at
a time using the relational algebraic operations. The relational algebra
is therefore a high-level database language.

  Our third example illustrates the use of the join operation. In this
case, we want to know the names of all those managers who have at least
one employee with a salary greater than $25,000. We give a solution in
part (*i*) of Figure 4.2.6(c). We join the EMPLOYEE and DEPARTMENT
tables, then select those rows for which the salary is greater than $25,000,
and finally project on MANAGER. We note that this solution is not as
efficient as it could be; if the tables are large, the program may take a
long time to perform a join. The reason is that for the join, one or more
elements from each row of one table must be compared with one or more
elements from each row of the other table. Section 7.2 will deal in
more detail with query optimization. Here we just indicate an alternate
solution, in part (*ii*) of Figure 4.2.6(c), that is more efficient because the
join is performed on smaller tables.

  It is worthwhile mentioning here that in the relational algebra, there
are expressions for the empty set and the universal set. Actually, since
different attributes have different domains (some may be the set of inte-

FIGURE 4.2.6
Relational Algebra Programs

(a) Print the name of the manager of the Sales department.

```
(i)  TEMP  := SELECT(DEPARTMENT: DNAME = 'Sales')
     RESULT := PROJECT(TEMP; MANAGER)
     PRINT RESULT
(ii) PRINT PROJECT(SELECT(DEPARTMENT: DNAME =
         'Sales'); MANAGER)
```

(b) Print the name and salary of every employee in the Sales department.

```
TEMP   := SELECT(EMPLOYEE: DNAME = 'Sales')
RESULT := PROJECT(TEMP; ENAME,SALARY)
PRINT RESULT
```

(c) Print the names of all managers who have at least one employee in their department with salary > 25000.

```
(i)  TEMP1  := JOIN(EMPLOYEE,DEPARTMENT)
     TEMP2  := SELECT(TEMP1: SALARY > 25000)
     RESULT := PROJECT(TEMP2; MANAGER)
     PRINT RESULT
(ii) TEMP1  := SELECT(EMPLOYEE: SALARY > 25000)
     TEMP2  := PROJECT(TEMP1; DNAME)
     TEMP3  := JOIN(TEMP2,DEPARTMENT)
     RESULT := PROJECT(TEMP3; MANAGER)
     PRINT RESULT
```

(d) Delete "TV Set" from ITEM

```
TODELETE := SELECT(ITEM: INAME = 'TV Set')
ITEM := DIFFERENCE(ITEM,TODELETE)
```

(e) Insert the row <Radio,79.50,45> into the ITEM table.

```
NEWITEM := <Radio,79.50,45>
ITEM    := UNION(ITEM,NEWITEM)
```

gers, while others may be the set of allowable character strings of some length), we assume that we can refer to such sets as needed. For an attribute A, we write dom(A) for the set of allowable values for that attribute.

Finally, we look at how to do updates using the relational algebra. Because a modification can be achieved by a deletion and an insertion, these two operations are illustrated. A deletion can be done by using set difference. If we wish to delete the row for "TV Set" in the ITEM table (see Figure 4.1.1), we can create a table containing that row and then subtract it from ITEM. This method is illustrated in Figure 4.2.6(d). Then, for insertion, we use the union operation. Again we form a new table (maybe containing one row) and use union to add it to the old one. For example, to add the row <Radio,79.50,45> to the ITEM table, we form a new table and use union, as shown in Figure 4.2.6(e).

If we restrict ourselves to queries, we find that the most common operations are SELECT, PROJECT, and JOIN. SELECT and PROJECT are used to obtain a portion of a table. JOIN is used to glue two tables together so that we can obtain connecting information between the tables. In fact, SELECT, PROJECT, and JOIN are sufficient for almost all the reasonable queries that one would ask of a database.

4.3 Introduction to SQL

In this section, we discuss a very important language for relational databases called **SQL (Structured Query Language).** This language has been implemented for relational databases and has become probably the most important language for them. In particular, it is the language used at present for the IBM relational database systems SQL/DS and DB2. ORACLE is another relational database system which uses SQL; it is available for a wide variety of mainframes, minicomputers, and microcomputers and is marketed by ORACLE Corporation. Also, the American National Standards Institute has formalized SQL as the standard language for relational databases. Because the syntax of the proposed standard is oriented toward an embedded version of SQL (which we discuss in Section 4.5), we will use the syntax of the interactive version from DB2 and ORACLE, while following most of the rules of the ANSI SQL. The syntax rules for the schema and query statements that we will use are shown in Figure 4.3.1.

In SQL, each user can access and manipulate a set of tables according to various restrictions. The totality of these tables and access privileges is the user's view of the database. However, the term "view" is used in SQL in a specific way, as we will see in Section 4.5. Privileges will be considered later, when we deal with aspects of security in Section 6.1. In any case, users have complete access to all the tables that they have created. Figure 4.3.2 gives a schema, which we will use for the rest of this chapter, and an instance for this schema.

For any attribute, we may specify that its corresponding column is not allowed to have null values by using the phrase NOT NULL. A null value is a special value, different from a blank or 0, that indicates that a particular value is unknown or inapplicable. In our example of Figure 4.3.2(b), we do not include any null values. However, it is conceivable, for example, that an employee's address may be unknown at some point. A null value can be used in that type of situation. We will discuss null values further in Section 11.1.

FIGURE 4.3.1
Syntax Rules for SQL Schema and Query Statements

Notes: 1. Additional syntax rules for SQL are presented in Figures 4.5.1, 4.5.3, 4.5.5, 6.1.5, 6.4.3, and 7.1.7.
2. All names are identifiers, which must start with a letter and may contain letters, digits, and underscores.
3. *Length, precision,* and *scale* are integers.
4. *Constant* is a number, and *string* is a character string.

```
<create table statement>   ::=   CREATE TABLE <table name>
                                  ( <column definition>
                                  [ { , <column definition> } . . . ] ) ;

<column definition>   ::=   <column name> <data type> [NOT NULL]

<data type>   ::=   DECIMAL [ ( <precision> [, <scale> ] ) ] |
                    INTEGER | FLOAT | CHAR ( <length> )

<drop table statement>   ::=   DROP TABLE <table name> ;

<alter table statement>   ::=   ALTER TABLE <table name> { ADD | MODIFY }
                                <alter table clause> ;

<alter table clause>   ::=   { <column name> <data type> } |
                             { ( <column name> <data type>
                             [ { , <column name> <data type> } . . . ] ) }

<select statement>   ::=   <query expression> [ <order by clause> ] ;

<query expression>   ::=   <query term> |
                           { <query expression> UNION <query term> }

<query term>   ::=   SELECT [ DISTINCT ] <select list> <table expression>

<select list>   ::=   * |
                      { <value expression> [, <value expression> ] . . . }

<value expression>   ::=   <term> | { <value expression> { + | − } <term> }

<term>   ::=   <factor> | { <term> { * | / } <factor> }

<factor>   ::=   [ + | − ] <primary>

<primary>   ::=   <constant> | <column specification> |
                  <set function specification> | ( <value expression> )

<column specification>   ::=   [ <table name>  ] <column name>

<set function specification>   ::=   COUNT (*) | <set function>

<set function>   ::=   { AVG | MAX | MIN | SUM | COUNT }
                       ( [DISTINCT ] <column specification> )

<table expression>   ::=   <from clause> [ <where clause> ]
                           [ <group by clause> [ <having clause> ] ]

<from clause>   ::=   FROM <table name> [ { , <table name> } . . . ]

<where clause>   ::=   WHERE <search condition>

<search condition>   ::=   <boolean term> |
                           <search condition> OR <boolean term>

<boolean term>   ::=   <boolean factor> |
                       <boolean term> AND <boolean factor>
```

(continued)

FIGURE 4.3.1 *(continued)*

```
<boolean factor>   ::=   [ NOT ] <boolean primary>
<boolean primary>   ::=   <predicate> | { ( <search condition> ) }
<predicate>   ::=   <comparison predicate> | <between predicate> |
                    <in predicate> | <like predicate> |
                    <quantified predicate> | <exists predicate>
<comparison predicate>   ::=   <value expression> <comparison operator>
                               { <value expression> | <subquery> }
<comparison operator>   ::=   < | <= | = | >= | > | <>
<subquery>   ::=   ( SELECT [ DISTINCT ] { <value expression> | * }
                   <table expression> )
<between predicate>   ::=   <value expression> [ NOT ] BETWEEN
                            <value expression> AND <value expression>
<in predicate>   ::=   <value expression> [ NOT ] IN
                       { <subquery> | ( <value list> ) }
<value list>   ::=   <literal> [ { , <literal> } . . . ]
<like predicate>   ::=   <column specification> [ NOT ] LIKE <string>
<quantified predicate>   ::=   <value expression> <comparison predicate>
                               { ALL | ANY } <subquery>
<exists predicate>   ::=   EXISTS <subquery>
<group by clause>   ::=   GROUP BY <column specification>
<having clause>   ::=   HAVING <search condition>
<order by clause>   ::=   ORDER BY <sort specification>
                          [ { , <sort specification> } . . . ]
<sort specification>   ::=   { <integer> | <column> } [ DESC ]
```

Users may change their schemas by various schema manipulation statements. The **CREATE statement** is used to add a table to the schema, while the **DROP statement** is used to delete an existing table from the schema. In fact, the table definitions in Figure 4.3.2(a) must have been initially defined by CREATE statements. For example, we can add the table INSURANCE to the schema as shown in part (a) of Figure 4.3.3, and we can delete the STATUS table as shown in part (b). The **ALTER statement** is used to change the description of a table. We are allowed to add a new column to the table, or change the data type of a column by increasing the maximum length of an item in the table. Part (c) of the figure shows how we add a column for NAME in the STATUS table. All commands end with a semicolon.

Next we consider data manipulation. The most important statement for querying in SQL is the SELECT statement. It is important not to confuse the SQL SELECT statement with the selection operation of

FIGURE 4.3.2
A Database Schema and an Instance for the Schema

(a) The schema

```
SCHEMA
  TABLE   DEPARTMENT
    ITEM   DNAME       CHAR (15)   NOT NULL
    ITEM   LOCATION    CHAR (2)
    ITEM   MANAGER     CHAR (15)
  TABLE   TASK
    ITEM   DNAME       CHAR (15)   NOT NULL
    ITEM   TASKNO      INTEGER     NOT NULL
    ITEM   TASKNAME    CHAR (15)
  TABLE   EMPLOYEE
    ITEM   DNAME       CHAR (15)   NOT NULL
    ITEM   SSNO        CHAR (9)
    ITEM   NAME        CHAR (15)
    ITEM   SALARY      INTEGER
    ITEM   ADDRESS     CHAR (20)
  TABLE   STATUS
    ITEM   DNAME       CHAR (15)   NOT NULL
    ITEM   SSNO        CHAR (9)
    ITEM   TASKNO      INTEGER     NOT NULL
    ITEM   ST          CHAR (10)
```

(b) An instance

DEPARTMENT		
DNAME	LOCATION	MANAGER
Engineering	12	Simon L
Sales	05	Johnson M
Word processing	03	Miller T
Service	10	Williams B

TASK		
DNAME	TASKNO	TASKNAME
Engineering	1	micro
Engineering	2	math
Engineering	3	stat
Sales	4	big sale
Service	5	fixit
Word processing	6	letters

(continued)

FIGURE 4.3.2 *(continued)*

EMPLOYEE				
DNAME	SSNO	NAME	SALARY	ADDRESS
Engineering	111111111	Smith L	25000	1501 Roper St
Engineering	222222222	Rogers C	30000	2057 York Rd
Sales	333333333	Bailey D	27600	261 Pine Ave
Sales	444444444	Rivers F	21070	55 Penn St
Sales	555555555	Smith L	31280	1750 Burke Ave
Word processing	666666666	Adams M	17285	2121 Taylor St
Service	777777777	Davis D	20050	1280 Boston Dr
Service	888888888	Wood J	22075	1280 Boston Dr

STATUS			
DNAME	SSNO	TASKNO	ST
Engineering	111111111	1	started
Engineering	111111111	2	completed
Engineering	222222222	3	completed
Engineering	222222222	1	midway
Word processing	666666666	6	completed
Sales	555555555	4	started
Service	777777777	5	midway

FIGURE 4.3.3
Schema Manipulation Statements

(a) Add the INSURANCE table to the schema.

```
CREATE  TABLE  INSURANCE
   ( SSNO    CHAR (9)  NOT NULL,
     NAME    CHAR (15),
     INS_CO  CHAR (20),
     POLICY  CHAR (13) );
```

(b) Delete the STATUS table from the schema.

```
DROP  TABLE  STATUS;
```

(c) Add a column for NAME in the STATUS table.

```
ALTER  TABLE  STATUS
   ADD  NAME  CHAR (15);
```

the relational algebra (even though we use SELECT for both). The SQL **SELECT statement** is complex and, with various options, includes the capabilities of the three basic operations of the relational algebra, JOIN, PROJECT, and SELECT. The general format of this statement is

SELECT attribute(s) FROM table(s) WHERE condition;

The SELECT statement prints the result which is always a table. Next we give examples of queries in SQL in Figure 4.3.4. In each case the SQL statement is shown in part (i) and the result is indicated in part (ii). All queries are shown for the database in Figure 4.3.2(b).

Let's consider projection first. Suppose that we wish to obtain the names of all the departments in the DEPARTMENT table. Figure 4.3.4 shows how to do this in query (a). After the word SELECT, we list the attributes on which we project. In this case there is only one attribute, DNAME. This list is followed by the word FROM and the name(s) of the table(s) from which the data is to be retrieved. Here we are dealing with the DEPARTMENT table. It is customary (but not necessary) to write the FROM clause on a new line. In Figure 4.3.4, query (b) gives another example of projection.

In order to accomplish selection we add another clause, the WHERE clause. Suppose that we wish to obtain data from the EMPLOYEE table about each employee whose salary is greater than $25,000. The corresponding SQL statement is given in query (c). The condition after WHERE may include relational operators such as $<, <=, >, >=, =, <>$, as well as the Boolean operators AND, OR, NOT. In many cases, selection is done in conjunction with projection in a query. For example, in the previous case, we may only want to know the department name, name, and salary of each employee whose salary is greater than $25,000. Such a request is shown as query (d).

Suppose that in the previous case we were only interested in the department names. That query is shown in query (e) of Figure 4.3.4. Note that Sales is repeated. To avoid such repetition, we may use the word DISTINCT in the SELECT clause. This approach is shown in query (f). Character string matching can also be used in the WHERE clause, as illustrated in query (g). The percent sign (%) matches any sequence of characters; an underscore can be used to match a single character. In many cases we would like to obtain the result in some ordered fashion, such as alphabetically or in numerical order. If, in the example of query (d), we wish to order the result in increasing order on SALARY, we can do so by using the ORDER BY clause as shown in query (h). Then, in query (i), we use DESC to indicate descending order and a second attribute for breaking ties. Our last example, query (j), shows a SELECT clause, which indicates a computation.

FIGURE 4.3.4
SQL Queries

(a) Print the name of each department in the DEPARTMENT table.

(i) ```
SELECT   DNAME
FROM   DEPARTMENT;
```

(ii)

| DNAME |
|---|
| Engineering |
| Sales |
| Word processing |
| Service |

(b) Print the name and salary of every employee.

(i) ```
SELECT   NAME,SALARY
FROM     EMPLOYEE;
```

(ii)

NAME	SALARY
Smith L	25000
Rogers C	30000
Bailey D	27600
Rivers F	21070
Smith L	31280
Adams M	17285
Davis D	20050
Wood J	22075

(c) Print all data about each employee whose salary is greater than $25,000.

(i) ```
SELECT   DNAME,SSNO,NAME,SALARY,ADDRESS
FROM   EMPLOYEE
WHERE   SALARY > 25000;
```

(ii)

| DNAME | SSNO | NAME | SALARY | ADDRESS |
|---|---|---|---|---|
| Engineering | 222222222 | Rogers C | 30000 | 2057 York Rd |
| Sales | 333333333 | Bailey D | 27600 | 261 Pine Ave |
| Sales | 555555555 | Smith L | 31280 | 1750 Burke Ave |

(d) Print the department name, name, and salary for each employee whose salary is greater than $25,000.

(i) ```
SELECT   DNAME,NAME,SALARY
FROM     EMPLOYEE
WHERE    SALARY > 25000;
```

(ii)

DNAME	NAME	SALARY
Engineering	Rogers C	30000
Sales	Bailey D	27600
Sales	Smith L	31280

(continued)

(e) Print all names of departments that have an employee whose salary is greater than $25,000.

(*i*)
```
SELECT   DNAME
FROM     EMPLOYEE
WHERE    SALARY > 25000;
```

(*ii*)

DNAME
Engineering
Sales
Sales

(f) Print, without repetition, all names of departments that have an employee whose salary is greater than $25,000.

(*i*)
```
SELECT   DISTINCT DNAME
FROM     EMPLOYEE
WHERE    SALARY > 25000;
```

(*ii*)

DNAME
Engineering
Sales

(g) Print the department name, name, and address for each employee whose name begins with "R."

(*i*)
```
SELECT   DNAME,NAME,ADDRESS
FROM     EMPLOYEE
WHERE    NAME LIKE 'R%';
```

(*ii*)

DNAME	NAME	ADDRESS
Engineering	Rogers C	2057 York Rd
Sales	Rivers F	55 Penn St

(h) Print the department name, name, and salary for each employee whose salary is greater than $25,000. Present the result in ascending order on salaries.

(*i*)
```
SELECT   DNAME,NAME,SALARY
FROM     EMPLOYEE
WHERE    SALARY > 25000
ORDER    BY SALARY;
```

(*ii*)

DNAME	NAME	SALARY
Sales	Bailey D	27600
Engineering	Rogers C	30000
Sales	Smith L	31280

(continued)

FIGURE 4.3.4 *(continued)*

(i) Same as item (h), but present the result in descending order on departments and break
ties in ascending order on salaries.

(*i*)
```
SELECT   DNAME,NAME,SALARY
FROM     EMPLOYEE
WHERE    SALARY > 25000
ORDER    BY DNAME DESC, SALARY;
```

(*ii*)

DNAME	NAME	SALARY
Sales	Bailey D	27600
Sales	Smith L	31280
Engineering	Rogers C	30000

(j) Print the name and new salary of everyone in the Sales department if they are all given
a $1000 raise.

(*i*)
```
SELECT   NAME,SALARY+1000
FROM     EMPLOYEE
WHERE    DNAME = 'Sales';
```

(*ii*)

NAME	SALARY + 1000
Bailey D	28600
Rivers F	22070
Smith L	32280

4.4 More Complex Queries in SQL

In the previous section, we discussed the implementation of the projection and selection operations of the relational algebra in SQL. We continue now with the third major operation of the relational algebra, the
join. Our first example involves the join of the DEPARTMENT and
TASK tables, and is given in Figure 4.4.1(a). The same SELECT statement that we used for expressing projection and selection is used for
expressing the join operation. In fact, we can express any type of join by
using the various relational operations within the SELECT statement.
When a column name appears in more than one table, like DNAME in
this example, it must be qualified by the appropriate table name to avoid
ambiguity. Again, in all the examples we give the answers to the queries
on the database of Figure 4.3.2(b).

Recall how in the previous section we were able to combine projection and selection. Because the same SELECT statement is also used for
the join operation, we can combine the three operations in one statement.
Our next example in Figure 4.4.1(b) illustrates this point. This query
finds the names of all employees in the Engineering department who

FIGURE 4.4.1
SQL Retrieval from More Than One Table

(a) Combine and print all department and task information.

```
(i) SELECT    DEPARTMENT.DNAME,LOCATION,MANAGER,TASKNO,
              TASKNAME
    FROM      DEPARTMENT,TASK
    WHERE     DEPARTMENT.DNAME = TASK.DNAME;
```

(*ii*)

DNAME	LOCATION	MANAGER	TASKNO	TASKNAME
Engineering	12	Simon L	1	micro
Engineering	12	Simon L	2	math
Engineering	12	Simon L	3	stat
Sales	05	Johnson M	4	bigsale
Word processing	03	Miller T	6	letters
Service	10	Williams B	5	fixit

(b) Print the names of all employees in the Engineering department who have completed a task.

```
(i) SELECT    NAME
    FROM      EMPLOYEE,STATUS
    WHERE     EMPLOYEE.DNAME = STATUS.DNAME
          AND EMPLOYEE.SSNO = STATUS.SSNO
          AND EMPLOYEE.DNAME = 'Engineering'
          AND ST = 'completed';
```

(*ii*)

NAME
Smith L
Rogers C

(c) Print the salary, task names, and manager of the employee whose social security number is 222-22-2222.

```
(i) SELECT    SALARY,TASKNAME,MANAGER
    FROM      EMPLOYEE,STATUS,TASK,DEPARTMENT
    WHERE     EMPLOYEE.SSNO = '222222222'
          AND DEPARTMENT.DNAME = EMPLOYEE.DNAME
          AND EMPLOYEE.SSNO = STATUS.SSNO
          AND STATUS.TASKNO = TASK.TASKNO
          AND EMPLOYEE.DNAME = STATUS.DNAME
          AND STATUS.DNAME = TASK.DNAME;
```

(*ii*)

SALARY	TASKNAME	MANAGER
30000	stat	Simon L
30000	micro	Simon L

have completed a task. Here we need to join the EMPLOYEE and STATUS tables, select on the Engineering department and completed status, and project on name. The join is indicated by the two tables in the FROM clause and the first two equality predicates in the WHERE clause. The projection is indicated by the column name after SELECT, and selection is indicated by the last two equalities in the WHERE clause.

We can also obtain the join of more than two tables by using a single SELECT statement. Suppose that we wish to know the salary, task names, and manager of the employee whose social security number is 222-22-2222. In this case, we join all four tables to get MANAGER from the DEPARTMENT table, SALARY from the EMPLOYEE table, and TASKNAME from the TASK table via TASKNO, which is in the STATUS table. This query is shown in Figure 4.4.1(c).

Before we consider the nesting of SELECT statements, we learn how to use the **IN clause.** IN is used as part of WHERE to indicate a subset relationship. Suppose that we wish to obtain the social security number and name of every employee who is either in the Sales department or the Service department. Figure 4.4.2 shows the query written in three different ways. First, part (a) gives a type of query that we discussed in the previous section. The query in part (b) illustrates the use of the IN clause. IN is used for set membership, as we require that the DNAME value be in the set {"Sales","Service"}. Then, part (c) gives the third solution by using the UNION operation of SQL, which corresponds to the union operation of the relational algebra.

Now we are ready to consider a **nested SELECT statement.** Suppose that we wish to obtain the names of all managers who have a completed task in their department. We give two ways of expressing this query in SQL. The first one uses the standard SQL method to obtain a join, a method that we have just discussed and which we show in part (a) of Figure 4.4.3. Then, in part (b), we write the query using a nested SELECT statement. We read this as follows: Select the managers from the DEPARTMENT table where the DNAME value is in the set of DNAME values, which are obtained from the STATUS table by selecting on the ST value "completed". In this case, there are two such DNAME values, Engineering and Word processing. That is how we then obtain the result. In general, nesting may be applied for any number of levels.

Next we discuss the **built-in** aggregate **functions:** COUNT, SUM, AVG, MAX, and MIN. Each of these five functions operates on a column of a table as follows: **COUNT** yields the number of values in the column; **MAX** yields the largest value in the column; **MIN** yields the smallest value in the column; **SUM** yields the sum of the values in the column; and **AVG** yields the average of the values in the column. Clearly, SUM and AVG can be used only on columns that have numeric values. For nonnumerical values, MIN and MAX work in the standard lexicographical order.

FIGURE 4.4.2
Using IN in a WHERE Clause

Print the social security number and name of every employee who is either in the Sales department or the Service department.

(a)
```
SELECT   SSNO,NAME
FROM     EMPLOYEE
WHERE    DNAME = 'Sales'
   OR    DNAME = 'Service';
```

(b)
```
SELECT   SSNO,NAME
FROM     EMPLOYEE
WHERE    DNAME   IN
              ('Sales','Service');
```

(c)
```
SELECT   SSNO,NAME
FROM     EMPLOYEE
WHERE    DNAME = 'Sales'
   UNION
SELECT   SSNO NAME
FROM     EMPLOYEE
WHERE    DNAME = 'Service';
```

(d)

SSNO	NAME
333333333	Bailey D
444444444	Rivers F
555555555	Smith L
777777777	Davis D
888888888	Wood J

Now let's consider examples of the built-in functions. Part (a) of Figure 4.4.4 shows two ways of finding the number of departments using the COUNT function. Note that if we do the counting in the EMPLOYEE table, we need to indicate DISTINCT to eliminate duplicates. In both cases the result is 4. The next query, given in part (b), illustrates a use of the MAX function. We wish to find the highest salary of an employee in the Service department. The MIN function is applied in a similar way.

If we wish to find the name(s) of the individual(s) with the highest salary in the Service department, we can proceed in several ways. We can first find the maximum salary value and then write a query to find the individual(s) with that salary, or we can write one query as shown in part (c) of Figure 4.4.4. This query illustrates not only the MAX function but also a nested SELECT statement which is used here not for set membership with IN but with equality. The query for finding the sum of the salaries in the Sales department uses the SUM function and is given in

FIGURE 4.4.3
Nested SELECT Query

Print the names of all managers who have a completed task in their department.

```
(a)  SELECT   MANAGER
     FROM     DEPARTMENT,STATUS
     WHERE    DEPARTMENT.DNAME = STATUS.DNAME
          AND ST = 'completed';

(b)  SELECT   MANAGER
     FROM     DEPARTMENT
     WHERE    DNAME   IN
                     (SELECT   DNAME
                      FROM     STATUS
                      WHERE    ST = 'completed');
```

(c)

MANAGER
Simon L
Miller T

FIGURE 4.4.4
SQL Built-in Functions

(a) Print the number of departments.

```
(i)  SELECT   COUNT(DNAME)                    (iii)
     FROM     DEPARTMENT;
(ii) SELECT   COUNT(DISTINCT DNAME)
     FROM     EMPLOYEE;
```

Result
4

(b) Print the highest salary of an employee in the Service department.

```
(i)  SELECT   MAX(SALARY)                     (ii)
     FROM     EMPLOYEE
     WHERE    DNAME = 'Service';
```

MAX(SALARY)
22075

(c) Print the name of the highest paid employee in the Service department.

```
(i)  SELECT   NAME
     FROM     EMPLOYEE
     WHERE    DNAME = 'Service'
          AND SALARY = (SELECT   MAX(SALARY)
                        FROM     EMPLOYEE
                        WHERE    DNAME = 'Service');
```

(continued)

(*ii*)

NAME
Wood J

(d) Print the sum of the salaries in the Sales department.

(*i*)
```
SELECT   SUM(SALARY)
FROM     EMPLOYEE
WHERE    DNAME = 'Sales';
```

(*ii*)

SUM(SALARY)
79950

(e) Print the average salary in the Sales department.

(*i*)
```
SELECT   AVG(SALARY)
FROM     EMPLOYEE
WHERE    DNAME = 'Sales';
```

(*ii*)

AVG(SALARY)
26650

(f) Print the average salary in every department.

(*i*)
```
SELECT   DNAME,AVG(SALARY)
FROM     EMPLOYEE
GROUP    BY DNAME;
```

(*ii*)

DNAME	AVG(SALARY)
Engineering	27500
Sales	26650
Word processing	17285
Service	21063

(g) Print the average salary in every department for which the average salary is between $20,000 and $27,000. Present the result in order on department name.

(*i*)
```
SELECT   DNAME,AVG(SALARY)
FROM     EMPLOYEE
GROUP    BY DNAME
HAVING   AVG(SALARY) BETWEEN 20000 AND 27000
ORDER    BY DNAME;
```

(*ii*)

DNAME	AVG(SALARY)
Sales	26650
Service	21063

part (d). The query in part (e) shows how to use the AVG function to find the average salary in the same department. The result is the sum of the salaries divided by 3, for the three individuals in that department.

The GROUP BY and HAVING clauses are useful in connection with the built-in functions. **GROUP BY** rearranges a table into groups based on an attribute. We illustrate this in part (f) of Figure 4.4.4 to find the average salary in every department. The **HAVING** clause may be used with a GROUP BY clause to specify a condition. In part (g), we wish to obtain the answer for only those departments where the average salary is between $20,000 and $27,000. In this case, we require the answer to be printed in order on department name.

We next consider another very useful construct in SQL, called EXISTS. Later, when we discuss logic in Chapter 8, we will consider in more detail the existential quantifier. Here we note that the purpose of EXISTS is to test for a non-empty set, and we give some examples for its use. The first example is in Figure 4.4.5(a). We wish to find the names of all those tasks which have been completed by some employee. One way of writing the query is given in part (*i*); this is similar to earlier examples. We give the query using EXISTS in part (*ii*). The way to think of the execution of this query is as follows: take a row from TASK and if there is a row in STATUS which has the same task number and whose ST value is "completed", then project on TASKNAME for the answer. We write an asterisk, which is equivalent to writing *all the attributes*, because we are interested only in the existence of an element from STATUS satisfying the WHERE condition.

In Figure 4.4.5(b), we illustrate the use of NOT EXISTS. In this case we want to find the department name and name of every employee who has no completed tasks. The NOT EXISTS(. . .) is true if the set obtained by the SELECT clause in the parentheses is empty. For example, this is the case for Bailey but not for Rogers.

When a subquery returns a set of values, the words ANY and ALL may be used with comparison operators preceding the subquery. In part (*i*) of Figure 4.4.6(a), we write a query using ANY. This query retrieves information about employees who earn more than at least one employee in the Service department. We can also write this query using the MIN function, as we show in part (*ii*). Finally, we ask for the employees who earn more than everyone in the Service department. We write this query in Figure 4.4.6(b) and note that we could also have written this query using the MAX function. We make two comments about ANY and ALL. First, when writing a query, do not be misled by the idiomatic meaning of ANY and ALL in English; instead, use them according to their technical definition. Second, IN has the same meaning as =ANY, and NOT IN is the same as <>ALL.

We end this section by mentioning that the intersection and difference of tables can be obtained by using EXISTS and NOT EXISTS,

FIGURE 4.4.5
EXISTS in SQL

(a) Print the names of all tasks which have been completed by some employee.

(*i*)
```
SELECT   TASKNAME
FROM     TASK STATUS
WHERE    TASK.TASKNO = STATUS.TASKNO
    AND ST = 'completed';
```
(*ii*)
```
SELECT   TASKNAME
FROM     TASK
WHERE    EXISTS
            (SELECT  *
             FROM    STATUS
             WHERE   STATUS.TASKNO = TASK.TASKNO
                AND ST = 'completed');
```
(*iii*)

TASKNAME
math
stat
letters

(b) Print the department name and name of every employee who has no completed tasks.

(*i*)
```
SELECT   DNAME,NAME
FROM     EMPLOYEE
WHERE    NOT EXISTS
            (SELECT  *
             FROM    STATUS
             WHERE   EMPLOYEE.SSNO = STATUS.SSNO
                AND ST = 'completed');
```
(*ii*)

DNAME	NAME
Sales	Bailey D
Sales	Rivers F
Sales	Smith L
Service	Davis D
Service	Wood J

respectively. Because we have already shown how to do selections, projections, and joins (as well as arbitrary products), it is clear that any query which can be expressed in the relational algebra can also be expressed in SQL. A query language which has (at least) the power of the relational algebra is said to be (relationally) **complete.** Thus, SQL is a complete query language.

FIGURE 4.4.6
ANY and ALL in SQL

(a) Print the department name and name of every employee who earns more than at least one employee in the Service department.

```
(i)  SELECT   DNAME,NAME
     FROM      EMPLOYEE
     WHERE     SALARY > ANY
               (SELECT  SALARY
                FROM     EMPLOYEE
                WHERE    DNAME = 'Service');
(ii) SELECT   DNAME,NAME
     FROM      EMPLOYEE
     WHERE     SALARY >
               (SELECT  MIN(SALARY)
                FROM     EMPLOYEE
                WHERE    DNAME = 'Service');
```

(iii)

DNAME	NAME
Engineering	Smith L
Engineering	Rogers C
Sales	Bailey D
Sales	Rivers F
Sales	Smith L
Service	Wood J

(b) Print the department name and name of every employee who earns more than all employees in the Service department.

```
(i)  SELECT   DNAME,NAME
     FROM      EMPLOYEE
     WHERE     SALARY > ALL
               (SELECT  SALARY
                FROM     EMPLOYEE
                WHERE    DNAME = 'Service');
```

(ii)

DNAME	NAME
Engineering	Smith L
Engineering	Rogers C
Sales	Bailey D
Sales	Smith L

4.5 Some Additional Features of SQL

We start this section by considering **updates** in SQL. Recall that there are three types of updates: *insertion, deletion,* and *modification.* SQL uses the verbs **INSERT, DELETE,** and **UPDATE,** respectively. We write the syntax rules for the SQL update statements in Figure 4.5.1. With one statement we can update only one table.

  We start with insertions. The simplest type of insertion involves inserting a row into a table. In Figure 4.5.2(a) we show how to insert a row into the STATUS table. It is not necessary to follow the name of the table, STATUS in this case, with a list of attributes in parentheses and separated by commas, because we are inserting a value for each attribute in the proper order. When the list is used and one or more attributes are omitted, the database system places a null value into the inserted row for each omitted attribute value. (We will discuss null values for SQL in Section 11.1.) It is also possible to use a SELECT statement to obtain some values from a table and then insert them into another table.

  Next we consider deletions. One or more rows of a table can be deleted at one time. Suppose that we wish to delete the row with social security number 111-11-1111 from the EMPLOYEE table. This can be done as shown in part (b) of Figure 4.5.2. Note however, that even after the deletion, there is still data about this employee in the STATUS table. We can delete those two rows by writing a similar statement, as shown in part (c).

FIGURE 4.5.1
Syntax Rules for SQL Update Statements

Note: Additional syntax rules for SQL are presented in Figures 4.3.1, 4.5.3, 4.5.5, 6.1.5, 6.4.3, and 7.1.7.

```
<insert statement>   ::=   INSERT INTO <table name>
                             [ ( <insert column list> ) ]
                             { VALUES ( <insert value list> ) |
                             <query specification> } ;
<insert column list>   ::=   <column name> [ { , <column name> } . . . ]
<insert value list>   ::=   <literal> [ { , <literal> } . . . ]
<delete statement>   ::=   DELETE FROM <table name>
                             [ WHERE <search condition> ] ;
<update statement>   ::=   UPDATE <table name>
                             SET <set clause> [ { , <set clause> } . . . ]
                             [ WHERE <search condition> ] ;
<set clause>   ::=   <column name> = <value expression>
```

FIGURE 4.5.2
Updating in SQL

(a) Insert the row <Sales,444444444,4,completed> into the STATUS table.

```
INSERT
INTO    STATUS
VALUES ('Sales','444444444',4,'completed');
```

(b) Delete the row from the EMPLOYEE table with social security number 111-11-1111.

```
DELETE
FROM    EMPLOYEE
WHERE   SSNO = '111111111';
```

(c) Delete the rows from the STATUS table with social security number 111-11-1111.

```
DELETE
FROM    STATUS
WHERE   SSNO = '111111111';
```

(d) Modify the status of task 1 in the Engineering department for social security number 111-11-1111 to 'midway'.

```
UPDATE  STATUS
SET     ST = 'midway'
WHERE   DNAME = 'Engineering'
    AND SSNO = '111111111'
    AND TASKNO = 1;
```

(e) Add $1000 to every employee's salary in the Service department.

```
UPDATE  EMPLOYEE
SET     SALARY = SALARY+1000
WHERE   DNAME = 'Service';
```

The last type of update is modification. First, part (d) of Figure 4.5.2 shows how to change the status of task 1 in the Engineering department for social security number 111-11-1111 to "midway". Here is one more example of a modification; this time the modification involves several rows. We want to add $1000 to every employee's salary in the Service department. The UPDATE statement for this example is given in part (e).

Next we consider how SQL can be used embedded in a programming language rather than as a stand-alone language. In fact, the ANSI SQL language is oriented toward the embedded approach rather than the stand-alone approach that we have examined so far. For DB2, the high-level host languages at present are PL/I, COBOL, and FORTRAN. We have already discussed the interaction of database and programming languages in Section 1.4 and illustrated it for the network and hierarchic models in Chapters 2 and 3, respectively.

Figure 4.5.3 shows some additional syntax rules useful for **embedded SQL statements.** For a high-level database manipulation language like SQL, the additional problem is that typically a SELECT statement returns a set of rows, but the host (programming) language can handle only one row at a time. The basic solution for this problem is to use a cursor that references just a single row. Thus if the answer to a query is a set of rows, we can use a cursor and a loop in the programming language to deal individually with each row. Let's assume that the host language is Pascal. Then if we embed SQL in Pascal, we need to define record variables in Pascal for storing data from the database.

Suppose that with such a Pascal program we wish to print the social security number, name, and salary for the employees in the Sales department. We set up a cursor by using a cursor declaration as shown in Figure 4.5.4(a). The name of the cursor is SALESPEOPLE and the SELECT statement indicates how the cursor will be used. A cursor must be opened by an OPEN statement before it can be used. Into the Pascal variables (which must have been previously declared) of SS, NAME, and SAL, the FETCH statement reads the appropriate values for the next row of EMPLOYEE where DNAME = "Sales." Figure 4.5.4(b) illustrates this procedure. We place a colon before each programming language variable in the FETCH statement to distinguish it from objects in the database schema.

FIGURE 4.5.3
Additional Rules for Embedded SQL

Note: Additional syntax rules for SQL are presented in Figures 4.3.1, 4.5.1, 4.5.5, 6.1.5, 6.4.3, and 7.1.7.

```
<declare cursor>   ::=   DECLARE <cursor name>
                         CURSOR FOR <cursor specification> ;
<cursor specification>   ::=   <query expression> [ <order by clause> ]
<fetch statement>   ::=   FETCH <cursor name> INTO <fetch parameter list> ;
<fetch parameter list>   ::=   { : <parameter name> }
                               [ { , : <parameter name> } . . . ]
<open statement>   ::=   OPEN <cursor name> ;
<close statement>   ::=   CLOSE <cursor name> ;
<positioned update statement>   ::=   UPDATE <table name>
                                      SET <set clause>
                                      [ { , <set clause> } . . . ]
                                      WHERE CURRENT OF <cursor name> ;
<positioned delete statement>   ::=   DELETE FROM <table name>
                                      WHERE CURRENT OF <cursor name> ;
```

FIGURE 4.5.4
Cursors in Embedded SQL

(a) Declare a cursor for employees in the Sales department omitting department name and address.

```
DECLARE SALESPEOPLE CURSOR FOR
SELECT   SSNO,NAME,SALARY
FROM     EMPLOYEE
WHERE    DNAME = 'Sales';
```

(b) Position SALESPEOPLE on the next row and assign the values to the appropriate variables.

```
FETCH   SALESPEOPLE
INTO    :SS,:NAME,:SAL;
```

(c) List the employees in the Sales department omitting department name and address.

```
EXEC SQL FETCH  SALESPEOPLE   INTO :SS,:NAME,:SAL;
WHILE SQLCODE = 0 DO
  BEGIN
    WRITELN(SS,NAME,SAL);
    EXEC SQL FETCH  SALESPEOPLE   INTO :SS,:NAME,:SAL;
  END
```

(d) Increase every employee's salary by 1000 in the Sales department.

```
EXEC SQL DECLARE  SALESSALARY CURSOR FOR
    SELECT   SALARY
    FROM     EMPLOYEE
    WHERE    DNAME = 'Sales';
EXEC SQL OPEN SALESSALARY;
EXEC SQL FETCH  SALESSALARY   INTO :SAL;
WHILE SQLCODE = 0 DO
  BEGIN
    EXEC SQL UPDATE  EMPLOYEE
        SET  SALARY = SALARY + 1000
        WHERE CURRENT OF SALESSALARY;
    EXEC SQL FETCH  SALESSALARY   INTO :SAL
  END
```

If we wish to print these values, one on a line, we can set up a loop in the programming language as shown in part (c) of Figure 4.5.4. We write each SQL statement after EXEC SQL using the implicit procedure calls method for the programming language interface. We assume that SQLCODE is given the value 0 after an operation is performed successfully. The loop terminates when there are no more rows and thus the value of SQLCODE is changed. If, instead of printing these values, we wish to increase each of these salaries by $1000, we can proceed as in Figure 4.5.2(e). Another approach is to use a positioned UPDATE statement, as shown in Figure 4.5.4(d), where in the loop we fetch the next row for the Sales department and modify the salary.

SQL allows the creation of **views,** which are single derived tables. Only the definition of the view is stored; each time a view is used it has to be recreated from the actual tables by the database system. Therefore, updates to the tables of the database are reflected in the views. In terms of the three-level architecture of Section 1.2, an SQL view is not the same as an external view because it is defined by a user on top of that user's view, but it is a similar idea in that views are defined by their mappings to tables and do not themselves exist. An SQL view can be an external view if the database is such that only one user, the DBA, creates all the tables, which then compose the conceptual view. We give the syntax rules for SQL view creation in Figure 4.5.5.

Suppose that we wish to create a view that contains the employee data, without address, for those whose salary is at least $30,000. This can be done as shown in Figure 4.5.6(a). Again, it is the SELECT statement which specifies the projection and selection necessary to create the view.

Once a view has been created, we can write queries to it. In particular, in Figure 4.5.6(b) we write a query to find the name and salary of every employee in WELLOFF. Updating a view is usually more complicated and becomes impossible in certain cases, such as when a view is defined by a built-in function. The problem is that a view update must be transformed to the update of the actual tables, and that update of the tables may not be well defined. We will discuss the view update problem in a general framework in Section 10.3.

DB2 and ORACLE place severe restrictions on view updates: they are allowed only on views obtained by projection and selection from a single table. Even in such a case a curious phenomenon of the disappearing row may occur. Suppose that a user tries to insert a row into a view which does not satisfy the condition of the view. An example would be the attempted insertion of a row into the WELLOFF view for an individual whose salary is not greater than $30,000. Such an insertion is not allowed if WITH CHECK OPTION is stated in the view definition, but if WITH CHECK OPTION is not used, then the insertion is allowed

FIGURE 4.5.5
Syntax Rules for SQL View Statements

Note: Additional syntax rules for SQL are presented in Figures 4.3.1, 4.5.1, 4.5.3, 6.1.5, 6.4.3, and 7.1.7.

```
<view definition>   ::=   CREATE VIEW <table name>
                          [ ( <view column list> ) ]
                          AS <query term> [ WITH CHECK OPTION ] ;
<view column list>   ::=   <column name> [ { , <column name> } . . . ]
<drop view statement>   ::=   DROP VIEW <table name> ;
```

FIGURE 4.5.6
Views in SQL

(a) Create a view for employees whose salary is greater than $30,000, omitting address.

```
CREATE  VIEW  WELLOFF
    AS  SELECT  DNAME,SSNO,NAME,SALARY
        FROM    EMPLOYEE
        WHERE   SALARY > 30000;
```

(b) Print the name and salary of every employee in WELLOFF.

```
SELECT  NAME,SALARY
FROM    WELLOFF;
```

(c) Create a view combining employee and status data omitting salary and address.

```
CREATE  VIEW  EMPFIN
    AS  SELECT  EMPLOYEE.DNAME,EMPLOYEE.SSNO,NAME,
                    TASKNO,ST
        FROM    EMPLOYEE,STATUS
        WHERE   EMPLOYEE.DNAME = STATUS.DNAME
            AND EMPLOYEE.SSNO = STATUS.SSNO
            AND ST = 'completed';
```

(d) Delete the EMPFIN view.

```
DROP  VIEW  EMPFIN;
```

and the individual is inserted into the EMPLOYEE table *but is hidden from the user* of the WELLOFF view.

Sometimes null values must be introduced by the database system; for example, if we insert a row into WELLOFF, when the corresponding row is inserted into the EMPLOYEE table, the system places a null value for ADDRESS. Because we can use any SELECT statement, it is also possible to create a view that consists of a join. In Figure 4.5.6(c) we show how to create a view that contains both EMPLOYEE and STATUS data, omitting SALARY and ADDRESS, for all completed tasks. Views may be deleted by using the DROP statement; this is illustrated in Figure 4.5.6(d).

4.6 Exercises

4.1 Transform the network data structure diagrams given in the following figures, but omitting SYSTEM and the Codasyl set names, into relational database schemes:

(a) Figure 2.5.2.
(b) Figure 2.5.3.

(c) Figure 2.5.4.
(d) Figure 2.5.5.

4.2 Using the tables for TEACHER and STUDENT given in Figure 4.6.1, write relational algebra programs and show the results for the following:

(a) Print all the data about teachers and students using one PRINT statement.
(b) Print all the data about teachers who are also students.
(c) Print all the data about teachers who are not students.
(d) Print all the data about students who are not teachers.
(e) Print all the data about teachers who are older than 30.
(f) Print the name, age, and address for each student between the ages of 20 and 35.
(g) Insert the row <444555666,Kline,5533 Bird Dr,32> into the TEACHER table.
(h) Delete the row for Jones from the TEACHER table.

4.3 Using the tables for DEPARTMENT, EMPLOYEE, CUSTOMER, and SALE given in Figure 4.6.2, write relational algebra programs and show the results for the following:

(a) Print the name of each employee in the Shoe department.

FIGURE 4.6.1
The TEACHER and STUDENT Tables

TEACHER			
SSNO	NAME	ADDRESS	AGE
123401234	Stephens	123 Home St	43
234512345	Jones	41 Downing St	28
345623456	White	16 Georgia Rd	31
456734567	Thompson	23 Back Rd	27
567845678	Johnson	187 Thomas Ave	30

STUDENT			
SSNO	NAME	ADDRESS	AGE
678956789	Brown	10 Third Ave	25
789067890	Wood	85 Main St	21
567845678	Johnson	187 Thomas Ave	30
123401234	Stephens	123 Home St	43
012345678	Smith	201 Blank Dr	21

FIGURE 4.6.2
The DEPARTMENT, EMPLOYEE, CUSTOMER, and SALE Tables

DEPARTMENT		
DNAME	LOCATION	TELEPHONE
Sporting Goods	Floor 1	333-0001
Shoe	Floor 2	333-0002
Children	Floor 1	333-0003
Jewelry	Floor 2	333-0005
Furniture	Floor 4	333-0006
Appliance	Floor 3	333-0007

EMPLOYEE				
DNAME	SSNO	NAME	ADDRESS	SALARY
Sporting Goods	333221111	Miller	61 Apple La	17500
Shoe	333222222	Taylor	1127 Tree St	32005
Furniture	333220000	Murray	407 Ocean Dr	16850
Shoe	201221111	Walters	14 E St	18400
Jewelry	201331111	Kennedy	10 Main St	19900
Appliance	201441111	Roberts	2220 Ash Way	28700
Appliance	201551111	Henderson	198 Peach Rd	25555
Shoe	201661111	Ryan	36 Fifth Ave	14200

CUSTOMER	
ACCTNO	NAME
AB123CD456	Woods
CF806GQ932	Jones
BD162XP469	Barkley
KZ921NH253	Bridges
PE843SA896	Evans
RV286TK181	Chen

SALE				
DNAME	SSNO	ACCTNO	RECEIPTNO	DATE
Appliance	201551111	AB123CD456	1270	2/12/86
Sporting Goods	333221111	KZ921NH253	2981	3/1/86
Shoe	333222222	BD162XP469	1420	3/13/86
Furniture	333220000	PE843SA896	1019	4/10/86
Shoe	201661111	BD162XP469	1383	5/5/86
Jewelry	201331111	RV286TK181	0085	7/1/86

(continued)

. . .

. . .

. . .

ITEMNAME	QUANTITY	AMOUNT
Refrigerator	1	745.50
Basketball	3	59.40
Women 7	2	36.30
Table	5	888.40
Men 9	1	24.70
Watch	3	123.30

. . .

(b) Print the name, address, and salary of each employee who made a sale over $50.

(c) Print the name and account number of each customer who made a purchase over $100.

(d) Print the date of every purchase on Floor 2.

(e) Insert the row <QV258BC763, Davis> into the CUSTOMER table.

(f) Delete the row for the Children department.

4.4 Using the tables for OFFICE, EQUIPMENT, LAWYER, and CLIENT given in Figure 4.6.3, write relational algebra programs and show the results for the following:

(a) For each office, print its number and area and the serial number and cost of each piece of equipment in it.

(b) Print the name, address, sex, and age of every client who has a case presided over by Judge Steele.

(c) Print the name and salary of every lawyer.

(d) Print the name of each lawyer who has a client with a case presided over by Judge Steele.

(e) Print the area of office number 100.

(f) Print the types of equipment in the office of Gibson's lawyer.

(g) Insert the row <281,830> into the OFFICE table.

(h) Delete the rows involving the lawyer with social security number 444-55-5666 from the LAWYER and CLIENT tables.

4.5 Using the tables for BRANCH, BORROWER, EMPLOYEE, and TASK given in Figure 4.6.4, write relational algebra programs and show the results for the following:

(a) Print all the data for the borrowers in the Homeville branch.

(b) Print the name of every employee whose task is reshelving.

(c) Print the location of the branch for the borrower with ID number 46001.

FIGURE 4.6.3
The OFFICE, EQUIPMENT, LAWYER, and CLIENT Tables

OFFICE	
ONUMBER	AREA
200	650
100	1010
305	470

EQUIPMENT			
SERIALNO	TYPE	COST	ONUMBER
AAXYZ12398	Computer	1789	100
XPVQR15296	Xerox Machine	1250	200
RHABC12350	Telephone	225	200

LAWYER						
ONUMBER	LSSNO	LNAME	ADDRESS	SALARY	STATUS	TELNO
200	123456789	Peters	86 Front Rd	25000	Associate	555-6666
100	111223333	Williams	104 Green St	91500	Partner	420-3000
305	567123456	Murphy	2690 Valley Dr	48300	Associate	248-1000
200	444555666	Bingham	10 Leaf Pl	60000	Associate	258-2000

CLIENT						
ONUMBER	LSSNO	CNAME	ADDR	SEX	AGE	JNAME
200	123456789	Gibson	38 Park Ave	M	27	Steele
100	111223333	Jackson	1103 Candle St	F	31	Stone
100	111223333	French	29 Branch La	F	45	Burns
305	567123456	Ward	613 Hart Rd	M	39	Steele
200	444555666	Johnson	77 Sunset St	M	24	Burns

(d) For each branch, print the branch name and the name of each borrower and employee using one PRINT statement.

(e) Insert the row

    <Homeville, 54556,Breyer,6050 North Dr,8/15/54>

into the BORROWER table.

(f) Delete all data involving the Rivertown branch.

4.6 Using the tables for TEAM, EMPLOYEE, CUSTOMER, and RE-PAIR_ORDER given in Figure 4.6.5, write relational algebra programs and show the results for the following:

(a) Print the name of the manager of each employee whose salary is greater than $20,000.

FIGURE 4.6.4
The BRANCH, BORROWER, EMPLOYEE, and TASK Tables

BRANCH	
BRNAME	LOCATION
Homeville	Ocean Blvd
Piketown	Back St
Oakdale	Ace Rd
Rivertown	Indian Hwy

BORROWER				
BRNAME	IDNO	BNAME	BADDR	BIRTHDATE
Homeville	52698	Kirby	123 Berry Rd	8/8/60
Piketown	33175	Fisher	87 Broadway	4/5/72
Oakdale	46001	Schultz	605 High St	11/17/71
Homeville	53059	Chung	321 Evelyn Cir	4/5/53
Rivertown	29088	Myers	1011 Crest Pl	2/28/42

EMPLOYEE				
BRNAME	ESSNO	ENAME	EADDR	SALARY
Pikeville	888877777	Smith	153 Holly La	16500
Oakdale	555553331	North	220 Bank Rd	21050
Homeville	334455666	Baxter	11 Angel Ave	23540

TASK		
BRNAME	ESSNO	TNAME
Pikeville	888877777	checkin
Oakdale	555553331	checkout
Homeville	334455666	reshelving

(b) Print the year and model of every car that had a repair order on May 3, 1986.

(c) Print the location of each team that had a repair order on May 3, 1986.

(d) Print the name and address of each customer who has a car of a model year before 1983.

FIGURE 4.6.5
The TEAM, EMPLOYEE, CUSTOMER, and REPAIR_ORDER Tables

TEAM		
TNAME	LOCATION	MANAGER
Blue	Garage 1	Johnson
Red	Garage 2	Lopez
Green	Garage 1	Walters
Yellow	Garage 3	Jackson
Brown	Garage 2	Turner

EMPLOYEE				
TNAME	ESSNO	ENAME	EADDR	ESALARY
Blue	123123123	Peters	10 Main St	24500
Red	234234234	Watson	163 Ash Rd	19750
Blue	012312345	Evans	408 First St	26300
Green	975310246	Majors	613 8th Ave	17550
Brown	123455555	Girard	10312 King St	31005

CUSTOMER					
ESSNO	CNAME	CADDR	SERIALNO	YEAR	MODEL
123123123	Murray	901 Wood Rd	PXQR12SYT3	73	Pinto
123123123	Jones	46 Pearl St	XYZA48ABC7	84	Mustang
012312345	Winters	19 Baxter St	RSRE43PPC9	82	Omega
975310246	Redding	600 Brook Rd	KHRH97RHG3	86	Jetta
975310246	Gibb	14 Marble Way	AZQP12PBD9	85	Corolla

REPAIR_ORDER			
SERIALNO	RONUMBER	DATE	BALANCE
XYZA48ABC7	1004	4/7/86	136.88
RSRE43PPC9	1102	5/3/86	73.59
KHRH97RHG3	1103	5/3l86	105.45
AZQP12PBD9	1316	6/10/86	212.66

    (e) Print the name and address of each employee who has a customer with a car of a model year before 1983.

    (f) Print the serial number of every car handled by the Blue or the Green team.

(g) Insert the row <PXQR12SYT3,1388,6/15/86,44.75> into the REPAIR_ORDER table.

(h) Delete all the data involving the Green team, its employees, customers, and repair orders from the database.

4.7 Write a definition of each of the following relational algebra operations in terms of other relational algebra operations:

(a) INTERSECT(T_1,T_2).

(b) JOIN(T_1,T_2).

(c) THETA-JOIN(T_1,T_2).

(d) DIVIDE(T_1,T_2).

4.8 Using the tables for TEACHER and STUDENT given in Figure 4.6.1, write SQL SELECT statements for the following:

(a) Print all the data about teachers who are older than 30.

(b) Print the name, age, and address for each student between the ages of 20 and 35.

(c) Print all the data about teachers and students.

(d) Print all the data about teachers who are also students.

(e) Print all the data about teachers who are not also students.

(f) Print all the data about students who are not teachers.

4.9 Using the tables for DEPARTMENT, EMPLOYEE, CUSTOMER, and SALE given in Figure 4.6.2, write SQL SELECT statements for the following:

(a) Print the name of each employee in the Shoe department.

(b) Print the name, address, and salary of each employee who made a sale over $50, in descending order on salaries.

(c) Print the name and account number of each customer who made a purchase over $100, in alphabetical order.

(d) Print the date of every purchase on Floor 2.

(e) Print the number of account numbers.

(f) Print the total amount of sales by department.

4.10 Using the tables for OFFICE, EQUIPMENT, LAWYER, and CLIENT given in Figure 4.6.3, write SQL SELECT statements for the following:

(a) For each office, print its number and area and the serial number and cost of each piece of equipment in it.

(b) Print the name, address, sex, and age of every client who has a case presided over by Judge Steele.

(c) Print the name and salary of every lawyer.

(d) Print the name of each lawyer who has a client with a case presided over by Judge Steele.

(e) Print the area of office number 100.

(f) Print the types of equipment in the office of Gibson's lawyer.

(g) Print the average salary of lawyers grouped by status.

    (h) For all clients who are older than at least one client, print the name of the client and the client's lawyer.

4.11 Using the tables for BRANCH, BORROWER, EMPLOYEE, and TASK given in Figure 4.6.4, write SQL SELECT statements for the following:

    (a) Print all the data for the borrowers in the Homeville branch.

    (b) Print the name of every employee whose task is reshelving.

    (c) Print the location of the branch for the borrower with ID number 46001.

    (d) For each branch print the branch name and the name of each borrower and employee.

    (e) Print the branch name and ID number for each borrower whose name begins with "L."

    (f) Print, without repetition, the name and location of each branch that has a borrower and an employee.

4.12 Using the tables for TEAM, EMPLOYEE, CUSTOMER, and RE-PAIR_ORDER given in Figure 4.6.5, write SQL SELECT statements for the following:

    (a) Print, without repetition, the name of the manager of each employee whose salary is greater than $20,000.

    (b) Print the year and model of every car that had a repair order on May 3, 1986.

    (c) Print, without repetition, the location of each team that had a repair order on May 3, 1986.

    (d) Print the name and address of each customer who has a car of a model year before 1983.

    (e) Print the name and address of each employee who has a customer with a car of model year 1985 or 1986.

    (f) Print the serial number of every car handled by the Blue or the Green team.

    (g) Print the number of repair orders.

    (h) Print the names of the employee and customer with the highest balance on a repair order.

4.13 (a) Show how set intersection can be implemented in SQL using EXISTS.

    (b) Show how set difference can be implemented in SQL using NOT EXISTS.

4.14 Using the tables for TEACHER and STUDENT given in Figure 4.6.1, write SQL update statements for the following:

    (a) Insert the row <444555666,Kline,5533 Bird Dr,32> into the TEACHER table.

    (b) Delete the row for Jones from the TEACHER table.

(c) Delete Johnson from the database.

(d) Change the address for Johnson to 600 Parkway Dr.

4.15 Using the tables for DEPARTMENT, EMPLOYEE, CUSTOMER, and SALE given in Figure 4.6.2, write SQL update statements for the following:

(a) Insert the row <QV258BC763,Davis> into the CUSTOMER table.

(b) Insert the row <Hardware,Floor 4,333-0009> into the DEPARTMENT table.

(c) Delete the row for the Children department.

(d) Delete the rows for employees in the Shoe department.

(e) Change the amount of the sale with receipt number 2981 to $69.40.

(f) Add $100 to the salary of each employee who sold a refrigerator.

4.16 Using the tables for OFFICE, EQUIPMENT, LAWYER, and CLIENT given in Figure 4.6.3, do the following operations using embedded SQL:

(a) Declare a cursor for all lawyers in office 200, omitting telephone number.

(b) Use the cursor declared in item (a) to print the social security number, name, address, salary, and status for each lawyer in office 200.

(c) Use the cursor declared in item (a) to increase the salary of each associate in office 200 by $2500.

4.17 Using the tables for BRANCH, BORROWER, EMPLOYEE, and TASK given in Figure 4.6.4, do the following operations using embedded SQL:

(a) Declare a cursor for all borrowers of the Homeville branch.

(b) Use the cursor declared in item (a) to print the name of each borrower at the Homeville branch.

(c) Declare a cursor combining all employee and task data.

(d) Use the cursor declared in item (c) to print the social security number, name, and task name for each employee.

4.18 Using the tables for TEAM, EMPLOYEE, CUSTOMER, and RE-PAIR_ORDER given in Figure 4.6.5, do the following:

(a) Create a view AFTER82 combining all customer and repair order information for cars with a model year later than 1982.

(b) Using the view from item (a), print the name, address, and serial number for each customer in AFTER82.

(c) Using AFTER82 from item (a), create a view called MAJOR-REPAIRS for cars with a balance greater than $100 on a repair order and with a model year later than 1982.

(d) Using the view from item (c), print the serial number, repair order number, and date for each car in MAJORREPAIRS.

4.7 Guide to Further Reading

The relational database model is discussed in detail in [1.1] Chapters 9 and 10, [1.2] Parts 2 and 3, [1.4] Chapters 5 and 6, and [2.4] Chapter 5. Our description of embedded SQL is taken from [4.1]. [4.2] contains a thorough discussion of SQL within the framework of the DB2 system.

[**4.1**] Database Language SQL. New York: American National Standards Institute, 1986.

[**4.2**] Date, C. J. *A Guide to DB2*. Reading, Mass.: Addison-Wesley, 1984.

Chapter 5

Database Design

5.1 Functional Dependencies

This chapter deals with integrity constraints for databases and the use of these constraints in designing the structure of a relational database. It also examines the entity-relationship database model, which is particularly useful for database design, and which is different from the database models discussed previously. In this section, we discuss functional dependencies, which represent probably the most important type of database integrity constraint. We also begin the study of database normalization, a method for improving database design. Recall from Chapter 4 that E. F. Codd, the originator of the relational database model, devised the relational algebra and relational calculus data manipulation languages. He also introduced the study of functional dependencies and database normalization. He showed that database integrity constraints, which deal with restrictions on the data allowed in the tables, are closely connected to database design issues.

Before we discuss functional dependencies, consider one possible problem in designing relational databases. Hierarchic and network databases contain explicit connections between files, but this is not so for the relational case. Thus, it is very important to make sure that these connections are included in some form. For example, recall the relational representation of the one-to-many relationship between EMPLOYEE and JOBHISTORY from Figure 1.3.3(c). If we forget to include the connection between EMPLOYEE and JOBHISTORY, we would wind up with these two tables as shown in Figure 5.1.1. There is now no way to find

153

out what job history record is associated with an employee, even though the attributes in the database are the same as before.

Recall that we have already considered and used the notion of a key for a table in Section 1.6. Recapitulating, a **key** *is an attribute or set of attributes whose value(s) uniquely determine the rest of the attributes.* Thus, if T(A,B,C,D,E) is a table (schema) for which A is a key, then there cannot be two rows in any instance of T with the same A value. Keys are important in virtually all the database models, not just the relational model. The notion of functional dependency, which we next define, is a generalization of the notion of key.

A **functional dependency** (often written as **fd** in the database literature) *is a database constraint which states that one or more attributes uniquely (or functionally) determine one or more attributes.* If, for a table (schema) T (not necessarily the same T as above), the attribute A determines the attribute B, then we write T:A→B. This means that any two rows in (an instance of) T which have the same A value must have the same B value. (Similarly, we write T:AC→BE if the combination of the attributes A and C uniquely determine the attributes B and E. We say that AC are the attributes on the left-hand side and BE are the attributes on the right-hand side of this functional dependency.) Note that T:A→B does not, by itself, imply that A is a key, or that there can be only one row in (an instance of) T with a particular value for A.

Consider, for example, the relational database description given in Figure 5.1.2 (taken from Figure 1.2.2). We call *the combination of database schema and constraints* a **view.** (This use of the word "view" is different from the notion of view in SQL or in the three-level architecture.) Views will be discussed in more detail in Section 10.1. The figure gives three functional dependencies. STNO is *not* a key for this view because one student may take many courses; hence, there may be many rows for each

FIGURE 5.1.1
A Lost Connection

```
TABLES            ATTRIBUTES
  EMPLOYEE          E#,NAME,ADDRESS,SALARY,AGE
  JOBHISTORY        COMPANY,DATES-OF-EMPLOYMENT,JOBTITLE
```

FIGURE 5.1.2
Functional Dependencies

```
STUDENT(STNO,STNAME,STADDRESS,COURSE,GRADE,CREDITS)
STUDENT:STNO->STNAME,STADDRESS
STUDENT:COURSE->CREDITS
STUDENT:STNO,COURSE->GRADE
```

STNO value. However, for each such row, the corresponding STNAME and STADDRESS values must be the same.

Let's examine the claim that STNO,COURSE forms the key. The analysis is as follows. For a given pair of STNO and COURSE values, there can be only a single STNAME value and a single STADDRESS value by the first functional dependency; we don't even need the COURSE value for this. Similarly, there can be only one CREDITS value by the second functional dependency—STNO is not even needed here—and only one GRADE value by the third functional dependency. The last functional dependency is the only one where exactly the key is on the left-hand side of the arrow.

Next, we investigate some design problems associated with functional dependencies whose left-hand side is not exactly (or does not include) the key. Note that there is not necessarily a unique key for every table. In particular, if we add to our example the functional dependency

$$\text{STUDENT:STNAME,STADDRESS->STNO}$$

—that is, if a name and an address uniquely determine a student number—then STNAME,STADDRESS,COURSE also forms a key.

If a set of attributes S forms a key, then so does every set containing S, according to our definition. However, we use key to mean a set of attributes S which forms a key *such that no subset of S also forms a key.* (Supersets of keys are sometimes called superkeys.) We observe also that some functional dependencies always hold: those where the left-hand side contains the right-hand side. We call such functional dependencies trivial and usually ignore them. In this regard we will assume that a functional dependency does not contain superfluous attributes, and so we do not write, for example, STUDENT:COURSE,GRADE→ CREDITS, because GRADE is superfluous here.

The problems concerning functional dependencies like the first and second ones in Figure 5.1.2 are of two related kinds: redundancies and anomalies. To see this, let's take a look at the STUDENT table of Figure 5.1.3. Note that each time we duplicate a student number, we must duplicate the name and address also, as we do for Smith and Rivers. Also, when we duplicate a course we must duplicate the credit value. We are *repeating values when the repetition seems to be unnecessary:* this is the **redundancy problem.**

The **anomaly problem** refers to difficulties that may occur in updating a table. Assume for now that no null values are allowed. In that case, if we wish to insert a row for a student that gives a student's grade in a course, we cannot do so if we don't know the credit value—even though that value may be considered extraneous to the insertion. The same problem occurs if we don't know a student's address. Even if null values are permitted and we place a null value for the address, then later, when

FIGURE 5.1.3
A STUDENT Table

STUDENT					
STNO	STNAME	STADDRESS	COURSE	GRADE	CREDITS
111111111	Smith L	1501 Roper St	COSC 236	B	3
222222222	Rogers C	2057 York Rd	COSC 236	C	3
111111111	Smith L	1501 Roper St	COSC 336	A	3
333333333	Rivers F	55 Penn St	COSC 336	C	3
333333333	Rivers F	55 Penn St	COSC 431	C	4
444444444	Bailey D	261 Pine Ave	COSC 236	A	3

the address is determined, we have to change the null value everywhere for the student. Also, if null values are permitted for non-key attributes only (as is usually the case), then there is no way to insert information about the number of credits assigned to a course before the registration of a student in it. The problems that occur because of such functional dependencies in the case of insertion are called **insertion anomalies.**

Next we consider deletion. If we delete all rows containing the course COSC 236, we also lose the separate fact that COSC 236 is 3 credits. Similarly, if we delete all courses for a student, we lose that student's name and address also. These problems are called **deletion anomalies.** Finally, suppose that a student has a new address. This is one change, so we would like to make one change in the database. However, we have to change the address in each row that contains information about the student. Similarly, if the number of credits for a course is changed, that change must be made in every row where the course appears, although conceptually it is a single change. These problems are called **update anomalies.**

The redundancy and anomaly problems can be eliminated by modifying the database view via a process called normalization. But before we show how to do database normalization, let's observe why the redundancy and anomaly problems occurred in the first place. The reason is that we were trying to model a network situation within a relational framework, and we placed all the attributes in a single table. The data structure diagram appears in Figure 5.1.4. The two parent files correspond to the first two functional dependencies as follows: STNO is the key for STUDENTINFO, and COURSE is the key for COURSEINFO. The last functional dependency reflects the parent-child relationship.

If we had started with the network structure of Figure 5.1.4, then we would have converted it to the relational view of Figure 5.1.5 with

FIGURE 5.1.4
Data Structure Diagram for STUDENT

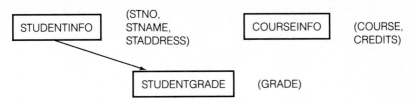

FIGURE 5.1.5
The Normalized Relational View

```
STUDENTINFO(STNO,STNAME,STADDRESS)
COURSEINFO(COURSE,CREDITS)
STUDENTGRADE(STNO,COURSE,GRADE)
STUDENTINFO:STNO->STNAME,STADDRESS
COURSEINFO:COURSE->CREDITS
STUDENTGRADE:STNO,COURSE->GRADE
```

three tables, where each child table inherits its key attributes from the parent table. In this case, each functional dependency represents a **key constraint;** that is, it determines a key for the table. We say that the relational view of Figure 5.1.2 has been *normalized.* In this example, we have normalized a relational database view by first going to a network structure. Our use of the network model illustrates the point that often anomaly problems in a relational database design are due to the modeling of a network or hierarchic structure within the relational model *in an improper manner.* But it is not necessary to leave the framework of the relational model to accomplish database normalization, as we will demonstrate. Our goal is to create a database view where all the constraints, functional dependencies for now, represent key constraints—as in Figure 5.1.5.

   Normalization by decomposition can be applied to a relational database view where some of the tables have too many attributes. By decomposing the original view into another database view with more tables, we can eliminate functional dependencies that cause anomaly and redundancy problems. For example, assume that the database view contains a generic relation T(A,B,C,D,E) with the constraints as shown in Figure 5.1.6(a). Clearly, AC (when we use single-letter names for attributes, we just write two or more names together) is the key for this view. But there are two additional functional dependencies that do not represent key constraints, and these are the ones that cause difficulties. The

FIGURE 5.1.6
Normalization by Decomposition

(a) Original database view

```
T(A,B,C,D,E)
T:AC->DE
T:A->B
T:D->E
```

(b) First step in the normalization

```
T₁(A,C,D,E)
T₂(A,B)
T₁:AC->DE
T₁:D->E
T₂:A->B
```

(c) Normalized database view

```
T₁(A,C,D)
T₁'(D,E)
T₂(A,B)
T₁:AC->D
T₁':D->E
T₂:A->B
```

second functional dependency, T:A→B, states that a proper portion of the key determines some attribute; the last one, T:D → E, states that an attribute, not in the key, determines another attribute, also not in the key.

The latter two types of functional dependencies, which don't represent key constraints, are the ones that usually come up in practice and cause the anomaly and redundancy problems. When a table has such functional dependencies, the solution is to decompose it. One systematic method (which does not necessarily give a unique solution because we can take the functional dependencies in any order) is given informally below as Algorithm 5.1. (We will discuss the lossless join property in the next section and BCNF later in this section.)

Algorithm 5.1   Lossless join decomposition to BCNF
For a functional dependency on a table whose left-hand side is not a key, obtain two tables as follows. Let the first contain the set of all attributes of the table except for the ones on the right-hand side of the functional dependency and let the second contain the set of attributes in the functional

dependency. Continue in this manner until all functional dependencies represent key constraints for all the tables.

We note that some functional dependencies may get lost in the process if their attributes no longer are included in a single table; we will come back to this problem in the next section. Let's apply this process now to the example of Figure 5.1.6(a). Because T:AC→DE has a key on the left-hand side, we ignore it. For T:A→B, we obtain T_1(A,C,D,E) and T_2(A,B), with the functional dependencies as shown in Figure 5.1.6(b). Now, applying the same process to T_1 with T_1:D → E, we obtain the result of Figure 5.1.6(c).

There are two important normal forms involving functional dependency constraints: **BCNF (Boyce-Codd Normal Form)** and **3NF (Third Normal Form).** 3NF is the one originally proposed by Codd; later he suggested BCNF. Originally, 3NF was obtained by placing the database view into First Normal Form, then Second Normal Form, and finally Third Normal Form. We go to Third Normal Form directly by using an alternate definition. All of our databases contain only atomic values for attributes and hence are in First Normal Form.

A relational database view is said to be in **BCNF** if *all the functional dependencies represent key constraints.* The procedure we gave above yields a view in BCNF. A relational database view is said to be in **3NF** if *for every functional dependency X→Y either X is a key or every attribute in Y is an attribute of some key.* It follows from the definitions that a relational database view in BCNF is automatically in 3NF. In most cases in practice, a view in 3NF is also in BCNF; differences may occur if a table has several keys. Consider the database view of Figure 5.1.7, in which both AB and BC are keys. This view is not in BCNF because T:C→A is a functional dependency that does not represent a key constraint. It *is* in 3NF, however, because A is an attribute of the key AB. Because it is probably reasonable not to decompose such a table, many people consider a 3NF database view as sufficiently normalized. We end this section by observing that while database normalization can lead to a better database design, this process has disadvantages also. In particular, answering queries may be slower for a normalized database, because more queries require a join for their evaluation.

FIGURE 5.1.7
3NF vs BCNF

```
T(A,B,C)
T:AB->C
T:C->A
```

5.2 Database Normalization

We start this section by considering decompositions in more detail and thereby finding two important properties that we would like decompositions to possess. In Figure 5.2.1, which shows an example relational database and several decompositions, the original database view of part (a) has a single table, TASK1, with one functional dependency. Because the key for TASK1 is the pair EMP,TASKID, this database view is not in 3NF or BCNF. Our method from the previous section can normalize the view, as shown in part (b). The attribute on the right-hand side is deleted from the original table and the attributes in the functional dependency are placed in another table. Note that whenever we decompose a database, we obtain the new database instance *by projection from the old one*. If we wish to recapture the original instance, we can do so by taking the join of the two new tables, EMPTASKID1 and TASKINFO1 in this case.

In Figure 5.2.1(c), we give another decomposition (again the new view is in BCNF). However, now let's take the join of EMPTASKNAME1 and TASKINFO1. In addition to the original rows of TASK1, we obtain three more. The extra rows appear because two different task IDs have the same name; so, by joining on TASKNAME, we obtain the other task ID value for each employee who works on a task with that name. A decomposition like this, *where the join of the projections contains additional rows* (it cannot have fewer rows) is said to have a **lossy join**—*the original table has been lost.* We prefer the type of decomposition, called **lossless join,** where *the join of the projections is identical to the original table.* The lossless join property, which holds for the first decomposition, is one that we would like to have when we decompose a view.

FIGURE 5.2.1
Decompositions

(a) Original database

    (*i*) View

```
TASK1(EMP,TASKID,TASKNAME)
TASK1:TASKID->TASKNAME
```

    (*ii*) Instance

TASK1		
EMP	TASKID	TASKNAME
Smith L	X26	Transfer
Jones B	X26	Transfer
Taylor T	R12	Safety
Smith L	R12	Safety
Kramer R	B01	Transfer

(continued)

(b) First decomposition

(*i*) View

```
EMPTASKID1(EMP,TASKID)
TASKINFO1(TASKID,TASKNAME)
TASKINFO1:TASKID->TASKNAME
```

(*ii*) Instance

EMPTASKID1	
EMP	TASKID
Smith L	X26
Jones B	X26
Taylor T	R12
Smith L	R12
Kramer R	B01

TASKINFO1	
TASKID	TASKNAME
X26	Transfer
R12	Safety
B01	Transfer

(c) Second decomposition

(*i*) View

```
EMPTASKNAME1(EMP,TASKNAME)
TASKINFO1(TASKID,TASKNAME)
TASKINFO1:TASKID->TASKNAME
```

(*ii*) Instance

EMPTASKNAME1	
EMP	TASKNAME
Smith L	Transfer
Jones B	Transfer
Taylor T	Safety
Smith L	Safety
Kramer R	Transfer

TASKINFO1	
TASKID	TASKNAME
X26	Transfer
R12	Safety
B01	Transfer

(*iii*) The join

JOIN(EMPTASKNAME1,TASKINFO1)		
EMP	TASKID	TASKNAME
Smith L	X26	Transfer
Smith L	B01	Transfer
Jones B	X26	Transfer
Jones B	B01	Transfer
Taylor T	R12	Safety
Smith L	R12	Safety
Kramer R	X26	Transfer
Kramer R	B01	Transfer

(continued)

FIGURE 5.2.1 *(continued)*

(d) Third decomposition

    (*i*)   View

```
EMPTASKID1(EMP,TASKID)
EMPTASKNAME1(EMP,TASKNAME)
```

    (*ii*) Instance

EMPTASKID1	
EMP	TASKID
Smith L	X26
Jones B	X26
Taylor T	R12
Smith L	R12
Kramer R	B01

EMPTASKNAME1	
EMP	TASKNAME
Smith L	Transfer
Jones B	Transfer
Taylor T	Safety
Smith L	Safety
Kramer R	Transfer

    (*iii*) The join

JOIN(EMPTASKID1,EMPTASKNAME1)		
EMP	TASKID	TASKNAME
Smith L	X26	Transfer
Smith L	X26	Safety
Jones B	X26	Transfer
Taylor T	R12	Safety
Smith L	R12	Transfer
Smith L	R12	Safety
Kramer R	B01	Transfer

      Our last decomposition for this view appears in part (d) of Figure 5.2.1. As was the case in part (c), it does not have the lossless join property. However, this decomposition is, in a sense, even worse than the previous one, because the functional dependency is also lost in the process. In the first two decompositions, because we did not split up TASKID and TASKNAME, we preserved the functional dependency TASK1: TASKID →TASKNAME on the new database as TASKINFO1: TASKID →TASKNAME. If no functional dependencies are lost in the decomposition, we call it **dependency preserving.**

      Now we show that it is possible for a decomposition to have the lossless join property without the dependency preserving property. The view of Figure 5.2.2(a) is obtained by adding a functional dependency

FIGURE 5.2.2
Another Decomposition Example

(a) The original database view

```
TASK2(EMP,TASKID,TASKNAME)
TASK2:EMP->TASKID
TASK2:TASKID->TASKNAME
```

(b) A lossless join, dependency preserving decomposition

```
EMPTASKID2(EMP,TASKID)
TASKINFO2(TASKID,TASKNAME)
EMPTASKID2:EMP->TASKID
TASKINFO2:TASKID->TASKNAME
```

(c) A lossless join, non-dependency preserving decomposition

```
EMPTASKID2(EMP,TASKID)
EMPTASKNAME2(EMP,TASKNAME)
EMPTASKID2:EMP->TASKID
```

to the view of Figure 5.2.1(a). The first decomposition for it appears in Figure 5.2.2(b); it has both the lossless join and dependency preserving properties. In contrast, Figure 5.2.2(c) shows the decomposition corresponding to the one in Figure 5.2.1(d); in this case the decomposition is lossless join but not dependency preserving. Section 8.5 will deal with implications of dependencies and show that for this last decomposition, the functional dependency

```
EMPTASKNAME2:EMP->TASKNAME
```

should be added to the view in Figure 5.2.2(c). In any case, the decomposition is lossless join but not dependency preserving.

Thus we have found two properties, lossless join and dependency preserving, that we would like a decomposition to possess. The reasons for their desirability should now be clear. If the decomposition is not lossless join, then the join may produce a table with extraneous rows and so give incorrect answers to queries on the new database. If the decomposition is not dependency preserving, then it may be easier to enter incorrect data. Figure 5.2.3 gives an example of this phenomenon. Using the database view of Figure 5.2.2(a) and its decomposition of Figure 5.2.2(c), Figures 5.2.3(a) and (b) give the original and decomposed instances. Suppose that we try to insert <Brown L,X26> into

FIGURE 5.2.3
The Dependency Preserving Property

(a) Original instance

TASK2		
EMP	TASKID	TASKNAME
Smith L	X26	Transfer
Taylor T	R12	Safety

(b) Decomposed instance

EMPTASKID2	
EMP	TASKID
Smith L	X26
Taylor T	R12

EMPTASKNAME2	
EMP	TASKNAME
Smith L	Transfer
Taylor T	Safety

(c) Decomposed instance after insertion

EMPTASKID2	
EMP	TASKID
Smith L	X26
Taylor T	R12
Brown L	X26

EMPTASKNAME2	
EMP	TASKNAME
Smith L	Transfer
Taylor T	Safety
Brown L	Systems

(d) The join

JOIN(EMPTASKID2,EMPTASKNAME2)		
EMP	TASKID	TASKNAME
Smith L	X26	Transfer
Taylor T	R12	Safety
Brown L	X26	Systems

EMPTASKID2 and <Brown L,Systems> into EMPTASKNAME2. The result appears in Figure 5.2.3(c). No constraint is violated. However, when we take the join, we obtain a table in which the dependency that was not preserved—namely, TASK2:TASKID→TASKNAME, is violated.

Next, let's reconsider the view of Figure 5.1.7. We stated before that this view is in 3NF but not in BCNF. Now we see what problem is created if we decompose this view. No matter how we do the decomposition, as long as we leave out an attribute, we cannot preserve T:AB→C. This example shows that it is not always possible to obtain a lossless join, dependency preserving decomposition of a view into BCNF. As we will see in the next section, the decomposition method given in Algorithm 5.1 *always* yields a lossless join decomposition into BCNF, but it does not always preserve dependencies. For example, for the view of Figure 5.1.7, Algorithm 5.1 gives the decomposed view as $T_1(B,C)$, $T_2(A,C)$, $T_2:C→A$.

Although it is not always possible to obtain a lossless join, dependency preserving decomposition into BCNF, it is always possible to obtain such a decomposition into 3NF. We will shortly describe this decomposition informally as Algorithm 5.2. First, let's assume, without loss of generality, that all functional dependencies are written with a single attribute on the right-hand side. (For example, we can rewrite T:AB→CD as T:AB→C and T:AB→D.) We also assume that the set of functional dependencies is **minimal:** *there are no unnecessary functional dependencies in the list, and the dependencies remaining in the list are in the simplest form* (we will come back to this idea in Section 8.5). We claim that if a view contains a functional dependency involving every attribute of a table T, then, as far as table T is concerned, the view is in 3NF. What is our proof? Suppose that we have T:ABC→D for T(A,B,C,D). We cannot have T:B→C, because then we could get a simpler functional dependency, T:AB→D, contradicting minimality. A functional dependency like T:D→A is allowed, because A is a part of a key. Now we are ready to describe the algorithm.

Algorithm 5.2 Lossless join, dependency preserving decomposition to 3NF (where the set of functional dependencies is minimal and where each functional dependency has a single attribute on the right-hand side)

Proceed as follows within the view for each table T that is not in 3NF. For each functional dependency whose set of attributes is not contained in the set of attributes of another functional dependency, form a table with exactly the attributes in that functional dependency. Finally, if no table contains the attributes of a key of T, add such a table. (At the end, several tables obtained from functional dependencies with identical left-hand sides may be recombined into one table.)

FIGURE 5.2.4
A Dependency Preserving, Lossless Join Decomposition into 3NF

(a) Original view   (b) Decomposed view

```
T(A,B,C,D,E)         T₁(A,B,C)
T:AB->C              T₂(A,D)
T:C->A               T₃(B,D,E)
T:D->A               T₁:AB->C
                     T₁:C->A
                     T₂:D->A
```

Figure 5.2.4 gives an example for the application of this algorithm. The original view is in part (a). The second functional dependency contains the attributes (A and C) that are also included in the first functional dependency, and so we ignore it. The result is a table T_1 for the attributes of the first functional dependency, and a table T_2 for the attributes of the third functional dependency. We add the table T_3, whose attributes form a key for T. Note that the new view, given in part (b), is not in BCNF.

5.3 Additional Dependencies and Normal Forms

Functional dependencies are the best-known and most thoroughly studied integrity constraints, but they are not the only ones. We saw, in the previous two sections, that extraneous functional dependencies—that is, functional dependencies not based on key constraints—can cause redundancy and anomaly problems. Our solution for a better database design was to decompose the database view into a view in 3NF or, preferably, BCNF. We demonstrate in this section that there are other kinds of dependencies that can cause similar problems. (Eventually, we will introduce a very strong normal form called DKNF.) We also discuss some methods of checking for integrity in database systems.

Consider the view given in part (a) of Figure 5.3.1. This view represents information about an employee: each row contains the name of an employee, the name of a child of the employee, and the name of a task assigned to the employee. There are no (nontrivial) functional dependencies. As we take a look at an instance in part (b), however, notice that there is a constraint: each child name must appear with each task name for each employee. Because L. Smith has two children and works on three tasks, there are six rows for her in the table. Here we have an example of a **multivalued dependency.** We write this multivalued dependency as EMPINFO:EMP→→CHILD, and say that EMP *multidetermines* CHILD. That is, an EMP value determines a *set* of CHILD values (rather than a unique value as in the case of functional dependencies) irrespective of the other attributes.

FIGURE 5.3.1
Multivalued Dependency

(a) View

```
EMPINFO(EMP,CHILD,TASK)
```

(b) Instance

EMPINFO		
EMP	CHILD	TASK
Smith L	Bill	System1
Smith L	Margaret	System1
Smith L	Bill	Transfer
Smith L	Margaret	Transfer
Smith L	Bill	Traffic
Smith L	Margaret	Traffic
Bailey D	Susan	System1
Bailey D	Cathy	System1
Rivers F	John	Transfer
Rivers F	John	Traffic

(c) Data structure diagram

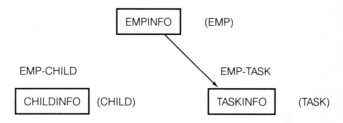

(d) Decomposition

    (*i*) Original view

```
EMPINFO(EMP,CHILD,TASK)
EMPINFO:EMP->->CHILD
```

    (*ii*) Decomposed view

```
EMPINFO₁(EMP,CHILD)
EMPINFO₂(EMP,TASK)
```

        Multivalued dependencies are symmetric in the following way: if $T(A,B,C,D,E)$ is the table and $T:AB \twoheadrightarrow C$ holds, then $T:AB \twoheadrightarrow DE$ must also hold; we call the latter the complementary multivalued dependency to the former (and vice versa). The reason is that if AB determines a set of C values, then it must also determine a set of DE values. In our case, EMPINFO:EMP$\rightarrow\rightarrow$ CHILD yields EMPINFO:EMP$\rightarrow\rightarrow$TASK by symmetry. So, because an EMP value determines a set of CHILD values, it also determines a set of TASK values.

We claim that this multivalued dependency presents the same types of redundancy and anomaly problems as does a functional dependency that is not the result of key constraints. We get redundancy because each child is repeated for each task for an employee. We have the insertion anomaly because if we want to insert another task for L. Smith, we have to do it once for each of her children. Similarly, if we want to delete one of L. Smith's tasks, we have to delete it separately for each of her children; hence we get the deletion anomaly. Finally, if we wish to change the name of a task for L. Smith, again we have to do it once for each of her children. This results in the update anomaly.

In the previous section, we noted that extraneous functional dependencies are often obtained by improperly designing a network or hierarchic database structure into a relational structure. This is also the case for multivalued dependencies. The hierarchic structure is shown as a data structure diagram in Figure 5.3.1(c). The multivalued dependency results from our squeezing two one-to-many relationships with the same parent into one table. If, instead, we chose to have two tables—EMP-CHILD(EMP,CHILD) and EMPTASK(EMP,TASK)—then we would not have these multivalued dependencies and the corresponding redundancy and anomaly problems.

Next we show how we can stay within the framework of the relational model and avoid these problems. But first, consider that there is a multivalued dependency corresponding to every functional dependency. That is, if A functionally determines B, then, in a trivial way, A also multidetermines B (where the set of B values associated with an A value is a singleton). Thus, not all multivalued dependencies cause problems, most certainly not the ones obtained from functional dependencies that represent key constraints. In any case, following our general minimality principle, we do not deal with multivalued dependencies that are the direct consequence of functional dependencies.

The solution in the case of extraneous functional dependencies was normalization by decomposition. We follow the same solution for multivalued dependencies. Although the situation can be complex when there are several multivalued dependencies in a table, often there is only one—in which case, we decompose the table by placing the attributes of the multivalued dependency in one table and the attributes of the complementary multivalued dependency in another table. Figure 5.3.1(d) shows the decomposition for our example. We do not write multivalued dependencies involving all the attributes of a table, like EMP-INFO1:EMP$\rightarrow\rightarrow$CHILD, because such multivalued dependencies are trivial—that is, they always hold.

In Section 5.1, we introduced 3NF and BCNF, normal forms that we tried to achieve by decomposition. Observe that the original view EMPINFO, as given in part (*i*) of Figure 5.3.1(d), is both in 3NF and BCNF, because there are no functional dependencies. Still, redundancy and anomaly problems remain, as we showed above. There is a more powerful normal form, however, that takes into account both functional and multivalued dependencies. We say that a database view is in **4NF (Fourth Normal Form)** *if it is in BCNF and there are no (nontrivial) multivalued dependencies.* (Recall that we ignore the multivalued dependencies obtained from functional dependencies.) Thus, the view of part (*i*) of Figure 5.3.1(d) is not in 4NF, but the one in part (*ii*) is.

In the previous section, we discussed the lossless join and dependency preserving properties for decompositions. We now show that the notion of a multivalued dependency holding in a view is equivalent to the lossless join property of the decomposition we gave for it above. We write the theorem in the simplest case with three attributes, but it holds in general.

> **Theorem 5.3** The decomposition $T(A,B,C)$ into $T_1(A,B)$ and $T_2(A,C)$ is lossless join if and only if $T:A \twoheadrightarrow B$ holds.
>
> *Proof:* Assume that the decomposition has the lossless join property. This assumption is equivalent to saying that if a row $<a,b>$ is in T_1 and a row $<a,c>$ is in T_2, then $<a,b,c>$ (which we obtain by taking the join) must be in T. That is, for every A value a there is a set of B values which appears in T with every C value for a. This relationship is equivalent to the multivalued dependency $T:A \twoheadrightarrow B$.

To begin our application of this theorem, recall Algorithm 5.1 from Section 5.1. We illustrate one step in this algorithm on a generic table $T(A,B,C,D,E)$ with $T:AB \rightarrow C$; the decomposition yields $T_1(A,B,D,E)$ and $T_2(A,B,C)$. The previous section claimed that such a decomposition always has the lossless join property, and we can now justify this claim as follows. Because $T:AB \rightarrow C$ holds, $T:AB \twoheadrightarrow C$ must also hold, as explained earlier. But then, by Theorem 5.3, the decomposition is lossless join.

In all of our decomposition examples so far, we have decomposed a table into two tables at one time. It is possible, however, to go further. Part (a) of Figure 5.3.2 gives an example of a table that may reasonably be decomposed into three tables at once. A triple, $<A,C,I>$, is in Retail if Agent A works for Company C and sells Item I manufactured by C. The decomposition shown in part (b) yields three meaningful tables. This decomposition has the lossless join property exactly if the following condition holds: whenever Agent A is employed by Company C, and Company C manufactures Item I, and Agent A sells Item I, then Agent A sells the Item I manufactured by Company C.

FIGURE 5.3.2
A Decomposition into Three Tables

(a) Original view

```
RETAIL(AGENT,COMPANY,ITEM)
```

(b) Decomposed view

```
EMPLOY(AGENT,COMPANY)
SELL(AGENT,ITEM)
MANUFACTURE(COMPANY,ITEM)
```

(c) Original instance

RETAIL		
AGENT	COMPANY	ITEM
Smith L	ABC Co	TV Set
Jones B	XYZ Co	TV Set
Smith L	Best Co	Freezer
Roberts L	ABC Co	Freezer

(d) Decomposed instance

REPRESENT	
AGENT	COMPANY
Smith L	ABC Co
Jones B	XYZ Co
Smith L	Best Co
Roberts L	ABC Co

SELL	
AGENT	ITEM
Smith L	TV Set
Jones B	TV Set
Smith L	Freezer
Roberts L	Freezer

MANUFACTURE	
COMPANY	ITEM
ABC Co	TV Set
XYZ Co	TV Set
Best Co	Freezer
ABC Co	Freezer

(e) The join

JOIN(JOIN(REPRESENT,SELL),MANUFACTURE)		
AGENT	COMPANY	ITEM
Smith L	ABC Co	TV Set
Smith L	ABC Co	Freezer
Jones B	XYZ Co	TV Set
Smith L	Best Co	Freezer
Roberts L	ABC Co	Freezer

The lossless join property need not always hold, as we show in parts (c) through (e) of Figure 5.3.2, by giving the original instance, the corresponding decomposed instance, and then the join (taken twice over the three tables). We can see from the original instance that although L. Smith represents the ABC Company which manufactures freezers, and L. Smith sells freezers, *L. Smith does not sell freezers manufactured by the ABC Company.* Therefore, this is not a lossless join decomposition.

Now, in analogy to multivalued dependencies in the sense of Theorem 5.3, it is possible to define the notion of **join dependency.** Let T be a table whose set of attributes is U, and let $X_1, X_2, \ldots, X_n$ be subsets of U. We say that for the table T(U) the join dependency $T:*[X_1, X_2, \ldots, X_n]$ holds if the decomposition of T to $T_1(X_1), T_2(X_2), \ldots, T_n(X_n)$ is lossless join. For example, for a table T(A,B,C,D), the join dependency T:*[AB,BC,CD] holds if the decomposition of T to $T_1(A,B), T_2(B,C),$ and $T_3(C,D)$ is lossless join. In the RETAIL example discussed above,

```
RETAIL:*[AGENT COMPANY, AGENT ITEM, COMPANY ITEM]
```

holds if the decomposition of

```
RETAIL(AGENT,COMPANY,ITEM)
```

to

```
REPRESENT(AGENT,COMPANY)
SELL(AGENT,ITEM)    and
MANUFACTURE(COMPANY,ITEM)
```

is lossless join. By Theorem 5.3, a multivalued dependency is a special case of a join dependency; in particular, for a table T(A,B,C), T:A→→B if and only if T:*[AB,AC].

Redundancy and anomaly problems are caused not just by multivalued dependencies, but also by join dependencies in general, which are *not* obtained from key constraints. Thus, it seems that key constraints are fundamental, and perhaps other constraints should be eliminated. Actually, there are reasons to leave in another type of constraint—the constraint which defines the *domain* of an attribute. We may want to specify, for example, that the domain for the attribute AGE is the set of integers between 0 and 100. Such **domain constraints** do not cause redundancy or anomaly problems.

Now we are ready to define our last normal form. We say that a database view is in **DKNF (domain-key normal form)** *if all the constraints are (obtainable from) domain constraints and key constraints.* The useful thing about DKNF is that it gives a straightforward structure to a database. Also, database views that are in DKNF have minimal redundancy and anomaly problems. There is no way to eliminate all redundancies, because when a hierarchic structure is flattened to a relational one, repetition is introduced. For example, in any instance for the relational view of Figure 5.3.1(d), which is in DKNF, an employee's name is repeated for each child and each task of that employee.

So far in our discussion of database constraints, we have only considered constraints that involve a single table. Sometimes databases have constraints that involve more than one table. **Inclusion dependencies** occur fairly often; we give an example in Figure 5.3.3. There are two tables, EMPLOYEE and DEPARTMENT, with a key constraint for each. We also have a subset constraint (inclusion dependency) because every manager is also an employee, and so the set of names obtained by projecting DEPARTMENT on MANAGER must be a subset of the set obtained by projecting EMPLOYEE on NAME. It is reasonable to allow inclusion dependencies, in addition to domain and key constraints, because they are useful and usually do not cause additional redundancy or anomaly problems. For example, if we delete a row for a manager in the EMPLOYEE table, then we must also delete the row for that DEPARTMENT (or update it by changing the manager). We do not consider this requirement a deletion anomaly.

There are several ways in which integrity constraints can be classified. For dependencies on a table, we studied functional and join (multivalued is an example of join) dependencies; in the preceding, we distinguished between constraints involving one table and more than one table. There is an even more general classification, however: static versus dynamic integrity constraints. All of the constraints that we have considered so far are static. A **static constraint** *is a statement about a database instance,* while a **dynamic constraint** *is a statement involving two database instances.* The latter type of constraint deals with the transition between instances.

Consider again the view of Figure 5.3.3. We may wish to state a constraint to the effect that an employee's salary may not be decreased. Then, whenever we do an update to change an employee's salary, the new salary must be greater than the old one. Note that we cannot check

FIGURE 5.3.3
An Inclusion Dependency

Database View:

```
EMPLOYEE(NAME,ADDRESS,SALARY,DEPT)
DEPARTMENT(DEPT,LOCATION,MANAGER)
EMPLOYEE:NAME->ADDRESS,SALARY,DEPT
DEPARTMENT:DEPT->LOCATION,MANAGER
DEPARTMENT[MANAGER]  SUBSET  EMPLOYEE[NAME]
```

such a constraint on a single database instance; we must look at both the before and after instances. Dynamic constraints are an aspect of the problem of including time in databases, a topic which we will study in Section 11.2.

Note that in spite of the substantial available theory concerning integrity constraints, most existing database systems do little in terms of allowing a user to specify constraints. In present versions of SQL, for example, a key can be specified only when an indexing (see Section 7.1) is created for a table. However, the ANSI SQL language allows the user to enter a key specification by using the CONSTRAINTS UNIQUE clause in the CREATE statement. Figure 5.3.4 illustrates this capability; we add the INSURANCE table to the schema, as in Figure 4.3.3(a), but make SSNO a key at the same time. The only other constraint that can be defined in SQL is the specification that no null values are allowed for an attribute. The constraints are checked by the database system whenever the database is updated. If an update would violate a constraint, an error condition occurs, and the user is provided with an error message.

Keys are also important for hierarchic and network databases. In IMS, the sequence field is the key field for its segment. In NDL, the record uniqueness clause is used for establishing a key. In addition, a record check clause can be specified for any expressible condition. (We did not discuss the record check clause in Chapter 2.) Figure 5.3.5 illustrates both the record uniqueness clause and the record check clause by showing a record name clause. For the EMPLOYEE file, SSNO is the key, and a domain constraint is given for AGE. In NDL, the insertion and retention clauses can be thought of as additional integrity constraints. Furthermore, for both the hierarchic and network models, the explicit formulation of the relationships between files also represents integrity constraints.

In this chapter, we have given algorithms for database normalization and stressed the advantages of normalized database views. We end this section by noting that there is also a disadvantage associated with database normalization. This is due to the fact that normalization creates smaller tables, which must be joined to answer certain queries. Since the

FIGURE 5.3.4
Example of Key Specification in ANSI SQL

```
CREATE   TABLE   INSURANCE
  ( CONSTRAINTS   UNIQUE   SSNO,
    SSNO    CHAR (9)  NOT NULL,
    NAME    CHAR (15),
    INS_CO  CHAR (20),
    POLICY  CHAR (13) );
```

FIGURE 5.3.5
Example of the Record Uniqueness Clause and the Record Check Clause in NDL

```
RECORD  EMPLOYEE
  UNIQUE  SSNO
  ITEM  SSNO   CHARACTER 9
  ITEM  NAME   CHARACTER 15
  ITEM  ADDRESS   CHARACTER 20
  ITEM  SALARY  FIXED 8 2
  ITEM  AGE   INTEGER
  CHECK  AGE > 15 AND AGE < 75
```

computation of a join may take a substantial amount of time, the processing of some queries may take longer for a normalized database than for an unnormalized one.

5.4 The Entity-Relationship (ER) Model for Database Design

So far this chapter has concentrated on two related topics, integrity constraints and database design. The major questions in designing a database are what data is to be included and how the data is to be represented. We are dealing here primarily with the conceptual view (see Section 1.2) because the choices are more limited for external views—which, after all, are constructed from the conceptual view. Designing a database of substantial size and complexity from scratch is a difficult task. The reader must be familiar with the data that is available and the needs of the people who (will) use the database system. Often, however, one does not start from scratch because the available files and their uses provide at least some indications of the data and the applications involved. The designer should realize that there is not necessarily a single best database design; even if there is such a one at a particular time, needs change over time, and a design that was best at one time may no longer be best after a while.

In previous chapters we examined three database models: network, hierarchic, and relational. These are the most popular models in terms of implementation. However, these models are not necessarily optimal for the database designer who first wants to construct a general description of the database. Recall, for example, that in the network model we cannot directly represent many-to-many relationships. (The connection file was introduced as a way to avoid this problem.) The situation for representing such relationships is even more problematic for the hierarchic and relational models. It would be preferable to start the design process by listing the files with their attributes and the relationships between the files without restrictions. It is possible to do this in the database model which we now present.

The **entity-relationship (ER) database model** was introduced by P. P. Chen in 1976 and is based on the idea that the fundamental concepts for a database *are* the entities and the relationships between them. These concepts are captured in a diagrammatic form called the **entity-relationship (ER) diagram.** Figure 5.4.1 presents such a diagram to illustrate what can be represented this way. The entities are enclosed in rectangular boxes, the relationships in diamond-shaped boxes, and the attributes are in ovals. Straight lines represent the connections. In the database literature, several variations of the ER model appear; the one that we give here is close to the original definition.

In this particular example, the entities (sometimes called entity sets) are DEPARTMENT, EMPLOYEE, WORK-HISTORY, TASK, EQUIPMENT, CLIENT, and CLIENTREP. There are five relationships (sometimes called relationship sets). Two of these are one-to-many relationships, namely, the ones on the left between DEPARTMENT and EMPLOYEE and between EMPLOYEE and WORK-HISTORY. We indicate one-to-many relationships by writing 1 and N, respectively, on the lines leading from the relationship to the entities. The attributes are connected to their respective entities by straight lines. It is also possible to indicate the domain of each attribute, as shown in Figure 5.4.2 for just the DEPARTMENT entity. In this case the ovals contain the domains and the attributes are labels on the connecting lines. We could have drawn Figure 5.4.1 this way, but placing the attributes in the ovals is the more common method of drawing ER diagrams.

Note two other things about the entities that have been considered so far. First, the key attribute(s) is (are) underlined for each entity. Second, the WORK-HISTORY entity is in a double box and an arrowhead is placed toward it from the relationship EMP-HAS-WH. The reason for this is that WORK-HISTORY is what is called a **weak entity:** *each instance of this entity has a meaning only according to the instance* (EMPLOYEE, in this case) *that is connected to it.* Thus, each WORK-HISTORY entity is *dependent* on the corresponding EMPLOYEE entity.

We indicate many-to-many relationships by writing distinct letters on the lines leading from the relationship to the entities. Our example has two many-to-many relationships. One is a standard many-to-many relationship between EMPLOYEE and TASK; each employee may be assigned to several tasks, and each task may have several employees assigned to it. Note that a relationship may also have attributes. In this case, the ASSIGNMENT relationship has the attribute STATUS to indicate the status of each employee for each task. The second many-to-many relationship is in fact a many-to-many-to-many relationship because it is

FIGURE 5.4.1
An Entity-Relationship Diagram

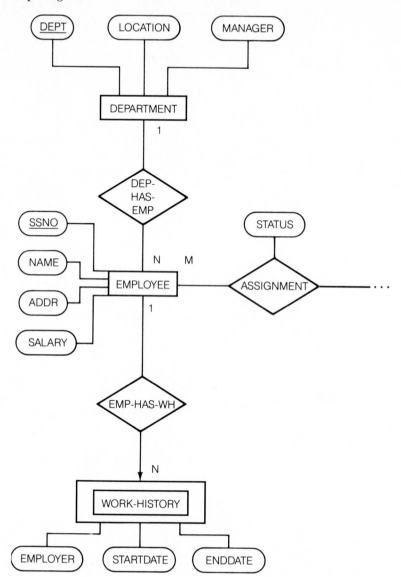

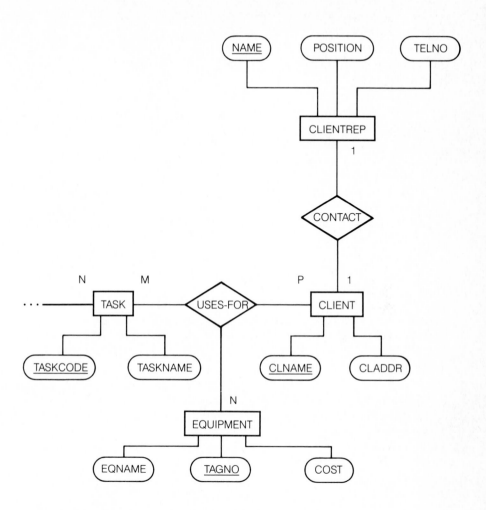

FIGURE 5.4.2
Representing Attributes and Domains

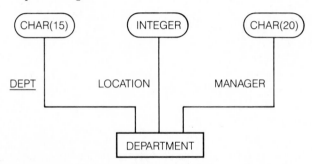

between three entities. Tasks use equipment for clients, hence the ternary relationship. The ER model allows us to directly represent such relationships. Finally, we show a one-to-one relationship between a client and the representative of the client.

The ER diagram can be rewritten in schema form, without pictures, much like the schemas we have written for the network, hierarchic, and relational models. There is no standard schema syntax for ER diagrams; in Figure 5.4.3 we show one possible way of writing the schema for the diagram of Figure 5.4.1.

The ER diagram is an excellent, intuitive way to represent the conceptual database. In the next section we will consider direct implementations for the ER model. However, database systems at present are usually based on a different database model, and so we must transform such a diagram to one in conformity with the database model of a particular system. In Figure 5.4.4, we show a representation of the ER diagram as a data structure diagram for the network model. Our general approach is to make entities into files and relationships into Codasyl sets. This can be done directly for the one-to-many (including one-to-one) relationships. For the many-to-many relationships we use the CODASYL approach of defining a connection file. The number of Codasyl sets is equal to the number of entities in the relationship: two for EMPLOYEE-TASK and three for TASK-EQUIPMENT-CLIENT. For the EMPLOYEE-TASK relationship, we use the attribute STATUS from the ASSIGNMENT relationship for the connection file. For the ternary relationship we introduce a WORK-ORDER file to connect the tasks, equipment, and clients.

Chapter 3 showed how to convert a network data structure diagram into one that is hierarchic; Chapter 4 showed how to remove the pointers between files to obtain a relational database schema. Thus, since we know how to convert an ER diagram to a data structure diagram, we can also convert it to a hierarchic or a relational schema by using the techniques from those chapters. But we can also convert an ER diagram *directly* to a relational schema. Figure 5.4.5 does this for the ER diagram of Figure 5.4.1.

Our method is as follows. Make every entity into a table with its corresponding attributes. Also make every relationship, which either contains at least one attribute or which is involved in some type of many-to-many relationship, into a table. In the case of a one-to-one or a one-to-many relationship, place the key attribute(s) of the entity indicated by 1 as (an) additional attribute(s) into the table constructed for the entity indicated by the N or the other 1. Thus the attribute DEPT is placed in the EMPLOYEE table and the attribute SSNO is placed in the WORK-HISTORY table. Note, in particular, how the USES-FOR table contains the keys for TASK, EQUIPMENT, and CLIENT.

This is not the only way to go from an ER diagram to a relational database schema. We could treat one-to-one and one-to-many relationships as many-to-many relationships and introduce an extra table. Or we

FIGURE 5.4.3
Schema for the Entity-Relationship Diagram

```
SCHEMA  COMPANY
  ENTITY  DEPARTMENT
    KEY  DEPT
    ATTRIBUTE  DEPT  DOMAIN  CHAR(15)
    ATTRIBUTE  LOCATION  DOMAIN  INTEGER
    ATTRIBUTE  MANAGER  DOMAIN  CHAR(20)
  ENTITY  EMPLOYEE
    KEY  SSNO
    ATTRIBUTE  SSNO  DOMAIN  CHAR(9)
    ATTRIBUTE  NAME  DOMAIN  CHAR(20)
    ATTRIBUTE  ADDR  DOMAIN  CHAR(25)
    ATTRIBUTE  SALARY  DOMAIN  REAL
  ENTITY  WORK-HISTORY
    WEAK ENTITY  DEPENDS ON EMPLOYEE
    ATTRIBUTE  EMPLOYER  DOMAIN  CHAR(20)
    ATTRIBUTE  START-DATE  DOMAIN  DATE
    ATTRIBUTE  END-DATE  DOMAIN  DATE
  ENTITY  TASK
    KEY  TASKCODE
    ATTRIBUTE  TASKCODE  DOMAIN  CHAR(5)
    ATTRIBUTE  TASKNAME  DOMAIN  CHAR(15)
  ENTITY  EQUIPMENT
    KEY  TAGNO
    ATTRIBUTE  EQNAME  DOMAIN  CHAR(15)
    ATTRIBUTE  TAGNO  DOMAIN  CHAR(12)
    ATTRIBUTE  COST  DOMAIN  REAL
  ENTITY  CLIENT
    KEY  CLNAME
    ATTRIBUTE  CLNAME  DOMAIN  CHAR(15)
    ATTRIBUTE  CLADDR  DOMAIN  CHAR(20)
  ENTITY  CLIENTREP
    KEY  NAME
    ATTRIBUTE  NAME  DOMAIN  CHAR(15)
    ATTRIBUTE  POSITION  DOMAIN  CHAR(12)
    ATTRIBUTE  TELNO  DOMAIN  CHAR(10)
  RELATIONSHIP  DEP-HAS-EMP
    ENTITY  DEPARTMENT  ONE
    ENTITY  EMPLOYEE  MANY
  RELATIONSHIP  EMP-HAS-WH
    ENTITY  EMPLOYEE  ONE
    ENTITY  WORK-HISTORY  MANY
  RELATIONSHIP  ASSIGNMENT
    ENTITY  EMPLOYEE  MANY
    ENTITY  TASK  MANY
    ATTRIBUTE  STATUS  DOMAIN  CHAR(10)
  RELATIONSHIP  USES-FOR
    ENTITY  TASK  MANY
    ENTITY  EQUIPMENT  MANY
    ENTITY  CLIENT  MANY
  RELATIONSHIP  CONTACT
    ENTITY  CLIENT  ONE
    ENTITY  CLIENTREP  ONE
```

FIGURE 5.4.4
The Corresponding Network Data Structure Diagram (with Codasyl Sets)

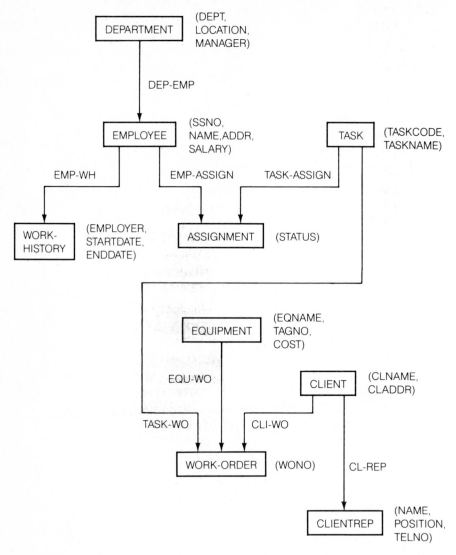

could treat many-to-many relationships as one-to-many relationships and place the key attribute(s) from one or more entities into the other tables.

We end this section by presenting a four-step database design methodology using the ER model in Figure 5.4.6. The first step involves identifying the data and user needs. This step may include a requirements formulation and analysis, interviews with users, and learning organi-

FIGURE 5.4.5
The Corresponding Relational Schema

```
TABLES                  ATTRIBUTES
   DEPARTMENT              DEPT,LOCATION,MANAGER
   EMPLOYEE                DEPT,SSNO,NAME,ADDR,SALARY
   WORK-HISTORY           SSNO,EMPLOYER,START-DATE,END-DATE
   TASK                   TASKCODE,TASKNAME
   ASSIGNMENT             SSNO,TASKCODE,STATUS
   EQUIPMENT              EQNAME,TAGNO,COST
   CLIENT                 CLNAME,CLADDR
   USES-FOR               TASKCODE,TAGNO,CLNAME
   CLIENTREP              CLNAME,NAME,POSITION,TELNO
```

FIGURE 5.4.6
A Relational Database Design Methodology

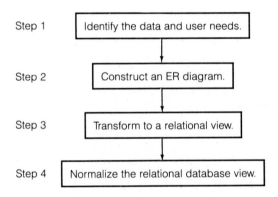

zational policies or business practices. At this point, the designer should know the entities and the relationships between them. The second step is the construction of the ER diagram. We have just seen indications of several ways in which the third step, to transform the ER diagram into a relational schema, can be accomplished. The constraints can be inferred from the ER diagram. Finally, the first three sections have already shown how to normalize a relational database view, as required by the fourth step.

5.5 Data Manipulation for the ER Model

In the previous section, we looked at the ER database model as a tool for database design. We saw that after a designer creates an initial database design using the ER model, he or she has to translate this model to the model provided by the database system in use. In recent years, a number of proposals and efforts have been made to implement the ER model directly. Such an implementation requires that data structures be provided for the ER model and that a data manipulation language be defined for it. This section discusses some features that such a data manipulation language *might* possess. At present, there does not exist a standard language for the ER model.

Recall, from Section 1.4, the distinction between a low-level query language and a high-level query language: in a low-level query language, one record is processed at a time, while in a high-level query language, a set of records is processed at a time. Although the proposals for languages associated with the ER model are usually high-level, we consider first the types of retrieval that might be provided by a low-level language in the spirit of NDL. Then we consider how the operations of the relational algebra can be extended to the ER model.

For the network database model, NDL uses the Codasyl sets for navigation in the database. For the ER database model, a low-level navigational language would use the relationships between the entities for navigation. There would be a cursor for the most recently accessed record in each entity and appropriate cursors for the most recently accessed records associated with each relationship. Using the ER diagram of Figure 5.4.1 for illustration, Figure 5.5.1 gives examples of the operations using, in an intuitive way, a language based on NDL without specifying the syntax or the semantics completely. (It may be helpful to refer to Figure 2.3.3, which gives examples of the various types of FIND statements for the ER model.)

We start in part (a) of Figure 5.5.1 by finding a record within an entity. If there is only one employee named F. Smith, then the first statement finds the record for that person. In any case, the first statement finds the record of an employee named F. Smith and we can find additional employee records for the same name (if any) by using the second statement. Note that for a weak entity, like WORK-HISTORY, it is not possible to find a record only through the entity WORK-HISTORY: the FIND must navigate through the relationship EMP-HAS-WH. In part (b), we consider the one-to-one relationship, CONTACT, between CLIENT and CLIENTREP. We show how to find the CLIENTREP record associated with a CLIENT record and vice versa.

Part (c) shows how to deal with a one-to-many relationship. A department may have many employees; this example shows how to find the first employee record, as well as any additional ones, for that department, which satisfy a condition. Example (*iii*) shows how to go backward to find the department of an employee. We consider the case of a many-to-many relationship with an attribute, namely, ASSIGNMENT, in part (d). An employee may have many tasks and a task may be assigned to many employees; the example in part (d) shows how to find a record for

FIGURE 5.5.1
Database Navigation for the ER Model

(a) Within an entity

    (*i*)   Find the record of an employee whose name is F. Smith.

```
FIND FIRST EMPLOYEE WHERE NAME = "Smith F"
```

    (*ii*)   Find the record of another employee whose name is F. Smith.

```
FIND NEXT EMPLOYEE WHERE NAME = "Smith F"
```

(b) For a one-to-one relationship

    (*i*)   Assume that the current record is the one for the client ABC Company. Find the record of this company's representative.

```
FIND CLIENTREP IN CONTACT
```

    (*ii*)   Assume that the current record is the one for L. Johnson, who represents a client. Find the record of the client represented by L. Johnson.

```
FIND CLIENT IN CLIENTREP
```

(c) For a one-to-many relationship

    (*i*)   Assume that the current record is the one for the Service department. Find the record of an employee in the Service department whose salary is less than $20,000.

```
FIND FIRST EMPLOYEE IN DEP-HAS-EMP WHERE
   SALARY < 20000
```

    (*ii*)   Find the record of another employee in the Service department whose salary is less than $20,000.

```
FIND NEXT EMPLOYEE IN DEP-HAS-EMP WHERE
   SALARY < 20000
```

    (*iii*)   Assume that the current record is the one for the employee whose social security number is 123-45-6789. Find the record of the department of this employee.

```
FIND DEPARTMENT FOR DEP-HAS-EMP
```

(d) For a many-to-many relationship with an attribute

    (*i*)   Assume that the current record is the one for the employee whose social security number is 123-45-6789. Find the record for a task associated with this employee.

```
FIND FIRST TASK IN ASSIGNMENT
```

    (*ii*)   Find the record for the status of this task.

```
FIND ASSIGNMENT FOR EMPLOYEE TASK
```

(continued)

FIGURE 5.5.1 *(continued)*

(*iii*)   Find the record of another task associated with this employee.

```
FIND NEXT TASK IN ASSIGNMENT
```

(e)   For a many-to-many-to-many relationship

(*i*)   Assume that the current record is the one for the client ABC Company and that there is no current record for EQUIPMENT. Find the record for a task associated with this client.

```
FIND FIRST TASK IN USES-FOR
```

(*ii*)   Find the record of a piece of equipment associated with this client and task.

```
FIND FIRST EQUIPMENT IN USES-FOR
```

(*iii*)   Find the record of another piece of equipment associated with this client and task.

```
FIND NEXT EQUIPMENT IN USES-FOR
```

(f)   The cursors

(*i*)   Find the most recently accessed EMPLOYEE record.

```
FIND EMPLOYEE
```

(*ii*)   Find the most recently accessed ASSIGNMENT record.

```
FIND ASSIGNMENT
```

a task and the status of the task for this employee as well as how to find additional tasks.

Part (e) of Figure 5.5.1 deals with many-to-many relationships in general. The first example shows how to find a task associated with a client assuming that equipment is not considered. The next two examples show how to find an equipment record for a given client record and task record. (In dealing with this type of situation it is useful to have a command for deleting the cursor for an entity or a relationship.) Finally, part (f) illustrates commands for finding the most recently accessed record for an entity and a relationship.

Next we consider a high-level query language based on the relational algebra. Recall from Section 4.2 that the major operations for the relational algebra are UNION, DIFFERENCE, PRODUCT, PROJECT, SELECT, and JOIN. Our next figure shows how to extend these operations to the ER model by applying them to entities and relationships. Usually the result is a new entity that inherits relationships from the original entities involved. Figure 5.5.2 describes the operations for this ER algebra.

FIGURE 5.5.2
Operations for the ER Algebra

Notes: 1. We use E (with subscripts) for entities and R for relationships.
   2. For UNION and DIFFERENCE, E_1 and E_2 must have the same structure.
   3. New entities obtained by the operations inherit relationships from the original entities. These relationships are assumed to be given new names.
   4. C is a condition involving attribute names, constants, and standard relational and Boolean operations.
   5. For the JOIN, $E_1, E_2, \ldots, E_n$ are entities in the relationship R.

UNION(E_1, E_2)—the set union of E_1 and E_2 with all relationships inherited both from E_1 and E_2.

DIFFERENCE(E_1, E_2)—the set difference of E_1 and E_2 with all relationships inherited from E_1.

PRODUCT(E_1, E_2)—the Cartesian product of E_1 and E_2 with all relationships inherited from both E_1 and E_2.

PROJECT(E; sequence of attributes)—the vertical subentity of E containing only the columns for the attributes specified in the sequence (the columns may be reordered this way by specifying a new sequence) with all relationships inherited from E.

SELECT(E: C)—the horizontal subentity of E containing those rows for which the condition is true with all relationships inherited from E.

JOIN($R; E_1, E_2, \ldots, E_n$)—the entity which contains attributes from $E_1, E_2, \ldots, E_n, R$, each of whose rows is obtained from the rows of $E_1, E_2, \ldots, E_n$ which are in the relationship R, including the attributes of R; all relationships, except R, are inherited from $E_1, E_2, \ldots, E_n$.

UNION, DIFFERENCE, PRODUCT, PROJECT, and SELECT are defined much as they are in the relational algebra—that is, with the entities substituted for the tables. The relationships are inherited from the original entities. We define a special JOIN operation for entities in a relationship R by "gluing" together the related rows from the various entities. For example,

```
JOIN(ASSIGNMENT;EMPLOYEE,TASK)
```

is an entity which contains rows with the attributes

```
STATUS,SSNO,NAME,ADDR,SALARY,TASKCODE,TASKNAME.
```

Each such row contains data about an employee, a task that the employee is working on, and the status for that task. Similarly,

```
JOIN(USES-FOR;TASK,EQUIPMENT,CLIENT)
```

contains rows that connect a piece of equipment with a task for a client with the attributes

```
TASKCODE,TASKNAME,EQNAME,TAGNO,COST,CLNAME,CLADDR.
```

We end this section by noting that a number of different database manipulation languages have been proposed for the ER model. These languages tend to be high-level languages based on SQL and the relational calculus. Section 8.2, which discusses the relational calculus, will briefly indicate how it can be extended to the ER model. The extension of SQL may be accomplished by using a SELECT statement with the following format:

```
SELECT attribute(s) FROM entity(ies) THRU
    relationship(s) WHERE condition;
```

In addition to the standard update statements INSERT, DELETE, and UPDATE for entities, it is necessary to add CONNECT and DISCONNECT for relationships.

In general, the ER model has become popular not just for database design but also as a unifying framework for database manipulation that contains aspects of the network and relational database models. Another uniform framework for the major database models, called database logic, will be discussed in Section 10.1.

5.6 Exercises

5.1 Identify a key for each of the following table schemas:
- (a) SALE(DNAME,ACCTNO,RECEIPTNO,DATE,ITEMNO, QUANTITY,AMOUNT.
- (b) LAWYER(SSNO,NAME,ADDRESS,SALARY,STATUS, TELNO).
- (c) EQUIPMENT(SERIALNO,TYPE,COST,LOCATION).
- (d) BORROWER(BNAME,IDNO,BADDR,BIRTHDATE).
- (e) REPAIR_ORDER(RONUMBER,CUSTOMER,DATE, AMOUNT).
- (f) STUDENT(NAME,ADDRESS,COURSE,SECTION, GRADE).

5.2 (a) For a table schema and a set of attributes, write an algorithm to determine whether or not the set forms a key.
- (b) Write an algorithm to find all the keys for a table schema.

5.3 For each view in Figure 5.6.1, determine if it is in BCNF; if not, use Algorithm 5.1 to transform it to BCNF. Which decompositions (if any) are dependency preserving?

5.4 Same as Exercise 5.3 for the views in Figure 5.6.2.

FIGURE 5.6.1
Views

(a) T(A,B,C,D,E,F,G)
   T:BD->A
   T:C->E
   T:A->C
   T:D->FG

(b) T(A,B,C,D,E,F,G)
   T:A->DE
   T:F->G
   T:C->BF

(c) T(A,B,C,D,E,F,G)
   T:B->E
   T:A->G
   T:CD->F

FIGURE 5.6.2
Additional Views

(a) CUSTOMER(CNAME,CADDR,MODEL,YEAR,SERIALNO)
   CUSTOMER:CNAME->CADDR
   CUSTOMER:SERIALNO->MODEL,YEAR

(b) MECHANIC(SSNO,NAME,EXPERIENCE,SALARY)
   MECHANIC:SSNO->NAME,EXPERIENCE,SALARY
   MECHANIC:EXPERIENCE->SALARY

(c) TEACHER(SSNO,NAME,COURSE,SECTION,TITLE)
   TEACHER:SSNO->NAME
   TEACHER:COURSE->TITLE

(d) EQUIPMENT(SERIALNO,TYPE,COST,LOCATION)
   EQUIPMENT:SERIALNO->TYPE,COST

(e) LAWYER(SSNO,NAME,ADDRESS,SALARY,STATUS)
   LAWYER:SSNO->NAME,ADDRESS

5.5 For each view in Exercise 5.3, determine if it is in 3NF; if not, use Algorithm 5.2 to transform it to 3NF.

5.6 For each view in Exercise 5.4, determine if it is in 3NF; if not, use Algorithm 5.2 to transform it to 3NF.

5.7 Explain why Algorithm 5.2
   (a) Provides a lossless join decomposition.
   (b) Transforms a schema to 3NF.

FIGURE 5.6.3
Views with Multivalued Dependencies

(a) `INSTRUCTOR(NAME,DEGREE,COURSE)`
`INSTRUCTOR:NAME->->DEGREE`

(b) `OFFICE(OFFICENO,AGENTNAME,AGENTADDR,STAFFNAME,`
`   STAFFSALARY)`
`OFFICE:OFFICENO->->AGENTNAME,AGENTADDR`
`OFFICE:AGENTNAME->AGENTADDR`
`OFFICE:STAFFNAME->STAFFSALARY`

(c) `COURSE(CNO,SECTION,STNAME,EQUIPMENT)`
`COURSE:CNO,SECTION->->STNAME`

5.8 Transform each of the views in Figure 5.6.3 to 4NF.

5.9 Represent the sets of entities and relationships in Figure 5.6.4 in the form of an ER diagram. Use the information provided with each example. You may make additional reasonable assumptions, such as keys for entities and attributes for relationships.

5.10 (a) Write a schema for the entity-relationship diagram of Figure 5.6.5.
  (b) Represent the entity-relationship diagram of Figure 5.6.5 as
   (*i*) A network data structure diagram.
   (*ii*) A relational schema.

5.11 Use the low-level query language for the ER model on the ER diagram of Figure 5.6.5 for the following database retrievals:
  (a) Find the record of a teacher whose social security number is 121-23-4567.
  (b) Find the most recently accessed student record.
  (c) Find the record of a piece of equipment for the current classroom whose cost is less than $100.
  (d) Find the record of another piece of equipment for the current classroom.
  (e) Find the record of a class for the current classroom.
  (f) Find the day and time for this class.
  (g) Find the record of a class for the current teacher and student.
  (h) Find the year, semester, and grade for this class.
  (i) Find the most recently accessed maintenance record.

5.12 Given an instance of the ER diagram of Figure 5.6.5, indicate what the following objects contain:
  (a) PROJECT(PRINCIPAL; SCHOOL,NAME).
  (b) SELECT(EQUIPMENT: COST > 50). (*Continued on page 191.*)

FIGURE 5.6.4
Entities and Relationships

(a) ENTITIES   ATTRIBUTES

ENTITIES	ATTRIBUTES
DEPARTMENT	DNAME,LOCATION,TELEPHONE
EMPLOYEE	SSNO,NAME,ADDRESS,SALARY
CUSTOMER	ACCTNO,NAME
SALE	RECEIPTNO,DATE,ITEMNAME,QUANTITY, AMOUNT

Each department has employees. A sale is between an employee and a customer.

(b)
ENTITIES	ATTRIBUTES
OFFICE	ONUMBER,AREA
EQUIPMENT	SERIALNO,TYPE,COST
LAWYER	SSNO,NAME,ADDRESS,SALARY,STATUS, TELNO
JUDGE	NAME
CLIENT	NAME,ADDR,SEX,AGE
CASE	CASENO,COURTHOUSE,ROOMNO,DATE
DOCUMENT	TYPE,DATE

Each office has lawyers and equipment. Each client has a lawyer and a judge for a case. There are documents for each case.

(c)
ENTITIES	ATTRIBUTES
BRANCH	NAME,LOCATION
VOLUNTEER	VNAME,VADDR
IN-MATERIAL	NUMBER,TYPE,TITLE,AUTHOR, PUBLISHER
BORROWER	IDNO,BNAME,BADDR,BIRTHDATE
OUT-MATERIAL	NUMBER,TYPE,TITLE,AUTHOR, PUBLISHER,DUEDATE
EMPLOYEE	ESSNO,ENAME,EADDR,ESALARY
EQUIPMENT	SERIALNO,TYPE
TASK	TNAME

Each library branch may have volunteers and lends in-materials which borrowers borrow, at which time the materials become out-materials. Each branch has employees and equipment used by employees for various tasks.

(d)
ENTITIES	ATTRIBUTES
TEAM	NAME,LOCATION,MANAGER
EMPLOYEE	ESSNO,ENAME,EADDR,ESALARY
CUSTOMER	CNAME,CADDR,SERIALNO,YEAR,MODEL
PARTS-AND-SUPPLIES	SALESPERSON
REPAIR-ORDER	RONUMBER,DATE,BALANCE
EQUIPMENT	SERIALNO,TYPE
PART	IDNO,STOCKNO,DESCRIPTION,COST

Each team has employees who service customers' cars. Equipment and parts are associated with PARTS-AND-SUPPLIES. A repair order relates customers with PARTS-AND-SUPPLIES.

FIGURE 5.6.5
An Entity-Relationship Diagram

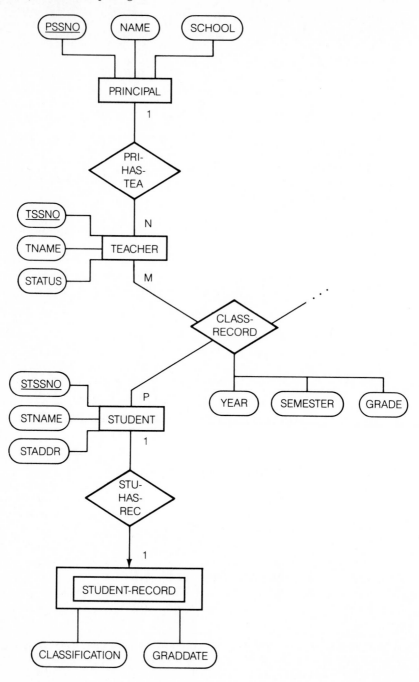

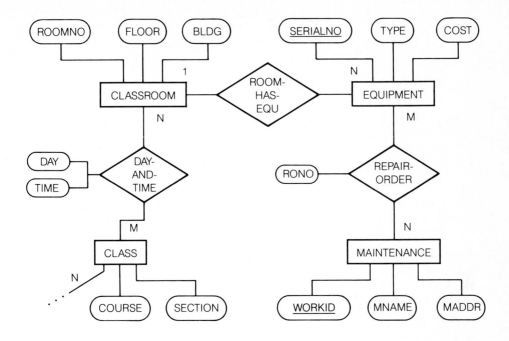

(c) PRODUCT(TEACHER,CLASSROOM).
(d) PRODUCT(PRODUCT(TEACHER,STUDENT),CLASS).
(e) JOIN(CLASS-RECORD;TEACHER,STUDENT,CLASS).
(f) JOIN(DAY-AND-TIME;CLASS,CLASSROOM).

5.7 Guide to Further Reading

Database dependencies and normalization are discussed in [1.1] Chapter 12, [1.2] Chapter 17, and [1.4] Chapter 7. [5.3] contains a great deal of information on these topics. The Domain-Key Normal Form is introduced in [5.1]. Database integrity is studied in detail in [5.2] as well as in [1.1] Chapter 13, [1.3] Chapter 2, [1.4] Chapter 10, and [2.4] Chapter 3. The entity-relationship database model is discussed in [1.1] Chapter 3, [1.2] Chapter 25, [1.4] Chapter 1, and [2.4] Chapter 8. The various conference proceedings, [5.4], contain collections of papers devoted to this topic.

[5.1] Fagin, R. "A Normal Form for Relational Databases That Is Based on Domains and Keys." ACM TODS 6(1981), pp. 387–415.

[5.2] Fernandez, E. B., R. C. Summers, and C. Wood. *Database Security and Integrity.* Reading, Mass.: Addison-Wesley, 1981.

[5.3] Maier, D. *The Theory of Relational Databases.* Rockville, Md.: Computer Science Press, 1983.

[5.4] *Proceedings* of Conferences on the Entity-Relationship Approach (held biennially beginning in 1979), published by North-Holland and the ER Institute.

Chapter 6

Database Components

6.1 Database Security

A database system is a complex piece of software with possibly many components. This chapter covers some of the important subsystems. The security component prevents unauthorized access to the database. The database dictionary, sometimes called the catalog, stores information about the database. The recovery manager, in conjunction with the transaction manager, recovers the database from failures. Concurrency, the simultaneous use of the database by several transactions, must be handled in such a way that the results of the transactions remain correct. Some other components provide assistance to users in various ways, such as for report writing, screen setup, and graph construction. Although not all database systems contain all of these components, the trend is toward including them.

In this section, we look at an important component of many database systems, the one that deals with database security. Databases may contain sensitive or confidential information such as salaries, credit reports, health histories, client lists, marketing strategies, or military secrets. It is therefore important that a database system which contains this type of information be secure. There are two main types of security abuse: unauthorized disclosure (retrieval) and unauthorized alteration (update) of information. While there are always some people who have legitimate rights to get to the information, it may be necessary to prohibit others from obtaining it. In particular, we may want to allow individuals to see their credit report, but not to destroy it or to change it.

The database system cannot be expected to handle many aspects of database security. Examples of safeguards outside the capabilities of databases include guards controlling physical access to a computer or a terminal and data encryption to protect against wiretapping the communications line of a legitimate user. Users may need to destroy or safeguard confidential reports obtained from a database. (This problem has become a more serious one in recent years, as the proliferation of microcomputers allows many users to download data to a floppy disk, which thereafter is often poorly guarded.) Many authorization schemes involve passwords that need to be kept secret. Finally, there must be security *built into the operating system*. Because a database system is built on top of the operating system, a user of the computer, who is not authorized to use a database system, may be able to get into it anyway through the operating system.

Thus there are many aspects of database security that really are beyond the capabilities of any database system, and which must be handled by other means. In the rest of this section, we will discuss only those aspects of security that are at the level of the database system. It should be recognized, however, that when we build security features into a database system, the system becomes more complex, uses additional storage, and processes information more slowly. Some database systems contain a useful feature that allows the database administrator to *disable* security features for nonsensitive data. Someone, or some group in the organization, must decide what security is appropriate based on the available features and sensitivity of data. Another aspect of security is the proper response in the case of an attempted security violation. At the very least the security violation should not be allowed. It is also helpful if the database system keeps a log file of attempted security violations, and alerts the computer operator, if there is one, so that possible security problems can be resolved.

We are now ready to examine the main issues involved in database security. Basically, the system must know who is authorized to do what. For this purpose, an **authorization matrix** can be set up. A very simple example appears in Figure 6.1.1. We indicate the authorizations of the users (they may be individuals or groups) horizontally and the access to the objects vertically. The element in the matrix at a particular row and column indicates the authorization of a user for an object.

In this case the authorization for the objects is at the level of tables and programs. A user may read (retrieve) a table (indicated by R), or write to (update) a table (indicated by W), or both, or neither. Also, a user may or may not run a program. For example, User 1 is allowed to read table T_4, but is not allowed to read or write to tables T_2 and T_3. User 1 is also allowed to both read from and write to tables T_1 and T_5. Additionally, User 1 may run program P_1 but not program P_2. There are several variations on this sort of scheme. We could subdivide W into I for Insert, D for Delete, and M for Modify. Sometimes the data items

FIGURE 6.1.1
An Authorization Matrix

	T_1	T_2	T_3	T_4	T_5	P_1	P_2
User 1	RW	—	—	R	RW	Y	N
User 2	R	R	—	—	—	Y	Y
User 3	R	—	—	—	RW	N	N
User 4	—	W	RW	—	—	N	Y

are set up hierarchically in the form of trees; then an access to an item at a node provides automatic access to all descendant nodes.

An authorization matrix can become very large, filled mostly with dashes. An alternative to such a table is to list what each user is authorized to do; these authorizations are called **user profiles.** Figure 6.1.2 gives an example for the authorization matrix of Figure 6.1.1. A table which is accessible only for read or write is so indicated. Another approach is to indicate authorization rights under the objects as **object profiles.** Figure 6.1.3 provides an example for the authorization matrix of Figure 6.1.1. Each user is indicated by a number; qualification on table accessibility is indicated as in Figure 6.1.2. In all cases, the security subsystem must check the authorization matrix, or user profile, or object profile, before the database system executes any user request. The database system must know at all times who its users are. It may cooperate with the operating system for this purpose.

FIGURE 6.1.2
User Profiles

```
User  1    T1; T4:R; T5; P1
User  2    T1:R; T2:R; P1; P2
User  3    T1:R; T5
User  4    T2:W; T3; P2
```

FIGURE 6.1.3
Object Profiles

```
T1    1; 2:R; 3:R          T5    1; 3
T2    2:R; 4:W             P1    1; 3
T3    4                    P2    2; 4
T4    1:R
```

In many cases, a finer distinction of authorizations is required. We may wish to restrict a user to read or write to only selected rows of the table. For example, a manager of a department may be allowed access to the records of the employees in that department, but not to the records of employees in other departments. We may also want to restrict a user to see only certain columns. Again, for a table of employees, we may not want to allow a user to see salary information. We may, however, want to allow a user to see statistical information about salaries, such as the average salary. Security problems involving statistical queries will be discussed when we deal with statistical databases in Section 11.3.

The view mechanism can be used to take care of many aspects of database security. We have already discussed external views as part of the three-level database architecture in Section 1.2, stressing their role as a convenience to users who want to access only a portion of the database. However, external views can also be set up so that users *cannot* access certain information in the database. By way of example, recall our discussion of the view mechanism for SQL in Section 4.5. Suppose that the schema is the one in Figure 4.3.2(a) and that we need to set up a view for a user who is allowed access to all of the EMPLOYEE table except for the SALARY column. Part (a) of Figure 6.1.4 indicates a view definition for that user. Part (b) gives a second view for a user who can access the EMPLOYEE table only for employees in the Sales and Delivery departments.

One attractive feature of using views for database security is that if the database system supports them, then they are available without having to add another mechanism to the system. While views are available in many relational database systems, the network database model also supports the similar notion of subschema—see Figure 2.2.6 for an example—and IMS supports a similar notion of logical database defined by a

FIGURE 6.1.4
Authorization Views

(a) First view

```
CREATE   VIEW   EMPLOYEE1
     AS   SELECT   DNAME,SSNO,NAME,ADDRESS
          FROM     EMPLOYEE;
```

(b) Second view

```
CREATE   VIEW   EMPLOYEE2
     AS   SELECT   DNAME,SSNO,NAME,SALARY,ADDRESS
          FROM     EMPLOYEE
          WHERE    DNAME = 'Sales'
               OR DNAME = 'Delivery':
```

program communication block (PCB)—see Figure 3.2.2(b) for an example. If views are used for the security system, then the authorization matrix would contain view access as well as table access. Again, the matrix could indicate whether a user can only use a view for reading it, or can also write to it.

At various times, the user profiles need to be updated. For example, when a new table is created, certain users will get access to it. Similarly, some users may be allowed to run a new program. It is also important that user authorizations be compatible. If a user is not allowed to see a table, then it makes little sense to allow that user to run a program which, among other things, prints the contents of the table. It is also useful to establish time- and location-dependent authorizations. This makes it possible, for example, to restrict the use of a PAYROLL view to terminals in the Payroll office between 9 a.m. and 5 p.m. Monday through Friday.

We now consider how security concepts are applied in SQL in addition to the view mechanism. The syntax rules for the statements involving privileges are indicated in Figure 6.1.5. The basic notion here is the **authorization identifier,** which refers to *a collection of privileges;* it is essentially a name associated with a user (profile), called a username. Users who may create tables have all privileges on the tables that they have created. Privileges may be granted to other users by means of the GRANT statement. Figure 6.1.6 shows examples of this statement in SQL. PUBLIC refers to all users, while ALL refers to all privileges. The phrase WITH GRANT OPTION allows the grantee (Jones, in this case) to grant privileges to others on the named data object (the EMPLOYEE table, in this case). There is also an example of a modification privilege that is restricted here to one attribute. Additionally, it is possible to give INSERT and DELETE privileges for a table.

FIGURE 6.1.5
Syntax Rules for SQL Privilege Statements

Note: Additional syntax rules for SQL are presented in Figures 4.3.1, 4.5.1, 4.5.3, 4.5.5, 6.4.3, and 7.1.7.

```
<grant statement>       ::=     GRANT <privileges> ON <table name> TO
                                { <grantee> [ { , <grantee> } . . . ] }
                                [ WITH GRANT OPTION ] ;
<privileges>      ::=     ALL | { <action> [ { , <action> } . . . ] }
<action>      ::=     SELECT | INSERT | DELETE | ALTER | INDEX |
                      { UPDATE [ ( <column name> [ { , <column name> } . . . ] ) ] }
<grantee>      ::=     PUBLIC | <authorization identifier>
<revoke statement>       ::=     REVOKE <privileges> ON <table name> FROM
                                 { <grantee> [ { , <grantee> } . . . ] } ;
```

FIGURE 6.1.6
The GRANT Statement in SQL

(a) Allow everyone to read the EMPLOYEE table.

```
GRANT SELECT ON EMPLOYEE TO PUBLIC;
```

(b) Allow Jones read and write privileges on the EMPLOYEE table. Also allow Jones to grant privileges on the EMPLOYEE table to others.

```
GRANT ALL ON EMPLOYEE TO JONES WITH GRANT OPTION;
```

(c) Allow Taylor to modify the SALARY attribute in the EMPLOYEE table.

```
GRANT UPDATE (SALARY) ON EMPLOYEE TO TAYLOR;
```

FIGURE 6.1.7
The REVOKE Statement

Revoke the modification privilege on the EMPLOYEE table from Jones.

```
REVOKE UPDATE ON EMPLOYEE FROM JONES;
```

The REVOKE statement is used to revoke privileges from users, as shown in Figure 6.1.7. Revocation cascades, for example, if we revoke a privilege from Jones, and Jones has already granted that privilege to Smith, then Smith's privilege is also revoked. The ALTER and INDEX privileges refer to the permission of adding and indexing attributes of a table. Additionally, note that there is another version of the GRANT/ REVOKE statements (whose syntax has not been given), which can be used by the database administrator to grant and revoke general privileges to and from a user. A user must have at least CONNECT authority to log onto the database system. RESOURCE authority is required to create tables. A user with DBA authority can add new users to the database system.

6.2 Data Dictionary

We use a database to store information about an enterprise. In our discussion of many database concepts throughout the book we have observed that a database itself is a complex object. A **data dictionary** is *a database that stores information about the objects in a database.* In this section, we discuss the contents and features of data dictionaries. Note that a data dictionary can be useful even to an organization that does not have a database system, just to keep track of its programs, files, data objects, and users. However, we consider data dictionaries in conjunction with database systems.

A data dictionary may come as part of a database system, but there are stand-alone dictionaries also. Having a database-independent dictionary is particularly useful if an organization wishes to convert from one database system to another one. The advantage of a database-specific dictionary is that it is integrated with the database system and usually provides more automatic features. A data dictionary includes several different types of objects. It should contain descriptions of the internal view, conceptual view, and external views, assuming the three-level architecture.

For the internal view, the data dictionary should include information about the files, data items, and indexings. It should contain the conceptual and external views in such a way that it is easy to find out information such as what tables contain a particular attribute and what attributes a particular table contains. Information from the schema, such as the relationships between tables and the types of attributes, needs to be available. In many cases, the units, such as feet or meters for length, need to be stored also. Synonyms, which are different names for the same object, should be listed as well. Additional information may include the list of database users, user profiles on database security, and the names of commonly used database programs along with their users.

A data dictionary can be helpful to users of the database system, to the database administrator, and to the database system itself. Users of the database system can find out what they can access in the database. In general, users are not allowed to gain access to the whole data dictionary, just as they cannot see the whole database, for security reasons. The database administrator has access to the complete data dictionary, and thereby can monitor the use of the database system. Finally, the database system itself can also use the data dictionary. (In Section 7.1, we will discuss the file structures and indexings about which data is stored in the data dictionary. Then, when we discuss query optimization in Section 7.2, we will see what type of data the optimizer needs from the dictionary.)

Because a data dictionary is in fact a database, a data dictionary system, if separate from the database system, must provide some database facilities. In particular, a data definition language is needed for defining the structure of the dictionary, and a data manipulation language is necessary for querying and updating the dictionary. If the data dictionary is part of the database system, then the DDL and DML of the database system can be used for that purpose. This is what is usually done in relational database systems. However, for hierarchic and network systems, which have more complex languages associated with them, it may be preferable to use a simpler language for the data dictionary. In connection with data dictionaries, it should also be recognized that such a dictionary can take up a substantial amount of storage for a large database system, and can possibly become a bottleneck itself.

To illustrate some of the concepts concerning data dictionaries, we now describe some aspects of the ORACLE Data Dictionary. Section 4.3 identified ORACLE as a relational database system which uses SQL. The data dictionary is a part of the database system, so it is set up as a relational database itself and can be queried using SQL. Users do not update the data dictionary; the system does the updates automatically. For example, when a user creates a table, data about that table is inserted into the dictionary. The revocation of a privilege is represented by a deletion (of the appropriate privilege) from the dictionary. The tables of the dictionary are fixed and are created by the database system at the time that the database is created. The ORACLE Data Dictionary does not contain data about programs, and is similar in style and function to the CATALOG in IBM's DB2 database system.

Figure 6.2.1 lists some of the tables in the ORACLE Data Dictionary. Part (a) indicates tables that users may access, and part (b) indicates tables that only the database administrator may access. Users may obtain information about their tables, views, columns, synonyms, data storage, and access authorization. Essentially, SYSTABAUTH is what we called the user profile in the previous section and SYSUSERAUTH is the authorization matrix. The objects created by a user are really prefixed by the user's username (or userid), but users do not need to write their own prefix. However, when a user wishes to obtain access to an object created by someone else, the user must employ the creator's username to do so. (An alternative to using the prefix is to create a synonym, which is then the user's name for that object and does not have to be prefixed.) Users may only obtain information from the data dictionary about objects that they are authorized to use.

FIGURE 6.2.1
Tables in the ORACLE Data Dictionary

(a) Some tables for users

CATALOG	tables, views, and clusters accessible to the user
COL	columns in tables created by the user
INDEXES	indexes created by the user and indexes on tables created by the user
VIEWS	definitions of views
SYSTABAUTH	access authorization granted by or to the user
STORAGE	data and index storage allocation for the user

(b) Some tables for the DBA

SYSSTORAGE	storage for all the data
SYSUSERAUTH	authorized users and their privileges

FIGURE 6.2.2
Attributes for ORACLE Data Dictionary Tables

```
TABLES              ATTRIBUTES
  CATALOG           TNAME,CREATOR,TABTYPE,TABID
  COL               TNAME,COLNO,CNAME,COLTYPE,WIDTH,SCALE,
                      NULLS
  INDEXES           INAME,ICREATOR,TNAME,CREATOR,COLNAMES,
                      INDEXTYPE
  VIEWS             VIEWNAME,VCREATOR,VIEWTEXT
  SYSTABAUTH        GRANTOR,GRANTEE,CREATOR,TNAME,TABTYPE,
                      AUTHORITY
  STORAGE           NAME,TYPE,WHICH,STORAGE,EXTENTS
  SYSSTORAGE        CREATOR,NAME,TYPE,STORAGE,EXTENTS
  SYSUSERAUTH       NAME,AUTHOR,AUTHORITY,PASSWORD
```

Figure 6.2.2 lists the attributes for the ORACLE Data Dictionary tables presented in Figure 6.2.1. For each table, view, and cluster (accessible to the user), the CATALOG table contains its name, creator (which may be the user), type (table, view, or cluster), and a special identification number. (**Cluster** here is used *in the sense of a join support,* which will be discussed in Section 7.1.) The COL table contains information about columns (attributes) of the user's tables. The COLTYPE attribute indicates if the column contains a numeric, character, or date value. Permission to use null values is also indicated. The INDEXES table lists the columns and tables on which indexes have been created. The INDEX-TYPE attribute indicates whether or not the indexed attribute is a key for the table. In the VIEWS table, the VIEWTEXT attribute contains an SQL view definition.

The SYSTABAUTH table contains the privileges granted by the user or to the user. There are four possible values for the AUTHORITY attribute: SELECT, DELETE, INSERT, and UPDATE. The STORAGE table contains storage information: the WHICH attribute, with two possible values, DATA and INDEX; the STORAGE attribute containing the number of pages; and the EXTENTS attribute indicating how many times storage was requested for the table or cluster. For the DBA, the SYSSTORAGE table lists storage information about all clusters and tables, and the SYSUSERAUTH table indicates the passwords and general authorizations (CONNECT,RESOURCE,DBA) for users.

In Figure 6.2.3, we examine a few SQL queries to the data dictionary with possible answers. For these examples, note that the user has the userid of Smith; Smith is authorized to access tables in the schema of Figure 4.1.1. A projection of the CATALOG table appears in part (a) of Figure 6.2.3. Note that Smith has access to the table ITEM, which was created by Jones. Next, suppose that Smith wants to get information about the attributes of the EMPLOYEE table. The SQL query and the answer appear in part (b). The next query, shown with the answer in

FIGURE 6.2.3
SQL Queries for the ORACLE Data Dictionary

(a) (*i*)   Query

```
SELECT   TNAME,CREATOR,TABTYPE
FROM     CATALOG;
```

· (*ii*)   Answer

TNAME	CREATOR	TABTYPE
DEPARTMENT	SMITH	TABLE
ITEM	JONES	TABLE
EMPLOYEE	SMITH	TABLE

(b) (*i*)   Query

```
SELECT   TNAME,CNAME,COLTYPE,WIDTH,SCALE
FROM     COL
WHERE    TNAME = 'EMPLOYEE';
```

(*ii*)   Answer

TNAME	CNAME	COLTYPE	WIDTH	SCALE
EMPLOYEE	SSNO	CHAR	9	
EMPLOYEE	ENAME	CHAR	15	
EMPLOYEE	DNAME	CHAR	12	
EMPLOYEE	SALARY	NUMBER	7	

(c) (*i*)   Query   (*ii*)   Answer

```
SELECT   AUTHORITY          AUTHORITY
FROM     SYSTABAUTH         ------------
WHERE    TNAME = 'ITEM';    SELECT
                            INSERT
```

(d) (*i*)   Query

```
SELECT   *
FROM     STORAGE;
```

(*ii*)   Answer

NAME	TYPE	WHICH	STORAGE	EXTENTS
DEPARTMENT	TABLE	DATA	30	2
DEPARTMENT	TABLE	INDEX	30	2
EMPLOYEE	TABLE	DATA	500	1
EMPLOYEE	TABLE	INDEX	250	1

part (c), asks for Smith's authority on the ITEM table. Note that Smith can query and insert into the ITEM table. Finally, a query about the storage of Smith's tables is shown in part (d). ORACLE automatically reserves space both for the data and the index. For the DEPARTMENT table, two requests were made, using default values, resulting in 30 (storage) pages of data and of index. For the EMPLOYEE table, one request was made initially, with 500 pages for the data and 250 for the index.

6.3 Transactions and Recovery

In this section, we discuss the problem of recovery from failure for database systems. A key concept here is the notion of **transaction,** which is *a consistent unit of work, such as an execution of a program.* A transaction may consist of a sequence of actions, such that either all of them must be executed, or none of them should be executed. A partial execution of a transaction may lead to an inconsistent state for the database. Consider, for example, a transfer of money from account X to account Y. We can think of such a transfer as consisting of a withdrawal from X and a deposit to Y. In this case, the transaction consists of the withdrawal and the deposit; we would not want just one of these operations to be performed without also doing the other one. Since transactions should not be left partially executed, they are taken as units of recovery in case some type of failure occurs. Transactions and recovery are managed by subsystems called the transaction manager and the recovery manager, respectively. Transaction and recovery management are important topics for operating systems in general; we will emphasize the aspects related to databases.

We start by considering the types of failures that can occur. For convenience, we divide failures into two kinds, **system failure** and **transaction failure.** System failures can also be divided into two types. The first and more serious type is where data is lost from the database; this may happen in the case of a *disk crash.* In the second type of system failure, data in memory is lost; this may happen through a power failure or internal problems within the operating or database system. Transaction failures can also be classified into two types; however, the recovery mechanism is the same for both. A transaction may fail because of an external problem such as a communication failure or a deadlock. The last case is an internal problem concerning a transaction: there may be an error in the program such as an attempted division by 0; the transaction may violate an integrity constraint; or a user may wish to cancel an operation.

Let's discuss the problem of transaction failures first. Each transaction will eventually succeed or fail. A transaction is called **committed** *after it terminates its execution successfully.* If a transaction fails, *its effects on the database are erased* in a process called the **rollback.** The recovery manager usually uses a **log** (also called **journal** or **audit trail**) which *contains* *information about the transactions.* (This log is different from the log of security violations mentioned in Section 6.1.) In particular, the commitment of a transaction is indicated there. In log-based recovery systems, the log contains data about each update of an object: a transaction identifier, the old value (if deleted), the new value (if inserted), and both the old and new values (if modified). The log may also contain additional items: for example, if there is a pointer for each transaction's log entry to the previous log entry of that transaction, then it is easier to do a rollback. Restarting after a system failure is simplified in the presence of separate lists for transactions that have been committed, rolled back, and which are active.

Buffers play an important part in the recovery process. A **buffer** is *an area in memory used for I/O processing.* The significance of buffers for recovery purposes is that an updated page of the database is placed into a buffer *before* it is actually written out on external storage (disk) into the database. This means that the time that the update is made in the database is not necessarily the time that the update command is executed according to the log, unless the buffers are immediately emptied. The opposite approach involves holding all updated pages of a transaction in the buffer area until the transaction commits. This latter case of deferred updates has the advantage that if the transaction fails, then during a rollback the database does not have to be changed. However, this approach may cause problems for buffer management. If the deferred updates method is not the one used, and updated pages are written out to the database by a transaction which is later rolled back, then an **undo operation** takes place. The undo operation consults the log to *recover the old database pages.* For this process to work correctly, the log pages must be written out to disk frequently, and an update should be written out to the log before the change is made in the database.

The case where only one transaction is being processed at the time of failure is the easiest one to handle; however, often many transactions are processed simultaneously. We will deal with concurrent processing in more detail in the next section, limiting the present discussion to the recovery problem associated with concurrent processing. Figure 6.3.1 illustrates the concurrent processing of two transactions, T_1 and T_2. T_1 changes the value of a data item which is subsequently read by T_2. Assume that the execution of T_2 comes to an end successfully. In our scenario, we cannot commit T_2 at this point. Suppose that T_1 fails later and must be rolled back. This means that T_2 used an incorrect value, and so must also be rolled back. We will see in the next section how locking resolves this problem.

Now we proceed to consider system failure. Let's begin with the case where system failure erases what is in memory, but the database on disk is kept intact. When the system is restarted, several actions must be taken. There are three types of transactions to consider: transactions which have been rolled back, ones which were active at the time of system failure,

FIGURE 6.3.1
A Rollback Problem

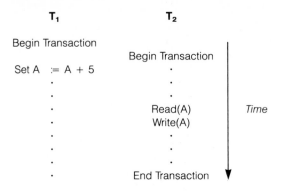

and those which have been committed. The recovery manager must undo those transactions which have been rolled back because the original roll-back may not have been complete at the time of system failure. Those transactions which were active at the time of system failure should also be rolled back; they can be restarted later. Finally, the recovery manager must **redo** those transactions which have been committed, because the updates may have been in the buffer at the time of the failure.

The problem with the method just described is that it is not clear how far back the recovery manager must go to redo or undo those trans-actions which were not active at the time of system failure. This problem can be solved by using checkpoints. At a **checkpoint,** *the system empties all the buffers for the committed transactions and completes the rollback for all failed transactions.* The taking of a checkpoint is then written into the log. When we use the checkpoint technique, it is not necessary at the time of system restart to consider any transactions which were committed or rolled back prior to the last checkpoint.

The last type of failure we consider is the one where data is lost from the database. In such a case, it is necessary to recover an older version of the database. This can be accomplished if backup (also called archival) copies of the database are made periodically. The **backup copy** *captures a specific database instance,* which we assume to be *correct.* For large databases, sometimes only a portion of the database is backed up at one time. In the case of this type of failure, it is then possible to retrieve the backup copy and use the log to do a **rollforward,** that is, *perform all the updates to the database for committed transactions as recorded in the log.*

Before briefly considering recovery methods which are not log-based, we note a few additional definitions concerning recovery. Storage in memory (including buffers) is called **volatile** because it *does not survive a system failure. Storage in external storage* (disk or tape) is called **stable.** It is particularly important to have the backup copy and the log in stable storage; often they are kept on tape for this reason. Another, unrelated, concept is the compensating transaction. Sometimes an erroneous transaction is committed with its effect known on the database. Since a committed transaction cannot be rolled back, it is necessary to perform another transaction which **compensates** for it. For example, an erroneous deposit can be compensated for by a withdrawal of the same amount.

The recovery methods that we have considered so far are called log-based, because the updates are placed into the log (in addition to the database). We now briefly consider two other recovery techniques. **Shadowing** *involves the maintenance of two copies of each page that is updated,* the current copy and the shadow copy. The shadow copy contains the old value and the current copy contains the new value. If the transaction is committed, the shadow copy is deleted; if the transaction is rolled back, the current copy is deleted. Unfortunately, shadowing tends to scatter the data on the disk. The **differential file** technique uses *a separate update file.* At various times the differential file is merged with the database; the old database then becomes the backup copy. This method involves additional searching since the differential file must be searched each time a lookup is done.

Whatever recovery method the database system applies, the database user is usually not concerned with recovery. Most systems automatically commit when a transaction terminates normally, and roll back when a program terminates abnormally. However, many database languages contain statements which allow the user to perform a commit or a rollback. In SQL, the statements used to commit and roll back a transaction are COMMIT WORK and ROLLBACK WORK, respectively. Since the default is automatic commit and rollback, AUTOCOMMIT must be turned off before applying the commit and rollback statements.

We end this section by mentioning that, in some cases, database applications are so essential that system failures which shut down the whole system must be avoided. Several so-called **fault-tolerant computer systems** exist today; these systems shield the users from system failure. Some of these systems, such as the ones by Tandem Computers, involve database applications. Such systems usually rely on duplication with multiple processors and disks, so that if one fails another one can take over. We will not go into the architecture of these systems. They tend to share some of the problems and complications involved with distributed database systems, which will be discussed in Section 7.3

6.4 Concurrent Processing

In this section, we deal with aspects of databases related to their simultaneous use by more than one transaction. Such use of a database system is called **concurrent processing.** Although most database systems on microcomputers are presently single-user systems, concurrency is essential for many database systems now in use. There are a number of problems and proposed solutions concerning concurrency. Like security and recovery, concurrency is a general problem for operating systems also, although we consider the problems as they pertain to databases only. We start by considering an example.

Suppose that two individuals, X and Y, have a joint bank account C, containing $10,000, from which both need to withdraw money. Assume that they go to different branches of the bank and make their withdrawal requests at about the same time. X wishes to withdraw $2000 at Branch 1, while Y requests $1000 at Branch 2. We would expect both requests to be honored, with the bank account balance left at $7000. Figure 6.4.1 indicates what could go wrong. Since the withdrawals take place concurrently, both branches read the same initial balance, $10,000. The modification is done first in a separate workspace for each withdrawal request. After Branch 1 writes the new balance of $8000, Branch 2 rewrites it as $9000, so that at the end the final balance is incorrect.

The problem was caused by the fact that there were two transactions simultaneously changing the same record. The second transaction did not see the effect of the first transaction, and so the effect of that first transaction was lost. **Lost update** is not the only possible problem, however. Suppose that a transaction is computing the average salary for employees, while another transaction is concurrently updating some sal-

FIGURE 6.4.1
Concurrent Bank Withdrawals

Branch 1	Branch 2	
Read balance of account C = $10,000.		
	Read balance of account C = $10,000.	
Perform withdrawal of $2000 from account C—New balance in workspace = $8000.		
	Perform withdrawal of $1000 from account C—New balance in workspace = $9000.	*Time*
Write new balance to account C = $8000.		
	Write new balance to account C = $9000.	
Give A $2000.		
	Give B $1000.	

End result: $3000 withdrawn, new balance shows $1000 withdrawn.

Figure 6.4.2
A Concurrent Read and Update

```
Salary 1    Salary 2    Salary 3    Salary 4    Salary 5    Running Total
15000       20000       25000       30000       35000       0
15000       20000       25000       30000       35000       15000
17000       20000       25000       30000       35000       35000
17000       20000       25000       33000       35000       60000         Time
17000       20000       25000       33000       35000       93000
17000       20000       25000       33000       35000       128000

              Average = 128000/5 = 25600
```

aries. An example is shown in Figure 6.4.2. Initially, the salaries are $15,000, $20,000, $25,000, $30,000, and $35,000; thus the average is $25,000. At the end, the salaries are $17,000, $20,000, $25,000, $33,000, and $35,000; so the new average is $26,000. But the transaction computing the average misses the first change of salary and catches the second one, while it is adding up the salary values. The result is an **incorrect answer.**

Without any mechanism to handle concurrent access to a database, it is possible to lose updates and to obtain incorrect answers to queries. There are several solutions to these problems. First we consider those methods that involve **locking.** When locking is used, a component of the database system, called the **lock manager,** handles the locks. The principle of locking is that a transaction may place a **lock** on an object to prevent its access by another transaction. There are several questions about locks, such as what to lock, for how long, and what type of lock to use. An extreme solution is for a transaction to exclusively lock the whole database for its duration. This certainly avoids all the problems, but it also defeats the purpose of concurrent access. Ideally, we would like to lock as little of the database as possible for as short a time as possible.

The unit of locking is referred to as the **granularity** of the lock. Consider the previous two examples. For the bank transactions, it would suffice to lock a single customer record. For the salary example, we should lock the column of the table containing the salaries at the least, or possibly the whole table if we are computing the average salary for only selected individuals. Going from coarse to fine granularity, the unit may be the whole database, a set of tables, a page (of storage), a row (record), or an individual data item. **Coarse granularity** *limits concurrent access to the database;* **fine granularity** *requires more lock management overhead.*

There are two kinds of locks, exclusive and shared. An **exclusive lock** prohibits other transactions from accessing the locked unit; exclusive locks are used for objects that are being updated. A **shared lock** is useful when several transactions concurrently read values from the database; it prohibits other transactions only from updating the locked unit. Now that we have touched on what to lock and what type of lock to use, the next question concerns when and how long to lock an object. It is certainly safe to lock all needed objects for the duration of the transaction. However, it may not be necessary to do so. Consider, also, that the sooner we release locks, the more we improve concurrent access to the database. A shared lock may be released as soon as the object is read. However, if an exclusive lock is released before the end of the transaction which updates the locked unit, and if the transaction does not commit, then another transaction may concurrently obtain an incorrect value. This problem was mentioned in the previous section (without using the notion of locks).

Let's consider the general situation concerning a database when the locking mechanism is used. Various transactions are concurrently accessing portions of the database for reads and writes (updates). The system requires that a transaction must request and obtain a lock for an object (or possibly a bigger object depending on the granularity of the locks) from the lock manager (program) before it can access that object. The lock manager keeps track of the locked items and lock requests at all times. If the requested object is not locked, then there is no problem: the lock request is granted and the transaction locks the object. If the object is already locked with a shared lock, and the transaction requests a shared lock, then again, the request is granted. However, the transaction's request is not granted otherwise—that is, if the object is already locked with an exclusive lock, or if it is already locked with a shared lock and the transaction requests an exclusive lock. When a transaction requests a lock and the request is not granted, then the transaction goes into a waiting stage.

Locking, like commit and rollback, is usually done automatically. However, most database systems which use locking, such as DB2 and ORACLE, allow the user to write an explicit LOCK statement for tables. The syntax for the LOCK statement is indicated in Figure 6.4.3. The SHARED UPDATE mode allows multiple simultaneous updates for different rows of a table, so it is in fact an exclusive lock on rows.

Now let's see how locking can prevent the two problems we mentioned at the beginning of the section. In the case of the concurrent bank withdrawals, we see what happens in part (a) of Figure 6.4.4. Let T_1 be the transaction at Branch 1 and T_2 the transaction at Branch 2. If T_1

FIGURE 6.4.3
Syntax Rules for the SQL LOCK Statement

Note: Additional syntax rules for SQL are presented in Figures 4.3.1, 4.5.1, 4.5.3, 4.5.5, 6.1.5, and 7.1.7.

```
<lock statement>     ::=     LOCK TABLE <table list> IN <lock mode> MODE ;
<table list>    ::=     <table name> [ { , <table name> } . . . ]
<lock mode>     ::=     SHARE | SHARED UPDATE | EXCLUSIVE
```

FIGURE 6.4.4
The Use of Locks

(a) The concurrent bank withdrawal example

Branch 1	Branch 2	
T_1 requests exclusive lock on account C.		
T_1 locks account C.		
	T_2 requests exclusive lock on account C.	
	T_2 waits.	*Time*
T_1 reads balance of account C = $10,000.		
T_1 performs withdrawal of $2000 (new balance in workspace = $8000).		
T_1 writes new balance to account C = $8000.		
T_1 releases the lock on account C.		
	T_2 locks account C.	
A is given $2000.		
	T_2 reads balance of account C = $8000.	
	T_2 performs withdrawal of $1000 (new balance in workspace = $7000).	
	T_2 writes new balance to account C = $7000.	
	T_2 releases the lock on account C.	
	B is given $1000.	

End result: $3000 withdrawn, new balance shows $3000 withdrawn.

(b) The concurrent read and update example

Average Salary Computation	Update Salaries	
T_1 requests shared lock on the EMPLOYEE table.		
T_1 locks the EMPLOYEE table.		
	T_2 requests exclusive lock on the EMPLOYEE table.	*Time*
	T_2 waits.	
T_1 performs the calculation of the sum.		
T_1 releases its lock on the EMPLOYEE table.		
	T_2 locks the EMPLOYEE table.	
T_1 computes the average.		
	T_2 performs the update on the EMPLOYEE table.	
	T_2 releases the lock on the EMPLOYEE table.	

Average = $25,000

makes a request for a lock first on account C, its request is granted. Thus, when T_2 requests a lock on account C, its request is denied, and T_2 must wait until T_1 releases its lock on C. But by that time, account C has the new balance of \$8000, and after T_2 performs its withdrawal, the correct balance is obtained. Part (b) shows the situation for the salary example. In this case, let T_1 be the transaction computing the average salary and T_2 the updating transaction. Assume that T_1 obtains a lock first on the EMPLOYEE table. It is a shared lock, but T_2 needs an exclusive lock; hence it must wait until *after* T_1 obtains the sum of the salaries. The average obtained is the correct old average salary. If T_2's request is granted first, then T_1 would have to wait until T_2 releases its lock, and so T_1 would obtain the correct new average salary.

Locking provides a powerful mechanism for correctly handling concurrent processing. However, there are also some disadvantages associated with this method, in addition to the overhead required to implement it. One possible problem is called livelock. **Livelock** occurs when *a transaction is in a constant waiting stage,* as other transactions keep locking an item that it needs. We give an example of livelock in Figure 6.4.5(a). T_1 requests a lock on item A, but must wait because T_2 locked it earlier. Before T_2 releases its lock on A, T_3 requests a lock on it, which is then granted. Later, T_4 requests a lock on A, which is also granted after T_3 releases it. The solution to the livelock problem is simple: accept lock requests in the order in which they are made. If this is done, then T_3 would not be allowed to lock A until after T_1 locked it (and then released its lock on it).

A more difficult problem about locks is called deadlock. **Deadlock** occurs for *n* transactions *when each transaction holds a lock on an object needed by another transaction, and so all of them must wait.* An example of a deadlock for three transactions and three objects appears in Figure 6.4.5(b). There are two types of solutions to the deadlock problem: either do not allow a deadlock to occur, or detect and resolve deadlocks.

We consider **deadlock prevention** first. There are two main methods: we could require each transaction to request all its locks at once; or, we could order the objects in some way, and then require all transactions to request locks in that order. To continue our example, if each transaction had to request all its locks at once, then T_1 would request locks on A_1 and A_2, T_2 would request locks on A_2 and A_3, and T_3 would request locks on A_3 and A_1. Assuming, without loss of generality, that T_1's request is granted first, then T_2 and T_3 would have to wait until T_1 released a lock, thereby preventing deadlock. For the second method, if the objects are ordered as A_1, A_2, and A_3, for example, then T_3 would have to request its lock on A_1 *before* requesting its lock on A_3. Thus, T_3 would have to wait, and there would be no deadlock.

The methods to prevent deadlocks may be difficult to apply because some transactions may not be able to determine initially all the objects

FIGURE 6.4.5
Livelock and Deadlock

(a) Livelock

T_1	T_2	T_3	T_4
	Requests shared lock on A. Locks A.		
Requests exclusive lock on A. Waits.			
	⋮		
		Requests shared lock on A. Locks A.	
	.		
	Releases lock on A.		
			Requests exclusive lock on A. Waits.
		⋮	
		Releases lock on A.	
			Locks A. ⋮

Time ↓

(b) Deadlock

T_1	T_2	T_3
Requests exclusive lock on A_1. Locks A_1.		
	Requests exclusive lock on A_2. Locks A_2.	
		Requests shared lock on A_3. Locks A_3.
Requests shared lock on A_2. Waits.		
	Requests exclusive lock on A_3. Waits.	
		Requests exclusive lock on A_1. Waits.

Time ↓

(continued)

(c) Wait-for graph

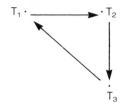

that they will need. The requirement for some objects may depend on processing (such as if a selection is done) during the transaction. Also, it may not always be obvious that two different transactions want to lock the same object. For example, suppose that T_1 needs to lock the record of the EMPLOYEE table with SSNO value 111-11-1111, while T_2 needs to lock the record of the EMPLOYEE table with ENAME value J. Smith. If J. Smith has the social security number 111-11-1111, then T_1 and T_2 will try to lock the same object.

Because there are problems with the deadlock prevention methods, we may instead allow a deadlock to occur, and then break it. But first, we must be able to **detect** a deadlock situation. This can be done by drawing a graph called the **wait-for graph.** The wait-for graph for the previous deadlock is shown in Figure 6.4.5(c). The nodes represent the transactions. A directed edge has been drawn from T_1 to T_2 because T_1 is waiting to lock an object presently locked by T_2. Similarly, there are directed edges from T_2 to T_3 and T_3 to T_1. In this graph, a cycle—which is a path starting and ending at the same node—represents a deadlock. When a deadlock is found, the system can roll back one of the transactions. The transaction that is rolled back can later be restarted.

When transactions are processed concurrently, several different answers may result, only some of which would be correct. In the concurrent read and update example of Figure 6.4.2, we said that intuitively both $25,000 and $26,000 may be considered to be correct, but not $25,600. The reason is that $25,000 is the old average and $26,000 the new average, while $25,600 was not the average at any point. Note that if we perform T_1 completely before T_2, we get $25,000, and if we perform T_2 completely before T_1, we get $26,000. The basic principle is this: if all the transactions are themselves individually correct, and if we perform them serially rather than concurrently, then we obtain correct answers.

The *order of the steps in an execution* is called a **schedule.** We say that a specific schedule of several transactions is **serializable** if *its effect is the same as that of some serial schedule.* The notion of serializability is important, because according to the basic principle just stated, we can take it as the criterion for the correctness of the concurrent execution. Neither of the two executions in Figures 6.4.1 and 6.4.2 are serializable, while both

FIGURE 6.4.6
Nonserializability

T_1	T_2
Requests exclusive lock on A_1.	
Locks A_1.	
	Requests exclusive lock on A_2.
	Locks A_2.
Set $A_1 := A_1 + 5$.	
Releases lock on A_1.	
	Set $A_2 := 2 * A_2$.
Requests exclusive lock on A_2.	
Waits.	
	Releases lock on A_2.
Locks A_2.	
	Requests exclusive lock on A_1.
	Locks A_1.
Set $A_2 := A_2 + 7$.	
	Set $A_1 := 2 * A_1$.
Releases lock on A_2.	
	Releases lock on A_1.

Time

executions in Figure 6.4.4 are. We may guess first that locking guarantees serializability; however, that is not so, as shown in Figure 6.4.6. Suppose that initially A_1 has the value 10 and A_2 has the value 20. T_1 adds 5 to A_1 and 7 to A_2, while T_2 doubles both A_1 and A_2. There are thus two correct answers for the serial executions: $A_1 = 30$ and $A_2 = 54$ if T_1 is done first, and $A_1 = 25$ and $A_2 = 47$ if T_2 is done first. The schedule of Figure 6.4.6 yields $A_1 = 30$ and $A_2 = 47$, which is not correct: that is, it could not be obtained by a schedule which does one transaction completely before the other one.

A **protocol,** in connection with concurrency control, *is a restriction on the order of steps for a transaction.* A very important one is the **two-phase lock protocol,** which *requires every transaction to obtain all of its locks before releasing any lock.* If a transaction obeys this protocol, then, in the first phase it acquires the locks, and in the second phase it releases the locks. Note that the transactions in Figure 6.4.6 do not obey the two-phase lock protocol. One convenient way to apply the two-phase lock protocol is by releasing the locks for a transaction only after the transaction is committed or rolled back. Using this method in Figure 6.3.1, T_2 must wait to get a lock on A until T_1 completes its execution, so T_2 will get the correct value of A: the new one if T_1 is committed, the old one if T_1 is rolled back. The importance of the two-phase lock protocol is due to the following theorem, which assures the correctness of transactions obeying it.

Theorem 6.1 Every schedule of transactions, all of which obey the two-phase lock protocol, is serializable.

We mentioned at the beginning of the section that locking is one important method of controlling concurrent access to a database. However, locking may require substantial overhead in execution time, an investment that may really be unnecessary if requests for the same object rarely occur. Additionally, problems like livelock and deadlock must be handled. Locking is considered a pessimistic approach to concurrency control because it assumes many requests for the same object. Instead, if we are optimistic, we may assume that concurrent requests for an object by several transactions will rarely occur, and so avoid the overhead involved in locking.

The **optimistic method** *allows a transaction to proceed until the commit time, at which point the system must validate the transaction by checking for possible conflicts.* This can be done by constructing the conflict graph. As in the wait-for graph, the nodes represent the transactions. A directed edge is drawn from T_1 to T_2 if T_2 reads or updates an object after T_1 updated it, or if T_2 updates an object after T_1 read it. In this graph, a cycle represents a conflict. If a conflict occurs at that point for a transaction, it is solved as in the case of a deadlock: the system rolls back the transaction, and then restarts it from the beginning.

Another approach is to use the **timestamping method,** where *each transaction is given a unique timestamp as it initiates.* In this case the transactions run concurrently, but their effect must be the same as if they were executed in the order of their timestamps. This is even a stronger notion than that of serializability, because it *guarantees* a unique answer. Of course, the problem is that transactions may interact. The solution to that problem is much like the solution for the optimistic method: the system rolls back the transaction, and then restarts it with a new timestamp.

In the timestamping method each object is usually given two times, its read time and its update time. All times are initialized to 0. At any point during execution, the read time and the update time of an object are respectively the timestamp of the latest transaction which read it and which updated it (or 0). We assume that a transaction reads an object before updating it. Under these assumptions, if a transaction T_1 with timestamp t_1 tries to read an object with update time t_2 where $t_2 > t_1$, or if T_1 tries to update an object with read or update time t_2 where $t_2 > t_1$, then the system rolls back T_1.

Now let's see how timestamping would solve the problems in the examples given at the beginning of the section. For the concurrent bank withdrawal problem of Figure 6.4.1, let $t_1 < t_2$, where t_i is the timestamp of T_i. The result appears in part (a) of Figure 6.4.7. When T_1 tries to do the update with time t_1, C already has read time t_2. Therefore, the system rolls back T_1 and gives T_1 a new timestamp, t_3, such that $t_3 > t_2$. This

FIGURE 6.4.7
Timestamping

(a) The concurrent bank withdrawal example

Account C		Time of T₁ = t₁ < t₂ = Time of T₂

Read Time	Update Time	Action
0	0	Start.
t_1	0	T₁ tries to read C—allowed.
t_2	0	T₂ tries to read C—allowed.
		T₁ tries to update C—not allowed.
t_2	0	Roll back T₁ and give it new timestamp = t_3.
t_2	t_2	T₂ tries to update C—allowed.
t_3	t_2	T₁ tries to read C—allowed.
t_3	t_3	T₁ tries to update C—allowed.

End result: $3000 withdrawn, new balance shows $3000 withdrawn.

(b) The concurrent read and update example

EMPLOYEE Table		Time of T₁ = t₁ < t₂ = Time of T₂

Read Time	Update Time	Action
0	0	Start.
t_1	0	T₁ tries to read Salary 1—allowed.
t_1	0	T₁ tries to read Salary 2—allowed.
t_2	0	T₂ tries to read Salary 1—allowed.
t_2	t_2	T₂ tries to update Salary 1—allowed.
		T₁ tries to read Salary 3—not allowed.
t_2	t_2	Roll back T₁ and give it new timestamp = t_3.
t_2	t_2	T₂ tries to read Salary 4—allowed.
t_2	t_2	T₂ tries to update Salary 4—allowed.
t_3	t_2	T₁ tries to read Salary 1—allowed.
t_3	t_2	T₁ tries to read Salary 2—allowed.
t_3	t_2	T₁ tries to read Salary 3—allowed.
t_3	t_2	T₁ tries to read Salary 4—allowed.
t_3	t_2	T₁ tries to read Salary 5—allowed.

Average = $26,000.

way T₂ can complete its task before T₁ does its work. In the case of the concurrent read and update example of Figure 6.4.2, Figure 6.4.7(b) shows what happens. Here T₁ cannot proceed when it tries to read the salary $25,000. Again, T₂ completes its task before T₁. We note that even with timestamping, a situation resembling livelock may occur, as illustrated in Figure 6.4.8. Because of the pattern of the executions, T₁ and T₂ keep getting terminated and restarted before completion.

FIGURE 6.4.8
A Timestamping Problem

A_1		A_2		Time of $T_1 = t_1 < t_2 =$ Time of T_2
Read Time	Update Time	Read Time	Update Time	Action
0	0	0	0	Start
0	0	t_1	0	T_1 tries to read A_2—allowed.
t_2	0	t_1	0	T_2 tries to read A_1—allowed.
t_2	0	t_1	t_1	T_1 tries to update A_2—allowed.
t_2	t_2	t_1	t_1	T_2 tries to update A_1—allowed.
				T_1 tries to update A_1—not allowed.
t_2	t_2	0	0	Roll back T_1 and give it new timestamp = t_3.
t_2	t_2	t_3	0	T_1 tries to read A_2—allowed.
t_2	t_2	t_3	t_3	T_1 tries to update A_2—allowed.
				T_2 tries to read A_2—not allowed.
0	0	t_3	t_3	Roll back T_2 and give it new timestamp = t_4.

.
.
.
.

6.5 Assistance for Users

Database systems provide various features to assist their users. Depending on the system, some of these features may be additional programs that do not come as part of the package, but are purchased separately. We start by considering utilities. The notion of utility is not always used in the same way by different systems, but generally, a **utility** is *a program that involves only a specific activity.* For example, some database systems consider the recovery manager a utility. Another utility loads data into the database, possibly from files set up in a different format. Often, a utility makes backup copies. Usually, the database administrator is given a utility program to monitor activity on the database. Such a program can be helpful in redesigning and reorganizing the database. Some of the information needed by an optimizer, which will be discussed in Section 7.2, may be gathered by another utility. Also, a utility may be used to assign data to specific storage media.

Next, we touch on some functions which database systems usually provide. In Section 1.4, we discussed host language interfaces, for writing programs involving the database in a programming language; the features that we note next may be available within the database system or can be programmed in the host language. Sorting a table based on a column or a column combination is an essential function for databases.

Simple statistical functions, such as SUM and AVERAGE, are very important for applications. It is also convenient to have functions on character strings, such as *substring* and *concatenation*. Additional useful features for users may indicate how many rows a table contains, and may allow users to easily scroll through their tables.

With the advent of microcomputers and the large number of non-computer professionals using them, the notion of user friendliness has become important. One possibility, natural language interfaces, will be discussed in Section 9.5. Many (microcomputer) database systems provide user friendliness by giving menus and prompts. A **menu** *is a list of items from which the user can choose one by a keystroke.* A sample menu is shown in part (a) of Figure 6.5.1. Here, pressing the F key stands for choosing the FIND command. At this point, the user may get another menu, or perhaps a prompt. Menu items may also be presented by num-

FIGURE 6.5.1
Menus and Prompts

(a) Using the first letter of a command in a menu

```
H(ELP) F(IND) I(NSERT) D(ELETE) M(ODIFY) T(ABLE) Q(UIT)

                    Enter Command:
```

(b) Using numbers in a menu

```
                    1. HELP
                    2. FIND
                    3. INSERT
                    4. DELETE
                    5. MODIFY
                    6. TABLE
                    7. QUIT

                 Enter Command Code:
```

(c) Some prompts

```
    Tablename: employee

    SSNO:   111111111
    DNAME:
    ENAME:
    SALARY:

    111111111
    Smith J
    Sales
    22500
```

bering them, in which case the appropriate number must be entered, as shown in part (b). Sometimes the cursor must be moved to the chosen item and a key pressed. Instructions on the screen explain what needs to be done. Some systems feature pictures, called *icons,* for the menu items, and selection is made by a device called a *mouse.*

A **prompt** is *a question for the user.* In Figure 6.5.1(c), we give an example of several prompts. The user's response is shown in boldface. For the first prompt, after the user presses F for FIND, the database system requests the name of the table. After the user names the table, the database system prompts with the attributes, so that the user can indicate values for them. In this case, after the user types in the SSNO value 111-11-1111, the row with that value is found and displayed. All of these operations can be done without menus or prompts, but such helpful features make using a database system easy for novice or infrequent users—who thus do not have to look up or memorize the syntax of a language. However, menus and prompts may restrict users to performing only simple tasks.

Many different types of errors may occur when a database system is used, including compile time errors, execution time errors, and errors internal to the database or operating system. Different systems handle errors differently. Some merely give an error number and a name; others also give a message to indicate what may have gone wrong. Some propose solutions as part of the message. In the case of a spelling error, many systems require only the retyping of the misspelled word, rather than the whole statement. Some systems also provide tutorials and portions of the reference manual interactively to users.

Since users of databases often need written reports, many database systems provide report writing facilities. Usually a default report form is available which the user can then change in many ways. Report descriptions can be saved as files, and then modified if necessary. Database systems differ on how formats for reports can be generated: in some cases the user is prompted, while in others a file of formatting commands must be written. Figure 6.5.2(a) shows the printing of the EMPLOYEE table of Figure 4.1.1(b). The default format specifies the column headings, the width of each item, and the spaces between columns. In this case, it is assumed that the width of the columns are 9, 15, 12, and 9 spaces, respectively, with 3 spaces between columns, yielding a report width of 54 spaces total.

Consider the kinds of changes we may want to make to such a report. We may wish to suppress some columns (this suppression can also be done by a projection in the data manipulation statement). We may wish to change the width of a column, the order of the columns, or the number of spaces between columns. Often we wish to have page headings or page footers, such as page numbers. Many reports have titles that should be printed near the top of the first page, centered. We may prefer double spacing to single spacing. It is often useful to display sums not

FIGURE 6.5.2
Report Formats

(a) Default

```
SSNO            ENAME              DNAME               SALARY
---------       -----------------  --------------      ---------
111111111       Smith  J           Sales               22500
222333444       Jones  B           Sales               24750
667788990       Turner W           Sales               25005
555555555       Ford L             Delivery            21004
234567890       Cramer T           DP                  27790
```

(b) Specialized

```
        1986 Salary for Employees by Department
        ----------------------------------------
    DNAME                ENAME                  SALARY
    ------------         -----------------      -----------
    Delivery             Ford L                    $21,004
                                                   -----------
                         Total for Delivery        $21,004

    DP                   Cramer T                  $27,790
                                                   -----------
                         Total for DP              $27,790

    Sales                Jones  B                  $24,750
                         Smith  J                  $22,500
                         Turner  W                 $25,005
                                                   -----------
                         Total for Sales           $72,255


                                                   -----------
                         Total                    $121,049

                              -1-
```

just at the end but at various places in a report. Also, we may not want
consecutive duplicate values to be printed in a column.

The report shown in part (a) of Figure 6.5.2 is reprinted using
different format options in part (b). In particular, we omit the SSNO
column, reorder the ENAME and DNAME columns, and change the
number of spaces between them. We also sort the table on DNAME and
on ENAME within DNAME (this may have to be done outside of the
report writer in the database program). We also put in salary totals and
subtotals beginning with $, insert commas to indicate thousands, and
omit consecutive duplicate values for DNAME. Additionally, we now have
an underlined report title and a page number.

Several observations about reports are relevant here. Since reports
are often long, users may be allowed to specify page breaks. Most report

writers allow users to obtain reports which consist of certain summary information. Printing can also be set up to coincide with the format of a preprinted form. Many reports, like the one in Figure 6.5.2(b), look hierarchic. In fact, we will see in Section 10.1 (on the database logic representation of hierarchic views) that our report looks more like the representation of a hierarchic database view than of a relational database view. The formatting commands make it possible to represent a relational database in this manner. But it may have been more natural to create and then format a hierarchic view, if the database system would allow it.

Some database systems allow the user to set up a graphic representation of data in addition to written reports. The different types of graphs include bar charts, pie charts, line charts, and scatter diagrams. An example of each appears in Figure 6.5.3. The user supplies the title and legend

FIGURE 6.5.3
Types of Graphs

(a) Bar chart

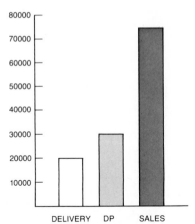

(b) Pie chart

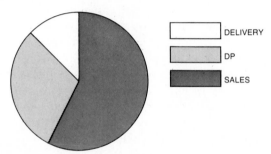

(continued)

FIGURE 6.5.3 *(continued)*

(c) Line chart

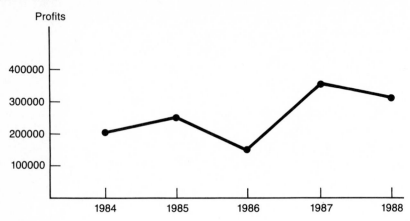

(d) Scatter diagram

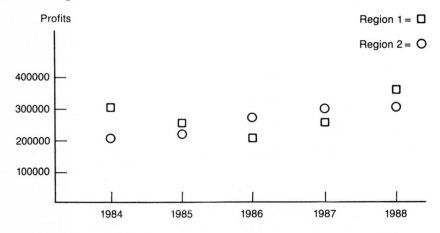

for the graph. Usually, both the type of the graph and the columns to be graphed must be specified by the user. Of course, only numerical values can be graphed. In a **bar chart** the ratio of values is represented by the height of the bars. A **pie chart** shows the ratios as sectors of a circle. A **line chart** is used for plotting values on a graph where the values are connected, such as for the fluctuation of profits from year to year. In a **scatter diagram** the points are not connected.

We end this section by making a distinction between direct and indirect users of database systems. **Direct users** *interact directly with the database system.* **Indirect users** *interact with the database system through programs written for them.* Such indirect users may be managers, clerks, or salespeople, for instance, who need to interact with a database in a spe-

FIGURE 6.5.4
A Form

```
Social Security Number:
Last Name:              First Name:              Initial:
Street Address:
City:                   State:          Zip:
Phone:(   )
Birthdate:   /  /
Date of Employment:   /  /
Yearly Salary:$
```

cialized way. Direct users can write programs for themselves and become indirect users also. It is common to give menus and prompts to indirect users. Many database systems have features enabling the programmer (direct user) to set up the screen for the indirect users in a specific manner. The screen may then look like a form which merely has to be filled in. An example of such a form is given in Figure 6.5.4. Database systems may have additional statements to facilitate the writing of such application programs.

6.6 Exercises

6.1 Write SQL statements for the following authorizations:
   (a) Allow Smith to insert into and to delete from the LIBRARY table.
   (b) Same as item (a), but also allow Smith to grant privileges on this table.
   (c) Allow everyone to read and insert into the LIBRARY table.
   (d) Allow Moore to update the DUEDATE attribute in the LIBRARY table.
   (e) Revoke the privilege of Smith to delete from the LIBRARY table.
   (f) Revoke all privileges from Evans concerning the LIBRARY table.

6.2 Write the SQL statements that the user Smith would write to the data dictionary for the following:
   (a) List the names of all tables created by Smith.
   (b) For the LIBRARY table that Smith has created, print the name and width of every attribute (column) whose data type is a character string.
   (c) List the name and text of each view created by Smith.
   (d) List the creator and name of every view on which Smith is granted a privilege.
   (e) List the privileges granted to Smith on the VOLUNTEER table.

6.3   Write the SQL statements that the DBA would write to the data dictionary for the following:

(a) List the name and type of each table (or view) created by Smith.
(b) List the creator and name of each view in the database.
(c) List the name of each user with DBA authority.
(d) List the name and password of each user with RESOURCE authority.

6.4   An operation "f" is called *idempotent* if f(f(x)) = f(x). Why must the undo and redo operations used in database recovery be idempotent?

6.5   Give an example of a deadlock with the minimum number of transactions and objects.

6.6   Give an example of three transactions, all of whose schedules are serializable.

6.7   (a) Consider the transactions in Figure 6.6.1(a). Assume that initially A = 5, B = 10, and C = 20. Find three serializable schedules and three nonserializable schedules. Indicate for each the final values of the variables.
(b) Same as item (a) for the transactions in Figure 6.6.1(b).
(c) Same as item (a) for the transactions in Figure 6.6.1(c).

FIGURE 6.6.1
Concurrent Transactions

(a) T_1

```
READ(A)
A := A + 2
READ(B)
B := B + 1
READ(C)
C := C + 3
```

T_2

```
READ(B)
B := B * 2
READ(A)
A := A * 5
```

(b) T_1

```
READ(A)
A := A + 2
READ(B)
B := B + 1
READ(C)
C := C * 2
```

T_2

```
READ(C)
C := C - 1
READ(B)
B := 5
```

(c) T_1

```
READ(A)
A := A + 2
READ(B)
B := B - 1
```

T_2

```
READ(B)
B := B * 5
READ(C)
C := C - 1
```

T_3

```
READ(C)
C := C * 2
```

6.8 Revise the schedules obtained in items (a) through (c) of Exercise 6.7 by adding locking. For each schedule, try to apply each of the following locking principles:

(i) The two-phase lock protocol.

(ii) Each transaction requests all its locks at once.

(iii) Locks must be requested on the objects A,B,C in that order.

6.9 For each schedule obtained in answer to Exercise 6.7, show what happens if the timestamping method is used. Indicate the read time and the update time for each object at all times.

6.10 For the salaries given in the EMPLOYEE table of Figure 4.3.2(b), draw a bar chart and a pie chart for total salary per department.

6.7 Guide to Further Reading

[1.1] covers security, concurrency, recovery, and utilities in Chapter 13, and data dictionaries in Chapter 14. [1.2] deals with the topics of this chapter in Chapters 18–20. [1.3] covers recovery in Chapter 1, concurrency in Chapter 3, and security in Chapter 4—all in more detail than [1.2]. [1.4] covers security in Chapter 10 and concurrency and recovery in Chapter 13. [5.2] is a comprehensive survey for security and integrity, which also deals with concurrency and recovery in Chapter 8. [4.2] deals with the topics of this chapter for the implementation of DB2. [6.1] is a comprehensive survey of concurrency and recovery techniques. [6.2] is the reference guide to ORACLE; in particular, it contains a complete list of the tables for the ORACLE Data Dictionary.

[6.1] Bernstein, P. A., N. Goodman, and V. Hadzilacos. *Concurrency Control and Recovery in Database Systems.* Reading, Mass.: Addison-Wesley, 1986.

[6.2] *ORACLE Terminal User Guide.* Menlo Park, Calif.: ORACLE Corporation, 1983.

Database Implementation

7.1 Physical Representation

In this book, we have dealt almost exclusively with what is often called the logical aspects of databases. The word "logical" is often used in the database literature as the opposite of "physical." In that sense, physical representation refers to the way that the database is stored in hardware, while logical representation refers to the way that we conceptualize the database. In the three-level database architecture of Section 1.2, the internal level deals with the physical aspects, while the conceptual and external levels deal with the logical aspects. This section discusses some characteristics of physical representation.

Recall from Section 1.5 that there are three major file access methods usually provided by operating systems: sequential, indexed sequential, and random. These basic structures are usually adequate for file management. However, because of the interrelationships between files, database systems tend to construct and use higher-level file organizations, such as linked lists and trees. We mentioned such structures briefly for network and hierarchic databases, where the logical organization tends to be closely paralleled in the physical organization. We assume that secondary storage must be used for the files in the database. Note, however, that as more memory becomes available at lower prices, it is now also reasonable to consider databases that can be brought *completely* into memory for processing.

Pointers, important in the higher-level file organizations, are discussed first. **Pointers** are used to find records; they represent the addresses of records. We distinguish among three methods for representing pointers: absolute address, relative address, and symbolic pointer (address). **Absolute address** refers to the actual physical address of a record. For a database stored on disks, for example, this may involve a volume number, cylinder number, track number, and record number. Using an absolute address pointer is certainly a fast way of getting to a record. The problem with this method is that if we want to move a record, because of an update, or for database reorganization, all the pointers to the record must be updated.

The **relative address** method is a popular one for database systems. One case is where the records of the database are numbered in some way, and the pointer is simply the number for a record. In many other systems, secondary storage is organized in the form of virtual memory with the unit of I/O (input/output) transfer being a page; that is, a whole page is fetched from and placed into secondary storage at a time. In this latter case, the database consists of certain pages of secondary storage, but all we need to use for a pointer is a relative page number and the position of the record on the page. In both cases, the file system does the translation between the relative address and the absolute address. The advantage of this method is that we can move records in secondary storage, and as long as the relative addresses are not changed, the pointers remain the same. In the case of paging, because a whole page is brought into memory at one time anyway, it may be sufficient to use only a single relative page number, as long as there is some way to identify the record once its page is in memory.

The last method uses **symbolic pointers.** In this method, records are identified not by an address but by some unique item. For example, a key value might identify a record in a file. In any case, there must be a method to convert a symbolic pointer to an actual address. This may be done by some hashing scheme or table lookup. (Recall that hashing is a technique whereby a randomizing function is applied to a value in order to obtain a location for it or to find its location.) Note that in this method, extra lookups or calculations (or both) must be made to find a record even after its symbolic address is known. Also, symbolic pointers sometimes take up more space than absolute or relative addresses. The advantage of symbolic pointers is that they provide independence from the actual locations of the records. We indicate the three methods of pointer representation and the trade-offs in Figure 7.1.1.

FIGURE 7.1.1
Pointer Representation

Absolute address	Immediate retrieval, great difficulty in moving records.
Relative address	Fast retrieval by system, less difficulty in moving records.
Symbolic pointer	Slower retrieval, complete flexibility in moving records.

For database systems oriented to ad-hoc queries to be practical, it is important to have fast access to records based on various criteria. Consider, for instance, a relatively simple query like the SQL query of Figure 4.3.4(c). One way to answer this query is to get all the records in the EMPLOYEE file and display those records for which the salary is greater than $25,000. If the EMPLOYEE file is large, this may take a long time. It would certainly be preferable if we could just get the records of those employees whose salary is greater than $25,000 in the first place. This ability is particularly important when the ratio of the number of target records to the total number of records is small.

An important technique used in database systems is **indexing;** its purpose is to locate particular records fast. We will now look at various aspects of this technique. Most operating systems provide indexed sequential files as a standard access method. We start there. In a **sequential file,** the *records are ordered sequentially on the key values.* For a large sequential file, however, it is time-consuming to find a particular record for a given key value. An **indexed sequential file** *has an additional index on the key values.* This notion is illustrated in Figure 7.1.2. There are two files, the data file and the index file. It is assumed that the data resides on twenty pages and so only the key value, which is a three-digit integer here, is indicated for each record. The index file contains both the largest key value (another method is to hold the smallest key value) for each page and the pointer (which we take to be a relative address), the page number.

Without the index file, if we search for a record with a particular key value, the number of page accesses would be about half the number of pages, ten in this case. But with the addition of the index file, there is only one page access, assuming that the index file is in memory. Suppose that we are given the key value 750. By searching the index file, we find the first key value that is at least 750, namely 764, on page 19. Hence the record must be there too. Even if the index file is not in memory, bringing it into memory, in this case, involves only one additional page access. Because the number of page accesses is closely related to the amount of time required to process a query, there is a substantial savings in time for an indexed sequential file as compared to a sequential file.

In many cases, queries refer to non-key attributes. In particular, for the EMPLOYEE file that we considered above, SSNO is the key, but the query refers to SALARY. Thus, an index on SSNO is not useful in answering the query—only an index on SALARY would be of help. But note that if the file is ordered on SSNO, we cannot assume that the records of employees whose salary is greater than some value starts at a particular address. Chances are that these values are scattered over the database. What is the solution? To help in the search, we can set up an index for SALARY. Note that a complete index file for SALARY must contain the addresses for all of the records and not just for some. Such

FIGURE 7.1.2
Indexed-Sequential File

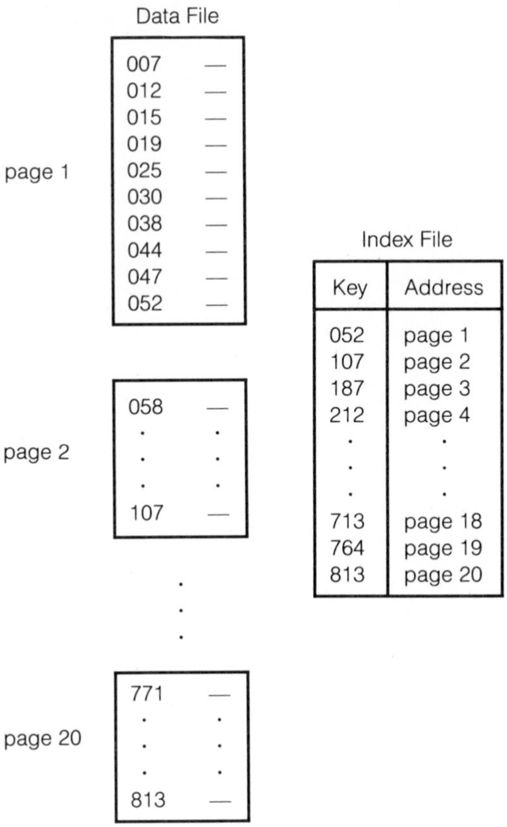

Data File

an index file has the form given in Figure 7.1.3. Dashes indicate each address. Two versions are shown: in part (a), each individual salary value is listed along with the address(es) of the record(s) with that salary value; in part (b), each salary entry indicates a range of salaries. Either index would help speed the answer to the query.

Now we can distinguish among different types of indexings. One distinction concerns the attribute on which the indexing is performed. A **primary index** *is an index on a key attribute* such as SSNO for the EMPLOYEE file, while a **secondary index** *is an index on a non-key attribute,* such as the one above on SALARY. Another distinction concerns the density of the index. A **dense index** is one that *contains an entry for each record,* such as the one for SALARY, while a **nondense index** *contains entries for only some of the records,* as in the main index for an indexed-

FIGURE 7.1.3
Indexing on Secondary Attributes

(a) Using individual values for the
attributes

(b) Using a range of values for an
attribute

Index File

Salary	Address
14528	—
	—
15615	—
15875	—
16110	—
16287	—
16715	—
16975	—
17008	—
.	.
.	.
.	.

Index File

Salary Range	Address
14000–14999	—
	—
15000–15999	—
	—
16000–16999	—
	—
	—
17000–17999	—
.	.
.	.
.	.

(c) Inverted organization

Index 1

Attribute 1	Address in data file
value 1	—
	—
	—
value 2	—
.	.
.	.
.	.

· · ·

Index *n*

Attribute *n*	Address in data file
value 1	—
	—
value 2	—
.	.
.	.
.	.

Data file

Key attribute only
key value 1
key value 2
.
.
.

sequential file. Thus, our examples so far consisted of a nondense primary index and a dense secondary index.

A dense primary index may be useful if there are several keys and if the orderings of the different keys are not the same. For example, the social security number, SSNO, may be one key, and a separate employee number, ENO, may be another key. If there is a nondense primary index based on SSNO, we may also want to have a dense primary index on ENO. A nondense secondary index may be useful if certain values often appear in queries. For example, we may have such an index on AGE values strictly for AGE > 60, if we expect to have queries involving such a condition.

Secondary indexes can substantially reduce the search time. Suppose that for an EMPLOYEE file we have indexes both on the attribute AGE and on the attribute SALARY, and a query involves employees within a certain age and salary range. Then we can obtain the addresses of the EMPLOYEE records for the AGE range, and intersect them with the addresses of the EMPLOYEE records for the SALARY range, to get the needed addresses within the index files, *before* going to the actual data files.

Suppose that we wish to have a dense index on every attribute. If we keep the original data file, then every single data value for every attribute is repeated in the index file. If the file is large, a lot of storage is used up this way. An alternative is the **inverted organization.** In this scheme, *the data file is abbreviated so that each record contains only the key value.* This file organization is illustrated in Figure 7.1.3(c). In fact, if symbolic pointers are used, then the data file is not needed at all. In any case, the inverted organization provides fast access to the key values for given attribute values, but it may take a long time to recreate the original records.

A disadvantage of the index representation that we have been using is that there may be many pointers in the index file associated with a single attribute value. There is another way of representing an index file where only one pointer is associated with one attribute value. The idea is to set up a linked list within the data file. Figure 7.1.4 illustrates this approach for the example of Figure 7.1.3(b). Each record contains an extra pointer for the index, which contains the address of the next record within its list or a null pointer. In general, there may be indexes on several attributes, in which case each record has several pointers and is located on several lists. Such a representation is called a **multilist organization.**

Indexing is commonly used in database systems for fast access. However, there are some drawbacks to the use of indexes. For one thing, they take up storage space. Also, updates are more complicated in the presence of indexes. Not only must a record be updated in the file, but updates also must be made for the indexes. For the multilist organization, this involves updating the *links* for the record under consideration. In all other cases, and sometimes even in the multilist organization case, the appropriate updates must be made to the index file. Because of the expense in time and storage of keeping indexes, many database systems require the user to request indexes. This way a user may place indexes on those attributes for which selection often occurs in queries, but not on those attributes which appear less frequently.

The indexing that we have considered so far is called **single-level indexing.** When the index file is large, it may be convenient to construct an index file for the index file. This type of construction, which can go on for several levels, is called **multilevel indexing.** A common way of

FIGURE 7.1.4
Multilist Organization

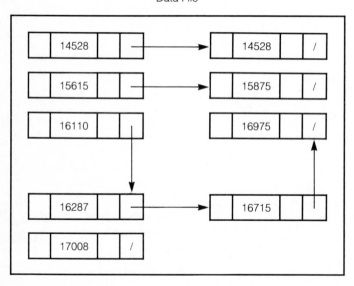

Index File

Salary Range	Address
14000–14999	—
15000–15999	—
16000–16999	—
17000–17999	—
⋮	⋮

Data File

doing this is by using a B-tree or some variant of a B-tree, such as a
B+-tree. Each **B-tree** has an order, m, which refers to the maximum
number of children that a node may have. Thus, the minimum number
of children is ceil($m/2$), where ceil(n) is the smallest integer greater than
or equal to n; that is, ceil(n) rounds a number up to the next integer—
except for the root and the leaf nodes. A B-tree is balanced in the sense
that all leaf nodes appear at the same level. A node with k children
contains $k - 1$ values.

Let's see how these rules apply to the B-tree, drawn horizontally, in
Figure 7.1.5. Each thin arrow is a pointer to a child node. In this case
we use numerical values for the indexed attribute. There are three levels.

FIGURE 7.1.5
B-Tree

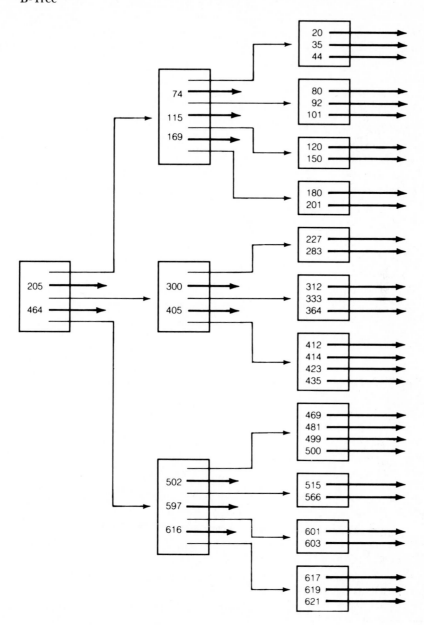

This B-tree is of order five, so that every node contains between two and four key values. We may think of each node as containing some unit (like a page or block) of storage. Each value is followed by a thick arrow which indicates the locations of all the records with that value for the indexed attribute. A B-tree is searched by starting at the root and looking for the requested value. If it is found, then we get the address of the record (or records) and we are through. Otherwise, we follow a (thin) pointer to another index block. For example, suppose that we want to look up the records with the value 423. Since 423 is between 205 and 464, we follow the arrow between 205 and 464. In the next block, since 423 is bigger than the largest value, 405, we follow the arrow after 405. The value 423 is found in this block.

Now we briefly discuss insertion and deletion for B-trees. Consider insertion first. We start by searching for the given attribute value. If this value is found in the B-tree, then a pointer to the new record must be included with the other pointers pointing to records with the same attribute value. Otherwise, the search leads to a leaf node. If this node has fewer than $m - 1$ values, then the new value is added to it. If the node already has $m - 1$ values, then it splits into two nodes and the median value is inserted in a similar way into the parent node. Insertion may propagate up to the root; when the root has $m - 1$ values already, it splits and the level of the B-tree is increased by one.

Now we consider deletion. If the value to be deleted has more than one record associated with it, then the pointer is simply deleted from the pointer list associated with that value. Otherwise, if the value to be deleted is not in a leaf node, then it is replaced by its immediate successor in the ordering; that value must be in a leaf node. This reduces deletion to deletion from a leaf node. A problem occurs when a value is deleted from a leaf node that has ceil($m/2$) $- 1$ values in it. In that case, either a value is moved from an adjacent node to the parent node and a value is moved down from the parent node, or two adjacent nodes are combined into one. This process may also propagate up to the root, and if the root has only one element, then it is removed, and the level of the B-tree is decreased by one.

One popular variant of a B-tree is a B+-tree. The difference between the two versions is that in a B + -tree, all the values appear at leaf nodes, and adjacent leaf nodes are connected by pointers. This leads to some redundancy as some values appear in more than one node. Also, for each search the B + -tree must be traversed to a leaf node, since the locations of the records with a specific value are indicated only at leaf nodes. A B + -tree is a convenient structure if a sequential traversal of the records based on the indexed attribute is required.

As mentioned before, data files may be large, and even indexes can take up a lot of storage. The term **data compression** refers to various techniques for *storing only portions of data values in order to reduce storage* *space.* Data compression is often used with indexing. The reason is that two consecutive index values are often almost identical. So, rather than writing out all of the index values, it is possible just to indicate the differences between them. Both the front and the rear of the index values can be compressed. An example of front compression appears in Figure 7.1.6. Part (a) indicates the original list of numbers, and part (b) shows the compressed list. The number n to the left of the dash indicates that the first n digits of this value are identical to those digits for the previous value.

We end this section by discussing a few more topics related to indexing. So far we have assumed that the indexes are constructed on single attributes. However, in some cases it is worthwhile to have a **multi-attribute index,** which *is an index on a combination of attributes.* For example, if we have information on a list of people that contains zip code and salary, and if many queries use those two attributes, then we may want to set up a combined index on zip code and salary. For a multi-attribute index we form tuples of index values, so that for, say, a two-attribute index for attributes A and B, $<a_1, b_1>$ precedes $<a_2, b_2>$ if a_1 precedes a_2, or if $a_1 = a_2$, and b_1 precedes b_2 in the ordering of attribute values for A and B, respectively.

Consider an index file like the one in Figure 7.1.3(b). If we are looking for employees whose salary range is \$16,000–\$16,999, we obtain four addresses. It would be nice if these four records were on the same page, because that would reduce the search time. Unfortunately, in general, the closeness of addresses in an index file does not guarantee the closeness of the corresponding records in the data file. However, it is always possible to achieve this goal for one index by placing the elements in order based on the index. Such an index is called a **clustering index;** it speeds up the search, particularly if much of the file must be traversed in an order based on the index values.

SQL-based systems, like DB2 and ORACLE, allow the user to create various types of indexes. Figure 7.1.7 gives the syntax rules for SQL

FIGURE 7.1.6
Data Compression

(a) Original list of numbers   (b) Compressed list

(a) Original list of numbers	(b) Compressed list
11257	0-11257
11259	4-9
11262	3-62
11264	4-4
11269	4-9
11272	3-72
11301	2-301

FIGURE 7.1.7
Syntax Rules for SQL Statements for Indexes and Clusters

Note: Additional syntax rules for SQL are presented in Figures 4.3.1, 4.5.1, 4.5.3, 4.5.5, and 6.1.5.

<create index statement>	:: =	CREATE [UNIQUE] INDEX <index name> ON <table name> [(<insert column list>)] ;
<drop index statement>	:: =	DROP INDEX <index name> ;
<create cluster statement>	:: =	CREATE CLUSTER <cluster name> (<column name> <data type> [{ , <column name> <data type> } . . .]) ;
<alter cluster statement>	:: =	ALTER CLUSTER <cluster name> ADD TABLE <table name> WHERE [<cluster name> .] <clusterkey column name> = [<table name> .] <column name> [{ AND [<cluster name> .] <clusterkey column name> = [<table name> .] <column name> } . . .] ;
<drop cluster statement>	:: =	DROP CLUSTER <cluster name> ;

statements involving indexes and clusters. Multi-attribute indexes are allowed; they are implemented in the form of a B-tree. One index may be a clustering index. An example of the creation of an index on a table in the database of Figure 4.3.2 appears in part (a) of Figure 7.1.8. A unique index signifies a key, as shown in part (b). (Recall from Section 5.3 that, in present SQL implementations, this is the only way to specify a key.) We remove the first index in part (c).

In our discussion of physical representation, we have stressed representations for individual files. However, databases may involve many files and links between them. As mentioned in Chapters 2 and 3, network and hierarchic databases suggest a certain link structure between files. For example, in a network database we can get to a record of a file which represents a child node by following a pointer from a record of the parent file.

In relational databases, we use the join operation to obtain connected information from several files (tables). A technique for speeding up the computation of the join is called **join support.** This *involves a simultaneous indexing on two tables.* For example, let $T_1(A,B,C)$ and $T_2(C,D)$ be two tables, with the common attribute C, which are often joined. The join support is a double indexing on elements c for the attribute C, with one set being the addresses of all records in T_1 with third value c, and the other set being the addresses of all records of T_2 with first value c. It is particularly helpful if the indexing is clustered between the two

FIGURE 7.1.8
Creating and Removing Indexes for the Database of Figure 4.3.2

(a) Create an index for DNAME on EMPLOYEE.

```
CREATE  INDEX DEPTINDEX  ON EMPLOYEE (DNAME);
```

(b) Create a unique index for SSNO on EMPLOYEE.

```
CREATE  UNIQUE INDEX  SSINDEX ON EMPLOYEE (SSNO);
```

(c) Remove the index created in part (a).

```
DROP  INDEX DEPTINDEX;
```

FIGURE 7.1.9
Creating and Removing a Cluster for the Database of Figure 4.3.2

(a) Create a cluster on DNAME for EMPLOYEE and DEPARTMENT.

```
CREATE  CLUSTER  DEPTCLUSTER (DNAME CHAR(15));
ALTER   CLUSTER DEPTCLUSTER
        ADD  TABLE  DEPARTMENT
        WHERE  DEPTCLUSTER.DNAME = DEPARTMENT.DNAME;
ALTER   CLUSTER DEPTCLUSTER
        ADD  TABLE  EMPLOYEE
        WHERE  DEPTCLUSTER.DNAME = EMPLOYEE.DNAME
```

(b) Remove the cluster created in part (a).

```
DROP  CLUSTER DEPTCLUSTER;
```

tables, so that *rows from the two tables which are equal in the join attribute are close together;* this is a **clustering join support.** ORACLE allows the user to create a CLUSTER, which can be used in such a way for any number of tables on a common attribute. Part (a) of Figure 7.1.9 illustrates the creation of a clustering join support between EMPLOYEE and DEPARTMENT on DNAME. First the cluster is created, and then it is modified to add the appropriate tables. Then, in part (b), the cluster is removed.

7.2 Query Optimization

Ever since the first database systems were implemented, efficiency has been a very important consideration. The low-level database languages for hierarchic and network database systems allow database users to make their programs efficient by database navigation. But for relational database systems, users have high-level database languages at their disposal; these make it more difficult to write efficient programs. Also, if we wish to make databases easy to use, then we do not even want users to have to concern themselves with efficiency. For this reason, a great deal of research has been devoted to the optimization of queries for relational databases. The term **optimization** refers to *the finding of an efficient method for executing the query;* the method obtained by optimization need not be the best one.

The general process of answering a query is shown in Figure 7.2.1. A query input to the system is usually checked for correct syntax and transformed to some internal representation by the **parser.** The **optimizer** constructs an efficient execution plan for the query. This plan is then executed, and the result is sent to the user. Note that there may be a question about what to optimize. Usually we wish to minimize the amount of time it takes to execute the query, but the amount of intermediate storage used may be another consideration. Note also that running the optimizer also takes time. Clearly, we would like the amount of time saved by the optimizer to be more than the amount of time taken up by running the optimizer.

Optimizers usually work in one of two ways. First, an optimizer may develop an execution plan for a query based on certain built-in rules. Generally, these rules manipulate the order of execution of various tasks to obtain a good solution. This method produces a single execution plan.

FIGURE 7.2.1
Steps in Answering a Query

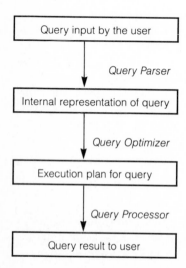

Another possibility is for the optimizer to generate many different solutions and then to choose the best one among them. To do so, it needs to use formulas to calculate the time taken by the various operations. We now take a look at how this may be done. It is implicitly assumed that every execution plan considered yields the same correct solution to the query.

The second type of optimizer needs to be able to estimate the amount of time spent on executing various primitive operations. There are two aspects, CPU time and I/O time. Much of the CPU time is spent on comparisons and on constructing rows for intermediate tables. The I/O time is taken up by moving storage blocks, which we take to be pages, between external and internal memory. When there is a lot of page swapping, I/O time is the dominant factor because the internal operations are executed much faster than page fetching. However, many database systems perform I/O processing efficiently; for them, CPU time is the dominant factor.

In this section, we develop formulas for some basic database operations in terms of various parameters. Consider some typical parameters as shown in Figure 7.2.2. The optimizer must be able to substitute specific values for these parameters to calculate the estimated times. Values needed include the number of rows and the number of pages for each table and the size of an element for each attribute of a table. The database system should keep this kind of information. For example, the optimizer can get size(A) and $n(A)$ for each attribute A from the type declarations. We assume that the components of the rows of a table are kept together; in other words, this is not the inverted organization. The indexing hierarchy for an attribute refers to the number of levels of indexing.

FIGURE 7.2.2
Parameters for the Optimizer

Note: We round all fractional values up in the computations. T is an arbitrary table and A is an arbitrary attribute.

$n(T)$ = the number of elements (rows) of T
$p(T)$ = the number of pages occupied by T
size(A) = the space (number of bytes) for each element of A
$n(A)$ = the number of different values for the type of A
comp(A) = the time to compare a value in A to another value in A
max(A) = the maximum possible value for the type of A
min(A) = the minimum possible value for the type of A
$h(A)$ = the indexing hierarchy of A
$i(A)$ = the space (number of bytes) for an index for A
page = the time to read or write a page
construct = the time to construct a new (projected) row
p = the space (number of bytes) per page

Now we find out how to estimate the time required for executing representative operations of the relational algebra. Then, if we have a query written in the relational algebra (or in another language that is transformed into a relational algebra query), we can estimate the time required to execute it. Since there may be many possible ways of executing such a program, we get many different time estimates. For these estimates, we assume that the intermediate tables are actually constructed and written out in external memory.

Let's start with the operations projection and selection on a single table T(A,B,C). Consider first the time estimate for projection, as given in Figure 7.2.3(a). The portion of the formula multiplied by page refers to I/O time. We need to read $p(T)$ pages into memory, and when we are through, the new table, whose size in pages we estimate by using the proportionality factor [size(A)]/[size(A) + size(B) + size(C)], is written out into storage. The CPU time is estimated by considering the time it takes to project one row at a time. Note that this formula represents only the time estimate for projection without duplicate elimination.

FIGURE 7.2.3
Time Estimation Formulas for Projection and Selection

(a) Time estimate for a projection

estimated time(PROJECT(T;A)) =
    {p(T) + p(T)*[size(A)/[size(A) + size(B) + size(C)]]} * page
    + construct * n(T)

(b) Time estimate for a selection with equality

estimated time(SELECT(T: A = c)) =
    {p(T) + p(T)*[1/n(A)]} * page + comp(A) * n(T)

(c) Time estimate for a selection with an inequality

estimated time(SELECT(T: A > c)) =
    {p(T) + p(T)*[[max(A) − c]/[max(A) − min(A)]]} * page + comp(A) * n(T)

(d) Time estimate for a selection using a clustering index

estimated time(SELECT(T: A = c)) =
    {h(A) + [i(A)*n(T)]/[p*n(A)] + p(T)/n(A) + p(T)/n(A)} * page
    + comp(A) * [n(T)/n(A)]

(e) Time estimate for a selection using a nonclustering index

estimated time(SELECT(T: A = c)) =
    {h(A) + [i(A)*n(T)]/[p*n(A)] + n(T)/n(A) + p(T)/n(A)} * page
    + comp(A) * [n(T)/n(A)]

Next we consider selection. With selection, we also need to estimate the number of rows that are retrieved. We do this here by assuming a uniform distribution of all the elements in the domain for the type of the attribute, although this may not always be a reasonable assumption. For example, if the attribute is AGE for an EMPLOYEE table, and the type is Integer, then the value 25 is much more likely to occur than the value 15. (Such errors can be compounded in later estimates as we use previously estimated values to continue with the operations.) The formula for computing the time estimate for an equality selection appears in Figure 7.2.3(b). We assume that each value for the attribute A occurs $1/n(A)$ times. Similarly, the formula for the time estimate for an inequality selection appears in Figure 7.2.3(c). We figure the ratio of selected elements as $[\max(A) - c]/[\max(A) - \min(A)]$.

In the previous section, we saw how indexing may help speed up the evaluation of queries. We assume now the presence of a clustering index, and obtain the estimated time for the selection of Figure 7.2.3(b) in Figure 7.2.3(d). First we read $h(A)$ pages, one for each level of the index. We estimate the number of index pages as $[i(A) * n(T)]/[p * n(A)]$. We estimate the number of data pages read as $p(T)/n(A)$, which is also the number of pages written. For the CPU time we consider a comparison for each element brought into memory. If the index is nonclustering, then the formula must be modified as we show in Figure 7.2.3(e). We replace the term $p(T)/n(A)$ by $n(T)/n(A)$ for the number of pages read in, as each row which satisfies the condition may be on a separate page. A sample calculation for selection is shown in Figure 7.2.4. Note that we get the best estimate by using a clustering index, but that even a non-clustering index is very helpful. However, a nonclustering index may not help much if the selection condition is an inequality.

So far we have obtained three different estimates for just one operation depending on the existence and type of indexing. But we did not

FIGURE 7.2.4
Actual Time Estimates for Selection

(a) Initial values for the parameters

p(T) = 40	n(T) = 1000		
n(A) = 100	h(A) = 2	i(A) = 8	comp(A) = 1
p = 4000	page = 50		

(b) Time estimate for the formulas of Figure 7.2.3

(b):	[41]*50 + 1000	= 3050
(d):	[5]*50 + 10	= 260
(e):	14*50 + 10	= 710

even consider the possibility of a more complex selection, such as a selection which involves more than one attribute. Consider a statement like SELECT(T: A > c & B = d), where c and d are constants. If T is indexed on both A and B, then we have several choices: use both indexings, one indexing, or no indexing. Again, we can write formulas for the different possibilities.

Next we consider those operations which involve more than one table. The most important such operation is the join, since union and difference are not used often. There are two main methods for executing the join: nested loops and merge sort. Assume the existence of two tables S(A,B,C) and T(C,D), so that the join is done on attribute C. The idea of the **nested loops method** is to read an element of one of the tables, say S, for the outer loop, and then to read each element of the other table, T in this case, for the inner loop. As each element of T is read, its C value is compared to the C value of the present element of S; if the two values are the same, then a new row is added to the join. Actually, since the elements of a table are usually concentrated on certain pages, we get many elements of the table by reading in a page of the table. We can therefore substitute a page of a table for an element of a table in the description of this method.

For the **merge sort method,** the first step is to sort the tables S and T on the join attribute. We can then merge the two tables by comparing an element from S with an element from T at a time starting at the beginning of both tables. Whenever the C values are not the same, we continue the process with the next element in the table with the smaller C value. For the rows of S and T with identical C values, we apply the nested loops method to obtain the rows for the join.

Actually, there are more than two choices for the join: for example, for the nested loops method we need to choose which table is used for the outer loop. Additionally, there may be indexings or join support available.

We write a formula for the nested loops method in Figure 7.2.5(a). First we read in $p(S)$ pages of table S, then $p(S) * p(T)$ pages of table T, as we assume that we perform the join for all elements of a page of S and a page of T at one time. The total time for the comparisons is $n(S) * n(T) * comp(C)$. A general problem for the join concerns the estimation of the number of rows in the result, which can vary from 0 to $n(S) * n(T)$. We use the formula $[n(S) * n(T)]/n(C)$ for this purpose. The join is then written out.

The merge sort method formula appears in Figure 7.2.5(b) under the assumption that all rows with identical C values are on one page both for S and T. We write separately the estimated time for sorting a table on an attribute. There are various techniques of sorting files (tables) in external storage using merging. We estimate $\log(n(S))$ passes, where each pass involves the reading and writing of the pages of S. During each pass,

FIGURE 7.2.5
Time Estimation Formulas for Join

(a) Nested loops method

estimated time(JOIN(S,T)) =
{p(S) + p(S)*p(T) + [[n(S)*n(T)]/n(C)]*
[[size(A) + size(B) + size(C) + size(D)]/p]} * page
+ n(S)*n(T)*comp(C) + construct*[[n(S)*n(T)]/n(C)]

(b) Merge sort method

estimated time(JOIN(S,T)) =
sort(S,C) + sort(T,C)
+ {p(S) + p(T) + [[n(S)*n(T)]/n(C)]*
[[size(A) + size(B) + size(C) + size(D)]/p]} * page
+ n(S)*n(T)*comp(C) + construct*[[n(S)*n(T)]/n(C)]

estimated time(sort(S,C)) =
[2*p(S)*log(n(S))]*page + log(n(S))*[n(S)/2]*comp(c)

(c) Nested loops method with join support

estimated time(JOIN(S,T)) =
{[n(C)*[size(C) + 2*i(C)]]/p + [[n(S) + n(T)]*i(C)]/p + n(S) + n(T)
+ [[n(S)*n(T)]/n(C)]*[[size(A) + size(B) + size(C) + size(D)]/p]} * page
+ construct*[[n(S)*n(T)]/n(C)]

each element of S may be compared to another element. (If the tables are already sorted, then we skip the sort.) With the merge sort method, we eliminate the term *p*(S) * *p*(T) for reading each page of T for each page of S. For large files, the merge sort method may give a better result.

We have not yet used indexing in the calculation of the formulas for the join. Actually, instead of indexing, we will use the special case of join support. The formula is given in Figure 7.2.5(c). The first term is the estimate of the number of pages of join index, as each value for C is followed by two pointers to the addresses of the elements in S and T. The second term represents the estimate for the total number of pages of the addresses. We do not assume clustering on the attribute C, so that for any value of C, the elements of S (and also of T) with that C value are effectively on different pages. This gives the term *n*(S) + *n*(T). The term for the comparisons from Figure 7.2.5(a) is no longer needed.

We have seen that indexes on attributes can be helpful in the execution of selections and joins. In our calculations, we used an index only if it already existed. However, it is possible to dynamically create an index by reading in a table. Of course, it takes time to create such an index, but even so, it may still save time in computing the answers to a query. Such an index is temporary: it is discarded at the end of the execution of the query. The advantage of such **dynamic indexing** is that it need not be maintained during updates.

It must be emphasized that all of our formulas are estimates only. Although we should be able to get precise figures for items such as the number of pages for a table, or the size of a row of a table, our estimate for the number of elements that satisfy a selection condition or that are involved in a join may be quite inaccurate in any one instance. We may try to make these estimates more accurate by keeping additional information about the database, but that involves more overhead. In any case, as we get to operations on intermediate temporary tables, our estimates will tend to differ more from the actual figures. (To get around this problem, it is possible to dynamically recompute estimates during query execution, but that involves interleaving the optimization and the execution of the query.) Nonetheless, because of the large number of possible execution plans, access path optimization is an important technique.

In our discussion of join evaluation we considered only the join of two tables. But often *more* than two tables must be joined. The ordering of joins can be significant in terms of the time that is involved. Suppose that we need to join R, S, and T. We may decide to join R and S first and then join the result to T using the nested loops method. But it is not really necessary to complete the first join before starting the second one. For as soon as we get a row for JOIN(R,S), we can start its join with T. This avoids having to write JOIN(R,S) out to secondary storage and then bring it back to memory.

In general, the order of operations has a significant effect on query evaluation time. Recall the example from Figure 4.2.6(c), where we gave two different relational algebra programs for a query. In the first case, we started with a join, followed by a selection and a projection. In the second case, we started with a selection, followed by a projection, a join, and another projection. We claimed that the second solution was more efficient. Now we want to see how we can tell if one solution is more efficient than another one.

Note first that it is preferable to perform several operations at the same time, if possible. We have already indicated how this may be useful in the case of multiple joins. Now consider the first solution in the above example. If we do one operation at a time, then after performing the join, we write it out as a temporary table and then read it back into memory to do the selection. After the selection we create another temporary table, which will have to be brought back into memory for the projection. The creation and storage of these complete intermediate tables is unnecessary. Instead, while we are doing the join, as soon as we obtain a row for the join, we can do the selection for that row as well as the projection. This way we save the time required to create the temporary tables as well as their subsequent reading into memory. By the way, it is not always possible to coalesce operations this way. In particular, if we

FIGURE 7.2.6
Coalesced Relational Algebra Programs

(a) The relevant tables with their attributes.

```
EMPLOYEE(SSNO,ENAME,DNAME,SALARY)
DEPARTMENT(DNAME,LOCATION,MANAGER)
```

(b) Print the names of all managers who have at least one employee in their department with a salary greater than $25,000.

> (*i*) PRINT JOIN-SELECT-PROJECT(EMPLOYEE,DEPARTMENT -:
>   SALARY > 25000 -; MANAGER)
> (*ii*) PRINT SELECT-PROJECT-JOIN-PROJECT(EMPLOYEE:
>   SALARY > 25000 -; DNAME -, DEPARTMENT -;
>   MANAGER)

take the join of S and T, followed by the join of S′ and T′, then there is no coalescing.

Figure 7.2.6 indicates the structure of the tables and the query, and shows the rewritten programs of Figure 4.2.6(c). When operations are hyphenated, it indicates that as they are being performed, from left to right, no temporary table is created; instead, the next operation is performed on the elements as they are obtained. (The order of the operations in Figure 4.2.6 was written from right to left without coalescing.) Then we estimate the time required for both programs in Figure 7.2.7, assuming no indexing and using the nested loops method for the join. The I/O cost is smaller for the second program, unless just about all the employees have a salary greater than $25,000. Suppose that each comp and construct has unit cost, while $n(J) = n(E) * n(D)$—that is, each EMPLOYEE row can be joined with one DEPARTMENT row. Then the CPU time for the first program is $2 * n(E) * n(D) + n(R)$, while for the second program it is $n(E) + n(S) + n(S) * n(D) + n(R)$. The I/O time estimate is also better for the second program.

We want to devise some general rules to execute a relational algebra program in the most efficient possible manner. We already stated one rule: coalesce operations whenever possible. Assuming the coalescings, we can still do better if we do selections before joins. The reason is that a join tends to take much longer than the single scan needed for a selection, and since selection reduces the size of a table, the consequent join should take less time.

So far we have been considering optimization of queries written in the relational algebra. Suppose now that a query is written in SQL. One method for the evaluation of such a query is to compile it into a relational algebra query, and then to optimize the latter. But there are also more direct methods for optimizing a query in such a language. Here we briefly consider the evaluation of nested SELECT statements by rewriting three

FIGURE 7.2.7
Effect of the Ordering of Operations in Relational Algebra Programs

(a) The parameters

p(E) = the number of pages for EMPLOYEE
p(D) = the number of pages for DEPARTMENT
p(R) = the number of pages for RESULT
p(S) = the number of pages for SELECT(EMPLOYEE: SALARY > 25000)
n(E) = the number of rows for EMPLOYEE
n(D) = the number of rows for DEPARTMENT
n(J) = the number of rows for JOIN(EMPLOYEE,DEPARTMENT)
n(R) = the number of rows for RESULT
n(S) = the number of rows for SELECT(EMPLOYEE: SALARY > 25000)
comp(DNAME) = the time to compare a DNAME value to another DNAME value
comp(SALARY) = the time to compare a SALARY value to another SALARY value
construct = the time to construct a projected row
page = the time to read/write a page

(b) Time estimate for the first program

[p(E) + p(E)*p(D) + p(R)]*page + n(E)*n(D)*comp(DNAME)
+ n(J)*comp(SALARY) + construct*n(R)

(c) Time estimate for the second program

[p(E) + p(S)*p(D) + p(R)]*page + n(E)*comp(SALARY) + construct*n(S)
+ n(S)*n(D)*comp(DNAME) + construct*n(R)

examples from Chapter 4 in Figure 7.2.8. Consider first the query in part (a). The inner SELECT statement is used to obtain a single value, MAX(SALARY), which is used in the WHERE condition of the outer SELECT statement. Because both SELECT statements refer to the same table, they can be performed simultaneously. In the query of part (b), the inner SELECT statement is used to obtain a set of DNAME values that is used in the outer SELECT statement. The inner SELECT statement should be done first here.

The situation gets more complicated in a case like part (c) of Figure 7.2.8, where the inner SELECT statement references an attribute from the outer SELECT statement. In such a case, it is not possible to perform an inner SELECT entirely before doing the outer SELECT. In general, nested queries can become quite complicated, particularly if there are many levels of nesting.

We end this section by considering some additional aspects of optimization. Suppose that some queries for a database system need not be answered immediately. Such queries can be collected for execution at some later time, perhaps when computer use is light. It may be the case that some queries require identical operations; such a situation can be

FIGURE 7.2.8
SQL Queries

```
(a) SELECT   NAME
    FROM     EMPLOYEE
    WHERE    DNAME = 'Service'
         AND SALARY = (SELECT  MAX(SALARY)
                       FROM     EMPLOYEE
                       WHERE    DNAME = 'Service');

(b) SELECT   MANAGER
    FROM     DEPARTMENT
    WHERE    DNAME  IN
                (SELECT  DNAME
                 FROM    STATUS
                 WHERE   ST = 'completed');

(c) SELECT   TASKNAME
    FROM     TASK
    WHERE    EXISTS
             (SELECT  *
              FROM    STATUS
              WHERE   STATUS.TASKNO = TASK.TASKNO
                  AND ST = 'completed');
```

optimized by performing those operations only once. Even if the operations are not identical, it may be possible to save time by doing several operations simultaneously. When a query requires a selection on a large table, we need to scan the table; this can be time-consuming. Suppose now that two queries require different selections on the same table. The table can be scanned once rather than twice, thus saving time. In this situation, we do better by optimizing on the set of queries, rather than by optimizing each query separately. We will discuss some additional aspects of query optimization for the relational calculus in Section 8.2.

7.3 Distributed Databases

So far in our presentation we have implicitly assumed that the database system is centralized. This means that the database system runs in one computer which contains all the data (in external storage). This situation is represented in Figure 7.3.1(a). In recent years, distributed systems, involving mini- and microcomputers, have gained in prominence. Distributed database systems have also been implemented. The corresponding diagram for a distributed database system appears in Figure 7.3.1(b). In this case, there are several computers connected by communication links; each computer contains the database system and its own local data-

FIGURE 7.3.1
Centralized vs. Distributed Databases

(a) Centralized database system

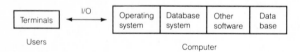

(b) Distributed database system

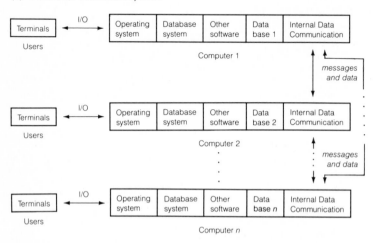

base. There are also scenarios which would fall between these two cases; for example, several computers may be connected for distributed processing where the database system or the database (or both) resides in one computer. In this section, we consider some aspects of database systems related to the situation represented by the diagram of Figure 7.3.1(b).

Let's see first why a distributed database system may be preferable to a conventional one. Many organizations have branches in different locations. Each location may have substantial local database needs, but may also require data used primarily at other locations. Communications can become a bottleneck if everyone is connected to a centralized database system. Suppose now that a distributed database system is set up with a computer at each location. This allows for the efficient processing of local data. Also, local autonomy makes it easier for users to resolve problems with the database system without depriving them of remote data. A distributed database system can also be more reliable than a centralized system: if one of the computers goes down, or one communication link fails, the rest of the system can continue functioning. Finally, it may be more economical to obtain and operate several small machines than a big one.

Sometimes it is convenient to represent a distributed database system without indicating the various software components. We then obtain a graph like the one in Figure 7.3.2. Each node in the graph represents a site in the network. Each edge represents the communication link between the two sites. It is not necessary to have a communication link between every pair of sites; in our diagram we can get from site 1 to site 3 via site 2 or site 4. The graph should be connected so that every node may communicate with every other node.

We emphasized physical and logical data independence in connection with the three-level database architecture presented in Section 1.2. In the extension of this type of independence, which is very desirable, to distributed databases, *the users should not have to know where various data items are located.* This notion is called **location** (or **distribution**) **transparency.** Because the location of the data is an aspect of its physical representation, it can be indicated in the internal view. If the database system possesses the location transparency property, then we can shift data from one location to another as needs change, without having to change programs on any external (or even the conceptual) view.

One complication in a distributed database system involves **data replication.** This refers to *the storage of some data at more than one site.* The advantage of data replication is the speed gained in processing at the sites where the duplicate data exists. However, there are also some disadvantages associated with this scheme. For one thing, such duplication of data requires the use of extra storage space. Another problem involves updates. When replicated data is updated, such updates must be performed at each participating site. In fact, the whole database is really

FIGURE 7.3.2
Graphic Representation of a Distributed Database

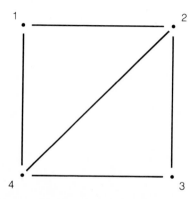

inconsistent whenever replicated data has been updated at some, but not all, sites.

This section now considers the various database components discussed in the previous chapter and briefly discusses some additional complications that occur for distributed databases. Let's start with database security. If not all the sites maintain the same level of security controls, then users at the less secure sites may have to be more restricted than other users. Like the data, the user profiles may also be distributed to the site associated with each user. In a distributed database, the data dictionary should now describe the distribution of the data at various sites. Usually, the data dictionary is itself distributed, so that each site contains a portion of it.

Transaction processing and recovery become more difficult when a database is distributed. In such a system, usually each site keeps its own log. When a transaction is processed in a distributed database, it may need to read and update data at different sites and send messages between sites. In order to commit a transaction, the system must make sure that all the relevant sites have done their processing. One site, possibly the last one in the processing, or the one where the transaction originated, can act as the coordinator, and send messages to all the participating sites. Each site must then send a message back to the coordinator. Only if processing has terminated normally at each site should the transaction be committed. Otherwise, the transaction should be rolled back at each participating site.

In a distributed system, both **site failure,** where *a site must shut down,* and **link failure,** where *communications between sites is lost,* are possibilities. A site failure is the distributed system's version of a system failure, except that here the other nodes can continue processing. That is, transactions, whose actions involve the working nodes and links, should be allowed to continue and to commit. If required data from a failed site is duplicated at an active site, then processing should switch there. However, if a transaction is running at a working site S and needs data from a failed site or from a site with a link failure to S, it may have to be rolled back. In any case, data replication among sites presents additional problems. In particular, if data is updated at one site while another site with duplicate data is down, then the same update must take place at the second site after its recovery.

A distributed system needs to be able to determine if a site or a link has failed. This is usually discovered when messages are not acknowledged. Let's consider what happens to a transaction if its coordinating site fails while it is transmitting commit messages to the participating sites. The sites that have not received a message have to communicate with the other sites. If any one site has received a commit message, then all the sites may commit the transaction.

Next we briefly discuss concurrency control for distributed database systems. This is a complex subject. When data is replicated at various sites, for example, and locking is used, there is the question of which copy (or possibly all copies) should be locked. Another problem in connection with locking is the large number of time-consuming messages that may be generated in a distributed environment. The location of the lock manager is another concern: should it be at one site only, or distributed, with a lock manager at each site? The latter approach may lead to a global deadlock, where no lock manager is aware of the deadlock. In the case of timestamping, the system must assure that the timestamp is globally unique for each transaction, and must carefully handle the read and update times of objects when several transactions access different copies of an object at different sites. Based on how these and other issues are resolved, many algorithms exist for distributed concurrency control.

This section ends with a brief discussion of the optimization of queries in a distributed database system. In such a system, if the execution of a query requires data from several sites, then there must be data transmission. Therefore, in calculating estimated times for query execution, we need to include transmission time. Usually, transmission time is expressed by the formula $Tt = St + c * s$, where Tt = transmission time, St = startup time for a transmission (including message passing), c = some constant, and s = the size of the transmitted data. Compared to operations in memory and even page fetches, data transmission tends to be very slow. Therefore, it is important to send as little data as possible, as few times as possible.

An operation that is very useful in distributed database query processing is the **semijoin.** We define it as follows:

$$\text{SEMIJOIN}(S,T) = \text{PROJECT}(\text{JOIN}(S,T) \text{ ;attributes of S}).$$

We give an example of two semijoin operations on the EMP and ELIGIBILITY tables of Figure 4.2.5(a) in Figure 7.3.3(a). Note that SEMIJOIN(S,T) is always a subtable of S.

Semijoins are useful when it is necessary to obtain the join of two tables that are at different sites. One way to do such a join is to ship one table (say the smaller one) to the site of the other table and to do the join at the second site. But the time needed to ship a table to a site may be substantial. Because the semijoin involves subtables of the original tables, if we ship the semijoins, we may be able to reduce the data transmission time substantially. Figure 7.3.3(b) shows the steps involved in performing the join of S(A,B,C) and T(C,D,E) by using a semijoin, where S is at site 1 and T is at site 2. If the time required to ship TEMP1 and TEMP2 plus the startup time is smaller than the time required to ship S, then there is less data transmission time involved using this method than by

FIGURE 7.3.3
The Semijoin Operation

(a) Semijoin examples

(*i*)

SEMIJOIN(EMP,ELIGIBILITY)		
NAME	AGE	YRSWORKED
Brown	30	3

(*ii*)

SEMIJOIN(ELIGIBILITY,EMP)	
YRSWORKED	BENEFIT
3	B

(b) Performing JOIN(S(A,B,C),T(C,D,E)) by using a semijoin

```
TEMP1 := PROJECT(T;C) (AT SITE2);
  (*C is the join attribute*)
SHIP TEMP1 TO SITE 1;
TEMP2 := JOIN(S,TEMP1) (at SITE1);
  (*TEMP2 is SEMIJOIN(S,T)*)
SHIP TEMP2 TO SITE 2;
RESULT := JOIN(TEMP2,T) (at SITE 2)
```

shipping S to site 2 and performing the join there (assuming that the join is needed at site 2).

Performing semijoins is not the only way that the amount of transmitted data can be reduced. Time can also be saved by doing all local selections and projections first. Additionally, if several copies of a table exist at different sites, it is usually advantageous to use a copy at a site where local processing must be done anyway. Query optimization for distributed databases is a very complex task.

Here is a final comment on query optimization in distributed databases. There are actually two times to consider, response time and total time. Total time refers to the total amount of time spent on processing at all the nodes and transmitting data. Response time refers to the amount of time spent on executing the query as seen by the user. These two values need not be the same because processing may be done simultaneously at different sites. However, such processing is possible at a node *only* if any needed results from other nodes have already been transmitted and received by the processing node.

7.4 Database Machines and Fifth Generation Computers

A database system can use up a lot of resources, even on a mainframe computer, and so may seriously impact other types of processing. It should also be recognized that the architecture of conventional computers is not particularly v ell suited, and in fact was not designed for, database processing. Hence, in the last ten years, a number of proposals have been made for computers specifically designed for database processing, called **database machines.** At the present time, some database machines are being marketed commercially. We may also think of a database machine as an instrument for database optimization.

This section deals with the architecture of various database machines. One idea is for a **backend computer** dedicated to database processing. We illustrate the difference between a conventional system and a system with a dedicated backend in parts (a) and (b) of Figure 7.4.1. In the backend system, the bulk of the database work takes place in the database machine, while the host computer contains some interface to the backend. Thus, the host computer is free to run other applications, without being tied up by the database system. In such a system, the user or application program deals only with the host computer, just as if there were no database machine. However, the database system interface intercepts the requests and sends them to the backend computer, which does the actual processing. The answers come back to the user through the host computer. There can also be a particularly complex configuration, as shown in Figure 7.4.1(c), where there are several host computers, of which more than one has its own database system. Now, the backend, which may be several machines, serves several hosts. It is a standard backend for some of the machines, and a part of a distributed database system for those hosts that have their own database system.

A backend computer, in the sense that we are discussing the concept, does only database processing. One hardware implementation for it is a standard minicomputer that is dedicated to database work, so that only the operating system and the database system run on it. However, a conventional computer may not be the best choice for a backend computer, because a standard operating system may not be the most appropriate one for strictly database applications. In fact, some of the tasks done by such an operating system, like job stream management, may not be needed for a dedicated machine. Also, the file system management may be done better by the database system than by the operating system. Thus, it is advantageous to construct such a machine with a specialized operating system.

We have not yet mentioned the possibility of specialized hardware for a database machine. If a computer is going to be used only for data-

FIGURE 7.4.1
Backend Computers

(a) Conventional system

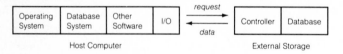

(b) Backend computer system

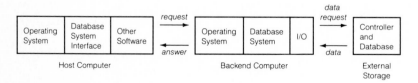

(c) Multiple hosts with backend computer

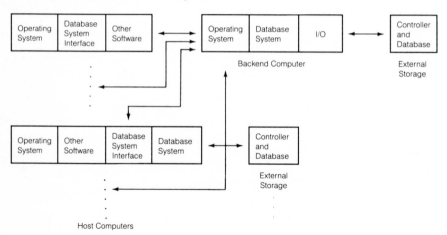

base work, it seems reasonable to build database functions into the hardware. The usual terminology for this specialized hardware is **associative processor.** The idea is to apply processing right at the storage (typically disk) level. Searching is a common database task, and conventional hardware is not particularly well suited for it. In Section 7.1, we saw how indexing can speed up the search. However, even with indexing, much unneeded data on pages gets swapped between internal and external storage. Because an associative processor has search capabilities at the storage level, only the required data need to be brought into memory. This way the amount of data transfer can be substantially decreased.

FIGURE 7.4.2
Associative Processors

(a) With a conventional system

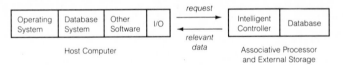

(b) With a backend computer system

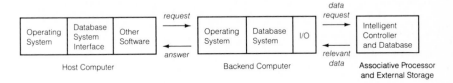

Associative processors may be used with a host computer or with a backend computer system. Diagrams for both types are given in Figure 7.4.2. There are various implementations for associative processors. A standard disk pack contains a certain number of identical surfaces that contain tracks on which the data are actually recorded. A cylinder contains one track from each surface in such a way that the circular tracks line up to form a cylindrical structure; these tracks can be accessed together without moving the read-write heads of a moving-head disk. The associative processors are microprocessors that are added to a disk pack. One method is to add a processor for each track. This way, all the processors can search in parallel. Such a system is often referred to as a **cellular-logic system,** as *each cell (track) contains a processor* which can perform logical operations. The entire disk can be searched in one rotation.

Another implementation involves one processor per disk surface. In this case, one cylinder can be searched in one rotation. The difference between the cellular-logic system and this one is analogous to the difference between a fixed-head disk, with a read-write head for each track, and a moving-head disk, with a read-write head for each surface. But now, in both cases, a processor is added to each read-write head. It is also possible to have one processor for a disk, but the improvement in performance is substantially less that way.

Another type of database machine involves the introduction of an additional level of storage. There are two standard methods. One method adds *an intermediate level of storage between internal memory and disk.* This is usually called **disk cache** or **cache memory.** It is slower than main memory, but cheaper; it is faster than disk storage, but more expensive because

FIGURE 7.4.3
Additional Levels of Storage

(a) Conventional system

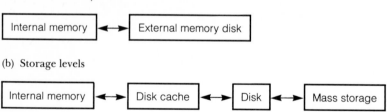

(b) Storage levels

additional microprocessors are involved. Usually, each processor handles one data page. The cache is managed so that the pages that are used most frequently remain in it; this reduces page swapping. The second method adds *a level of storage beyond the disk* in the form of a **mass storage system.** Such a system is slower than the disk, but can store massive amounts of data. One or both of these levels of storage can be used with a conventional database system running on a general-purpose computer or with a backend computer system. The storage levels are shown in Figure 7.4.3.

Probably the best-known database machine at the present time is the IDM (Intelligent Database Machine) from Britton-Lee, Inc., available in different versions since 1981. IDM is a backend machine whose operating system is dedicated to database management. It contains a relational database system and can interface with many different mainframe and minicomputers as well as the IBM PC. The host machine interfaces with the user, accepting the commands in the language IDL (Intelligent Database Language), which is similar to QUEL (see Section 12.2), as well as formatting and transmitting the results to the user. IDM also contains some cache memory.

Teradata Corporation is another manufacturer of database machines. It markets the DBC (Data Base Computer) primarily for the IBM large mainframe environment. This machine is fault-tolerant and can be attached to multiple host systems. It uses the SQL language for its relational database system.

The Japanese Fifth Generation Computer Systems Project is an attempt to synthesize developments in VLSI (very large-scale integration), artificial intelligence, and databases, to construct knowledge information processing systems. Such computer systems will be small in size, will contain a large amount of data, and will have intelligent reasoning capabilities that go way beyond the already complex matter of efficiently

FIGURE 7.4.4
Fifth Generation Computer System

Standard Computer	Fifth Generation Version
Memory	Knowledge-Base Machine (Database)
CPU	Inference Machine (Prolog)
I/O	Intelligent Interface Machine (Natural Language, Graphics, Speech)

entering and then retrieving data. Users will be able to interact with these systems through natural language, speech, graphs, and pictures. Figure 7.4.4 indicates the analogies between standard computer systems and the proposed computer system. The Knowledge-Base Machine is fundamentally a machine for the storage and processing of a deductive database. It interfaces with the Inference Machine, which is essentially a Prolog machine. The general plan also calls for a heavy use of parallel processing by means of a dataflow computer architecture. (We will discuss deductive databases, Prolog, and natural language interfaces in Chapter 9.)

As part of the project for the Knowledge-Base Machine, two relational database machines, called Grace and Delta, have been designed. Grace is used to study efficient hardware implementation for the join operation. It uses a hash and sort technique to organize data into buckets —a bucket is a group of usually adjacent storage locations, such as a block—in such a way that only data hashed to the same bucket can be joined. Since the buckets are independent of one another, it is possible to process them in parallel. We end this section by indicating some features of Delta, which is a more general database machine.

Delta is a backend database machine, which is planned to be used in a local-area network environment. The host computer will be a number of what are called SIMs (Sequential Inference Machines) connected in a network. A major aspect of the Delta design is hardware for the efficient execution of operations of the relational algebra. The basic architecture of Delta is shown in Figure 7.4.5. The Interface Processor manages the connection to the host machine or network. The Control Processor coordinates various subsystems. The Hierarchic Memory uses a semiconductor disk for cache storage. The Maintenance Processor maintains reliability and serviceability.

The idea of the Relational Database Engine is to implement the relational algebra as much as possible in hardware. Thus, Delta has primitive commands which are database operations. A portion of the Delta command set appears in Figure 7.4.6. Note that all the standard opera-

FIGURE 7.4.5
The Delta Architecture

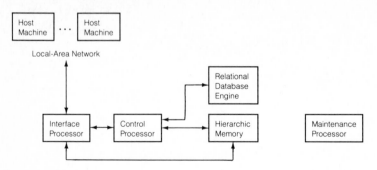

FIGURE 7.4.6
Some Delta Commands

Relational Algebra	Built-in Function
Projection	Count
Selection	Summation
Natural-Join	Maximum
Semi-Join	Minimum
Union	Average
Difference	Set Comparison
Intersection	Equal
Cartesian-Product	Contain
Update	I/O
Insert	Get
Delete	Put
Update	Miscellaneous
Definition	Sort
Create-Relation	Copy
Purge-Relation	Group-by
Append-Attribute	Transaction Control
Drop-Attribute	Start-Transaction
Arithmetic	End-Transaction
Add	Abort-Transaction
Subtract	Commit-Transaction
Multiply	
Divide	

tions of the relational algebra, even the Cartesian product, are included. Additionally, three update commands are available. Commands also exist for creating and modifying tables. Both arithmetic and the standard aggregate operations are included. Equal and Contain are used for set comparison, while Get and Put are I/O commands. Transaction control commands are also available.

The basic hardware algorithm is merge sort, which we discussed in Section 7.2 for the join. Two or more queues are used for this purpose. The tables are stored in a special version of the inverted organization, using a range of values for each attribute and symbolic pointers. The merge sort method is also used for selection. For example, if the selection condition is $A < c$, where A is an attribute and c is a constant value, c is placed in the first queue and the actual values for attribute A in the other queue, outputting those items from the second queue that satisfy the criterion.

7.5 Database Administration

So far, this book has dealt with many technical aspects concerning database systems. In this chapter, we have considered various topics related to the implementation of database systems. An important concern about any complex system must be its administration. In this section we discuss briefly the functions and responsibilities of the individual or group of individuals called the DBA (database administrator). There is not necessarily one single approach to the management of a database system. Much depends on the size of the organization and the use of the database system. The focus here will be on those aspects that are common to most situations. Figure 7.5.1 lists the major functions of the DBA.

Planning is an important aspect of the job of the DBA. Initially, the DBA may be involved in the original selection process for a database system. This process includes performing a cost/benefit analysis, specifying requirements, and evaluating various database packages. After a database system is installed, the DBA must deal with the growth in database usage which may involve both hardware and software upgrades. The DBA needs to keep up with new versions of the database system as well as with new developments in database technology. Usually, the DBA takes classes offered by the database vendor. Attending meetings of user groups is a good way of finding out how other people have solved similar problems, what is new and coming up, and what things should be avoided.

The DBA is usually also in charge of designing the database. Assuming the three-level architecture as presented in Section 1.2, database design involves the design of the internal view and the conceptual view. The conceptual view contains a complete logical description of the data stored in the database, while the file structures, indexings, and other aspects of the physical implementation are in the internal view. External views are written for users; in some cases an individual user or group of users may design their own external view. In such a case the user(s) may need assistance, which is provided by the DBA. Additionally, the mappings between the conceptual view and the internal view and between

FIGURE 7.5.1
The Major Functions of the Database Administrator (DBA)

Planning
Database design
Operation of the database system
Development of application systems
Monitoring performance
Enforcing standards
Documentation
Education
Liaison with management, users, vendors, and DP staff

each external view and the conceptual view must be written. (In many cases, such a mapping must be specified in the definition of the view itself.)

One important function of the DBA is the actual operation of the database system. This involves topics such as integrity, security, recovery, and concurrency for the system. We have already discussed these topics in previous chapters. The DBA is in charge of setting up procedures to ensure the proper functioning of these database components. Integrity checks are usually defined in the schema. Security involves passwords and authorizations. The DBA should be aware of privacy considerations concerning the data in the database. The DBA must also be familiar with recovery procedures for the database system. These procedures may involve making backup copies and then restarting the database operations after a crash, as well as applying the commit and rollback processes. The DBA should monitor locking if the system uses that method for concurrency control. Certainly, deadlocks must be resolved.

Typically, the DBA develops the primary application systems. The database system, basically a powerful tool, must be *applied* to enter and update data and to pose queries. For some systems, particularly the older ones, complicated programs must be written in a low-level database language. The DBA then must maintain these programs and develop new ones as requirements and circumstances change.

The DBA monitors the performance of the database system. Some people are on-line and need rapid response to queries and performance of updates. Others may be able to wait longer. Usually the DBA has some leeway to reorganize internal structures, such as indexings, in order to improve performance. The DBA has to recognize payoffs; for example, indexings may be helpful in answering queries, but may slow down updates and require extra space. It may also happen that an internal change, to improve the performance of some application for one user, makes the performance of an application for another user worse. The method of changing internal structures is called **tuning** the database. The DBA can obtain performance statistics by using utilities to monitor the database system.

In the database environment, it is important for the DBA to enforce standards. This usually involves naming conventions as well as standard data types for various objects. The data dictionary is an important tool for this purpose. The DBA is also in charge of documentation for the database system and the application programs. The DBA must give the users clear instructions about using the database system. Some users should only have to use a few keystrokes, while other users may be required to write some programs in order to use the database system. In general, the DBA is in charge of database education for users and may have to set up training classes for this purpose.

So far, we have dealt primarily with the technical aspects of the DBA's job. But part of the DBA's job is organizational. The DBA must interface with the management, the users, the vendors, and the data processing staff. The management of the company or organization must support the DBA and give the DBA the authority to resolve conflicts between users. The DBA deals with the vendors primarily through their representatives. We have already indicated the many ways in which the DBA interfaces with the users. Usually a computer is used for many tasks; database processing is one of these. For this reason, the DBA must work with the data processing staff, especially since a database system often uses a substantial amount of computer resources.

We have discussed the DBA in the singular, as one person. However, the job of the DBA for large database systems is too much for one person to handle. In such a case, the DBA comprises a group of individuals. Different individuals specialize in various aspects of the DBA tasks, and the person with the title "database administrator" may be the manager of the group. For distributed database systems, each site may have its own DBA to handle local database processing.

We end this section by briefly discussing the impact of *microcomputers* on database administration, because we have so far dealt primarily with the DBA's tasks for mainframe and minicomputer systems. Microcomputers are the cause of some changes in database administration. Many users wish to download their external views to their microcomputers for additional processing, often by spreadsheet systems. The DBA should know how to do these tasks and must deal with the security aspect of someone storing possibly sensitive data on unguarded floppy disks. Additionally, there are now many microcomputer database systems on the market. For some of these systems, the user is the DBA but may need help from others or an expert in using the database system. Many of the microcomputer database systems are for a single user, but in an increasing number of cases, microcomputers are connected by (usually local-area) networks so that several users may share the data in the database. When several users work with the database, more administration of the database becomes necessary.

7.6 Exercises

7.1 Construct an index file for the sequential file of Figure 7.6.1.

7.2 Explain how an index file is used to retrieve an element from an indexed-sequential file if the index file contains the smallest key value from each page.

7.3 Draw the new B-tree if the following action is performed to the B-tree of Figure 7.1.5:
   (a) 153 is inserted.
   (b) 394 is inserted.
   (c) 450 is inserted.
   (d) 435 is deleted.
   (e) 120 is deleted.
   (f) 405 is deleted.

7.4 Compress the following lists of numbers and words:
   (a) 123456, 123567, 123571, 125891, 125895, 125990.
   (b) 1110, 1115, 1135, 1138, 1157, 1159.
   (c) 34187, 34189, 34289, 34299, 34567, 34569.
   (d) have, haven, haver, haversack, havoc, haw, hawk.
   (e) multiple, multiplex, multiplication, multiply, multitude, multi-valent, mum.
   (f) Kraus, Krausch, Krause, Krauss, Kravetz, Kravitz, Krawitz.

7.5 Using the tables of Figure 4.6.3, write SQL statements for the following:
   (a) Create an index for EQUIPMENT on TYPE.
   (b) Create an index for CLIENT on JNAME.
   (c) Create a unique index for LAWYER on LSSNO.
   (d) Remove the index created in item (a).
   (e) Create a cluster on ONUMBER for EQUIPMENT and LAWYER.
   (f) Remove the cluster created in item (e).

7.6 Using the inverted organization, show the representation of the TEACHER and STUDENT tables of Figure 4.6.1. Use the symbolic pointers method.

FIGURE 7.6.1
A Sequential Data File

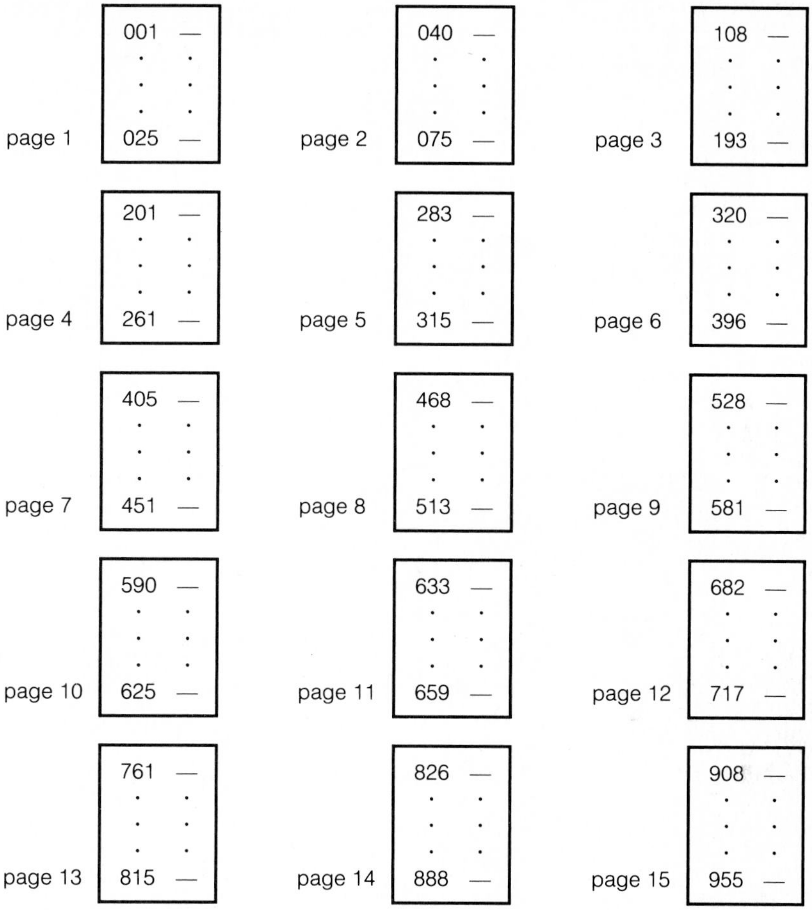

page 1 001 — ⋮ 025 —	page 2 040 — ⋮ 075 —	page 3 108 — ⋮ 193 —
page 4 201 — ⋮ 261 —	page 5 283 — ⋮ 315 —	page 6 320 — ⋮ 396 —
page 7 405 — ⋮ 451 —	page 8 468 — ⋮ 513 —	page 9 528 — ⋮ 581 —
page 10 590 — ⋮ 625 —	page 11 633 — ⋮ 659 —	page 12 682 — ⋮ 717 —
page 13 761 — ⋮ 815 —	page 14 826 — ⋮ 888 —	page 15 908 — ⋮ 955 —

7.7 Using the parameters in Figure 7.2.2, write a time estimation formula for the following:

(a) Projection with duplicate elimination: PROJECT(T; A).

(b) More complex selection: SELECT(T: $A > c$ & $B = d$), no indexing is used.

(c) Same as item (b) but use indexing on B.

7.8 Use the three methods in Figure 7.2.5 to obtain time estimation formulas for the join. The initial values for the parameters are as follows:

$p(S) = 25$, $p(T) = 40$, $n(S) = 600$, $n(T) = 2550$, $n(C) = 100$, $p = 1000$, page $= 50$, size(A) $= 20$, size(B) $= 10$, size(C) $= 10$, size(D) $= 5$, comp(C) $= 1$, construct $= 1$, $i(C) = 10$.

7.9 For each query in Exercise 4.3, write several coalesced relational algebra programs (if possible) and indicate which one is the most efficient.

7.10 Same as Exercise 7.9, but for Exercise 4.4.

7.11 Same as Exercise 7.9, but for Exercise 4.5.

7.12 For each query in Exercise 4.9, write a nested SQL SELECT statement (if possible) and indicate whether or not it is possible to perform the two SELECT statements simultaneously or the inner SELECT first.

7.13 Same as Exercise 7.12, but for Exercise 4.10.

7.14 Same as Exercise 7.12, but for Exercise 4.12.

7.15 For the database of Figure 4.6.4, perform the following semijoins:
  (a) SEMIJOIN(BRANCH,EMPLOYEE).
  (b) SEMIJOIN(TASK,BRANCH).
  (c) SEMIJOIN(BRANCH,BORROWER).
  (d) SEMIJOIN(TASK,EMPLOYEE).

7.16 For the database of Figure 4.6.5, perform the following semijoins:
  (a) SEMIJOIN(TEAM,EMPLOYEE).
  (b) SEMIJOIN(EMPLOYEE,TEAM).
  (c) SEMIJOIN(CUSTOMER,REPAIR_ORDER).
  (d) SEMIJOIN(REPAIR_ORDER,CUSTOMER).

7.7 Guide to Further Reading

The physical representation of databases is discussed in [1.1] Chapter 2, [1.2] Chapter 3, and [1.4] Chapter 2. Query optimization is discussed in [1.2] Chapter 16, [1.4] Chapter 8, and [5.3] Chapter 11. [7.2] is a recent survey of this topic. Some of our formulas for executing database operations are based on the formulas in [7.1]; this paper also discusses optimization for deductive databases, which we cover in Chapter 9. Distributed databases are covered in [1.1] Chapter 16, [1.2] Chapter 24, [1.3] Chapter 7, and [1.4] Chapter 12. Database machines are discussed in [1.1] Chapter 15 and [1.3] Chapter 8. [7.3] contains collections of papers devoted to the Fifth Generation Computer Systems Project. Database administration is discussed in [1.1] Chapter 13 and [1.2] Chapter 2. [7.4] is devoted to this topic.

[7.1] Grant, J., and J. Minker. "Optimization in Deductive and Conventional Relational Database Systems." In *Advances in Database Theory.* Vol. 1. Edited by H. Gallaire, J. Minker, and J. M. Nicolas. New York: Plenum Press, 1981, pp. 195–234.

[7.2] Jarke, M., and J. Koch. "Query Optimization in Database Systems." *ACM Computing Surveys* 16(1984), pp. 111–152.

[7.3] Proceedings of Conferences on Fifth Generation Computer Systems, published by ICOT and North-Holland.

[7.4] Weldon, J.-L. *Data Base Administration*. New York: Plenum Press, 1981.

Logic for
Relational Databases

8.1 First-Order Logic

Logic is the branch of mathematics and philosophy that deals with the rules of reasoning. Logic also provides a foundation for the study of computer science. However, the connection between logic and databases was not really well-understood until Codd formalized the relational database model and defined a query language, the relational calculus, based on logic. In this chapter we demonstrate some of the fundamental connections between logic and databases.

Many people are familiar with a branch of logic called **propositional logic** (or **Boolean logic**). This is the logic of propositions connected by "and," "or," "not," "implies," and possibly some additional connectives. Truth tables are used to determine the truth or falsity of formulas. This logic is also the one applied in binary circuits which are used for computer hardware. An example of the use of propositional logic is given in Figure 8.1.1(a). There are two hypotheses which can be expressed as $p \rightarrow q$ and p, where p stands for the proposition "It's Sunday," and q stands for the proposition "I don't go to work." The conclusion, namely q, follows logically from the hypotheses: that is, if the hypotheses are true, then the conclusion must also be true.

Propositional logic, while extremely useful in some applications, is not powerful enough to handle many types of logical reasoning. Consider, for example, the reasoning expressed in part (i) of Figure 8.1.1(b). The sentences "All men are mortal" and "Socrates is a man" are certainly

FIGURE 8.1.1
The Use of Logic in Reasoning

(a) Propositional logic

Hypotheses:
    (1) If it's Sunday, then I don't go to work. $p \rightarrow q$
    (2) It's Sunday. p
Conclusion: —————
      I don't go to work. q

(b) First-order logic

    (*i*)   Hypotheses:
           (1) All men are mortal.   Ax (Man(x) → Mortal(x))
           (2) Socrates is a man.   Man(Socrates)
          Conclusion: ————————————————
              Socrates is mortal.   Mortal(Socrates)
    (*ii*) Hypotheses:
           (1) No tiger eats grass.   Ax (Tiger(x) → −Grasseater(x))
           (2) Some animals that eat grass   Ex (Animal(x) & Grasseater(x) &
                are tame.   Tame(x))
          Conclusion: ————————————————————
              Some tame animals are not   Ex (Animal(x) & Tame(x) & −Tiger(x))
              tigers.
    (*iii*) Hypothesis:
              Every horse is an animal.   Ax (Horse(x) → Animal(x))
          Conclusion: ————————————————
              A horse's tail is an animal's AxAy (Tail(x,y) & Horse(x) →
              tail.   Tail(x,y) & Animal(x))

related, but this relationship cannot be expressed using the propositional connectives. Two slightly more complex examples appear in parts (*ii*) and (*iii*) of the figure. We will come back later to the formulas given beside the sentences. These formulas are written in **first-order logic** (sometimes called **predicate logic** or **predicate calculus**), which allows for this more complex, logical reasoning.

    Next we will begin to learn a formal language for first-order logic. Such a language is similar to a programming language or query language: it has symbols which have to be put together according to certain rules of syntax. The syntax rules of first-order logic are given in Figure 8.1.2. We use the binary connectives "&" for "and" (conjunction), "∨" for "or" (disjunction), "→" for "implies" (implication), and "−" for "not" (negation). There are really infinitely many different first-order languages: one for each combination of predicate, function, and constant symbols. However, the results that we formulate hold for any first-order language.

FIGURE 8.1.2
Syntax Rules for First-Order Logic

Notes: 1. Subscripts are allowed for predicate, constant, variable, and function symbols.
2. The number of terms in a term list is determined by the assignment of a positive integer to each predicate and function symbol.

```
<formula>   ::=   <atomic formula>|
                  {<quantifier> <variable symbol> <formula>}|
                  {(<formula> <binary connective> <formula>)}|
                  {<unary connective> <formula>}
<atomic formula>   ::=   {<predicate symbol> (<term list>)}|
                         {<term> <built-in predicate symbol> <term>}
<term list>   ::=   <term> { [ , <term> ] . . . }
<term>   ::=   <constant symbol> | <variable symbol> | <functional term>
<constant symbol>   ::=   a | b | c
<variable symbol>   ::=   x | y | z
<functional term>   ::=   <function symbol> ( <term list> )
<function symbol>   ::=   f | g | h
<predicate symbol>   ::=   P | R
<built-in predicate symbol>   ::=   =
<quantifier>   ::=   A | E
<binary connective>   ::=   & | ∨ | →
<unary connective>   ::=   −
```

It turns out to be convenient to relax some of the restrictions for the symbols used: in particular, we allow arbitrary identifiers for predicate, constant, and variable symbols, as long as we can tell from context what a symbol represents. We also generally omit parentheses by setting precedence rules for the connectives in the order −, &, ∨, and →. A **predicate symbol** stands for a relationship, which may be set membership. In part (*i*) of Figure 8.1.1(b), we use Man as a predicate symbol that reflects set membership, since every object is either a man or not a man.

The meaningful statements of first-order logic are called **formulas**. Each predicate symbol in a formula is followed by a set of objects, called **arguments**, inside parentheses and separated by commas. These arguments must be terms. **Terms** are usually constants or variables in our applications; however, functions may also be applied to terms to form more complex terms. The number of arguments must be specified for each predicate symbol. A predicate symbol with a single argument, such as Horse in part (*iii*) of Figure 8.1.1(b), is called unary; while one with two arguments, like Tail in the same example, is called binary; in general, a predicate symbol with n arguments is called n-ary.

Constant symbols stand for individual objects. For example, Socrates is a constant symbol in part (*i*) of Figure 8.1.1(b). Variable symbols are usually used with quantifiers. Ax is read "for all x"; Ex is read "there exists an x." Sometimes we use other words in English such as "every" or "each" instead of "all," and "some" instead of "exists." (Note that some logical symbols used in this book are slight modifications of standard notation. In particular, formal logic's "∀" [meaning "for all"] and "∃" [meaning "there exists"] are shown here simply as "A" and "E", respectively. This modification is a matter of convenience only.) Equality, "=", is a special predicate symbol. We should now be able to read the formulas given for the logical deductions in Figure 8.1.1(b). Tail(x,y) is read as "y is the tail of x": that is, the relationship between x and y is that y is the tail of x.

Part (a) of Figure 8.1.3 gives some examples of terms, with the assumption that f is a binary function symbol and g is a unary function symbol. (Function symbols, just like predicate symbols, must have the number of arguments specified.) Part (b) of the figure displays examples of atomic formulas. Here we assume that P is binary and R is ternary. Examples of formulas appear in part (c). In the first formula, x appears but is not quantified; that is, there is no Ax or Ex applied to it. Such a variable is said to be **free**. In the second formula, there are two variables, x and y. Note that these variables also appear with a quantifier applied to them, E for x and A for y. Such variables are said to be **bound**. The second formula reads, "There is an x, such that for all y, P(x,a) is true and R(b,y) is true." A formula with no free variables is called a **sentence**.

Having considered the syntax for first-order logic, we next consider the semantics. The syntax merely indicates the legal combinations of symbols; **semantics** *deals with the meanings assigned to these symbols.* An **interpretation** consists of a nonempty set D, called the domain, an assignment of each constant symbol to an element of the domain, an assignment of each function symbol to a function on the domain, and an assignment of each predicate symbol to a predicate (relation) on the domain. An *n*-ary predicate is (identified with) a subset of the *n*-ary Cartesian product, $D \times \ldots \times D_n$. In Figure 8.1.4(a), we give an interpretation for a

FIGURE 8.1.3
Terms, Atomic Formulas, and Formulas

(a) Terms	(b) Atomic formulas	(c) Formulas
(*i*) a	(*i*) P(a,x)	(*i*) P(a,x) → R(b,a) ∨ P(b,b)
(*ii*) x	(*ii*) R(b,a,y)	(*ii*) ExAy (P(x,a) & R(b,y))
(*iii*) f(a,b)		(*iii*) AxEyP(x,y)
(*iv*) f(g(x),f(a,y))		(*iv*) AxEyR(x,y)

FIGURE 8.1.4
Interpretations

(a) D = the set of positive integers
   $I(P) = \{<m,n> \mid m < n\}$
   $I(R) = \{<m,n> \mid m > n\}$
   $I(a) = 2$
   $I(b) = 5$

(b) D = {mary,john,paul,susan,pat}
   $I(P) = \{<mary,pat>,<susan,paul>\}$
   $I(R) = \{<mary, john>,<john,pat>,<paul,susan>,<susan,susan>,<pat,mary>\}$
   $I(a)$ = john
   $I(b)$ = pat

FIGURE 8.1.5
Valid, Unsatisfiable, and Equivalent Sentences

(a) Valid

   (*i*) Ax (P(x) → P(x))
   (*ii*) ExEy (R(x,y) ∨ −R(x,y))

(b) Unsatisfiable

   (*i*) Ex (P(x) & −P(x))
   (*ii*) AxAy (R(x,y) & −R(x,y))

(c) Equivalent

   (*i*) AxEy (R(x,y) → P(x))
   (*ii*) AxEy (−R(x,y) ∨ P(x))

language which contains two binary predicate symbols, P and R, and two constant symbols, a and b.

There is a formal way to define the truth of a sentence for a given interpretation. We do this here informally by examples. Let's look again at the sentence, ExAy (P(x,a) & R(b,y)). In the interpretation of Figure 8.1.4(a), we read this sentence as, "There is a positive integer x, such that for all positive integers y, x is less than 2 and 5 is bigger than y." This sentence is false for the interpretation because 5 is not bigger than all y.

Let's consider now the same interpretation for the sentence AxEyP(x,y). This sentence says, "For all x there is a y, such that x is less than y"; in other words, it says that there is no largest element. This sentence is true under the above interpretation. However, the sentence AxEyR(x,y) is false because there is a smallest element in the set, namely 1. Figure 8.1.4(b) gives another (very different) interpretation. In this interpretation, the sentence in part (*iv*) of Figure 8.1.3(c) is true while the other two sentences in parts (*ii*) and (*iii*) are false. If a formula is not a sentence, then it has one or more free variables, and for an interpretation, its truth or falsity may depend on what elements of the domain are substituted for the variables.

There are some sentences whose truth or falsity does not depend on the interpretation. *A sentence which is true in every interpretation* is called **valid**. *A sentence which is false in every interpretation* is called **unsatisfiable**. We give examples of such sentences in parts (a) and (b) of Figure 8.1.5. Two sentences are said to be (logically) **equivalent** *if they have the same truth-value under every interpretation*. For example, all valid sentences are equivalent. An example of equivalent sentences is shown in Figure 8.1.5(c).

8.2 The Relational Calculus

In Section 4.2, we considered the relational algebra, one of the two languages that Codd proposed for database manipulation. Now we look at the second language, the relational calculus, which is based on first-order logic. By way of preparation, the previous section has defined the language of first-order logic and dealt both with syntax and semantics. As we will see, the application of logic to relational databases is based on the fact that tables can be thought of as predicates (relations), and so predicate symbols can be used to represent them. It becomes possible, then, to use logic both as a data definition language and as a data manipulation language. In fact, as Chapters 8–10 will show, logic can be used to describe integrity constraints (which can be thought of as part of data definition), to give deductive definitions, as well as to describe database transformations.

First let's see how facts about tables can be expressed in logic. Suppose that we wish to create a table EMPLOYEE, with attributes SSNO, ENAME, DNAME, and SALARY. We thus place a predicate symbol EMPLOYEE with four arguments into the language. To express the fact that <111222333,Barber C,Sales,21550> is a row in this table, we write the atomic formula EMPLOYEE(111222333,Barber C,Sales,21550). In this way, by writing an atomic formula for each row in each table, we can describe the database. If we wish to deal with a database consisting of the tables DEPARTMENT, ITEM, and EMPLOYEE, as in Figure 4.1.1, we can do so in logic by placing the predicate symbols DEPARTMENT, ITEM, and EMPLOYEE in the language. Constant symbols—essentially a constant symbol for every value that any attribute can take on, such as social security numbers, names, salaries, and so on—are also needed. In this way, we obtain the syntax needed for dealing with a particular database. Figure 8.2.1(a) indicates all the basic symbols of a language for the above-mentioned relational database. (Some additional built-in predicate symbols are included for convenience.)

Recalling how an interpretation defines a domain and the assignments of the constant and predicate symbols, look again at Figure 8.2.1. Part (b) presents an interpretation for the language given in part (a). In

FIGURE 8.2.1
First-Order Representation of a Relational Database

(a) First-order language

Predicate symbols: DEPARTMENT (3-ary) ITEM (3-ary) EMPLOYEE (4-ary)
Constant symbols: all (representable) integers, real numbers, and character strings of
                    lengths 2, 9, 12, 15, and 20
Variable symbols: x y z
Quantifiers: E A
Connectives: − & ∨   →
Punctuation: ( ) ,
Built-in predicate
        symbols: = < <= > >=

(b) An interpretation

D = all the representable integers, real numbers, and character strings of length 2, 9,
      12, 15, and 20
The interpretation of each constant symbol is itself.
The interpretation of each built-in predicate symbol is the standard interpretation of that
symbol.
I(DEPARTMENT) = {<Sales,15,Smith L>,<Delivery,07,Jones B>,
                     <DP,29,Borden T>}
I(ITEM)   = {<Printer,455.69,23>,<TV Set,599.00,10>,
                     <Camera,127.50,70>}
I(EMPLOYEE)   = {<111111111,Smith J,Sales,22500>,
                     <222333444,Jones B,Sales,24750>,
                     <667788990,Turner W,Sales,25005>,
                     <555555555,Ford L,Delivery,21004>,
                     <234567890,Cramer T,DP,27790>}

dealing with databases in logic, we usually interpret each constant symbol as itself; in fact, we place these constant symbols in the language in the first place with this interpretation in mind. The interpretation of each predicate is a set of rows, which are exactly the ones that appear in the corresponding table. Hence, we can think of an interpretation of such a language as a representation for a database instance.

There is actually a deficiency in this representation. Nothing prevents us, given the definitions, from placing the row <10,599.2,DP> into I(DEPARTMENT)—but such a row would not make sense for the DEPARTMENT table. The problem is that we are using a single domain for all attributes. It is possible to define a more complex version of first-order logic, called **many-sorted logic** (or **typed logic**), where individual constant symbols fall into types; a type is associated with each variable symbol; and for each predicate and function symbol, a specific type is associated with each position that a term can occupy. We deal with many-sorted logic in an informal way by using the attribute names. Figure 8.2.2 displays these attributes by giving a typed first-order representation and

FIGURE 8.2.2
Typed First-Order Representation of a Relational Database

(a) Typed first-order language

Predicate symbols: DEPARTMENT(DNAME,LOCATION,MANAGER)
ITEM(INAME,PRICE,VOLUME)
EMPLOYEE(SSNO,ENAME,DNAME,SALARY)

Constant symbols:

for DNAME	:	all character strings of length 12
for LOCATION	:	all character strings of length 2
for MANAGER	:	all character strings of length 20
for INAME	:	all character strings of length 15
for PRICE	:	all real numbers
for VOLUME	:	all integers
for SSNO	:	all character strings of length 9
for ENAME	:	all character strings of length 20
for SALARY	:	all integers

Variable symbols:
$DNAME_1$, $DNAME_2$, . . .
$LOCATION_1$, $LOCATION_2$, . . .
$MANAGER_1$, $MANAGER_2$, . . .
$INAME_1$, $INAME_2$, . . .
$PRICE_1$, $PRICE_2$, . . .
$VOLUME_1$, $VOLUME_2$, . . .
$SSNO_1$, $SSNO_2$, . . .
$ENAME_1$, $ENAME_2$, . . .
$SALARY_1$, $SALARY_2$, . . .

Quantifiers:	E A
Connectives:	$-$ & $\vee$ $\rightarrow$
Punctuation:	( ) ,
Built-in predicate symbols:	$=$ $<$ $<=$ $>$ $>=$

(b) An interpretation

D(DNAME)	=	all character strings of length 12
D(LOCATION)	=	all character strings of length 2
D(MANAGER)	=	D(ENAME) = all character strings of length 20
D(INAME)	=	all character strings of length 15
D(PRICE)	=	all real numbers
D(VOLUME)	=	D(SALARY) = all integers
D(SSNO)	=	all character strings of length 9

The interpretation of each constant symbol is itself.
The interpretation of each built-in predicate symbol is the standard interpretation of that
symbol.

I(DEPARTMENT) = {<Sales,15,Smith L>,<Delivery,07,Jones B>,
<DP,29,Borden T>}
I(ITEM) = {<Printer,455.69,23>,<TV Set,599.00,10>,
<Camera,127.50,70>}
I(EMPLOYEE) = {<111111111,Smith J,Sales,22500>,
<222333444,Jones B,Sales,24750>,
<667788990,Turner W,Sales,25005>,
<555555555,Ford L,Delivery,21004>,
<234567890,Cramer T,DP,27790>}

interpretation for the database of Figure 8.2.1. In particular, part (a) shows the attributes associated with each predicate symbol and the constant symbols associated with each attribute; note that attribute names with subscripts are used for variable symbols. For the interpretation, part (b) indicates a domain for each attribute.

Our discussion of the relational calculus, which is the data manipulation language in first-order logic, begins with the query language. Each query is expressed as a formula of first-order logic. A yes-no query is expressed by a formula which is a sentence. Such a formula is evaluated in a database instance to be true or false; true means "yes" and false means "no". When a formula contains free variables, constants (of the appropriate type) can be substituted for the free variables to obtain a sentence, which can then be evaluated to be true or false. Thus, any formula can be thought of as a query whose answers are the constants, or rows of constants, whose substitution for the free variable(s) makes the formula true.

Figure 8.2.3 gives examples of queries and answers on the interpretation (database instance) of Figure 8.2.2(b). To emphasize that we are dealing with database retrieval we use the word GET. (We assume that the GET command retrieves and prints the answer.) We write a retrieval as GET $(x_1, \ldots, x_n) \mid F(x_1, \ldots, x_n)$ where $x_1, \ldots, x_n$ are the free variables in the formula $F(x_1, \ldots, x_n)$. A sequence of constants, $<c_1, \ldots, c_n>$, is retrieved by the GET statement if the sentence $F(c_1, \ldots, c_n)$ (that is, c_i substituted for x_i) is true in the database. Although we use subscripts in our figures, in an actual database language where subscripts are not allowed, a consistent substitution can be done. For example, MANAGER$_1$ may be represented by MANAGER[1]. (The arrow symbol, "→", can be represented as "−>"; the logical *or*, "$\lor$", can be represented as the letter "v"; and the vertical bar, "|", as "❘".)

Query (a) of Figure 8.2.3 retrieves the manager of the Sales department. In this formula, there is one free variable of type MANAGER, so the answer must be a set of manager names; in this case, that set consists of a single element. Note that in this formula, LOCATION must be present and existentially quantified, because it is needed in the atomic formula DEPARTMENT. The value "Sales" is a constant. We can thus read the retrieval as, "Get all managers' names which appear in a row of the DEPARTMENT table with a DEPARTMENT value of Sales and with some LOCATION value." Query (b) is a similar one involving the Sales department. In this case, there are two free variables, so the answer consists of pairs of ENAME and SALARY values.

Query (c) involves a formula which is a conjunction of two atomic formulas. The next query contains a conjunction of three atomic formulas, two of which represent tables, while the third one is the built-in predicate ">". Query (e) is a yes-no query; it has no free variables. Query (f) illustrates the case where one atomic formula appears more than once

FIGURE 8.2.3
Retrievals in the Relational Calculus

(a) Print the name of the manager of the Sales department.

  (*i*) GET (MANAGER$_1$) :
            E LOCATION$_1$ DEPARTMENT(Sales,LOCATION$_1$,MANAGER$_1$)

  (*ii*)

MANAGER
Smith L

(b) Print the name and salary of every employee in the Sales department.

  (*i*) GET (ENAME$_1$,SALARY$_1$) :
            E SSNO$_1$ EMPLOYEE(SSNO$_1$,ENAME$_1$,Sales,SALARY$_1$)

  (*ii*)

ENAME	SALARY
Smith J	22500
Jones B	24750
Turner W	25005

(c) Print the name of the manager of L. Ford.

  (*i*) GET (MANAGER$_1$) :
            E SSNO$_1$ E DNAME$_1$ E SALARY$_1$ E LOCATION$_1$
            (EMPLOYEE(SSNO$_1$,Ford L,DNAME$_1$,SALARY$_1$)
            & DEPARTMENT(DNAME$_1$,LOCATION$_1$,MANAGER$_1$))

  (*ii*)

MANAGER
Jones B

(d) Print the names of all managers who have at least one employee in their department with salary greater than $25,000.

  (*i*) GET (MANAGER$_1$) : E SSNO$_1$ E ENAME$_1$ E SALARY$_1$
            E DNAME$_1$ E LOCATION$_1$
            (EMPLOYEE(SSNO$_1$,ENAME$_1$,DNAME$_1$,SALARY$_1$)
            & DEPARTMENT(DNAME$_1$,LOCATION$_1$,MANAGER$_1$)
            & SALARY$_1$ > 25000)

  (*ii*)

MANAGER
Smith L
Borden T

(continued)

FIGURE 8.2.3 (*continued*)

(e) The price of a printer is less than $500.

    (*i*) GET ( ) ! E PRICE$_1$ E VOLUME$_1$
             (ITEM(Printer,PRICE$_1$,VOLUME$_1$)
             & PRICE$_1$ < 500.0)

    (*ii*)

RESULT
Yes

(f) Print the name of every department with more than one employee.

    (*i*) GET (DNAME$_1$) ! E SSNO$_1$ E ENAME$_1$ E SALARY$_1$
             E SSNO$_2$ E ENAME$_2$ E SALARY$_2$
             (EMPLOYEE(SSNO$_1$,ENAME$_1$,DNAME$_1$,SALARY$_1$)
             & EMPLOYEE(SSNO$_2$,ENAME$_2$,DNAME$_1$,SALARY$_2$)
             & - (SSNO$_1$ = SSNO$_2$))

    (*ii*)

DNAME
Sales

(g) Print the name of the item with the lowest price.

    (*i*) GET (INAME$_1$) ! E PRICE$_1$ E VOLUME$_1$
             (ITEM(INAME$_1$,PRICE$_1$,VOLUME$_1$)
             & A INAME$_2$ A PRICE$_2$ A VOLUME$_2$
               (ITEM(INAME$_2$,PRICE$_2$,VOLUME$_2$) ->
               PRICE$_1$ <= PRICE$_2$))

    (*ii*)

INAME
Camera

in the query. We must include the literal $-(SSNO_1 = SSNO_2)$, because otherwise the formula would be true even for a department with one employee, as the same constant value can be substituted for two different variables (of the same type). The last query illustrates the use of the universal quantifier.

    Essentially, the relational calculus is just a query language, but we can also introduce update statements into it. Examples of updates appear in Figure 8.2.4. The words INSERT, DELETE, and MODIFY operate as their names imply. Values which are irrelevant to the update are omitted, but the missing values are indicated by including the commas that would ordinarily separate them.

FIGURE 8.2.4
Updates in the Relational Calculus

(a) Insert information about Roberts into the EMPLOYEE table.

```
INSERT (EMPLOYEE) (123456789,Roberts P,Delivery,18870)
```

(b) Delete the information about cameras from the ITEM table.

```
DELETE (ITEM) (Camera, , )
```

(c) Change the volume of TV sets to 20 in the ITEM table.

```
MODIFY (ITEM) ( (TV Set, , ); (TV Set, ,20) )
```

Our version of the relational calculus is sometimes called the domain calculus. The word "domain" is used here in the sense of "attribute" since the **domain calculus** *has variables and constants for each attribute.* The other version of the relational calculus is called the tuple calculus. In fact, when Codd originally defined the relational calculus, he used the latter one. In the **tuple calculus**, *variables and constants stand for rows (tuples),* and a particular element of a row may be indicated by a number in brackets or the name of the attribute after the name of the row. For example, if r stands for a row (of constants) in the DEPARTMENT table, then r[1] is the DNAME value, r[2] is the LOCATION value, and r[3] is the MAN-AGER value. In Section 12.2, we will discuss the language QUEL, which is based on the tuple calculus.

Our definition of interpretation contained an implicit assumption that any legal row which is not in a table represents a negative fact. Thus, if the row <123456789,Jones,DP,20000> is not in the EMPLOYEE table, then for our interpretation, − EMPLOYEE(123456789,Jones,DP,20000) is true. As a matter of fact, this is how we represent negative information in a database—that is, by not including those rows in the table. But this is not the only possibility. Perhaps we have not included the row <123456789,Jones,DP,20000> in the EMPLOYEE table because we don't know if there is an employee whose social security number is 123-45-6789, whose name is Jones, who is in the DP department, and whose salary is $20,000. In this latter case, we would need a table, − EMPLOYEE, for placing *negative* facts about the EMPLOYEE table in the database.

The two approaches mentioned above are called the **Closed World Assumption (CWA)** (implicit negative facts) and the **Open World Assumption (OWA)** (explicit negative facts), respectively. With the CWA we can ask negative questions and obtain answers. With the OWA we get no answers to negative questions because there are no negative tables in a relational database. The distinction between the CWA and the OWA is illustrated in Figure 8.2.5 where part (a) is the query, part (b) the CWA

FIGURE 8.2.5
Closed World Assumption and Open World Assumption

(a) The query

```
GET (MANAGER₁) ! -DEPARTMENT(Sales,15,MANAGER₁)
```

(b) CWA answer

Result = All possible manager name values except L. Smith.

(c) OWA answer

Result = The empty set.

answer, and part (c) the OWA answer. We always assume the CWA, since that is the usual implicit understanding for databases in general. There is really a good reason for not including negative information in a database: there is usually much more negative information than positive information. Thus, for the EMPLOYEE table, every possible row that represents a legal social security number, employee name, department name, and salary, and that is not in the (positive) table, is assumed to be in the corresponding negative table. If we tried to actually store all the negative information in the database, unless the domains were very small, we would quickly overwhelm the available storage.

Chapter 10 will show how to extend the relational calculus to hierarchic and network databases using database logic. This extension provides a high-level database query language for hierarchic and network databases, in contrast to the low-level query languages that we studied in Chapters 2 and 3. The relational calculus can also be extended to the ER database model by treating the entities as tables. Such an extension involves the incorporation of relationships into the language.

We next deal with the implementation and optimization of relational calculus queries. The next section will show how to transform expressions of the relational calculus to equivalent programs in the relational algebra. Thus, one way to implement a relational calculus query is to transform it to a relational algebra program, which can then be optimized by the methods discussed in Section 7.2. As we will see, a conjunction S & T in the relational calculus is implemented in the relational algebra in the typical case by performing JOIN(S,T). We end this section by discussing the removal of unnecessary conjuncts from a relational calculus query. By removing a conjunct we usually eliminate a join. Eliminating a join is helpful because the join is a time-consuming operation.

Consider the relational calculus query of Figure 8.2.6(a) on the database of Figure 8.2.2(b). The way this query stands, it may require

FIGURE 8.2.6
Relational Calculus Query and its Simplification

(a) Original query

```
GET (ENAME₁,DNAME₁) ! E SSNO₁ E LOCATION₁ E MANAGER₁
      E ENAME₂ E DNAME₂ E SALARY₁ E SSNO₂ E DNAME₃
      E SALARY₂
      ( EMPLOYEE(SSNO₁,ENAME₁,DNAME₁,25000)
      & DEPARTMENT(DNAME₁,LOCATION₁,MANAGER₁)
      & EMPLOYEE(SSNO₁,ENAME₂,DNAME₂,SALARY₁)
      & EMPLOYEE(SSNO₂,ENAME₁,DNAME₃,SALARY₂) )
```

(b) Change an existentially quantified variable to a target variable, constant, or existentially quantified variable, and remove a duplicate conjunct.

```
GET (ENAME₁,DNAME₁) ! E SSNO₁ E LOCATION₁ E MANAGER₁
      E ENAME₂ E DNAME₂ E SALARY₁
      ( EMPLOYEE(SSNO₁,ENAME₁,DNAME₁,25000)
      & DEPARTMENT(DNAME₁,LOCATION₁,MANAGER₁)
      & EMPLOYEE(SSNO₁,ENAME₂,DNAME₂,SALARY₁) )
```

(c) Identify elements by a functional dependency and remove a duplicate conjunct.

```
GET (ENAME₁,DNAME₁) ! E SSNO₁ E LOCATION₁ E MANAGER₁
      ( EMPLOYEE(SSNO₁,ENAME₁,DNAME₁,25000)
      & DEPARTMENT(DNAME₁,LOCATION₁,MANAGER₁) )
```

(d) Remove a conjunct by an inclusion dependency.

```
GET (ENAME₁,DNAME₁) ! E SSNO₁
      EMPLOYEE(SSNO₁,ENAME₁,DNAME₁,25000)
```

three joins to evaluate (some of the joins are of EMPLOYEE with itself). But we can simplify the query by removing some of the conjuncts (which are really redundant). Clearly, if two conjuncts are identical, we can remove one of them without modifying the answer to the query. Unfortunately, in the present query, no two conjuncts are identical. However, we can obtain an equivalent query—that is, one that has the same answer—in which some of the conjuncts are identical. Then, as we remove one of the identical conjuncts, we also remove one join in the evaluation of the query.

Consider the claim that an existentially quantified variable, which does not occur in another conjunct, can be changed to a target variable, constant, or another existentially quantified variable to identify two conjuncts and so obtain an equivalent query. We represent the situation as

C_1 & C_2 & E, which we wish to reduce to C_1 & E by identifying C_2 with C_1. (C_2 is the conjunct which contains one or more such existentially quantified variables.) Note that any answer to C_1 & C_2 & E is certainly an answer to C_1 & E. Thus, for the removal of C_2, it suffices to show that any answer (row) to C_1 & E is an answer to C_2 also.

We now see why our claim holds in our example query by examining the first and fourth conjuncts. Note that for this query the fourth conjunct has three existentially quantified variables, $SSNO_2$, $DNAME_3$, and $SALARY_2$, none of which appears in another conjunct. By our rule we change $SSNO_2$ to the existentially quantified variable $SSNO_1$, $DNAME_3$ to the target variable $DNAME_1$, and $SALARY_2$ to the constant 25000.00. Suppose that <e,d> is an answer to the query in Figure 8.2.6(b), which is obtained by omitting the last conjunct. Then there must be a row in EMPLOYEE of the form <s,e,d,25000.00>, since the first conjunct of the query is satisfied. But this row provides an $SSNO_2$, namely s, a $DNAME_3$, namely d, and a $SALARY_2$, namely $25,000. Thus, <e,d> is also an answer to the last conjunct of the original query. This fact justifies the removal of the last conjunct.

Next, assume that the database view contains the functional dependency EMPLOYEE:SSNO→ENAME,DNAME,SALARY. Since the SSNO values are the same in the first and third conjunct, all the corresponding values for the other attributes, whether variable or constant, must be the same. Therefore, we can remove the third conjunct to obtain the query in part (c) of Figure 8.2.6. Suppose now that the database view contains the following inclusion dependency in the view: EMPLOYEE[DNAME] SUBSET DEPARTMENT[DNAME]. Note that since the other variables in DEPARTMENT are existentially quantified, the only purpose of the DEPARTMENT conjunct is to make sure that the DNAME value of EMPLOYEE appears in DEPARTMENT. Thus, the second conjunct also becomes unnecessary, and we obtain the final optimized query in part (d).

8.3 Relational Calculus and Relational Algebra

When Codd proposed the relational database model, he introduced two query languages, the relational algebra and the relational calculus. (SQL was introduced later for an implementation of the relational model.) In this section, we compare these two languages in terms of their expressive power. Codd originally showed that every query which is expressible in the relational calculus can also be expressed in the relational algebra. This result works in the opposite direction also, in the sense that a query, which can be expressed in the relational algebra, has an equivalent formulation in the relational calculus. We will not prove this result formally, but we will see some indications as to why it holds. Chapter 4 already showed how the operations of the relational algebra can be implemented in SQL.

Before we learn how to transform expressions from one language to the other one, let's compare the level of these languages. Because the relational algebra and the relational calculus each manipulate a set of elements at a time, both are high-level database languages. However, in the relational algebra, we must specify the order of operations, while in the relational calculus, we write a formula without specifying how it is to be evaluated. For this reason, we say that the relational algebra is a **procedural** high-level database language, while the relational calculus is a **nonprocedural** high-level database language. In this regard, we group SQL with the relational calculus as a nonprocedural high-level database language, since an SQL query also does not specify an order for the operations.

We start by showing how queries in the relational algebra can be expressed in the relational calculus. Recall that the basic operations of the relational algebra are union, difference, projection, selection, product, and join. These operations are applied to tables, which can be created in any relational database language. All of these operations are binary, so we will assume that the two tables to be worked on already exist.

For all the operators, we assume that $F(X1_1, \ldots, Xn_1)$ is the formula for the table S with attributes $X1, \ldots, Xn$; and $G(Y1_1, \ldots, Ym_1)$ is the formula for the table T with attributes $Y1, \ldots, Ym$. Thus, for a database instance DB, the row $<a_1, \ldots, a_n>$ is in S if and only if $F(a_1, \ldots, a_n)$ is true in DB, and, similarly, $<b_1, \ldots, b_m>$ is in T if and only if $G(b_1, \ldots, b_m)$ is true in DB. The relational calculus expressions for the relational algebra operations appear in Figure 8.3.1.

The two union-compatible operations UNION and DIFFERENCE are transformed using disjunction, and conjunction followed by negation, respectively. Projection is transformed by existentially quantifying on the nonprojected attributes. For selection, C is expressible in first-order logic—something the discussion of the allowed conditions in Chapter 4 did not mention, because we did not study logic until this chapter. PRODUCT and JOIN are transformed by using conjunction. Figure 8.3.2 shows the transformation of two queries from Figure 4.2.6, written as a single expression, and without PRINT. The results are equivalent to the corresponding queries in Figure 8.2.3.

So far we have seen that expressions of the relational algebra can be transformed to the relational calculus. Thus, any query that is expressible in the relational algebra is expressible also in the relational calculus. But recall that the relational calculus is a nonprocedural language, while the relational algebra is procedural. Thus, it is more likely that we would want to transform a relational calculus query, written by a user, to a relational algebra query for implementation. Figure 8.3.3 shows how to do such a transformation by indicating the appropriate operations of the relational algebra for an expression of the relational calculus. For the query, F contains the free variables $X1_1, \ldots, Xn_1$, and may contain additional bound variables.

FIGURE 8.3.1
Transformation of Relational Algebra Operations to Relational Calculus
Expressions

Notes: 1. S is the table obtained by GET $(X1_1, \ldots, Xn_1) \mid F(X1_1, \ldots, Xn_1)$, T is the table
obtained by GET $(Y1_1, \ldots, Ym_1) \mid G(Y1_1, \ldots, Ym_1)$.
2. For UNION and DIFFERENCE substitute $(X1_1, \ldots, Xn_1)$ for $(Y1_1, \ldots, Ym_1)$ by
union-compatibility.
3. For PROJECT let $Z = \{Z1, \ldots, Zj\}$, $W = \{W1, \ldots, Wk\}$, $Y = \{Y1, \ldots, Ym\}$, X
$= \{X1, \ldots, Xn\}$. Then Z is a subset of Y, W is a subset of Y, and the union of Z
and W is Y.
4. For PRODUCT we assume that the intersection of X and Y is empty.
5. For JOIN we assume that $X(i + 1) = Y1$, $\ldots$, $Xn = Y(n - i)$, and that the
other Xs and Ys are pairwise distinct.
6. D(X) is the domain for the variable X.

UNION(S,T)   —   GET $(X1_1, \ldots, Xn_1) \mid F(X1_1, \ldots, Xn_1) \vee G(X1_1, \ldots, Xn_1)$
DIFFERENCE(S,T)   —   GET $(X1_1, \ldots, Xn_1) \mid F(X1_1, \ldots, Xn_1)$ & $-G(X1_1, \ldots, Xn_1)$
PROJECT(T; Z1, ... ,Zk)   —   GET $(Z1_1, \ldots, Zk_1) \mid EW1 \ldots EWk_1\ G(Y1_1, \ldots, Ym_1)$
SELECT(S : C)   —   GET $(X1_1, \ldots, Xn_1) \mid F(X1_1, \ldots, Xn_1)$ & C
PRODUCT(S,T)   —   GET $(X1_1, \ldots, Xn_1, Y1_1, \ldots, Ym_1) \mid$
$\qquad\qquad F(X1_1, \ldots, Xn_1)$ & $G(Y1_1, \ldots, Ym_1)$
JOIN (S,T)   —   GET $(X1_1, \ldots, Xi_1, Y1_1, \ldots, Ym_1) \mid F(X1_1, \ldots, Xn_1)$ & $G(Y1_1, \ldots, Ym_1)$
D(A)   —   GET $(X) \mid X = X$
EMPTY   —   GET $(X) \mid - (X = X)$

FIGURE 8.3.2
Transformation of Relational Algebra Queries to Relational Calculus Queries

(a) (*i*)   Relational algebra query

```
PROJECT(SELECT(DEPARTMENT: DNAME = 'Sales');
    MANAGER)
```

(*ii*)   Transformation to relational calculus query

```
GET (MANAGER₁) : E DNAME₁ E LOCATION₁
    ( DEPARTMENT(DNAME₁,LOCATION₁,MANAGER₁)
    & DNAME₁ = 'Sales' )
```

(b) (*i*)   Relational algebra query

```
PROJECT(SELECT(JOIN(EMPLOYEE,DEPARTMENT):
    SALARY > 25000); MANAGER)
```

(*ii*)   Transformation to relational calculus query

```
GET (MANAGER₁) : E SSNO₁ E ENAME₁ E DNAME₁
    E SALARY₁ E LOCATION₁
    ( EMPLOYEE(SSNO₁,ENAME₁,DNAME₁,SALARY₁)
    & DEPARTMENT(DNAME₁,LOCATION₁,MANAGER₁)
    & SALARY₁ > 25000 )
```

FIGURE 8.3.3
Transformation of Relational Calculus Expressions to Relational Algebra Operations

The relational calculus query is GET $(X1_1, \ldots, Xn_1) \mid F(X1_1, \ldots, Xn_1)$.

Case 1. F is an atomic formula.
(a) The atomic formula contains a standard predicate symbol and no constants.

```
GET (X1₁,...,Xn₁) : T(X1₁,...,Xn₁)   --   T
```

(b) The predicate symbol is a built-in predicate symbol.

```
GET (X1₁,X2₁) : X1₁ < X2₁  --
     SELECT(PRODUCT(dom(X1),dom(X2)): X1 < X2)
```

(c) The atomic formula contains a constant.

```
GET (X1₁) : T(X1₁,c)   --
     PROJECT(SELECT(T(X1,X2): X2 = c); X1)
```

Case 2. Negation
S is the table obtained by GET $(X1_1, \ldots, Xn_1) \mid G(X1_1, \ldots, Xn_1)$.

```
GET (X1₁,...,Xn₁) : -G(X1₁,...,Xn₁)   --
    DIFFERENCE(PRODUCT(...PRODUCT(dom(X1),dom(X2))
    ...dom(Xn)),S)
```

Case 3. Disjunction
S is the table obtained by GET $(Y1_1, \ldots, Ym_1) \mid G(Y1_1, \ldots, Ym_1)$, T is the table obtained by GET $(Z1_1, \ldots, Zk_1) \mid H(Z1_1, \ldots, Zk_1)$. $Y1 = X1, \ldots, Ym = Xm$; each Zi is some Xj.

```
GET (X1₁,...,Xn₁) : G(Y1₁,...,Ym₁) ∨ H(Z1₁,...,Zk₁)
    --   UNION(S',T')
```

where $S' = \text{PRODUCT}(\ldots(\text{PRODUCT}(S,\text{dom}(X(m + 1))) \ldots \text{dom}(Xn))$ and T' is obtained in a similar way from T.

Case 4. Conjunction
Same assumptions as for disjunction.

```
GET (X1₁,...,Xn₁) : G(Y1₁,...,Ym₁) & H(Z1₁,...,Zk₁)
    --   JOIN(S,T)
```

Case 5. Existential quantification
Same assumption as for negation.

```
GET (X1₁,...,Xn₁) : EY₁ G(X1₁,...,Xn₁,Y₁)
    --   PROJECT(S; X1,...,Xn).
```

We now consider three subcases in which the expression is an atomic formula. Other atomic formulas are handled similarly. We may assume that F is a more complex formula obtained by using $-$, $\vee$, &, or E, since a formula using $\rightarrow$ and A can be rewritten without those symbols. In particular, $AxG(x)$ is logically equivalent to $-Ex-G(x)$. (Actually, it is also not necessary to include $\vee$.)

To take negation first, we construct the complement (with respect to the domains) of the table represented by G. Next we do disjunction and conjunction. We assume that each Zi is some Xj, and that $Y1 = X1$, $Y2 = X2, \ldots, Ym = Xm$; if this is not the case then the Ys can be permuted by using PROJECT. The primed sets are obtained from the unprimed sets by expanding them using the other domains. In this way, S' and T' become union-compatible. If the Yi and Zj are pairwise distinct then the join is, in fact, a product. The existential quantifier is transformed by using PROJECT on the nonquantified variable. Figure 8.3.4 shows how to transform two relational calculus queries to relational algebra queries using our method. These relational algebra queries are not necessarily in a good form; in particular, two PROJECT operations can be cascaded into one.

FIGURE 8.3.4
Transformation of Relational Calculus Queries to Relational Algebra Queries

(a) (*i*) Relational calculus query

```
GET (ENAME₁,SALARY₁) :
     E SSNO₁ EMPLOYEE(SSNO₁,ENAME₁,Sales,SALARY₁)
```

(*ii*) Transformation to relational algebra query

```
PROJECT(PROJECT(SELECT(EMPLOYEE(SSNO,ENAME,
       DNAME,SALARY) : DNAME = 'Sales');
       SSNO,ENAME,SALARY); ENAME,SALARY)
```

(b) (*i*) Relational calculus query

```
GET (MANAGER₁) : E SSNO₁ E DNAME₁ E SALARY₁
     E LOCATION₁
     (EMPLOYEE(SSNO₁,Smith J,DNAME₁,SALARY₁)
     & DEPARTMENT(DNAME₁,LOCATION₁,MANAGER₁) )
```

(*ii*) Transformation to relational algebra query

```
PROJECT(PROJECT(PROJECT(PROJECT(JOIN(PROJECT
       (SELECT(EMPLOYEE: ENAME = 'Smith J'):
       SSNO,DNAME,SALARY),DEPARTMENT));
       MANAGER,SSNO,DNAME,SALARY);
       MANAGER,SSNO,DNAME);
       MANAGER,SSNO); MANAGER)
```

We have thus demonstrated that it is possible to go back and forth between relational calculus and relational algebra expressions. SQL may be considered to be between the relational calculus and the relational algebra in the sense that the relational calculus is somewhat more non-procedural than SQL. SQL is actually more powerful than the relational algebra, since it has some additional operators like the SUM function.

So far we have converted queries only, because that is how those languages were first defined. The translation of updates between the languages is relatively straightforward. Usually, queries in languages that may be based on the relational calculus are transformed to an internal form based on a sequence of operations in the relational algebra. A translation based on our method may not yield an optimal sequence of operations, however, and therefore should be optimized. Some optimization techniques for relational algebra queries have already been discussed in Section 7.2.

8.4 Mechanical Theorem Proving

Section 8.1 indicated that logic deals with the rules of reasoning and then discussed the syntax and semantics of first-order logic; Section 8.2 showed how first-order logic can be used as a data manipulation language in the form of the relational calculus. In this section, we examine how reasoning can be formalized within first-order logic, and how such a process can be automated. We assume throughout this section that we are working with an arbitrary and fixed first-order language.

The key notion in logical reasoning is **logical implication**. In fact, the examples in Figure 8.1.1 illustrate how certain hypotheses logically *imply* a conclusion. We now want to deal with this notion more formally. Our reason for doing so is that after we formalize logical implication, we can write a program to do such logical reasoning. We will see in the next chapter that the incorporation of such logical reasoning adds intelligence to a database system.

Suppose that S is a set of sentences, and B is a sentence. We say that **S logically implies B** (written as **S ⊨ B**) if for every interpretation in which every element of S is true, B is true also. Now let S = {A$_1$, ..., A$_n$}. The following theorem indicates the connection between implication, validity, and unsatisfiability.

Theorem 8.1   The following three conditions are equivalent:
(1) {A$_1$, ..., A$_n$} ⊨ B.
(2) A$_1$ & ... & A$_n$ → B is valid.
(3) A$_1$ & ... & A$_n$ & −B is unsatisfiable.

Proof: We show that (1) implies (2), (2) implies (3), and (3) implies (1). First we show that (1) implies (2). Suppose that $\{A_1, \ldots, A_n\} \models B$, and let I be any interpretation. If some A_i is false for I, then $A_1 \& \ldots \& A_n \rightarrow B$ is true. Otherwise, each A_i is true in I. Then, by the definition of $\models$, B must be true in I, and so $A_1 \& \ldots \& A_n \rightarrow B$ is true. Next we show that (2) implies (3). Suppose that $A_1 \& \ldots \& A_n \rightarrow B$ is valid, and let I be any interpretation. If some A_i is false for I, then $A_1 \& \ldots \& A_n \& -B$ is also false for I. Otherwise, each A_i is true for I. Then, by the validity of $A_1 \& \ldots \& A_n \rightarrow B$, B must be true, and so $A_1 \& \ldots \& A_n \& -B$ is false for I. Finally, we show that (3) implies (1). Suppose that $A_1 \& \ldots \& A_n \& -B$ is unsatisfiable, and let I be any interpretation for which $A_1, \ldots, A_n$ are all true. Since $A_1 \& \ldots \& A_n \& -B$ is unsatisfiable, B must be true for I.

Theorem 8.1 is useful because it allows us to test the logical implication of a set of sentences by testing the validity or unsatisfiability of a single sentence. Therefore, it is sufficient to construct a test for the unsatisfiability of a sentence in order to test for logical implication. This is, in fact, what we do in this section. But first we must learn how to transform a sentence into a special form—a form which allows for a more convenient mechanical method to check for unsatisfiability.

A **literal** *is an atomic formula or the negation of an atomic formula.* A formula is said to be in **conjunctive normal form** if it has no quantifiers, contains only the connectives $-$, &, $\vee$, and has the form $(L_{11} \vee \ldots \vee L_{1n_1}) \& \ldots \& (L_{m1} \vee \ldots \vee L_{mn_m})$, where each L_{ij} is a literal. Thus, a formula is in conjunctive normal form if it consists of a conjunction of conjuncts, where each conjunct is a disjunction of literals. Part (a) of Figure 8.4.1 gives an example of a formula in conjunctive normal form. Note that this formula is not a sentence because it has free variables. In fact, this formula has no quantifiers at all. For sentences (although the definition can be applied to formulas in general) we define a special form called prenex conjunctive normal form. A sentence is said to be in **prenex conjunctive normal form** *if all of its quantifiers* (if any) *are in front and the rest of the formula is in conjunctive normal form.* The quantifiers form the **prefix**, and the rest of the formula is called the **matrix**. We give an example of a sentence in prenex conjunctive normal form in part (b) of Figure 8.4.1.

It turns out to be convenient to deal only with sentences in prenex conjunctive normal form. Therefore, we would like to be able to transform any sentence into a sentence in that form. But such a transformation is useful only if the new sentence has the same truth-value as the original sentence in every interpretation: in other words, only if the new sentence is logically equivalent to the original one. The next theorem, which we do not prove formally, gives the key result about prenex conjunctive normal form.

Theorem 8.2 For every sentence S there is a sentence S′ which is in prenex conjunctive normal form and which is logically equivalent to S.

FIGURE 8.4.1
Prenex Conjunctive Normal Form

(a) A formula in conjunctive normal form

$(P(x,a) \vee P(y,z))$ & $(-P(a,b) \vee R(a,y,z))$

(b) A sentence in prenex conjunctive normal form

AxEyAz $(\ (P(x,a) \vee R(x,y,z))$ & $(-P(a,b) \vee R(a,y,z)\ )$

(c) Transformations that preserve logical equivalence

(*i*) Propositional transformations

Transform	To	Reason
$F \to G$	$-F \vee G$	definition of $\to$
$--F$	F	double negation cancels
(F)	F	extraneous parentheses
$F \vee G$	$G \vee F$	commutativity of $\vee$
F & G	G & F	commutativity of &
$(F \vee G) \vee H$	$(F \vee G \vee H)$	associativity of $\vee$
$(F$ & $G)$ & H	$(F$ & G & $H)$	associativity of &
$-(F$ & $G)$	$-F \vee -G$	De Morgan's law
$-(F \vee G)$	$-F$ & $-G$	De Morgan's law
$F \vee G$ & H	$(F \vee G)$ & $(F \vee H)$	distributivity of & over $\vee$

(*ii*) Predicate transformations

Rule	Transform	To
1	$-AxF(x)$	$Ex-F(x)$
2	$-ExF(x)$	$Ax-F(x)$
3	$AxF(x) \vee G$	$Ax(F(x) \vee G)$
4	$AxF(x)$ & G	$Ax(F(x)$ & $G)$
5	$ExF(x) \vee G$	$Ex(F(x) \vee G)$
6	$ExF(x)$ & G	$Ex(F(x)$ & $G)$
7	$AxF(x)$ & $AxH(x)$	$Ax(F(x)$ & $H(x))$
8	$ExF(x) \vee ExH(x)$	$Ex(F(x) \vee H(x))$
9	$AxF(x) \vee AxH(x)$	$AxAz(F(x) \vee H(z))$
10	$ExF(x)$ & $ExH(x)$	$ExEz(F(x)$ & $H(z))$
11	$AxF(x) \vee ExH(x)$	$AxEz(F(x) \vee H(z))$
12	$AxF(x)$ & $ExH(x)$	$AxEz(F(x)$ & $H(z))$
13	$ExF(x) \vee AxH(x)$	$ExAz(F(x) \vee H(z))$
14	$ExF(x)$ & $AxH(x)$	$ExAz(F(x)$ & $H(z))$

(continued)

FIGURE 8.4.1 (*continued*)

(d) Transformation of a sentence to prenex conjunctive normal form

$AxAy(Ex_1(P(x,x_1) \& P(y,x_1)) \rightarrow Ey_1R(x,y,y_1)) \& (P(a,b) \lor P(a,a))$

$AxAy(-Ex_1(P(x,x_1) \& P(y,x_1)) \lor Ey_1R(x,y,y_1)) \& (P(a,b) \lor P(a,a))$
   by the definition of $\rightarrow$

$AxAy(Ax_1 - (P(x,x_1) \& P(y,x_1)) \lor Ey_1R(x,y,y_1)) \& (P(a,b) \lor P(a,a))$
   by rule 2

$AxAy(Ax_1(-P(x,x_1) \lor -P(y,x_1)) \lor Ey_1R(x,y,y_1)) \& (P(a,b) \lor P(a,a))$
   by De Morgan's law

$AxAy(Ax_1(-P(x,x_1) \lor -P(y,x_1)) \lor Ey_1R(x,y,y_1))) \& (P(a,b) \lor P(a,a))$
   by rule 3

$AxAy(Ax_1Ey_1(-P(x,x_1) \lor -P(y,x_1) \lor R(x,y,y_1))) \& (P(a,b) \lor P(a,a))$
   by rule 5 and the commutativity of $\lor$

$AxAyAx_1Ey_1(-P(x,x_1) \lor -P(y,x_1) \lor R(x,y,y_1)) \& (P(a,b) \lor P(a,a))$
   by removing parentheses

$AxAyAx_1Ey_1((-P(x,x_1) \lor -P(y,x_1) \lor R(x,y,y_1)) \& (P(a,b) \lor P(a,a)))$
   by rules 3 and 4

Part (c) of Figure 8.4.1 presents rules which can be used to transform formulas into prenex conjunctive normal form while preserving logical equivalence. It is assumed that F and G are subformulas of a formula; that is, they are parts of the formula which themselves are formulas. We write F(x) to emphasize that x appears as a free variable in F, but we allow F to contain additional variables. We assume that G does not contain x. We write H(z) for the formula H(x), with z substituted for every occurrence of x. Note, for example, that it would be incorrect to transform ExF(x) & ExH(x) to Ex(F(x) & H(x)), because the second formula states the existence of a single x for both F and H, while the first one does not. In particular, if F is Tall and H is Short, then the first sentence states that there is somebody who is tall and somebody who is short, while the second sentence states that there is somebody who is tall and short. Part (d) of the figure gives an example showing the transformation of a sentence to prenex conjunctive normal form.

To obtain our method of checking for the unsatisfiability of a sentence, we must do an additional transformation. We need to eliminate existential quantifiers to transform the sentence to Skolem normal form. A sentence is said to be in **Skolem normal form** *if it is in prenex conjunctive normal form and contains no existential quantifiers.* To obtain Skolem normal form, we must eliminate each existential quantifier as follows: going from left to right, we omit the existential quantifier from the prefix, and in the matrix insert a term which is a (new) function—called a Skolem function—whose arguments are the universally quantified variables in front of the variable to be eliminated. If there are no universally quantified variables in front of the existentially quantified variable, then we replace it in the matrix by a (Skolem) constant. Figure 8.4.2 offers examples of transformations of sentences to Skolem normal form.

By Theorem 8.2, when a sentence is transformed to prenex conjunctive normal form, the new sentence is logically equivalent to the old one. However, this is not the case for the transformation to Skolem nor-

FIGURE 8.4.2
Transformation to Skolem Normal Form

(a) For the sentence of Figure 8.4.1(d)

    (*i*) Original sentence

$$AxAyAx_1Ey_1(\,(-P(x,x_1) \vee -P(y,x_1) \vee R(x,y,y_1)) \,\&\, (P(a,b) \vee P(a,a))\,)$$

    (*ii*) Transformed sentence

$$AxAyAx_1(\,(-P(x,x_1) \vee -P(y,x_1) \vee R(x,y,f(x,y,x_1)))$$
$$\&\, (P(a,b) \vee P(a,a))\,)$$

    Note: x, y, x_1 are universally quantified variables which precede y_1 in the prefix; f is a new function symbol.

(b) Another sentence

    (*i*) Original sentence

$$ExAyAy_1EzAy_2(\,(-R(x,y,y_1) \vee P(y,z))$$
$$\&\, (P(y_2,y_2) \vee -P(y,x) \vee R(x,y_1,z))\,)$$

    (*ii*) Transformed sentence

$$AyAy_1Ay_2(\,(-R(c,y,y_1) \vee P(y,f(y,y_1)))$$
$$\&\, (P(y_2,y_2) \vee -P(y,c) \vee R(c,y_1,f(y,y_1)))\,)$$

    Note: c is a new constant symbol and f is a new function symbol.

(c) Simple example for inequivalence

    (*i*) Original sentence

$$ExP(x)$$

    (*ii*) Transformed sentence

$$P(c)$$

mal form. Consider the sentences in part (c) of Figure 8.4.2. Let the interpretation be D = {d_1,d_2}, I(P) = {$<d_1>$}, I(c) = d_2. For this interpretation, ExP(x) is true, but P(c) is false. Fortunately, it is not necessary for the new sentence to be logically equivalent to the old one; Theorem 8.1 has reduced the question of logical implication to unsatisfiability. Thus, it is sufficient that if S' is the Skolem normal form of S, then S and S' are equivalent for unsatisfiability. We state this result as the next theorem.

> **Theorem 8.3**   Let S' be the Skolem normal form of S. Then S is unsatisfiable if and only if S' is unsatisfiable.

The idea of the proof is to show that each time an existential quantifier is eliminated, the new sentence is unsatisfiable if and only if the old sentence is unsatisfiable. Once we have sentences in Skolem normal form, we can write them in what is called clausal form, which is convenient for what we do next. **Clausal form** is obtained by eliminating all the universal quantifiers (we already know that all the variables are universally quantified), and eliminating all the conjunctions by writing each conjunct separately and calling it a clause. The clausal forms of the sentences in Figure 8.4.2 appear in Figure 8.4.3.

Now we are almost ready to understand the method of resolution, various versions of which are very commonly used in mechanical theorem proving. To illustrate this idea, first let's consider the case of propositional logic formulas. Suppose that $-A \lor B$ and $-B \lor C$ are such formulas. Since $-A \lor B$ is equivalent to $A \to B$, and $-B \lor C$ is equivalent to $B \to C$, by the transitivity of implication we obtain $A \to C$, which is equivalent to $-A \lor C$. Note that neither formula contains "&"; one for-

FIGURE 8.4.3
Clausal Form

(a) The two clauses for the sentence of Figure 8.4.2(a)

$C_1 = - P(x,x_1) \lor -P(y,x_1) \lor R(x,y,f(x,y,x_1))$
$C_2 = P(a,b) \lor P(a,a)$

(b) The two clauses for the sentence of Figure 8.4.2(b)

$C_1 = -R(c,y,y_1) \lor P(y,f(y,y_1))$
$C_2 = P(y_2,y_2) \lor -P(y,c) \lor R(c,y_1,f(y,y_1))$

(c) The clause for the sentence of Figure 8.4.2(c)

$C_1 = P(c)$

mula contains B and the other formula contains $-$ B. The result is obtained by putting together the two formulas with a disjunction, while eliminating the atom which appears in a positive form in one formula and in a negative form in the other. Resolution is essentially an extension of this idea to first-order logic.

We need a few more definitions before we get to resolution. A **substitution** is a finite set $\{t_1/v_1, \ldots, t_n/v_n\}$, where each t_i is a term, each v_i is a variable, and all the v_i's are distinct. When a substitution is applied to a formula, each v_i is simultaneously replaced by the corresponding t_i. We use s for substitutions and write s(F) for the formula obtained by applying the substitution s to F. Part (a) of Figure 8.4.4 shows a substitution. Given a set of formulas $\{F_1, F_2, \ldots, F_k\}$, a substitution s is called a **unifier** if $s(F_1) = s(F_2) \ldots = s(F_k)$. (Actually we assume that s is a most general unifier; this means essentially that no constants are introduced unless necessary.) Part (b) of the figure gives an example of a substitution that unifies three formulas. When two or more literals are unified within a single clause, the result is called a **factor** of the original clause.

Now we are ready to define resolution. Let C_1 and C_2 be two clauses which contain no common variables. (Common variables must be renamed first in one clause.) Suppose that L_1 is a literal in C_1, L_2 is a literal in C_2,

FIGURE 8.4.4
Substitution, Unification, and Resolution

(a) A substitution

Let $F = P(x) \vee -Q(y,a,f(z))$,
$\quad$ s $= \{f(a)/y,b/x\}$.
Then $s(F) = P(b) \vee -Q(f(a),a,f(z))$.

(b) A unification

Let $F_1 = P(x) \vee -Q(y,a,f(z))$,
$\quad F_2 = P(b) \vee -Q(f(a),u,f(z))$,
$\quad F_3 = P(x) \vee -Q(f(u),a,f(z))$,
and s $= \{f(a)/y,b/x,a/u\}$.
Then $s(F_1) = s(F_2) = s(F_3) = P(b) \vee -Q(f(a),a,f(z))$

(c) A resolvent

Let $F_1 = P(f(y)) \vee R(g(y))$,
$\quad F_2 = -P(f(g(a))) \vee R(b)$.
Apply the substitution s $= \{g(a)/y\}$ to obtain
$\quad s(F_1) = P(f(g(a))) \vee R(g(g(a)))$,
$\quad s(F_2) = -P(f(g(a))) \vee R(b)$.
The resolvent is $R(g(g(a))) \vee R(b)$.

and s unifies $\{L_1, -L_2\}$ (we assume that a double negation is removed). Then the clause obtained by taking the disjunction of $s(C_1)$ and $s(C_2)$, while omitting $s(L_1)$ and $s(L_2)$, is called a **resolvent** of C_1 and C_2. An example of a resolvent appears in Figure 8.4.4(c). If $C_1 = L_1$ and $C_2 = L_2$ (where s unifies $\{L_1, -L_2\}$), then the resolvent is the empty clause, written as [].

For the **resolution method** of theorem proving, the starting point is a set of clauses. Additional clauses are obtained by resolution: a new clause may be the resolvent of two clauses or the factor of a clause. The new clauses may be used in the resolution process. Resolution ends if it is impossible to obtain any more resolvents or if [] is obtained as a resolvent. The main result about the resolution method is stated in the next theorem.

> **Theorem 8.4** A set of clauses S is unsatisfiable if and only if [] is obtained in the resolution process.

Let's see now how the resolution method can be applied to check logical implication. Suppose that we have a set of sentences $S = \{A_1, \ldots, A_n\}$ (the hypotheses) and a sentence B (the conclusion). We would like to know whether or not B logically follows from S. We first apply Theorem 8.1 by forming the sentence A_1 & $\ldots$ & A_n & $-B$. This sentence is then transformed into clausal form. Then the resolution method is applied to this set of clauses. If [] is obtained, then A_1 & $\ldots$ & A_n & $-B$ is unsatisfiable, hence B logically follows from S. If there are no more resolvents and [] was not obtained, then B does not logically follow from S. Figure 8.4.5 gives some examples of the application of the resolution method. It should be understood that after any finite amount of time spent on doing resolutions, it may be the case that [] has not been obtained but there are still more resolutions to be performed. At any such point we don't know whether or not B logically follows from S.

This section concludes with two additional items. First, we were originally interested in the concept of logical implication. What we discussed was the resolution method of theorem proving. The symbol used for logical implication is $\models$; $A \models B$ means that A logically implies B. We use the symbol $\vdash$ to indicate the application of some theorem proving method, like resolution. We write $A \vdash B$ if B can be proved from A (by the resolution method as far as we are concerned). Thus, the effect of Theorem 8.4 is to indicate that $\models$ and $\vdash$ are equivalent; that is, $A \models B$ if and only if $A \vdash B$.

Second, the resolution method is not the only technique used in theorem proving. Many theorem provers are based on the resolution method but employ additional processes to gain efficiency. The resolution method, as we described it, is not efficient enough to prove complex theorems.

FIGURE 8.4.5
The Resolution Method

(a) Resolution proof for the logical implication of part (*iii*) of Figure 8.1.1(b)

A_1 = {Ax(Horse(x) → Animal(x))}
B = AxAy(Tail(x,y) & Horse(x) → Tail(x,y) & Animal(x))

A_1 & −B = Ax(Horse(x) → Animal(x))
& −AxAy(Tail(x,y) & Horse(x) → Tail(x,y) & Animal(x))

A_1 & −B in prenex conjunctive normal form =
ExEyAz((−Horse(z) ∨ Animal(z)) & Tail(x,y) & Horse(x)
& (−Tail(x,y) ∨ −Animal(x))

A_1 & −B in clausal form =
−Horse(z) ∨ Animal(z)
Tail(a,b)
Horse(a)
−Tail(a,b) ∨ −Animal(a)

Resolution:

−Horse(z) ∨ Animal(z)   Horse(a)   Tail(a,b)   −Tail(a,b) ∨ −Animal(a)
Animal(a)   −Animal(a)
[]

(b) Using resolution without finding a proof

A_1 = Ax(P_1(x) & P_2(x) → R(x))
A_2 = EyR(y)
B = Ex(P_1(x) ∨ −P_2(x))

A_1 & A_2 & −B = Ax(P_1(x) & P_2(x) → R(x)) & EyR(y)
& −Ex(P_1(x) ∨ −P_2(x))

A_1 & A_2 & −B in prenex conjunctive normal form =
EyAxAz((−P_1(x) ∨ −P_2(x) ∨ R(x)) & R(y) & −P_1(z) & P_2(z))

A_1 & A_2 & −B in clausal form =
−P_1(x) ∨ −P_2(x) ∨ R(x)
R(c)   c is a Skolem constant
−P_1(z)
P_2(u)

Resolution:

−P_1(x) ∨ −P_2(x) ∨ R(x) P_2(u)   R(c)   −P_1(z)
−P_1(x) ∨ R(x)

There are no more resolvents; it is impossible to obtain [].

8.5 Constraints in First-Order Logic

Section 8.2 showed that a relational database can be described in first-order logic, and that the relational calculus, which is based on first-order logic, provides a query language for relational databases. This section will show that integrity constraints can also be expressed in logic; thus, logic can be used to completely describe databases. Also in this section, mechanical theorem proving from the previous section will be used to study the implications of dependencies, a concept that we needed in Chapter 5 when we considered database normalization, but which we did not explicitly discuss there.

We start by learning how to express functional dependencies. Two of the functional dependencies given in Figure 5.1.2 are expressed in logic as Figure 8.5.1(a). The sentence for the first functional dependency can be read as saying that for any two rows of a STUDENT table, if the STNO values are the same, then the STNAME and STADDRESS values must be the same also. In other words, STNO uniquely determines both STNAME and STADDRESS. Similarly, the effect of the second sentence is to say that for any two rows of a STUDENT table, if both the STNO and COURSE values are the same, then the GRADE values must also be the same.

Next we examine the multivalued dependency of Figure 5.3.1(d) as written in logic in Figure 8.5.1(b). We need to express the fact that each EMP value determines a set of CHILD values irrespective of the TASK values. This means that if there are two rows with the same EMP value but different CHILD and TASK values, then there must be a row with the same EMP value, whose CHILD value comes from the first row and whose TASK value comes from the second row. In other words, for every EMP value, we must pair every CHILD value related to that EMP value with every TASK value related to that EMP value. Recall from our discussion of multivalued dependencies that if we have EMPINFO:EMP→→CHILD, then we get EMPINFOEMP→→TASK by symmetry. When we look at the second multivalued dependency in Figure 8.5.1(c), we see that the two formulas are equivalent: the only difference is *in the order* of the conjuncts in the hypothesis, which is immaterial.

We continue with the join dependency RETAIL:*[AGENT COMPANY,AGENT ITEM,COMPANY ITEM] (see Figure 5.3.2 and the related text) as written in Figure 8.5.1(d). We read the sentence as follows: If there are three rows in the RETAIL table—such that the first row's AGENT value is repeated in the second row, the first row's COMPANY value is repeated in the third row, and the second row's ITEM value is repeated in the third row—then there is a row which contains exactly the repeated AGENT, COMPANY, and ITEM values. We write this formula from the join dependency by making each attribute set into a hypothesis with the attributes in the set getting the subscript 1, and having all subscripts equal

FIGURE 8.5.1
Expressing Dependency Constraints in Logic

(a) Functional dependencies from Figure 5.1.2

```
STUDENT:STNO->STNAME,STADDRESS
```

A $STNO_1$ A $STNAME_1$ A $STNAME_2$ A $STADDRESS_1$
A $STADDRESS_2$ A $COURSE_1$ A $COURSE_2$
A $GRADE_1$ A $GRADE_2$ A $CREDITS_1$ A $CREDITS_2$
(STUDENT($STNO_1$,$STNAME_1$,$STADDRESS_1$,$COURSE_1$,$GRADE_1$,$CREDITS_1$)
& STUDENT($STNO_1$,$STNAME_2$,$STADDRESS_2$,$COURSE_2$,$GRADE_2$,$CREDITS_2$)
$\rightarrow$ $STNAME_1$ = $STNAME_2$ & $STADDRESS_1$ = $STADDRESS_2$)

```
STUDENT:STNO,COURSE->GRADE
```

A $STNO_1$ A $STNAME_1$ A $STNAME_2$ A $STADDRESS_1$
A $STADDRESS_2$ A $COURSE_1$ A $GRADE_1$
A $GRADE_2$ A $CREDITS_1$ A $CREDITS_2$
(STUDENT($STNO_1$,$STNAME_1$,$STADDRESS_1$,$COURSE_1$,$GRADE_1$,$CREDITS_1$)
& STUDENT($STNO_1$,$STNAME_2$,$STADDRESS_2$,$COURSE_1$,$GRADE_2$,$CREDITS_2$)
$\rightarrow$ $GRADE_1$ = $GRADE_2$)

(b) Multivalued dependency from Figure 5.3.1

```
EMPINFO:EMP->->CHILD
```

A EMP_1 A $CHILD_1$ A $CHILD_2$ A $TASK_1$ A $TASK_2$
(EMPINFO(EMP_1,$CHILD_1$,$TASK_2$) & EMPINFO(EMP_1,$CHILD_2$,$TASK_1$)
$\rightarrow$ EMPINFO(EMP_1,$CHILD_1$,$TASK_1$))

(c) Another multivalued dependency

```
EMPINFO:EMP->->TASK
```

A EMP_1 A $CHILD_1$ A $CHILD_2$ A $TASK_1$ A $TASK_2$
(EMPINFO(EMP_1,$CHILD_2$,$TASK_1$) & EMPINFO(EMP_1,$CHILD_1$,$TASK_2$)
$\rightarrow$ EMPINFO(EMP_1,$CHILD_1$,$TASK_1$))

(d) A join dependency (see Figure 5.3.2)

```
RETAIL:*[AGENT COMPANY,AGENT ITEM,COMPANY ITEM]
```

A $AGENT_1$ A $AGENT_2$ A $COMPANY_1$ A $COMPANY_2$ A $ITEM_1$ A $ITEM_2$
(RETAIL($AGENT_1$,$COMPANY_1$,$ITEM_2$)
& RETAIL($AGENT_1$,$COMPANY_2$,$ITEM_1$)
& RETAIL($AGENT_2$,$COMPANY_1$,$ITEM_1$)
$\rightarrow$ RETAIL($AGENT_1$,$COMPANY_1$,$ITEM_1$))

(e) Another join dependency

```
T:*[XY,YZ,ZV]
```

AX_1AX_2AX_3AY_1AY_2AZ_1AZ_2AV_1AV_2AV_3
(T(X_1,Y_1,Z_2,V_2) & T(X_2,Y_1,Z_1,V_3) & T(X_3,Y_2,Z_1,V_1)
$\rightarrow$ T(X_1,Y_1,Z_1,V_1))

(continued)

FIGURE 8.5.1 (*continued*)

(f) A domain dependency

```
EMP(NAME,ADDRESS,SALARY,AGE)
EMP:0<=AGE<=100
```

A NAME$_1$ A ADDRESS$_1$ A SALARY$_1$ A AGE$_1$
(EMP(NAME$_1$,ADDRESS$_1$,SALARY$_1$,AGE$_1$) $\rightarrow$ 0 <= AGE$_1$ & AGE$_1$ <= 100)

(g) An inclusion dependency

```
EMPLOYEE(NAME,ADDRESS,SALARY,DEPT)
DEPARTMENT(DEPT,LOCATION,MANAGER)
DEPARTMENT[MANAGER] SUBSET EMPLOYEE[NAME]
```

A DEPT$_1$ A LOCATION$_1$ A MANAGER$_1$ E NAME$_1$ E ADDRESS$_1$ E SALARY$_1$
(DEPARTMENT(DEPT$_1$,LOCATION$_1$,MANAGER$_1$)
$\rightarrow$ EMPLOYEE(NAME$_1$,ADDRESS$_1$,SALARY$_1$,DEPT$_1$) & NAME$_1$ = MANAGER$_1$)

to 1 in the conclusion. Another join dependency in Figure 8.5.1(e) illustrates that not all subscripts need to be 1 or 2.

Next we consider domain dependencies; these are important for DKNF. We usually need built-in predicates like <= to express them. An example of restricting the domain for AGE to between 0 and 100 appears in Figure 8.5.1(f). In Section 5.3, we also discussed inclusion dependencies; these are important types of dependencies relating tables. Figure 8.5.1(g) shows the inclusion dependency from Figure 5.3.3. Because the NAME and MANAGER attributes have the same domain, we can write an equality between their respective variables.

The fact that integrity constraints can be expressed in first-order logic allows us to study implications of integrity constraints in logic. Sections 5.2 and 5.3 suggested the importance of these implications. In particular, implications of functional dependencies were used to determine when a set of attributes forms a key for a table. Implications were needed again to define the notion of dependency preserving decomposition. Implications were also used in our requirement for dealing with a minimal set of functional dependencies. Finally, it was mentioned that functional dependencies imply their corresponding multivalued dependencies; this implication is very useful in connection with Theorem 5.3 concerning lossless join decompositions.

Since integrity constraints can be expressed in first-order logic, the implication of dependencies can be made into a theorem proving problem and the resolution method can be applied to it. Two examples illustrate this. The first example, in part (a) of Figure 8.5.2, shows what is called the **transitivity property** of dependencies; that is, if an attribute functionally determines another attribute, and the second attribute functionally determines a third attribute, then the first attribute also functionally determines the third attribute. (This works in the same way for sets of attributes.) We write the functional dependencies in clausal form. To prove the implication, we must form the negation of the conclusion, that is, the negation of $T:A \rightarrow C$. This is where Skolem constants are introduced; these we denote by lowercase symbols. Since we deal with equality in the proof, we also use axioms that express the symmetry and substitutivity of equality. We present the second example in part (b). This example proves that a functional dependency implies the corresponding multivalued dependency.

FIGURE 8.5.2
Implications of Dependencies

(a) Transitivity of functional dependencies

$T(A,B,C)$
$T:A \rightarrow B$ and $T:B \rightarrow C$ imply $T:A \rightarrow C$

$-T(A_1,B_1,C_1) \vee -T(A_1,B_2,C_2) \vee B_1 = B_2$ \qquad $T(a_1,b_1,c_1)$

$-T(a_1,B_2,C_2) \vee b_1 = B_2$ \qquad $T(a_1,b_2,c_2)$

$b_1 = b_2$ \qquad $-B_3 = B_4 \vee B_4 = B_3$

$b_2 = b_1$ \qquad $-T(A_5,B_5,C_5) \vee -B_5 = B_6 \vee T(A_5,B_6,C_5)$

$-T(A_5,b_2,C_5) \vee T(A_5,b_1,C_5)$ \qquad $T(a_1,b_2,c_2)$

$T(a_1,b_1,c_2)$ \qquad $-T(A_3,B_3,C_3) \vee -T(A_4,B_3,C_4) \vee C_3 = C_4$

$-T(A_4,b_1,C_4) \vee c_2 = C_4$ \qquad $T(a_1,b_1,c_1)$

$c_2 = c_1$ \qquad $-C_6 = C_7 \vee C_7 = C_6$

$c_1 = c_2$ \qquad $-c_1 = c_2$

$[ ]$

(continued)

FIGURE 8.5.2 (*continued*)

(b) Functional dependency implies multivalued dependency

$T(A,B,C)$
$T:A \rightarrow B$ implies $T:A \rightarrow\!\!\rightarrow B$

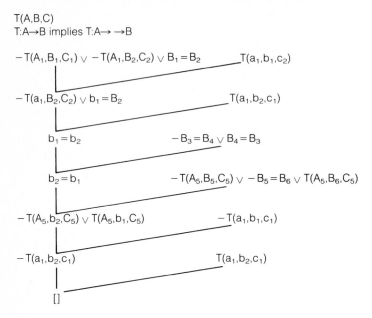

Because of the importance of the implications of dependencies, theorem proving can be a useful tool in database design. As an example, suppose that $D_1, D_2 \vdash D_3$, where the D_i are dependencies. This means that for every database where D_1 and D_2 hold, D_3 must hold also. In particular, if a view contains D_1 and D_2, and D_3 is a join dependency on T, then the decomposition of T into the tables represented by the attribute sets in D_3 is lossless join. (We stated in the previous section that logical implication, $\models$, and provability, $\vdash$, are equivalent.)

Now let's see how we can use implications to find a minimal set of functional dependencies, a notion used for Algorithm 5.2. Given the set of functional dependencies $S = \{D_1, D_2, \ldots, D_n\}$ (each with a single attribute on the right-hand side), we must make sure that $S - \{D_i\}$ does not imply D_i for any i. This means that no functional dependency can be proved from the others. Also, for each $D_i = T:W \rightarrow A$, where $W = B_1 \ldots B_m$ is a set of attributes, we must make sure that $(S - D_i) \cup \{T:W' \rightarrow A\}$ does not imply D_i for any W', where $W' = W - \{B_j\}$ for some j. In other words, we must make sure that each functional dependency has minimal hypotheses.

Next we will see how implication is used for the notion of dependency preserving decomposition, which we defined somewhat informally in Section 5.2. Suppose that there is a view with a set of functional dependencies F. Assume that we can generate the set of functional dependencies implied by F, which we call **F+**. (We will come back to this soon.) Now generate F+ and keep all those elements of F+ that are meaningful for the decomposition: that is, those functional dependencies for which all of the attributes are in one of the new projected tables. Call this set P; these are the projected functional dependencies. Thus, we can write a formal definition as follows: a decomposition is **dependency preserving** if P implies F; that is, *if the projected functional dependencies imply the original functional dependencies*. We used F+ to obtain P because if $T(A,B,C)$ contains $T:A{\rightarrow}B$ and $T:B{\rightarrow}C$, and if T is decomposed into $T_1(A,B)$, $T_2(B,C)$, $T_3(A,C)$, then we would want to have the dependencies $T_1:A{\rightarrow}B$, $T_2:B{\rightarrow}C$, and $T_3:A{\rightarrow}C$ in the new view, since $T:A{\rightarrow}C$ is implied by $T:A{\rightarrow}B$ and $T:B{\rightarrow}C$. This also explains the remark concerning the additional functional dependency for EMPTASKNAME2 in Figure 5.2.2(c).

Theoretically, it is also possible to apply theorem proving to check if a database instance is consistent with the integrity constraints in the database view. As shown in Section 8.2, we can describe the database as a set of atomic formulas. We can then add the formulas for integrity constraints and try to obtain [] by resolution. If [] is obtained, then the database is inconsistent with the integrity constraints. This may be useful as a check for illegal updates; in general, however, it is not an efficient method.

Similarly, we can solve all implication problems for integrity constraints by theorem proving. However, often we want to deal with implication only between certain special kinds of statements, such as functional dependencies. The resolution method, or some other general theorem proving technique, is not the most efficient one to use under those circumstances. In fact, special methods exist for obtaining implications among various classes of dependencies.

This section concludes by describing the **Armstrong rules** (after W. W. Armstrong, who proposed a similar set in 1974) for functional dependencies. (There exist rules for multivalued dependencies also, as well as for certain combinations of different kinds of dependencies.) These rules can be used, in particular, to obtain F+ from F. For these rules, assume that T is the table on which we are considering dependencies; U is the set of attributes of T (so we omit T:); and X, Y, Z are subsets of U. The rules are as follows:

1. (**Reflexivity**) If Y is a subset of X, then $X{\rightarrow}Y$ holds.
2. (**Augmentation**) If $X{\rightarrow}Y$ holds, then $XZ{\rightarrow}YZ$ holds.
3. (**Transitivity**) If $X{\rightarrow}Y$ and $Y{\rightarrow}Z$ hold, then $X{\rightarrow}Z$ holds.

Given a set of functional dependencies F, the Armstrong rules can be applied one at a time to obtain additional functional dependencies. It

FIGURE 8.5.3
An Application of the Armstrong Rules

T(A,B,C,E,G,H)
F = {AB→C, EC→GH},   D = ABE→H
Proof that F implies D:

Step 1—Apply rule 2 to AB→C to obtain ABE→CE.
Step 2—Apply rule 3 to ABE→CE and EC→GH to obtain ABE→GH.
Step 3—Apply rule 1 to obtain GH→H.
Step 4—Apply rule 3 to ABE→GH and GH→H to obtain ABE→H.

is not difficult to see that if we start with F and obtain a functional dependency D by applying the rules (a finite number of times), then F must imply D. An example of such a derivation appears in Figure 8.5.3. It turns out that these rules are also complete in the sense that if F implies D then D can be obtained from F by applying the rules. We end our discussion of the Armstrong rules by stating this result.

> **Theorem 8.5**   For any set of functional dependencies F, F+ is the set of functional dependencies that can be obtained by applying the Armstrong rules 1–3 to F.

8.6 Exercises

8.1   For all the interpretations in Figure 8.6.1 and each sentence in Figure 8.1.3(c), indicate and justify the truth or falsity of the sentence.

8.2   Among the sentences below, which are valid and which are unsatisfiable? Indicate the pairs of sentences which are equivalent.

(a) Ax (P(x) ∨ P(x)).   (d) AxAy (R(x,y) → R(y,x)).
(b) Ey (R(a,y) ∨ P(b)).   (e) Ax (P(x) & P(x)).
(c) AxAy (R(x,y) → R(x,y)).   (f) ExEy (R(x,y) & − R(x,y)).

8.3   Write a many-sorted first-order representation, including language and interpretation, for the relational databases in:

(a) Figure 4.6.1.   (d) Figure 4.6.4.
(b) Figure 4.6.2.   (e) Figure 4.6.5.
(c) Figure 4.6.3.

8.4   Using your answer to Exercise 8.3(a), write relational calculus queries and updates for the items in Exercise 4.2.

8.5   Using your answer to Exercise 8.3(b), write relational calculus queries and updates for the items in Exercise 4.3.

8.6   Using your answer to Exercise 8.3(c), write relational calculus queries and updates for the items in Exercise 4.4.

FIGURE 8.6.1
Interpretations

(a) D = {0,1,2,3}
  I(P) = {<m,n> | m < n}
  I(R) = {<m,n> | m < = n}
  I(a) = 1
  I(b) = 0

(b) D = {1,2,3,4}
  I(P) = {<1,1>}
  I(R) = {<2,1>,<2,2>,<2,3>,<2,4>}
  I(a) = 1
  I(b) = 2

(c) D = the set of all integers
  I(P) = {<m,n> | m < = n}
  I(R) = {<m,n> | m > = n}
  I(a) = -10
  I(b) = 5

(d) D = {1,2,3}
  I(P) = {<1,1>,<2,3>}
  I(R) = {<2,1>,<3,1>}
  I(a) = 2
  I(b) = 2

(e) D = {purple,red,yellow}
  I(P) = {<purple,red>,<red,yellow>,<yellow,purple>}
  I(R) = {<purple,red>,<red,yellow>,<yellow,purple>,
        <purple,purple>,<purple,yellow>}
  I(a) = red
  I(b) = purple

(f) D = {orange,apple,pear}
  I(P) = {<orange,apple>,<apple,pear>,<pear,orange>}
  I(R) = {<pear,orange>,<pear,apple>,<pear,pear>}
  I(a) = pear
  I(b) = pear

8.7 Using your answer to Exercise 8.3(d), write relational calculus queries and updates for the items in Exercise 4.5.

8.8 Using your answer to Exercise 8.3(e), write relational calculus queries and updates for the items in Exercise 4.6.

8.9 In Figure 8.6.2, simplify each query of part (b) on the view of part (a).

8.10 Use the method given in Section 8.3 to transform the following relational algebra queries on the view of Figure 8.6.2(a) to relational calculus queries:

(a) PROJECT(SELECT(EQUIPMENT: ONUMBER = '200'); TYPE,COST),

(b) PROJECT(JOIN(EQUIPMENT,LAWYER); SERIALNO,LSSNO),

(c) PROJECT(JOIN(SELECT(EQUIPMENT: COST < 5000), LAWYER); LNAME,TYPE).

8.11 Using the method given in Section 8.3, take the relational calculus queries obtained in Exercise 8.9 after simplification and transform them to relational algebra queries.

8.12 Transform the following sentences to clausal form. For each sen-

FIGURE 8.6.2
A View and Queries

(a) View

```
OFFICE(ONUMBER,AREA)
EQUIPMENT(SERIALNO,TYPE,COST,ONUMBER)
LAWYER(ONUMBER,LSSNO,LNAME,ADDRESS,SALARY,STATUS,TELNO)
OFFICE:ONUMBER->AREA
EQUIPMENT:SERIALNO->TYPE,COST,ONUMBER
LAWYER:LSSNO->ONUMBER,LNAME,ADDRESS,SALARY,STATUS,TELNO
EQUIPMENT[ONUMBER] SUBSET OFFICE[ONUMBER]
LAWYER[ONUMBER] SUBSET OFFICE[ONUMBER]
```

(b) Queries

```
(i) GET (LNAME₁,TYPE₁) ! E ONUMBER₁ E LSSNO₁ E ADDRESS₁
         E STATUS₁ E TELNO₁ E LSSNO₂ E ADDRESS₂
         E SALARY₁ E TELNO₂ E ONUMBER₂ E LNAME₂
         E SALARY₂ E STATUS₂ E TELNO₃ E SERIALNO₁
         E COST₁
         ( LAWYER(ONUMBER₁,LSSNO₁,LNAME₁,ADDRESS₁,45000,
           STATUS₁,TELNO₁)
         & LAWYER(ONUMBER₁,LSSNO₂,LNAME₁,ADDRESS₂,
           SALARY₁, STATUS₁,TELNO₂)
         & LAWYER(ONUMBER₂,LSSNO₁,LNAME₂,ADDRESS₂,
           SALARY₂, STATUS₂,TELNO₃)
         & EQUIPMENT(SERIALNO₁,TYPE₁,COST₁,ONUMBER₁) )
(ii) GET (SERIALNO₁) ! E ONUMBER₁ E AREA₁ E COST₁
          ( OFFICE(ONUMBER₁,AREA₁)
          & EQUIPMENT(SERIALNO₁,Computer,COST₁,ONUMBER₁)
          & COST₁ < 5000 )
(iii) GET (ONUMBER₁) ! E AREA₁ E SERIALNO₁ E COST₁ E TYPE₁
          E COST₂ E ONUMBER₂ E LSSNO₁ E LNAME₁ E ADDRESS₁
          E SALARY₁ E STATUS₁ E TELNO₁ E LNAME₂
          E ADDRESS₂ E STATUS₂ E TELNO₂
          ( OFFICE(ONUMBER₁,AREA₁)
          & EQUIPMENT(SERIALNO₁,Computer,COST₁,ONUMBER₁)
          & EQUIPMENT(SERIALNO₁,TYPE₁,COST₂,ONUMBER₂)
          & LAWYER(ONUMBER₂,LSSNO₁,LNAME₁,ADDRESS₁,
            SALARY₁,STATUS₁,TELNO₁)
          & LAWYER(ONUMBER₁,LSSNO₁,LNAME₂,ADDRESS₂,
            SALARY₁,STATUS₂,TELNO₂)
          & SALARY₁ > 50000 )
```

tence, indicate both the prenex conjunctive normal form and the
Skolem normal form.

(a) $Ax (P(x,a) \vee EyR(x,y,b))$ & $P(b,a)$.
(b) $AxEy (R(x,y,a) \rightarrow P(x,y) \vee EzP(x,z))$.
(c) $ExEyP(x,y)$ & $AzExR(x,x,z)$.

FIGURE 8.6.3
Implications

(a) A₁: Ax (Man(x) → Mortal(x))
    A₂: Mortal(Socrates)
    B : Man(Socrates)

(b) A₁: Ax (Tiger(x) → − Grasseater(x))
    A₂: Ex (Animal(x) & Grasseater(x) & Tame(x))
    B : Ex (Animal(x) & Tame(x) & − Tiger(x))

(c) A₁: AxEy(R(y) → P(x))
    A₂: AxEy(P(y) → R(x))
    B : Ex(R₁(x) & − R(x))

8.13 Use the resolution method to try to obtain proofs for the implications in Figure 8.6.3. In each case the A_i's are the hypotheses and B is the conclusion.

8.14 Express the functional dependencies of the views in Figure 5.6.2 in first-order logic.

8.15 Express the following dependencies on $T(X,Y,Z,V)$ and $T'(Y,V,W)$ in first-order logic:

    (a) T:XY→→Z.
    (b) T:X→→YZ.
    (c) T:*[XY,YZ,YV].
    (d) T:*[XYZ,XV].
    (e) T:10<=Y<=20.
    (f) T':0<=Y<=50.
    (g) T[Y] SUBSET T'[Y].
    (h) T[Y,V] SUBSET T'[Y,V].

8.16 Apply the Armstrong rules to show the following:

    (a) {AB→C, AB→D} implies {AB→CD}.
    (b) {AB→C, CD→F} implies {ABD→F}.
    (c) {AB→C, B→CD, D→FG} implies {AB→G}.

8.7 Guide to Further Reading

The relational calculus is discussed in [1.1] Chapter 9, [1.2] Chapter 14, [1.4] Chapter 5, and [5.3] Chapter 10. Optimization for relational calculus queries is presented in [1.4] Chapter 8 and [5.3] Chapter 11. There are many books on logic; a particularly nice introduction to logic and to theorem proving can be found in [8.1]. [8.2] investigates the formulation of database dependencies in first-order logic and gives applications.

[8.1] Chang, C.-L., and R. C.-T. Lee. *Symbolic Logic and Mechanical Theorem Proving*. New York: Academic Press, 1973.

[8.2] Grant, J., and B. E. Jacobs. "On the Family of Generalized Dependency Constraints." *Journal of the ACM* 29(1982), pp. 986–997.

Intelligent Databases

9.1 Deductive Databases

Database systems were originally designed and implemented for the efficient storage, management, and retrieval of large amounts of data. In this chapter, we consider additional capabilities that we may want more sophisticated database systems to possess. Along these lines, recall from Section 7.4 our brief discussion of the Fifth Generation Computer Systems Project; the basic (in some sense the machine) language for this project is Prolog, a language based on first-order logic. The topics of this chapter are deduction for database systems, the Prolog language, and natural language interfaces to database systems. These topics involve the interaction of two areas of computer science: artificial intelligence and databases.

Artificial intelligence *is the science of building computer systems that exhibit intelligent behavior.* Programs have been designed, for example, to play games of intellect such as go, chess, and checkers. There are programs that can be used to prove mathematical theorems. Some systems have been constructed which understand natural language, so that a user does not have to write a program in some (artificial) programming language. Expert systems are systems which are able to solve problems in a limited domain as well as a human expert; such systems have been constructed for the diagnosis of certain types of illnesses and for analyzing chemical structures, to name just a few applications.

We start our consideration of deductive databases with a simple example. Let's assume that our database consists of a single table

FIGURE 9.1.1
The Family Database as a Relational Database

(a) Using one table

    (*i*) Database instance

PARENT	
CNAME	PNAME
Smith John Jr	Smith John
Smith John Jr	Smith Mary
Rogers Charles	Rogers Linda
Rogers Linda	Jones David
Rogers Linda	Jones Mary
Smith Mary	Ford Albert
Cramer Steven	Cramer William

    (*ii*) Relational calculus query to find the parent(s) of Charles Rogers

```
GET (X) : PARENT(Rogers Charles,X)
```

(b) Using two tables

    (*i*) Database instance

PARENT	
CNAME	PNAME
Smith John Jr	Smith John
Smith John Jr	Smith Mary
Rogers Charles	Rogers Linda
Rogers Linda	Jones David
Rogers Linda	Jones Mary
Smith Mary	Ford Albert
Cramer Steven	Cramer William

GRANDPARENT	
CNAME	GPNAME
Rogers Charles	Jones David
Rogers Charles	Jones Mary
Smith John Jr	Ford Albert

    (*ii*) Relational calculus query to find the grandparent(s) of Charles Rogers

```
GET (X) : GRANDPARENT(Rogers Charles,X)
```

PARENT that contains the names of individuals and the names of (some of) their parents as in part (*i*) of Figure 9.1.1(a). Considering this as a relational database, we can write atomic queries to find the names of an individual's parents, as shown in part (*ii*), for example. (We are not using a many-sorted language here, because all the elements are names and so have the same type.) It would be convenient if we could write an atomic query to find an individual's grandparents using a grandparent predicate. One possibility is the addition of a table that lists grandparents. This is how we obtain the instance in part (*i*) of Figure 9.1.1(b); the atomic query to find grandparents appears as part of (*ii*). (We will discuss this example further in Section 9.3.)

The GRANDPARENT table contains redundant information, since we obtained it from the PARENT table by using our knowledge that a grandparent is a parent's parent. It would be better if we could just give the database a rule that uses precisely this definition, as well as the PARENT table, and then be able to write atomic queries involving the notion of grandparent. This is the type of thing that can be done in a deductive database system.

A **deductive database** instance consists of two components: an **extensional database**—*the tables*—and an **intensional database**—*the rules*. The rules are expressed in first-order logic and are used to define the intensional database in terms of the extensional database. We do not exclude the case where a table is defined both extensionally and intensionally: in that case the intensional component defines rows in addition to the extensional component. However, we do not consider such an example here.

Figure 9.1.2 represents the Family database as a deductive database; the extensional portion is the same as the table given before in part (*i*) of Figure 9.1.1(a). The intensional portion consists of a single axiom defining the GRANDPARENT table in terms of the PARENT table: that is, a grandparent is a parent of a parent, as shown in Figure 9.1.2(b). In part (c), we consider a query about grandparents which is identical to the query on the instance with two tables given in part (*i*) of Figure 9.1.1(b). The axiom, in a compact way, defines another table for the database. Note that such a definition is similar to the notion of view in SQL, discussed in Section 4.5. However, here the new predicate is not a separate view but becomes part of the original database. Also, SQL does not allow recursive definitions, which can be used to define intensional predicates, as will be illustrated in Section 9.3.

We could certainly make every database completely extensional, but the advantage of an intensional portion is the compactness of the representation: in large databases, we may be able to avoid having to store some big tables. Thus, we reduce redundancy and save on storage space. The problem now is how to evaluate a query in a deductive database. If the query contains only extensional tables, then there is no problem; it can just be evaluated as for a standard database system. But if the query contains one or more intensionally defined tables, then its evaluation must involve the appropriate intensional axiom(s).

It is convenient now to make a distinction between the so-called model-theoretic and proof-theoretic approaches to databases. In both cases, a first-order logic language appropriate to the database is defined initially. The **model-theoretic approach** is basically the one presented in Section 8.2. There, *a database instance is identified with a particular interpre-*

FIGURE 9.1.2
The Family Database as a Deductive Relational Database

(a) Extensional database

PARENT	
CNAME	PNAME
Smith John Jr	Smith John
Smith John Jr	Smith Mary
Rogers Charles	Rogers Linda
Rogers Linda	Jones David
Rogers Linda	Jones Mary
Smith Mary	Ford Albert
Cramer Steven	Cramer William

(b) Intensional database

AXAYAZ (PARENT(X,Y) & PARENT(Y,Z) → GRANDPARENT(X,Z))

(c) Relational calculus query to find the grandparent(s) of Charles Rogers

```
GET (X) ! GRANDPARENT(Rogers Charles,X)
```

tation. A query in the relational calculus is a formula whose answers are the substitutions of constants for the variables that make the formula true for that interpretation. In the **proof-theoretic approach**, *a database instance is identified with a set of formulas of the language.* A query in the relational calculus is a formula whose answers are the substitutions of constants for the variables that can be proved from the database instance. For dealing with deductive databases, and even with concepts such as the Closed World Assumption and null values, the proof-theoretic approach tends to be more useful, and we will follow it here.

Recall now our discussion of theorem proving from Section 8.4. We think of a database instance as a set of formulas in first-order logic, where each row of a table is represented as an atomic formula. This representation appears in Figure 9.1.3. Then the facts about the database are the ones that can be proved from the database. This criterion generalizes the notion of an ordinary relational database in the sense that since there are no axioms for such a database, only the original facts present in the tables can be proved.

Figure 9.1.4 shows two resolution proofs. The first is for the statement that Linda Rogers is a parent of Charles Rogers, and the second is for the statement that Mary Jones is a grandparent of Charles Rogers. In resolution theorem proving, the conclusion must be negated and all

FIGURE 9.1.3
The Family Database as a Set of Formulas of First-Order Logic

```
PARENT(Smith John Jr,Smith John)
PARENT(Smith John Jr,Smith Mary)
PARENT(Rogers Charles,Rogers Linda)
PARENT(Rogers Linda,Jones David)
PARENT(Rogers Linda,Jones Mary)
PARENT(Smith Mary,Ford Albert)
PARENT(Cramer Steven,Cramer William)
AXAYAZ (PARENT(X,Y) & PARENT(Y,Z) -> GRANDPARENT(X,Z))
```

FIGURE 9.1.4
Proof of Statements for the Family Database

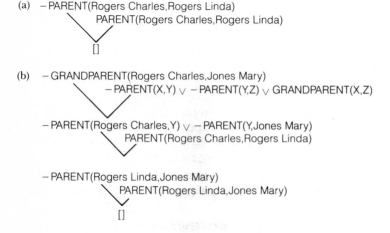

formulas must be converted into clausal form. The first case involves only one resolution with a fact in the extensional database. For the second example, we resolve the negation of the conclusion with the axiom defining GRANDPARENT. The clause obtained this way can be resolved with two facts from the extensional database for the proof. Suppose next that we ask for all the grandparents of Charles Rogers. In that case we try to prove GRANDPARENT(Rogers Charles,V) where V is a variable standing for a solution. The set of solutions comprises the set of constants which, when substituted for V in the proof, yield []. This outcome is shown in Figure 9.1.5. There are two ways to obtain [], either by substituting Mary Jones for V or by substituting David Jones for V. The set of substitutions for the unknown that lead to a solution forms the answer to the query.

Using a theorem prover is not necessarily the only way to implement a deductive database. In particular, for our grandparent example we can

FIGURE 9.1.5
Solving a Query in the Family Database

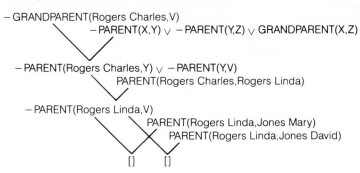

simply use a substitution: whenever GRANDPARENT(X,Z) appears in a query, we can substitute the formula EY(PARENT(X,Y) & PARENT(Y,Z)) for it. Thus, we reduce a search involving a theorem prover over a deductive database to a standard search over a relational (extensional) database. However, such a substitution cannot be done in a simple manner for tables that are defined recursively, such as the one for ancestor that we will look at later.

Recall the Closed World Assumption (CWA), which was discussed in Section 8.2. The CWA allows us to assume a negative fact if the corresponding positive fact is not in the database. This assumption works for the extensional database, but not for the intensional database. For example, since there are no rows in the GRANDPARENT table, by the original CWA we could assume that GRANDPARENT is false for every pair of names. But this assumption clearly cannot be correct, since we can prove statements such as GRANDPARENT(Rogers Charles, Jones Mary) from the database. Thus, in this case we have to modify the CWA by saying that we can assume a negative fact exactly if the corresponding positive fact is not *provable* from the database. Note that if the database is purely extensional, then the only positive facts provable from the database are the ones that are already in the tables. Therefore, for a standard relational database, this new definition of the CWA is identical to the old one.

Next our family relationship database is extended to show more examples of deduction. Assume that in addition to the PARENT table, there is a table called MALE which contains the names of all male individuals in the database, as shown in part (a) of Figure 9.1.6. This database has no direct facts relating children to fathers. Again, if we wanted this information, we could create another table FATHER to list the names of all the children and their fathers. But there is an easier way. Instead, for the intensional database we can write a rule for FATHER in terms of

FIGURE 9.1.6
An Extended Family Database

(a) Extensional database

PARENT	
CNAME	PNAME
Smith John Jr	Smith John
Smith John Jr	Smith Mary
Rogers Charles	Rogers Linda
Rogers Linda	Jones David
Rogers Linda	Jones Mary
Smith Mary	Ford Albert
Cramer Steven	Cramer William

MALE
NAME
Smith John Jr
Smith John
Rogers Charles
Jones David
Ford Albert
Cramer Steven
Cramer William

(b) Intensional database

AXAY (PARENT(X,Y) & MALE(Y) → FATHER(X,Y))
AXAYAZ (PARENT(X,Y) & PARENT(Y,Z) → GRANDPARENT(X,Z))
AXAYAZ (GRANDPARENT(X,Y) & FATHER(Z,Y) → GRANDFATHER(X,Y))

(c) Relational calculus query to find the grandfather(s) of Charles Rogers

```
GET (X) : GRANDFATHER(Rogers Charles,X)
```

(d) Executing the query using a theorem prover

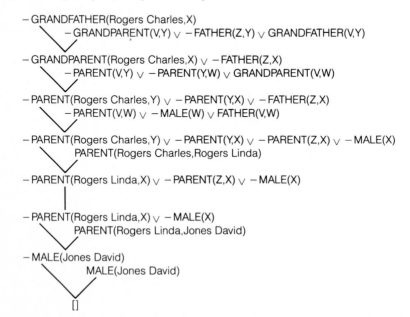

PARENT and MALE, as shown in part (b). Assume also that we still have the rule for GRANDPARENT. Now we can write a rule for GRAND-FATHER using the intensionally defined tables GRANDPARENT and FATHER. The definition for an intensionally defined table can use previously defined intensional tables. (There is a simpler way of defining GRANDFATHER in terms of GRANDPARENT and MALE; our method of definition is for illustrative purposes only.)

We end this section with a proof to show that an answer to the question, "Who is a grandfather of Charles Rogers?" is "David Jones." The query, written in the relational calculus, appears in part (c) of Figure 9.1.6; the resolution proof appears in part (d). In several places, variables are renamed in accordance with the resolution rule. First, GRAND-FATHER is reduced to GRANDPARENT and FATHER. Second, GRANDPARENT is reduced to PARENT (applied twice). (Alternatively, we could have reduced FATHER first. In general, there may be several alternatives for any step.) Next, we use the axiom for FATHER to reduce it to PARENT and MALE. After this point, facts from the PARENT and MALE tables are used. At some point, where both $-$PARENT(Rogers Linda,$GFNAME_1$) and $-$PARENT(Z,$GFNAME_1$) appear as disjuncts in a clause, we obtain a factor for the formula by unifying these two negations. Finally, we obtain [] by substituting the name "Jones David" for $GFNAME_1$. Hence, "David Jones" is a solution. For this database, that is the only solution.

Let's review our understanding so far. We learned in the previous chapter that first-order logic can be used to describe database views and to write database queries. In this section, we saw that we can expand the notion of relational database to that of deductive database by the addition of rules, written in first-order logic, to define additional tables intensionally. Thus, first-order logic can be used exclusively as a uniform language for relational databases. It would be convenient if there were a programming language in which we could write logical formulas and where we could do theorem proving. Such a language could then be used for implementing a deductive database system. There is, in fact, such a language. This language, Prolog, is the topic of the next section.

9.2 Introduction to Prolog

Prolog is a language whose statements are formulas of first-order logic. Its underlying mechanism is a special type of theorem prover. While Prolog can be used as a programming language, we will consider those aspects of Prolog which are related to databases. We noted before that Prolog is the foundation language for the Fifth Generation Computer

Systems Project, whose aim is to develop highly intelligent computer systems that can store vast amounts of information. The interaction between logic and databases, as exemplified in the application of the relational calculus and the notion of deductive database, is a key idea in the construction of a new generation of intelligent computers.

Often, in books and articles, Prolog is presented to people who have no knowledge of first-order logic. Since we have already considered the fundamental concepts of logic, the basic principles of Prolog will sound familiar. Prolog does not yet have a standard syntax; in this and the following sections we follow a syntax which is common to many Prolog systems. The basic statements of Prolog are special types of formulas of first-order logic written in a specific clausal form. In Figure 9.2.1(a), we see some examples of how facts are expressed in Prolog using the Family database of the previous section.

Except for some minor points of syntax, the Prolog statements concerning facts are the same as the first-order formulas presented in Figure 9.1.3. Since we write each name as a single constant, and since no blanks are allowed in an identifier, we place an underscore between the last and first name. There is another option, however; Prolog allows us to write a name in quotes instead, so that we could have written the first statement as parent("Smith John Jr","Smith John"). We begin names with a lower-case letter because Prolog (in most versions) assumes that a name which starts with a capital letter, if not enclosed within quotes, represents a variable. We end each statement with a period (as in English, but not as in first-order logic). In Prolog, unlike some other programming languages, there are no declarations; the meanings of objects are determined by the language interpreter or compiler based on context. In particular, the name "parent" is treated in Prolog as a binary predicate symbol.

Figure 9.2.1(b) shows the intensional axiom for grandparent—from Figure 9.1.2(b)—in Prolog. Note that there are some differences between the Prolog statement and the version in first-order logic. In particular, the universal quantifiers are missing. The reason is that the statements of Prolog correspond to a special class of formulas of first-order logic

FIGURE 9.2.1
Prolog Statements

(a) Facts

```
parent(smith_john_jr,smith_john).
parent(rogers_charles,rogers_linda).
```

(b) An axiom

```
grandparent(X,Z) :- parent(X,Y),parent(Y,Z).
```

called universal Horn formulas. A **universal Horn formula** *is a formula in prenex conjunctive normal form* (see Section 8.4), *where all the quantifiers are universal and the matrix is a single conjunct that contains at most one positive literal.* In clausal form, a universal Horn formula has the form $-A_1 \vee \ldots \vee -A_n \vee A_{n+1}$, where the A_{n+1} is optional.

Prolog statements that represent facts and axioms contain such an A_{n+1}, while the queries do not. A ":−" separates the two sides of an axiom. The conclusion (the portion to the right of the → in the formula, which is the same as the positive literal in the clausal form) is written to the left of the :−, while the hypotheses (the portion to the left of the → in the formula, or the negative literals in the clausal form) are written to the right. Atomic formulas in the hypotheses are separated by commas. Another way of thinking of these Prolog statements is by considering them as *if . . . then . . .* rules with the hypotheses on the right-hand side and the conclusion on the left-hand side, as $A_{n+1} \leftarrow A_1, \ldots, A_n$. We note here that many of the formulas that we wrote for integrity constraints in Section 8.5 can be expressed as universal Horn formulas, and can therefore be written in Prolog as axioms. In particular, we can write all join (and therefore multivalued) dependencies in Prolog for the database, thereby making Prolog generate (implicitly) the additional rows that may be required after an insertion or an update.

Let's see how we can use Prolog to answer a question about a database. First, in Figure 9.2.2(a), Prolog statements are written to describe the Family database (see Figures 9.1.2 and 9.1.3 for the deductive relational and the first-order logic representations, respectively). Then, in

FIGURE 9.2.2
The Family Database in Prolog

(a) Facts and axioms

```
parent(smith_john_jr,smith_john).
parent(smith_john_jr,smith_mary).
parent(rogers_charles,rogers_linda).
parent(rogers_linda,jones_david).
parent(rogers_linda,jones_mary).
parent(smith_mary,ford_albert).
parent(cramer_steven,cramer_william).
grandparent(X,Z) :- parent(X,Y),parent(Y,Z).
```

(b) Prolog query to find the parent(s) of Charles Rogers

```
?- parent(rogers_charles,X).
```

(c) Prolog query to find the grandparent(s) of Charles Rogers

```
?- grandparent(rogers_charles,X).
```

parts (b) and (c) of Figure 9.2.2, two queries are written to find the parent(s) and grandparent(s) of Charles Rogers, respectively. A "?–" begins each query.

Because Prolog queries are formulas in first-order logic, they are closely related to relational calculus queries. By comparing the queries in parts (b) and (c) of Figure 9.2.2 to the ones in parts (a) and (b) of Figure 9.1.1, we see that the main difference is that "GET( ) |" is not used in Prolog. Usually, the answer to a question is a (set of) substitution(s) for the variable(s) of the query. We can type a semicolon to request another answer. After all the answers have been displayed, Prolog's answer is "no" (this also happens at the beginning if there are no answers at all). Such a question-answer session for the Family database appears in Figure 9.2.3. The system's prompts and answers are shown in the darker typeface. Note that we decided not to ask for a second grandparent of John Smith, Jr., and that we included a yes-no query.

Recall that for Prolog, the underlying mechanism for getting the answers is a theorem prover. This internal Prolog theorem prover is based on the resolution rule, but it uses resolution in a specific, predetermined way. Reviewing our discussion on resolution theorem proving, we note that in many cases during the proof, several resolutions are possible. Prolog follows a specific rule, called its control structure, for doing the resolutions. The example that follows is for illustration.

In this example, the extended Family database of Figure 9.1.6 is written in Prolog, along with a query, in Figure 9.2.4. The use of variables within and among statements is the same in Prolog as in first-order logic. We may use the same variable X in several statements, such as the definitions of father, grandparent, and grandfather; the uses of X are local to each formula, hence they are distinct. But within each statement, the Xs represent the same variable; in particular, for the first Prolog statement which represents an axiom, the X in father must be the same as the X in parent.

FIGURE 9.2.3
Question-Answer Session in Prolog

```
?- parent(rogers_linda,X).
X=jones_david;
X=jones_mary;
no
?-parent(jones_mary,X).
no
?-grandparent(smith_john_jr,X).
X=ford_albert
?-parent(smith_john_jr,smith_john).
yes
```

FIGURE 9.2.4
The Extended Family Database in Prolog and Query

(a) The database in Prolog

```
parent(smith_john_jr,smith_john).
parent(smith_john_jr,smith_mary).
parent(rogers_charles,rogers_linda).
parent(rogers_linda,jones_david).
parent(rogers_linda,jones_mary).
parent(smith_mary,ford_albert).
parent(cramer_steven,cramer_william).
male(smith_john_jr).
male(smith_john).
male(rogers_charles).
male(jones_david).
male(ford_albert).
male(cramer_steven).
male(cramer_william).
father(X,Y) :- parent(X,Y),male(Y).
grandparent(X,Z) :- parent(X,Y),parent(Y,Z).
grandfather(X,Y) :- grandparent(X,Y),father(Z,Y).
```

(b) Prolog query to find the grandfather(s) of Charles Rogers

```
?- grandfather(rogers_charles,X).
```

In Figure 9.2.5, we see how a query is evaluated in Prolog, where we think of Prolog as a resolution theorem prover. (The next section will show that there is another way to analyze Prolog's action in answering queries.) As in Figure 9.1.6(d), we first negate the conclusion (this is the query now) and try to resolve this clause with the clauses in the database. Prolog looks for the first clause in the database that resolves with the leftmost literal in the query. Here the query has only one literal, and there is also only one clause in the database which resolves with it— namely, the clause which defines grandfather. We write each Prolog statement in clausal form with the hypotheses negated and the conclusion positive, to do the resolution proof, and indicate all the substitutions for unification.

Because, for resolution, the variables in different clauses must be distinct, we start by renaming X to V in the axiom. We obtain a negated clause with − grandparent and − father. Prolog next tries to resolve the leftmost negated atom. This involves the definition of grandparent in terms of parent. In forming the new clause, we place the new negative literals on the left in their original order. Prolog always tries to resolve the leftmost literal of the clause obtained by resolutions from the query. No other type of resolution is allowed.

FIGURE 9.2.5
Query Evaluation in Prolog Using Resolution

− grandfather(rogers_charles,X)
     − grandparent(V,Y) ∨ − father(Z,Y) ∨ grandfather(V,Y)

     {rogers_charles/V,X/Y}

− grandparent(rogers_charles,X) ∨ − father(Z,X)
     − parent(V,Y) ∨ − parent(Y,W) ∨ grandparent(V,W)

     {rogers_charles/V,X/W}

− parent(rogers_charles,Y) ∨ − parent(Y,X) ∨ − father(Z,X)
     parent(rogers_charles,rogers_linda)

     {rogers_linda/Y}

− parent(rogers_linda,X) ∨ − father(Z,X)
     parent(rogers_linda,jones_david)

     {jones_david/X}

− father(Z,jones_david)
     − parent(X,Y) ∨ − male(Y) ∨ father(X,Y)

     {Z/X,jones_david/Y}

− parent(Z,jones_david) ∨ − male(jones_david)
     parent(rogers_linda,jones_david)

     {rogers_linda/Z}

− male(jones_david)
     male(jones_david)

     []

       X = jones_david

When we get to the parent predicate, we can use the facts in the database. In the case of − parent(rogers_linda,X), two clauses in the database can be used for resolution: parent(rogers_linda,jones_david) and parent(rogers_linda,jones_mary). Prolog always chooses the one that comes earlier in the set of clauses. Note, by the way, that the clause parent(rogers_linda,jones_david) is used twice in the proof. Since jones_david was substituted for X, Prolog's answer to the query is X=jones_david. Note how we can draw a line from the top to the bottom so that each time we include one resolvent; this type of resolution is called

FIGURE 9.2.6
Prolog Representation for the Relational Database of Figures 8.2.1 and 8.2.2.

```
department(sales,15,smith_l).
department(delivery,07,jones_b).
department(dp,29,borden_t).
item(printer,455.69,23).
item(tv_set,599.00,10).
item(camera,127.50,70).
employee("111111111",smith_j,sales,22500).
employee("222333444",jones_b,sales,24750).
employee("667788990",turner_w,sales,25005).
employee("555555555",ford_l,delivery,21004).
employee("234567890",cramer_t,dp,27790).
```

linear resolution. As a theorem prover, Prolog uses a special type of linear resolution strategy.

We end this section by rewriting a previous relational database example—one that we used in our discussion of the relational calculus (see Figures 8.2.1 and 8.2.2)—in Prolog. This example appears in Figure 9.2.6. Note that Prolog has no types; thus, we could have written a Prolog statement such as item(25,sales,smith_j), even though that would not make much sense considering what we want the table ITEM to represent. In considering Prolog as a deductive database system, we are only dealing with queries. Prolog does not have specific database update statements. Insertion is achieved by placing a clause in the database. Deletion may be done outside of Prolog, or in Prolog by using the built-in predicate "retract", whose argument is the clause that is to be deleted.

Figure 9.2.7 shows the relational calculus queries given in Figure 8.2.3 as written for the Prolog version of the database. We use suggestive names for the variables, like "Manager"; we could have used X instead. Again we see the close relationship between the two versions. A variable whose value is not needed may be replaced by a single underscore character.

For query (c), we must include a variable for Dname to obtain the join. This query consists of two atoms separated by a comma (which stands for &). Two versions are shown. In the first version, both the department name and the manager of L. Ford will be printed. In the second version, we first define a predicate "fordsmanager", which contains only names of managers. Therefore, the department names are not printed in this version. We follow the second approach for the remaining queries. Prolog allows the use of ">" and other standard built-in predicates. As a matter of fact, most Prolog versions include many built-in predicates for the convenience of the programmer. Note that the result for query (d) will list the names of all managers the same number of

FIGURE 9.2.7
Prolog Queries for the Database

(a) Print the name of the manager of the Sales department.

```
?- department(sales,_,Manager).
```

(b) Print the name and salary of every employee in the Sales department.

```
?- employee(_,Ename,sales,Salary).
```

(c) Print the name of the manager of L. Ford.

```
(i)  ?- employee(_,ford_1,Dname,_),
     department(Dname,_,Manager).
(ii) fordsmanager(Manager) :- employee(_,ford_1,Dname,_),
                              department(Dname,_,Manager).
     ?- fordsmanager(Manager).
```

(d) Print the names of all managers who have at least one employee in their department with salary greater than $25,000.

```
somemanagers(Manager) :- employee(_,_,Dname,Salary),
                         department(Dname,_,Manager),
                         Salary > 25000.
?- somemanagers(Manager).
```

(e) Print the price of a printer if it is less than $500.

```
?- item(printer,Price,_), Price < 500.0.
```

(f) Print the name of every department with more than one employee.

```
somedepartments(Dname) :- employee(Ssno1,_,Dname,_),
                          employee(Ssno2,_,Dname,_),
                          not(Ssno1 = Ssno2).
?- somedepartments(Dname).
```

(g) Print the name of the item with the lowest price.

```
lowprice(Iname1) :- item(Iname1,Price1,_),
                    not(item(Iname2,Price2,_),
                    Price2 < Price1).
?- lowprice(Iname1).
```

times as the number of employees in their department with salaries greater than $25,000. We can write yes-no questions in Prolog, but our version of query (e) yields the price value also if it is less than $500. (A yes-no query without variables gets the answer "yes" or "no".) Query (f) uses both equality and negation; again, a department name may appear many times in the answer. The last query uses a more complex negation.

9.3 Additional Prolog Concepts

In this section, we continue our introduction to Prolog concepts which are useful in database applications. We know from the previous section that using resolution theorem proving is one way of explaining the Prolog query-solving mechanism. Now we present a second method, the one that is usually taught to people who do not know about resolution. This method is equivalent to the previous one, but it uses the terminology of goals and subgoals instead of clauses. This method is illustrated using the query to find the grandfather of Charles Rogers in Figure 9.3.1. (We showed how to evaluate this query using resolution in Figure 9.2.5.)

FIGURE 9.3.1
Answering a Question in Prolog

Goal   Prolog statement substitution

grandfather(rogers_charles,X)
          grandfather(X,Y) :− grandparent(X,Y),father(Z,Y).

                    {rogers_charles/X,X/Y}

grandparent(rogers_charles,X), father(Z,X)
          grandparent(X,Z) :− parent(X,Y),parent(Y,Z).

                    {rogers_charles/X,X/Z}

parent(rogers_charles,Y), parent(Y,X), father(Z,X)
          parent(rogers_charles,rogers_linda).

                    {rogers_linda/Y}

parent(rogers_linda,X), father(Z,X)
          parent(rogers_linda,jones_david).

                    {jones_david/X} substitution for the original X

father(Z,jones_david)
          father(X,Y) :− parent(X,Y),male(Y).

                    {Z/X,jones_david/Y}

parent(Z,jones_david), male(jones_david)
          parent(rogers_linda,jones_david).

                    {rogers_linda/Z}

male(jones_david)
          male(jones_david)

success   X = jones_david

We consider the question itself as a goal that needs to be solved. The only way to solve for grandfather is by using the rule for grandfather. Thus, we substitute rogers_charles for X, and X for Y, in that rule to obtain our next goal; there we have to solve two subgoals, one for grandparent and one for father. Since goal solving proceeds from left to right, we must solve for grandparent first. This is done using the rule for grandparent. At the next step there are three goals. Again we have to solve the leftmost one, namely parent(rogers_charles,Y). That is, we need to find the first Prolog statement, starting at the beginning of the database, that can match parent(rogers_charles,Y). Since the parent predicate is extensional, this statement must be a fact, not a rule. There is only one such statement, namely parent(rogers_charles,rogers_linda). At this time we substitute rogers_linda for Y and eliminate the solved subgoal.

Next we solve for parent(rogers_linda,X). We must start with the first solution in the database; this gives a substitution of jones_david for X. When we solve for father, we must use the rule for father. Note that when we solve for parent(Z,jones_david), the substitution for Z is immaterial, as Z does not appear anywhere else. We write "success" at the end to signify a successful solution of the goal; the answer is X=jones_david. Observe that each step corresponds to a step in the resolution proof if we replace the goal statement by its negation and write formulas in clausal form.

We next discuss an important concept in Prolog problem solving, called **backtracking**. Backtracking involves backing up; Prolog needs to do this when it gets into a blind alley and when it looks for additional solutions. To illustrate backtracking, our extended Family database is first modified, as shown in Figure 9.3.2. Our effort to answer the same question on this modified database appears in Figure 9.3.3 (pages 322–323). Because we switched the order of Linda Roger's parents in the database, we get to a point where the goal is male(jones_mary). Since Mary Jones is not male, we fail. But this does not mean that there are no solutions to the query; it just means that Prolog has to back up and choose another statement at some point to try to obtain a solution. In backing up, Prolog goes back to the last place where an alternate Prolog statement was available for solving the goal; here it can use parent(rogers_linda, jones_david) for solving the goal parent(rogers_linda,X). The rest of the process continues as before, and jones_david is obtained as the answer.

So, by backtracking, Prolog has obtained one solution. However, this query has a second solution. Recall from the previous section that after obtaining a solution to a query, we can try to obtain another solution. Again Prolog uses backtracking. This time it backtracks to the goal parent(rogers_charles,Y) to find another solution, Y=rogers_michael. At the end, we obtain a second solution, namely rogers_peter, as the other grandfather. There is a way to represent the backtracking process in the

FIGURE 9.3.2
Modified Family Database in Prolog

```
parent(smith_john_jr,smith_john).
parent(smith_john_jr,smith_mary).
parent(rogers_charles,rogers_linda).
parent(rogers_linda,jones_mary).
parent(rogers_linda,jones_david).
parent(smith_mary,ford_albert).
parent(cramer_steven,cramer_william).
parent(rogers_charles,rogers_michael).
parent(jones_mary,davis_margaret).
parent(rogers_michael,rogers_peter).
male(smith_john_jr).
male(smith_john).
male(rogers_charles).
male(jones_david).
male(ford_albert).
male(cramer_steven).
male(cramer_william).
male(rogers_michael).
male(rogers_peter).
father(X,Y) :- parent(X,Y),male(Y).
grandparent(X,Z) :- parent(X,Y),parent(Y,Z).
grandfather(X,Y) :- grandparent(X,Y),father(Z,Y).
```

form of a tree where we show at once how each goal can be solved. Look at the solution tree in Figure 9.3.4 (page 324). If we think of each Prolog statement as a node of the tree with grandfather (rogers_ charles,X) as the root, then the Prolog strategy is to search the solution tree in a depth-first, left-to-right manner (preorder traversal). This means that the next step in the solution is always to visit the leftmost successor of the node where we are, and if that node is a leaf (has no successor), then Prolog must back up until it becomes possible to follow the *next* leftmost, unused successor of a node.

One important topic in Prolog that we have not yet discussed is recursion. **Recursion** is important in computer science and mathematics because it *allows a concept to be defined in terms of itself without circularity.* Our example for recursion is the ancestor predicate, which is defined as a part of another Family database in Figure 9.3.5 (page 324). This definition consists of two parts. Y is an ancestor of X if Y is a parent of X. But also, Y is an ancestor of X if Z is a parent of X, and Y is an ancestor of Z. (This type of definition cannot be written as a view in SQL.) Figure 9.3.6 (page 325) shows a solution tree to find the ancestors of Charles Rogers.

We start by placing the query, ancestor(rogers_charles,X), at the top of the tree. There are two ways to solve for ancestor: either ancestor is parent, or ancestor is ancestor of parent. So the first solution (leftmost

FIGURE 9.3.3
Answering a Question on the Modified Family Database

Goal   Prolog statement substitution

grandfather(rogers_charles,X)
        grandfather(X,Y) : – grandparent(X,Y),father(Z,Y).

                    {rogers_charles/X,X/Y}

grandparent(rogers_charles,X), father(Z,X)
        grandparent(X,Z) : – parent(X,Y),parent(Y,Z).

                    {rogers_charles/X,X/Z}

parent(rogers_charles,Y), parent(Y,X), father(Z,X)
        parent(rogers_charles,rogers_linda).

                    {rogers_linda/Y}

parent(rogers_linda,X), father(Z,X)
        parent(rogers_linda,jones_mary).

                    {jones_mary/X} substitution for the original X

father(Z,jones_mary)
        father(X,Y) : – parent(X,Y),male(Y).

                    {Z/X,jones_mary/Y}

parent(Z,jones_mary), male(jones_mary)
        parent(rogers_linda,jones_mary).

                    {rogers_linda/Z}

male(jones_mary)

failure

(continued)

```
    :    :
    :    :
    └──▶ parent(rogers_linda,X), father(Z,X)
                  parent(rogers_linda,jones_david).

                                    {jones_david/X} substitution for the original X

          father(Z,jones_david)
                  father(X,Y) :− parent(X,Y),male(Y).

                                    {Z/X,jones_david/Y}

          parent(Z,jones_david), male(jones_david)
                  parent(rogers_linda,jones_david).

                                    {rogers_linda/Z}

          male(jones_david)
                  male(jones_david)

          success                   X = jones_david


    └──▶ parent(rogers_charles,Y), parent(Y,X), father(Z,X)
                  parent(rogers_charles,rogers_michael).

                                    {rogers_michael/Y}

          parent(rogers_michael,X), father(Z,X)
                  parent(rogers_michael,rogers_peter).

                                    {rogers_peter/X} substitution for the original X

          father(Z,rogers_peter)
                  father(X,Y) :− parent(X,Y),male(Y).

                                    {Z/X,rogers_peter/Y}

          parent(Z,rogers_peter), male(rogers_peter)
                  parent(rogers_michael,rogers_peter).

                                    {rogers_michael/Z}

          male(rogers_peter)


          success                   X = rogers_peter
```

FIGURE 9.3.4
Solution Tree for Answering the Question

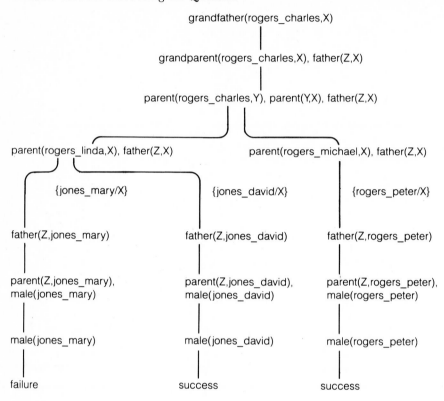

FIGURE 9.3.5
A Family Database with a Recursive Definition

```
parent(smith_john_jr,smith_john).
parent(smith_john_jr,smith_mary).
parent(rogers_charles,rogers_linda).
parent(rogers_linda,jones_mary).
parent(rogers_linda,jones_david).
parent(smith_mary,ford_albert).
parent(cramer_steven,cramer_william).
parent(rogers_charles,rogers_michael).
parent(jones_mary,davis_margaret).
parent(rogers_michael,rogers_peter).
ancestor(X,Y) :- parent(X,Y).
ancestor(X,Y) :- parent(X,Z), ancestor(Z,Y).
```

FIGURE 9.3.6
Solution Tree for Another Question

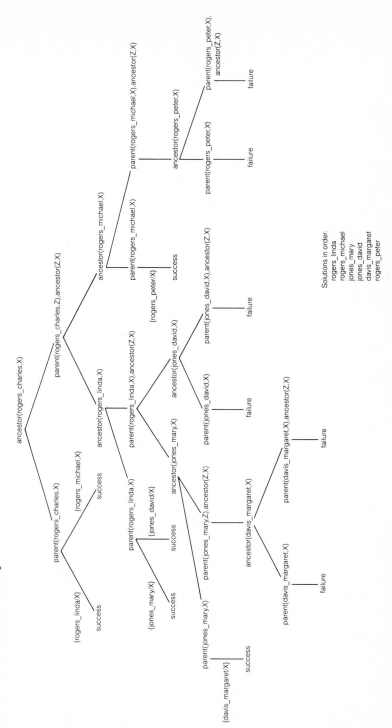

branch of the tree) yields Linda Rogers as an ancestor. (We would stop here if we only wanted one solution, but we assume that we wish to find *all* solutions.) The second solution is Michael Rogers. These are the only solutions that can be obtained in one step by using only parent. Next we use the second definition for ancestor which involves both parent and ancestor. In other words, here we start by looking for the parents of Linda Rogers. We get our third and fourth solutions this way, namely Mary Jones and David Jones. The fifth solution is a parent of Mary Jones, Margaret Davis. Since Margaret Davis has no parents listed in the database, we obtain failure nodes as we look for ancestors there. The last solution is obtained by finding a parent of Michael Rogers. Additional branches end in failure nodes.

Recursive definitions provide a very powerful tool for Prolog. First, let's recall the discussion of the definition of grandparent in logic from Section 9.1. There, to find the grandparent(s) of Charles Rogers in Figure 9.1.2 we wrote

```
GET (X) : GRANDPARENT(Rogers_Charles,X).
```

However, we could have handled this query by including the definition from the intensional database as part of the query, without actually using the intensional database, as

```
GET(X) : EY (PARENT(Rogers_Charles,Y) & PARENT(Y,X)).
```

Now suppose that in Figure 9.1.2 the intensional database contained the following two axioms:

```
AXAY (PARENT(X,Y) → ANCESTOR(X,Y)),
AXAYAZ (PARENT(X,Z) & ANCESTOR(Z,Y) → ANCESTOR(X,Y)).
```

Then we could write a query to find the ancestor(s) of Charles Rogers as follows:

```
GET(X) : ANCESTOR(Rogers_Charles,X).
```

This is where the power of recursive definitions becomes apparent. The reason is that in general, it is impossible to write an equivalent single query in the relational calculus using only the PARENT table. (It is possible to write such a query if we restrict the definition of ancestor to include up to only a certain level of ancestry, such as grandparents or great-grandparents.) In this sense Prolog, or another deductive database system, is a more powerful database retrieval language than the relational calculus.

Recall now our discussion in Section 9.1 about the Closed World Assumption in deductive databases, in which we had to introduce the notion of provability to be able to assume negative facts. Prolog uses a similar idea called **negation by failure** to answer negated queries. On finding a goal not(G), G is evaluated. If G succeeds, then not(G) is considered to have failed; if G fails, then not(G) is considered to have succeeded. In particular, for the database of Figure 9.3.2, if we write the query not(male(jones_mary)), the answer is "yes" because male(jones_mary) fails (it is not in the database). However, not(male(johnson_john)) succeeds also, giving the answer "yes", because male(johnson_john) is not in the database, while not(male(smith_john)) fails, and so gives the answer "no".

Section 8.4 on theorem proving mentioned that the resolution method is complete, so that if A → B is valid, then the resolution method yields a proof (although possibly after a very large number of steps). As we learned previously, Prolog uses a special kind of resolution, so we may wonder if Prolog is also complete in the sense that resolution is complete. The answer is no, and the reason is the Prolog method of resolving always on the left first. An example appears in Figure 9.3.7. The database is a simple modification of the one in Figure 9.2.2, with the addition of an extra predicate called child—which is defined in terms of parent (while parent is defined in terms of child). Part of the infinite solution tree is shown in Figure 9.3.7. Since the tree is traversed in a depth-first, left-to-right manner, Prolog never gets to the success nodes; instead, it gets stuck in an infinite loop trying to solve child for parent and parent for child. In this case, we can solve the problem easily by removing the definition of parent in terms of child; nevertheless, this example shows that Prolog may be surprisingly incapable of solving a simple query.

Our last point about Prolog in general is that at the present time, Prolog is not feasible for large databases. The reason for this is that Prolog is usually implemented without convenient access to external databases. In fact, one aspect of the Fifth Generation and various other computer projects is to couple Prolog to a database system; present Prolog implementations generally allow for the handling of only small databases. Another problem involves the depth-first, left-to-right strategy—which, as we just saw, can lead to an infinite loop. But even if this strategy does not lead to an infinite loop, it may make the search very slow if the success nodes are on the right while the failure nodes are on the left. So, although Prolog is a powerful language, various people have suggested extensions to Prolog involving different control strategies, including parallel processing. The term **logic programming** is a generic term which refers to *the use of logic as a programming language*; it includes the different versions of Prolog as well as suggested and implemented modifications.

FIGURE 9.3.7
Example Where Prolog Does Not Find a Proof

(a) Database

```
child(X,Y) :- parent(Y,X).
parent(X,Y) :- child(Y,X).
parent(smith_john_jr,smith_john).
parent(smith_john_jr,smith_mary).
parent(rogers_charles,rogers_linda).
parent(rogers_linda,jones_david).
parent(rogers_linda,jones_mary).
parent(smith_mary,ford_albert).
parent(cramer_steven,cramer_william).
```

(b) Infinite solution tree

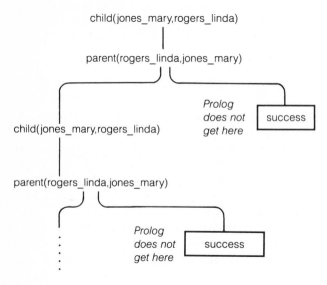

9.4 micro-PROLOG

In this section, we discuss some features of a Prolog implementation called micro-PROLOG, which is available on many popular microcomputers. (There are also various versions of standard Prolog available on microcomputers.) The syntax of micro-PROLOG differs somewhat from the standard Prolog syntax that we encountered in the previous two sections. It seems somewhat more English-like than standard Prolog, which is closer to the formalism of first-order logic.

We start with Figure 9.4.1, which shows how to enter the extended Family database of Figure 9.2.4 in micro-PROLOG. In this case, we have

FIGURE 9.4.1
Entering the Extended Family Database of Figure 6.2.4 in micro-PROLOG

```
&.add(Smith-John-Jr has-parent Smith-John)
&.add(Smith-John-Jr has-parent Smith-Mary)
&.add(Rogers-Charles has-parent Rogers-Linda)
&.add(Rogers-Linda has-parent Jones-David)
&.add(Rogers-Linda has-parent Jones-Mary)
&.add(Smith-Mary has-parent Ford-Albert)
&.add(Cramer-Steven has-parent Cramer-William)
&.add(Smith-John-Jr is-male)
&.add(Smith-John is-male)
&.add(Rogers-Charles is-male)
&.add(Jones-David is-male)
&.add(Ford-Albert is-male)
&.add(Cramer-Steven is-male)
&.add(Cramer-William is-male)
&.add(x has-father y if x has-parent y and y is-male)
&.add(x has-grandparent y if x has-parent z and
1.z has-parent y)
&.add(x has-grandfather y if x has-grandparent y
1.and z has-father y)
```

two predicates, has-parent and is-male, about which we add facts to the database. A binary predicate like has-parent is placed between its two arguments, while a unary predicate like is-male is placed after its argument, to better approximate English usage. Note that micro-PROLOG uses a hyphen to connect words in forming names of objects. For a predicate of more than two arguments—something which isn't shown in Figure 9.4.1—the standard syntax is used with the predicate name first, followed by the arguments in parentheses separated by commas. Rules are expressed using "if" and the hypotheses are connected by "and". The system's prompts appear in boldface. The "&." is the standard micro-PROLOG prompt. In some places the prompt "1." appears because micro-PROLOG is waiting for one right parenthesis on the new line.

In micro-PROLOG, facts and rules can be added and deleted by using the "add" and "delete" commands, respectively. To delete the fact that John Smith, Jr., has a parent called John Smith, we write delete(Smith-John-Jr has-parent Smith-John). Rules are deleted the same way. We saw in our discussion of the Prolog evaluation process that the placement of facts and rules is of great importance, because Prolog uses them in the order of their appearance. In micro-PROLOG, we can specify that a particular sentence should be placed as the nth sentence in the order of sentences for a particular predicate by writing the number n after the word "add". We can delete all the statements for a predicate by using the command "kill". We can list the sentences for a predicate by using the command "list".

The standard words used for querying are "is" and "which". As one would expect, "is" is used for yes-no type queries, while "which" is used for queries that yield names of objects for answers. Figure 9.4.2 gives the question-answer session presented for Prolog in Figure 9.2.3 in micro-PROLOG. Again, the system's prompts and answers appear in the darker typeface. In the queries, the variable name(s) is (are) given first, followed by a colon, followed by a statement. The answer(s) to the query is (are) obtained as in Prolog. Unlike Prolog, however, micro-PROLOG lists all

FIGURE 9.4.2
Question-Answer Session in micro-PROLOG

```
&.which(x : Rogers-Linda has-parent x)
Jones-David
Jones-Mary
No (more) answers
&.which(x : Jones-Mary has-parent x)
No (more) answers
&.which(x: Smith-John-Jr has-grandparent x)
Ford-Albert
No (more) answers
&.is(Smith-John-Jr has-parent Smith-John)
YES
&.
```

FIGURE 9.4.3
micro-PROLOG Representation for the Relational Database of Figures 5.2.1 and 5.2.2

```
&.accept Department
Department.(Sales 15 Smith-L)
Department.(Delivery 07 Jones-B)
Department.(DP 29 Borden-T)
Department.end
&.accept Item
Item.(Printer 455.69 23)
Item.(TV-Set 599.00 10)
Item.(Camera 127.50 70)
Item.end
&.accept Employee
Employee.('111111111' Smith-J Sales 22500)
Employee.('222333444' Jones-B Sales 24750)
Employee.('667788990' Turner-W Sales 25005)
Employee.('555555555' Ford-L Delivery 21004)
Employee.('234567890' Cramer-T DP 27790)
Employee.end
&.
```

the answers. It is possible to obtain one answer at a time by using "one" instead of "which". In micro-PROLOG, x, y, z, X, Y, and Z, optionally followed by a numeral, as in X2, are used for variables; thus, constant names may start with capital letters.

Figure 9.4.3 shows how to represent the relational database of Figures 8.2.1 and 8.2.2 in micro-PROLOG. (The Prolog representation was given in Figure 9.2.6.) Here we note the use of the "accept" command, which makes the system prompt the user for the arguments that are associated with that predicate. The word "end" indicates the end of the facts for that predicate. Figure 9.4.4 shows the queries of Figure 8.2.3

FIGURE 9.4.4
micro-PROLOG Queries for the Database

(a) Print the name of the manager of the Sales department.

```
which(X : Department(Sales y X))
```

(b) Print the name and salary of every employee in the Sales department.

```
which(name X salary Y : Employee(z X Sales Y))
```

(c) Print the name of the manager of L. Ford.

```
which(X : Employee(z1 Ford-L Z z2) and
          Department( Z z3 X))
```

(d) Print the names of all managers who have at least one employee in their department with salary greater than $25,000.

```
which(X : Employee(z1 z2 Z Y) and
          Department(Z z3 X) and 25000 LESS Y)
```

(e) Is the price of a printer less than $500?

```
is(Item(Printer X z) and X LESS 500.0)
```

(f) Print the name of every department with more than one employee.

```
which(X : Employee(Y1 z1 X z2) and
          Employee(Y2 z3 X z4)
          and not Y1 EQ Y2)
```

(g) Print the name of the item with the lowest price.

```
which(X1 : Item(X1 Y1 z1) and not
           (Item(X2 Y2 z2)
           and Y2 LESS Y1))
```

(see also Figure 9.2.7) in micro-PROLOG. In query (b), note that we put text in between or around the variables to make the answers easier to read. When micro-PROLOG answers the query, it just puts the text in as part of the answer, such as

```
name Smith-J salary 22500.
```

In query (d), we use the binary predicate LESS, which is a built-in predicate. Another built-in predicate is EQ, which stands for equality. Variables must be used, even if their values are not needed to answer the query, in place of the underscore in Prolog.

We end our brief consideration of micro-PROLOG by considering lists. In many programming problems involving non-numeric processing, lists are very useful. All Prolog implementations allow for the construction of a list, but we consider lists only in micro-PROLOG. A **list** is essentially *a sequence of objects,* some of which may be lists themselves. (Note that this is a recursive definition.) A simple example of a list is the list of all the item names from Figure 9.4.3, namely (Printer TV-Set Camera). In micro-PROLOG, we simply place the elements of a list inside parentheses. Lists are often processed an element at a time. It is convenient, therefore, to have some notation to deal with lists. The notation used in micro-PROLOG is similar to LISP notation. (LISP is a very important list processing language used in artificial intelligence.)

For example, we write (X|Y) to indicate that X is the head of the list (under consideration) and Y is the tail (where a list consists of two parts: the first element is the head, and the rest of the list, the tail). Many definitions involving lists are recursive. Treating a list as a set, we define list membership in part (a) of Figure 9.4.5. We may read this definition as follows: "An element is a member of a list if it is the first element or if it is a member of the rest of the list." We can use lists as a convenient way of grouping objects. In our Family database, for example, we can list the children for a parent, rather than create individual statements for each child-parent pair.

In part (b) of the figure, there are two sets of facts; the second set uses two lists. The six statements using individuals become one statement using lists. Now let's see how we can ask queries when we deal with such lists. Part (c) shows several queries involving the have-parents relation. Two versions of the query about Mary Taylor's children are shown. In the first version, the answer consists of a single element, the list (Taylor-Peter Taylor-Sally Taylor-Margaret), while in the second version, the answer consists of three individuals. In cases (*i*) and (*iv*), where there are single answers, we use "one" instead of "which". In general, list processing is important in many applications of artificial intelligence, and Prolog is a good language to use for handling lists.

FIGURE 9.4.5
Lists in micro-PROLOG

(a) List membership definition

X is-a-member-of (X|Z)
X is-a-member-of (Y|Z) if X is-a-member-of Z

(b) Using lists to represent facts

(*i*)   Without a list

Taylor-Peter has-parent Taylor-Mary
Taylor-Sally has-parent Taylor-Mary
Taylor-Margaret has-parent Taylor-Mary
Taylor-Peter has-parent Taylor-John
Taylor-Sally has-parent Taylor-John
Taylor-Margaret has-parent Taylor-John

(*ii*)   With lists

(Taylor-Peter Taylor-Sally Taylor-Margaret)
have-parents
(Taylor-Mary Taylor-John)

(c) Queries involving lists

(*i*)   Who are Mary Taylor's children? (The answer is a list of the children.)

```
one(x : x have-parents (Taylor-Mary z))
```

(*ii*)   Who are Mary Taylor's children? (The answer consists of the individual children separately.)

```
which(x : Y have-parents (Taylor-Mary z) and
          x is-a-member-of Y)
```

(*iii*) Is John Taylor a parent of Sally Taylor?

```
is(X have-parents Y and
   Taylor-Sally is-a-member-of X
   and Taylor-John is-a-member-of Y)
```

(*iv*) Who is Peter Taylor's father?

```
one(x : Taylor-Peter is-a-member-of X and
        X have-parents (y x))
```

9.5 Natural Language Interfaces

One aspect of adding intelligence to databases is to allow users to query a database in their natural language, such as English. In fact, one aim of the Fifth Generation Computer Systems Project is exactly this, so that individuals will be able to obtain information from large databases without having to learn a complex query language or to use intermediaries (programmers). In this section, we consider some of the problems associated with natural language interfaces to databases in general, and then briefly discuss one system in present commercial use, called Intellect. The general problem of getting a computer system to understand natural language is a complex one; however, the problem is considerably simplified when only a query interface to a database is required. We do not consider here the artificial intelligence techniques used in constructing such interfaces (for which, by the way, Prolog is a good language to use), or extensions to updates. We also do not discuss menu-based systems which prompt the user to put together a query.

Before starting our discussion, consider the fact that some people have criticized the natural language approach altogether. The main reason for their criticism is that questions posed in natural language can be ambiguous and vague, while queries in a formal language, such as SQL, are precise and structured. Additionally, a question phrased in English may be more wordy than the corresponding query in a formal language. Finally, we should recognize that each formal query language was designed for a specific purpose, and thus is likely to be more efficient than a natural language. Nevertheless, the possibility of natural language access to databases is attractive to many people, and a number of such interfaces have been constructed.

Let's go back to the non-Family database used in Figures 9.2.6 and 9.2.7. We can see some of the difficulties of constructing a natural language interface by taking a single question and writing it in many different ways. For example, we originally phrased the first question as: "Print the name of the manager of the Sales department." Figure 9.5.1 shows several other ways of writing the same query. Two of the queries are phrased as questions, while three are commands. A natural language processor must certainly know about synonyms like "print", "get", and "find". Even for the two queries phrased as questions, one is a "who" question, while the other one is a "what" question.

Now let's look at the different types of queries that a user may wish to ask. One type of query is the one we just gave: retrieval using selection and projection from a table. Another type of query is a yes-no question. In the latter case, sometimes such a one-word answer is misleading. For

FIGURE 9.5.1
Expressing a Query in Different Ways in English

Print the name of the manager of the Sales department.
Get the manager of the Sales department.
Find the Sales department's manager.
Who is the manager of the Sales department?
What is the name of the person managing the Sales department?

example, if we ask, "Is L. Roberts in the Sales department?" the answer for the database is "no". But this answer is not really complete: it may be interpreted as meaning that L. Roberts is in another department, while, in fact, there is no L. Roberts in the database.

Database users are often interested in questions involving counting, which is why database languages, like SQL, have the built-in functions COUNT, SUM, AVG, MAX, and MIN. Thus, another type of query is one which involves numerical calculations, often simple ones like a sum or an average. Sometimes the request is specified in terms of percentages. Examples for our database include "How many departments are there?" and "Who earns the highest salary in the Sales department?"

We end this section, and the chapter, by noting some features of Intellect, a natural language interface primarily used for IBM mainframes at present. One useful feature of Intellect (also found in other natural language systems) is the optional **echo** feature. This feature transforms a query into a more structured form, which it then prints for the user. This helps in avoiding misunderstandings, as a user may be able to recognize that something is wrong if the echo does not seem to quite match what was intended. In Figure 9.5.2, we look at some queries in English and see what the corresponding echo looks like; all-capital letters

FIGURE 9.5.2
The Echo in Intellect

(a) Get the manager of the Sales department.

```
PRINT THE MANAGER WITH DNAME = SALES.

MANAGER

SMITH L
```

(b) Give everyone's name and salary in the Sales department.

```
PRINT THE ENAME AND SALARY OF ALL EMPLOYEES WITH
     DNAME = SALES

ENAME               SALARY

SMITH J             $22,500
JONES B             $24,750
TURNER W            $25,005
```

(c) What is the average salary?

```
PRINT THE AVERAGE SALARY OF ALL EMPLOYEES.

AVERAGE   $24,210
```

FIGURE 9.5.3
Additional Features of Intellect

(a) Referring back with pronouns

```
How many employees are in the Sales Department?

COUNT THE EMPLOYEES WITH DNAME = SALES.

ANSWER: 3

NEXT REQUEST.

Name those who earn more than $24000.

PRINT THE NAME OF ALL EMPLOYEES WITH DNAME = SALES
    & SALARY > $24,000.

ENAME

JONES B
TURNER W
```

(b) Sorting

```
Sort the items by price.

PRINT THE INAME, PRICE, AND VOLUME SORTED BY PRICE.

INAME       PRICE        VOLUME

CAMERA      $127.50      70
PRINTER     $455.69      23
TV SET      $599.00      10
```

(c) Clarification

```
What is the printer's prce?

I'M NOT FAMILIAR WITH THE WORD "PRCE".
IF IT'S A WORD YOU EXPECT TO FIND IN THE DATABASE HIT
THE RETURN KEY.
OTHERWISE EITHER FIX ITS SPELLING OR ENTER A SYNONYM
FOR IT.

Price

        PRICE

        $455.69
```

designate Intellect's echoes and answers. We continue to use the database of Figure 4.1.1. Note that even the structured language of the echo is English-like.

It is very useful in a conversational natural language system for the user to be able to continue a query with a pronoun that refers to the previous set of objects or persons. An example appears in Figure 9.5.3(a). First we ask for the number of employees in the Sales department. In the second question, we refer back to the individuals considered in the first section by using the pronoun "those". For a large database, some queries take a long time to answer. Intellect has a feature called the expensive-query trap, which alerts the user to this fact and presents an opportunity to the user to cancel the request.

Often, when we pose a query, we would like the answers displayed in some sorted order. Intellect can sort records in ascending or descending order on some combination of fields; part (b) of Figure 9.5.3 gives a simple example. Additionally, Intellect permits arithmetic expressions to be used in queries, so that if we had salary stored for different years, we could ask for, say, all those employees whose 1985 salary plus 1986 salary is bigger than $50,000. If Intellect does not understand a word or words, it asks for clarification. An example of a misspelling is shown in part (c). Intellect can also be used to display the results in a graphic form, such as a bar graph, line graph, or pie chart, for instance.

One may wonder how Intellect knows about the tables that are used and the names of the attributes. Someone must first construct what is called the lexicon. The **lexicon** *contains the names of the tables, the relationships between tables* (join attributes), *the attribute types, as well as synonyms for words.* For a table, such as EMPLOYEE, we may enter synonyms like "people", "person", "everyone", and "anyone" for "employee". In general, the initial lexicon is modified over time, as more people use the system and get messages requesting clarification from Intellect; these messages are saved for the lexicon writer.

9.6 Exercises

9.1 Consider the extensional database given in Figure 9.6.1. Write axioms for the intensional database to define SIBLING (must have one parent in common), SISTER, AUNT, UNCLE, and COUSIN.

9.2 For the database given by the extensional database of Figure 9.6.1 and the intensional database which is the answer to Exercise 9.1, write relational calculus queries to find the following:

(a) Barbara Johnson's sibling(s).

(b) Peter Johnson's sister(s).

FIGURE 9.6.1
An Extensional Database

PARENT	
CNAME	PNAME
Johnson Barbara	Johnson Peter
Johnson Barbara	Johnson Grace
Johnson Francis	Johnson Peter
Johnson Francis	Johnson Grace
Johnson Peter	Johnson Ralph
Davis Susan	Johnson Ralph
Johnson Grace	Miller Helen
Miller Robert	Miller Helen
Miller Robert	Miller Thomas
Miller Ann	Miller Robert
Davis Carol	Davis Susan
Miller Lucy	Miller Robert

FEMALE
NAME
Johnson Barbara
Johnson Grace
Davis Susan
Miller Helen
Miller Ann
Davis Carol

   (c) Ann Miller's aunt(s).
   (d) Carol Davis's uncle(s).
   (e) Francis Johnson's cousin(s).

9.3   For each query in Exercise 9.2, show how to obtain its solution(s) using resolution proofs.

9.4   Write the database of Exercise 9.1, including facts and axioms, in Prolog.

9.5   Write Prolog queries to the database of Exercise 9.4 for the queries given in Exercise 9.2.

9.6   Show the Prolog query evaluation for the queries in Exercise 9.5 using both the resolution method and the terminology involving goals and subgoals.

9.7   Write in Prolog the relational databases in
   (a) Figure 4.6.1.   (d) Figure 4.6.4.
   (b) Figure 4.6.2.   (e) Figure 4.6.5.
   (c) Figure 4.6.3.

9.8   Using your answer to part (a) of Exercise 9.7, write Prolog queries for parts (b) to (f) of Exercise 4.2.

9.9   Using your answer to part (b) of Exercise 9.7, write Prolog queries for parts (a) to (d) of Exercise 4.3.

9.10 (a) Using your answer to part (b) of Exercise 9.7, write a Prolog predicate *bigspender,* which contains the names and account numbers of all customers who have a purchase over $100.

  (b) Using your answer to part (a), write a Prolog query to print the name of every individual in bigspender.

  (c) Using your answer to part (b) of Exercise 9.7, write a Prolog predicate *wellpaid,* which contains the social security number and name of each employee whose salary is greater than $25,000.

  (d) Using your answer to part (c), write a Prolog query to print the social security number and name of every individual in wellpaid.

9.11 Using your answer to part (c) of Exercise 9.7, write Prolog queries for parts (a) to (f) of Exercise 4.4.

9.12 Consider the extensional database given in Figure 9.6.2. Write the recursive axioms in Prolog for the intensional database to define the predicate *worksfor*(X,Y), where X works for Y if Y is a manager of X or if the manager of X works for Y.

9.13 (a) Use your answer to Exercise 9.12 to write a Prolog query to find all individuals for whom J. Smith works.

  (b) Show the answer to the query in part (a) for the database of Exercise 9.12.

  (c) Show the solution tree for your answer in part (b).

9.14 (a) Use your answer to Exercise 9.12 to write a Prolog query to find all individuals who work for P. Williams.

FIGURE 9.6.2
Another Extensional Database

MANAGER	
ENAME	MNAME
Baker L	Roberts M
Smith J	Roberts M
Colson H	Roberts M
Jones B	Taylor R
Gordon T	Taylor R
Roberts M	Becker R
Taylor R	Becker R
Becker R	Williams P
Powers T	Williams P
Olson J	Taylor R
Lewis M	Becker R

(b) Show the answer to the query in part (a) for the database of Exercise 9.12.

(c) Show the solution tree for your answer in part (b).

9.15 Show how to enter into micro-PROLOG the relational databases in

(a) Figure 4.6.1.　　(d) Figure 4.6.4.

(b) Figure 4.6.2.　　(e) Figure 4.6.5.

(c) Figure 4.6.3.

9.16 Using your answer to part (d) of Exercise 9.15, write micro-PROLOG queries for the exercises in parts (a) to (c) in Exercise 4.5.

9.17 Using your answer to part (e) of Exercise 9.15, write micro-PROLOG queries for the exercises in parts (a) to (f) in Exercise 4.6.

9.18 (a) Using your answer to part (e) of Exercise 9.15, enter into micro-PROLOG the predicate *Oldcar-owner*, which contains the name, address, year, and model for every customer who has a car with a year value less than 80.

(b) Using your answer to part (a), write a micro-PROLOG query to print the name of each individual in Oldcar-owner.

(c) Using your answer to part (e) of Exercise 9.15, enter into micro-PROLOG the predicate *Bestteam-member*, which contains the name and salary of every employee of the Blue team.

(d) Using your answer to part (c), write a micro-PROLOG query to print the name and salary of each individual in Bestteam-member.

9.7 Guide to Further Reading

[9.4] is a survey of the research that has been done in applying logic to databases; it contains a substantial amount of material and references on deductive databases. [9.3] and [9.2] are introductions to Prolog and micro-PROLOG, respectively. Both books give examples of the applications of logic programming. [9.1] and related publications from Artificial Intelligence Corporation describe Intellect.

[9.1] Artificial Intelligence Corporation. *Intellect Query System—User's Guide*. Waltham, Mass.: Artificial Intelligence Corporation, 1982.

[9.2] Clark, K. L., and F. G. McCabe. *micro-PROLOG: Programming in Logic*. Englewood Cliffs, N.J.: Prentice-Hall, 1984.

[9.3] Clocksin, W. F., and C. S. Mellish. *Programming in Prolog*. New York: Springer-Verlag, 1981.

[9.4] Gallaire, H., J. Minker, and J. M. Nicolas. "Logic and Databases: A Deductive Approach." *ACM Computing Surveys* 16 (1984), pp. 153–185.

Chapter *10*

Database Logic and Transformations

10.1 Views in Database Logic

In Chapters 2–4, we discussed in detail the three major database models: network, hierarchic, and relational. There are some major differences between the hierarchic and network models on the one hand, and the relational model on the other. The hierarchic and network models use explicit links between files; the relational model does not. The standard query languages for the hierarchic and network models are low-level, while the corresponding languages for the relational model are high-level. The last two chapters stressed the applicability of logic to relational databases. First-order logic provides a uniform language for expressing the schema, constraints, and queries on the relational model—and even provides for extending the relational model to the notion of a deductive (relational) database.

Even if we prefer the relational model, we should recognize the existence of very successful hierarchic and network database systems. Thus, it would be very useful to have a logical framework, like first-order logic for the relational model, which could be used in a uniform way to express the schema, constraints, and queries for the hierarchic and network models. Although the first-order logic formalism does not account for hierarchic and network structures, it can be extended to a higher-order logic, called **database logic,** to take care of such structures. Since database logic is an extension of first-order logic, this provides a uniform framework for the study of many issues and problems associated with all three models for database systems: relational, hierarchic, and network.

A basic idea behind the relational model is that a database is described in terms of tables. In first-order logic, each table is represented by a predicate; thus, formulas involving such predicates can be used to express information concerning these tables. Hierarchic and network databases cannot be so represented because they contain two kinds of objects, tables and links (between tables). But there is another way to visualize such databases: we can imagine them as having *tables within tables,* with the table of a child node inside the table of its parent node, instead of having links between tables.

Recall the hierarchic insurance company example from Chapter 3. Part (a) of Figure 3.1.1 gave the data structure diagram, and parts (a) and (b) of Figure 3.2.1 gave an instance. The corresponding representation in database logic appears in Figure 10.1.1(a). Note that two agents are added to the office at 1000 George Ave. The second agent there has no clients (at this time). According to our convention about embedded tables, CLIENT is inside AGENT and AGENT is inside OFFICE. Note

FIGURE 10.1.1
Hierarchic and Network Database Instances in Database Logic

(a) The hierarchic insurance company example of Figure 3.2.1

OFFICE									
OFFICE ADDRESS	TELE PHONE	MANAGER	AGENT						
			ANAME	ADDR	COMM ISSION	CLIENT			
						CNAME	CADDR	POLICY TYPE	POLICY NUMBER
500 Maple St	235-7799	Robbins C	Baker T	805 Hills Rd	25000.00	Taylor B	44 Fifth Ave	T	LLM581 GFRDD41
						West M	444 Second Ave	K	DGG498 HHBQW11
			Lewis J	35 Fall Ln	43590.75	Davis D	55 Flower Dr	L	ABD660 DKUYT29
						Johnson T	265 Pine Ave	K	FFT485 JDDRB75
						Kramer B	2342 F St	L	FFR641 JJYHH83
			Potter G	2673 Third Ave	37460.50	Falk R	33 Light Rd	K	AFF543 NNHMM43
						Rogers D	730 Harold St	F	XHF113 GTRNN23
1000 George Ave	777-5555	Smith B	Wayne A	260 First St	28050.70	Kennedy V	89 Paul Ave	T	ABC556 LFXBB31
			Maple C	800 River St	15000.00				

(continued)

(b) The network database example of Figure 2.1.6

DEPARTMENT						
DNAME	MANAGER	LOCATION	EMPLOYEE			
			SSNO	NAME	ADDR	SALARY
Sales	Smith G	10	112233445	Jones T	139 Safe St	24000
			254778000	Blake R	25 First Rd	28906
Service	Baker L	25	666666686	Johnson B	2611 Byron Ave	21500

HEALTHPLAN						
COMPNAME	ADDRESS	TELNO	EMPLOYEE			
			SSNO	NAME	ADDR	SALARY
Blue Cross	1000 Third St	3456789	112233445	Jones T	139 Safe St	24000
			333444555	West H	2121 York Ave	34510
Clinic 1	500 Maple Ave	2546999	254778000	Blake R	25 First Rd	28906

(c) A recursive network example

PREREQ											
CNO	CNAME	CRED	PREREQ								
			CNO	CNAME	CRED	PREREQ					
						CNO	CNAME	CRED	..		
COSC 236	STRUCTURED PROGRAMMING	3									
COSC 280	ASSEMBLY LANGUAGE PROGRAMMING	3	COSC 236	STRUCTURED PROGRAMMING	3						
COSC 336	DATA STRUCTURES	3	COSC 236	STRUCTURED PROGRAMMING	3						
COSC 338	COMPUTER ORGANIZATION	3	COSC 280	ASSEMBLY LANGUAGE PROGRAMMING	3	COSC 236	STRUCTURED PROGRAMMING	3 3			
COSC 355	SURVEY OF PROGRAMMING LANGUAGES	3	COSC 280	ASSEMBLY LANGUAGE PROGRAMMING	3	COSC 236	STRUCTURED PROGRAMMING	3 3 3			
			COSC 336	DATA STRUCTURES	3	COSC 236	STRUCTURED PROGRAMMING	3 3			

how grouping the agents within their office and the clients within their agent yields a natural representation.

Next we consider network databases. First, Figure 10.1.1(b) shows the database logic representation for the example of Figure 2.1.6: two hierarchic tables are created with EMPLOYEE inside DEPARTMENT in one and inside HEALTHPLAN in the other. There is another type of network structure also, the recursive network structure. This occurs when a subtable of a table has the same structure as the table itself. For example, there may be a table of parts, where the table includes the parts that are components of a part, as well as their components, and so on. We did not specifically discuss recursive network structures in Chapter 2, although the concept was mentioned in Exercise 2.18. Figure 10.1.1(c) gives an example of such a table for the data structure diagram of Figure 2.5.6. Note, for example, that COSC 355 has two prerequisites, each of which has a prerequisite. The depth of nesting within tables is finite for any database instance, but we place no a priori fixed limit on it. The duplication of objects, such as the repetition of employee records and course information, is in the conceptual database, and need not exist at the internal level, in the physical database.

In Section 9.1, we distinguished between the model-theoretic and proof-theoretic approaches to databases. In that chapter, as we discussed Prolog and deductive databases, we applied the proof-theoretic approach. However, in this chapter, as we consider views in database logic, we will use the model-theoretic approach, where the constraints are the axioms and an instance is an interpretation that satisfies the axioms. Section 5.1 defined the notion of view as a combination of database schema and constraints.

Now we will consider how to describe formally a database view in database logic. We do this first for the relational schema of Figure 4.1.1 as shown in Figure 10.1.2. The tables and types are the same as before. We merely added the constraints, which in this case are three functional dependencies representing key constraints for the three tables. The next example, given in Figure 10.1.3(a), is a hierarchic view for the database of Figure 10.1.1(a). Note that in a hierarchic view, some of the attributes are themselves tables. In particular, AGENT and CLIENT are both tables and attributes.

The constraints are functional dependencies in the hierarchic model. We previously considered keys for networks and hierarchies, but since we considered functional dependencies only in the relational model, we expand our coverage of this subject here. The first constraint indicates that for the OFFICE table, an OFFICEADDRESS value functionally (uniquely) determines a TELEPHONE value, a MANAGER value, and an AGENT value (where the AGENT value happens to be a table). In other words, OFFICEADDRESS is the key for the OFFICE table. The meaning of the second constraint is that for the AGENT table within the OFFICE table, which we write as OFFICE-AGENT, the OFFICEAD-DRESS and ANAME values together functionally determine an ADDR value, a COMMISSION value, and a CLIENT value, where the last one is a table. The final constraint refers to the CLIENT table within the AGENT table within the OFFICE table in a similar way. In the termi-nology of Section 3.2, ANAME is the sequence field for AGENT, and CNAME is the sequence field for CLIENT.

FIGURE 10.1.2
Relational View in Database Logic for the Database of Figure 4.1.1

```
VIEW   COMPANY
SCHEMA
   TABLES              ATTRIBUTES
      DEPARTMENT       DNAME,LOCATION,MANAGER
      ITEM             INAME,PRICE,VOLUME
      EMPLOYEE         SSNO,ENAME,DNAME,SALARY
   TYPES               ATTRIBUTES
      CHAR(2)          LOCATION
      CHAR(9)          SSNO
      CHAR(12)         DNAME
      CHAR(15)         MANAGER,ENAME
      CHAR(20)         INAME
      INTEGER          VOLUME,SALARY
      REAL             PRICE
CONSTRAINTS
   DEPARTMENT:DNAME->LOCATION,MANAGER
   ITEM:INAME->PRICE,VOLUME
   EMPLOYEE:SSNO->ENAME,DNAME,SALARY
```

FIGURE 10.1.3
Hierarchic and Network Views in Database Logic

(a) A hierarchic view for the database of Figure 10.1.1(a)

```
VIEW   OFFICES
SCHEMA
   TABLES              ATTRIBUTES
      OFFICE           OFFICEADDRESS,TELEPHONE,MANAGER,AGENT
      AGENT            ANAME,ADDR,COMMISSION,CLIENT
      CLIENT           CNAME,CADDR,POLICYTYPE,POLICYNUMBER
   TYPES
      CHAR(1)          POLICYTYPE
      CHAR(8)          TELEPHONE
      CHAR(13)         POLICYNUMBER
      CHAR(15)         MANAGER,ANAME,CNAME
      CHAR(20)         OFFICEADDRESS,ADDR,CADDR
      REAL             COMMISSION
CONSTRAINTS
   OFFICE:OFFICEADDRESS->TELEPHONE,MANAGER,AGENT
   OFFICE-AGENT:OFFICEADDRESS,ANAME->ADDR,COMMISSION,
                     CLIENT
   OFFICE-AGENT-CLIENT:OFFICEADDRESS,ANAME,CNAME->CADDR,
                     POLICYTYPE,POLICYNUMBER
```

(continued)

FIGURE 10.1.3 (*continued*)

(b) A network view for the database of Figure 10.1.1(b)

```
VIEW   EMPHEALTH
SCHEMA
   TABLES            ATTRIBUTES
      DEPARTMENT     DNAME,MANAGER,LOCATION,EMPLOYEE
      HEALTHPLAN     COMPNAME,ADDRESS,TELNO,EMPLOYEE
      EMPLOYEE       SSNO,NAME,ADDR,SALARY
   TYPES
      CHAR(2)        LOCATION
      CHAR(7)        TELNO
      CHAR(9)        SSNO
      CHAR(12)       DNAME,COMPNAME
      CHAR(15)       MANAGER,NAME
      CHAR(20)       ADDRESS,ADDR
      INTEGER        SALARY
   CONSTRAINTS
      DEPARTMENT:DNAME->MANAGER,LOCATION,EMPLOYEE
      HEALTHPLAN:COMPNAME->ADDRESS,TELNO,EMPLOYEE
      EMPLOYEE:SSNO->NAME,ADDR,SALARY
```

(c) A network view for the database of Figure 10.1.1(c)

```
VIEW   PREREQUISITES
SCHEMA
   TABLES            ATTRIBUTES
      PREREQ         CNO,CNAME,CRED,PREREQ
   TYPES
      CHAR(8)        CNO
      CHAR(30)       CNAME
      INTEGER        CRED
   CONSTRAINTS
      PREREQ:CNO->CNAME,CRED,PREREQ
```

A network view for the database of Figure 10.1.1(b) appears in Figure 10.1.3(b). Note that here the EMPLOYEE table is an attribute in two different tables. This indicates that the structure is a network; that is, a file has two parents in the graph representation. The first two constraints indicate the keys for the DEPARTMENT and HEALTHPLAN tables, respectively. The last constraint means that for all EMPLOYEE tables, the SSNO value functionally determines the NAME, ADDR, and SALARY values. This is a global constraint in the sense that it does not involve any additional attributes from DEPARTMENT or HEALTH-PLAN, unlike the constraints in the previous example for AGENT and CLIENT. This constraint ensures the consistency of the NAME, ADDR, and SALARY values over the entire database. Thus, we may not have, for example, a SALARY value for an employee within DEPARTMENT-

EMPLOYEE which is different from the SALARY value for the same employee within HEALTHPLAN-EMPLOYEE. (For network databases which do not contain such an identifier for the rows of a common inner table, it may be necessary to introduce an additional attribute for such a table to identify individual rows.)

Figure 10.1.3(c) presents a network view for the database of Figure 10.1.1(c). In this case, a table is an attribute within itself. This indicates that the structure is a recursive network. The single constraint is a powerful key constraint for the PREREQ table. It states that wherever the same CNO value appears in the table, the corresponding CNAME, CRED, and inner PREREQ values must be identical. For example, in the table of Figure 10.1.1(c), since COSC 280 appears three times, in all three places the CNAME and CRED values, as well as the PREREQ values (tables), must be identical.

Let's summarize the definition of views in database logic. A **view** *consists of a schema and constraints*. The **schema** *describes the structure of the database*. No attribute may be repeated for a table. Each atomic attribute, that is, each attribute which is not also a table, is given a type. If there are additional functions or predicates, such as SUM, they are listed also (although we usually omit the standard built-in predicates like $<$). A **relational schema** has no attributes which are also tables. A **hierarchic schema** has at least one attribute which is also a table, but a table may not appear as an attribute in two tables, and a table may not be embedded within itself. The last statement means that there cannot be a sequence of tables $T_1, T_2, \ldots, T_n$, such that T_2 appears in T_1, T_3 appears in $T_2, \ldots, T_n$ appears in T_{n-1}, and T_1 appears in T_n. There are no restrictions for a **network schema** (except for the distinctness of the attributes for each table).

This section ends with a general convention for hierarchic and network databases. We assume that, for any table, the set of atomic attributes always functionally determines the set of nonatomic attributes. Consider, for example, the hierarchic insurance company example of Figure 10.1.1(a). In the view description, we indicated the key constraint, OFFICE:OFFICEADDRESS $\rightarrow$ TELEPHONE,MANAGER,AGENT. Therefore, for each OFFICEADDRESS value, there is a unique AGENT value. But even if we did not have this key constraint, according to our convention, we would at least have the constraint OFFICE: OFFICEADDRESS,TELEPHONE,MANAGER$\rightarrow$AGENT. This simply means that, for a triple of OFFICEADDRESS, TELEPHONE, and MANAGER values, we do not break up the corresponding AGENT table. Incidentally, a set is also a table, one with a single column. Figure 10.1.4(a) modifies the hierarchic view of Figure 10.1.3(a) to one where each office has several telephones (but one manager). A corresponding instance appears in Figure 10.1.4(b). In this case, we have an example of a table, namely OFFICE, which has two tables inside of it. This situation corre-

FIGURE 10.1.4
A Set in a Hierarchic View

(a) The view

```
VIEW  OFFICES2
SCHEMA
   TABLES          ATTRIBUTES
      OFFICE       OFFICEADDRESS,MANAGER,TELNOS,AGENT
      TELNOS       TELEPHONE
      AGENT        ANAME,ADDR,COMMISSION,CLIENT
      CLIENT       CNAME,CADDR,POLICYTYPE,POLICYNUMBER
   TYPES
      CHAR(1)      POLICYTYPE
      CHAR(8)      TELEPHONE
      CHAR(13)     POLICYNUMBER
      CHAR(15)     MANAGER,ANAME,CNAME
      CHAR(20)     OFFICEADDRESS,ADDR,CADDR
      REAL         COMMISSION
   CONSTRAINTS
   OFFICE:OFFICEADDRESS->MANAGER,TELNOS,AGENT
   OFFICE-AGENT:OFFICEADDRESS,ANAME->ADDR,COMMISSION,
                   CLIENT
   OFFICE-AGENT-CLIENT:OFFICEADDRESS,ANAME,CNAME->CADDR,
                   POLICYTYPE,POLICYNUMBER
```

(b) An instance

OFFICE									
OFFICE ADDR ESS	MANAGER	TELNOS	AGENT						
		TELE PHONE	ANAME	ADDR	COMM ISSION	CLIENT			
						CNAME	CADDR	POLICY TYPE	POLICY NUMBER
500 Maple St	Robbins C	235-7797 235-7798 235-7799	Baker T	805 Hills Rd	25000.00	Taylor B	44 Fifth Ave	T	LLM581 GFRDD41
						West M	444 Second Ave	K	DGG498 HHBQW11
			Lewis J	35 Fall Ln	43590.75	Davis D	55 Flower Dr	L	ABD660 DKUYT29
						Johnson T	265 Pine Ave	K	FFT485 JDDRB75
						Kramer B	2342 F St	L	FFR641 JJYHH83
			Potter G	2673 Third Ave	37460.50	Falk R	33 Light Rd	K	AFF543 NNHMM43
						Rogers D	730 Harold St	F	XHF113 GTRNN23
1000 George Ave	Smith B	777-5555	Wayne A	260 First St	28050.70	Kennedy V	89 Paul Ave	T	ABC556 LFXBB31
			Maple C	800 River St	15000.00				

sponds to the case of a node with two children nodes in the data structure diagram. We follow the convention of writing attributes which are tables *after* the atomic attributes.

10.2 The Language of Database Logic

In the previous section, we saw how views are expressed in database logic. But we have not yet introduced the language of database logic. We merely considered how to describe the schema and used the arrow notation for expressing functional dependency constraints. In this section, we will learn how to write statements in database logic. In particular, we associate a language with a schema and use that language to write queries and constraints for the database.

Section 8.2 showed how to associate a (first-order logic) language with a relational database. There were two versions, an unsorted and a many-sorted one (see Figures 8.2.1 and 8.2.2). The idea is to use a predicate symbol for each table, so that an atomic formula expresses the fact that a row is in a table. For example, for the view of Figure 10.1.2, we can write the atomic formula EMPLOYEE(111222333,Barber C,Sales, 21550) to express the fact that the row <111222333,Barber C,Sales, 21550> is in the EMPLOYEE table. In first-order logic, predicates are not allowed within predicates; that is why we extend first-order logic to a higher-order logic, called database logic, to deal with hierarchic and network databases. (Note, however, that some aspects of hierarchic and network databases can be expressed by using functions within predicates in first-order logic and Prolog.)

We start by considering the hierarchic view of Figure 10.1.3(a). The (many-sorted) database logic language representation is indicated in Figure 10.2.1(a). Note that the predicate symbol AGENT is inside the predicate symbol OFFICE, and that CLIENT is inside AGENT, according to the hierarchic structure. We also have variables for the predicates AGENT and CLIENT, because there may be several AGENT and CLIENT tables in a database instance. We write the constant symbols for AGENT by placing an OFFICEADDRESS constant symbol in brackets after AGENT. Here we are using the constraint that OFFICEADDRESS functionally determines AGENT. Such a constant symbol stands for the AGENT table which is associated with that OFFICEADDRESS value. For CLIENT we need both an OFFICEADDRESS and an ANAME value. (Recall our remark, in the previous section, that for every inner table it is possible to find a set of atomic attributes which functionally determine it.) We give the interpretation corresponding to the instance of Figure 10.1.1(a) in Figure 10.2.1(b).

FIGURE 10.2.1
Database Logic Representation of a Hierarchic Database

(a) Database language

Predicate symbols: OFFICE(OFFICEADDRESS,TELEPHONE,MANAGER,AGENT)
           AGENT(ANAME,ADDR,COMMISSION,CLIENT)
           CLIENT(CNAME,CADDR,POLICYTYPE,POLICYNUMBER)

Constant symbols:
  for OFFICEADDRESS : all character strings of length 20
  for TELEPHONE   : all character strings of length 8
  for MANAGER   : all character strings of length 15
  for ANAME   : all character strings of length 15
  for ADDR   : all character strings of length 20
  for COMMISSION   : all real numbers
  for CNAME   : all character strings of length 15
  for CADDR   : all character strings of length 20
  for POLICYTYPE   : all character strings of length 1
  for POLICYNUMBER   : all character strings of length 13
  for AGENT   : AGENT[OFFICEADDRESS constant symbol]
  for CLIENT   : CLIENT[OFFICEADDRESS constant symbol,
                          ANAME constant symbol]

Variable symbols:
      $OFFICEADDRESS_1$, $OFFICEADDRESS_2$, . . .
      $TELEPHONE_1$, $TELEPHONE_2$, . . .
      $MANAGER_1$, $MANAGER_2$, . . .
      $AGENT_1$, $AGENT_2$, . . .
      $ANAME_1$, $ANAME_2$, . . .
      $ADDR_1$, $ADDR_2$, . . .
      $COMMISSION_1$, $COMMISSION_2$, . . .
      $CLIENT_1$, $CLIENT_2$, . . .
      $CNAME_1$, $CNAME_2$, . . .
      $CADDR_1$, $CADDR_2$, . . .
      $POLICYTYPE_1$, $POLICYTYPE_2$, . . .
      $POLICYNUMBER_1$, $POLICYNUMBER_2$, . . .

Quantifiers: E A
Connectives: $-$ & $\vee$ $\rightarrow$
Punctuation: ( ) [   ] ,
Built-in predicate symbols: $=$ $<$ $<=$ $>$ $>=$

(b) An interpretation

D(OFFICEADDRESS) = D(ADDR) = D(CADDR) = all character strings of length 20
D(TELEPHONE) = all character strings of length 8
D(MANAGER) = D(ANAME) = D(CNAME) = all character strings of length 15
D(COMMISSION) = all real numbers
D(POLICYTYPE) = all character strings of length 1
D(POLICYNUMBER) = all character strings of length 13
The interpretation of each individual constant symbol is itself.

(continued)

The interpretation of each built-in predicate symbol is the standard interpretation of that
  symbol.
I(OFFICE) = {<500 Maple St,235-7799,Robbins C,AGENT[500 Maple St]>,
                <1000 George Ave,777-5555,Smith B,AGENT[1000 George Ave]>}
I(AGENT[500 Maple St]) =
  {<Baker T,805 Hills Rd,25000.00,CLIENT[500 Maple St,Baker T]>,
  <Lewis J,35 Fall Ln,43590.75,CLIENT[500 Maple St,Lewis J]>,
  <Potter G,2673 Third Ave,37460.50,CLIENT[500 Maple St,Potter G]>}
I(AGENT[1000 George Ave]) =
  {<Wayne A,260 First St,28050.70,CLIENT[1000 George Ave,Wayne A]>,
  <Maple C,800 River St,15000.00,CLIENT[1000 George Ave,Maple C]>}
I(CLIENT[500 Maple St,Baker T]) =
  {<Taylor B,44 Fifth Ave,T,LLM581GFRDD41>,
  <West M,444 Second Ave,K,DGG498HHBQW11>}
I(CLIENT[500 Maple St,Lewis J]) =
  {<Davis D,55 Flower Dr,L,ABD660DKUYT29>,
  <Johnson T,265 Pine Ave,K,FFT485JDDRB75>,
  <Kramer B,2342 F St,L,FFR641JJYHH83>}
I(CLIENT[500 Maple St,Potter G]) =
  {<Falk R,33 Light Rd,K,AFF543NNHMM43>,
  <Rogers D,730 Harold St,F,XHF113GTRNN23>}
I(CLIENT[1000 George Ave,Wayne A]) =
  {<Kennedy V,89 Paul Ave,T,ABC556LFXBB31>}
I(CLIENT[1000 George Ave,Maple C]) = {}

Next we introduce some extra predicates, called cluster predicates,
that are useful in database logic applications. If we consider the tree
(graph) structure of a hierarchic (network) database, we see that each
predicate represents a node with the arrows emanating from the node.
Part (a) of Figure 10.2.2 indicates the tree structure for the hierarchic
database under consideration. Note, in part (b) of the figure, how each
primitive predicate represents a node with its arrows (in this case a single
arrow both for OFFICE and AGENT because each has one child). Often
it is convenient to be able to refer to a bigger portion of the tree (or
graph). The various cluster predicates for this case appear in part (c).
Each cluster predicate contains at least two nodes and the appropriate
arrows. The OFFICE-CLIENT combination is not allowed because all
connecting nodes must be included in a cluster.

Section 8.5 showed how to write constraints in first-order logic; now
we use the language of database logic to write constraints for hierarchic
and network databases. Let's consider some examples. The three constraints for the hierarchic view of Figure 10.1.3(a) are written in Figure
10.2.3(a). Note that when we write the cluster predicate OFFICE-AGENT,
we place an AGENT predicate inside, followed by its attributes. Although
there are two variables for TELEPHONE, MANAGER, and AGENT,
each pair must be equal by the first constraint. The global third constraint
for the network view of Figure 10.1.3(b) is shown in Figure 10.2.3(b).

FIGURE 10.2.2
Cluster Predicates

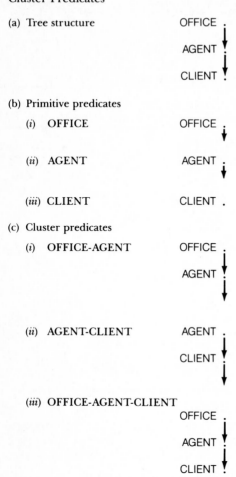

(a) Tree structure

(b) Primitive predicates

    (*i*)   OFFICE

    (*ii*)   AGENT

    (*iii*) CLIENT

(c) Cluster predicates

    (*i*)   OFFICE-AGENT

    (*ii*) AGENT-CLIENT

    (*iii*) OFFICE-AGENT-CLIENT

(We omit the database logic representation for this view.) Finally, the constraint for the recursive network view of Figure 10.1.3(c) appears in Figure 10.2.3(c).

This section ends with the writing of some queries in database logic for our databases. Recall from our discussion of the relational calculus that each formula of the appropriate first-order logic language represents a query. The answer to a query is then a (relational) table where each row is an individual answer; that is, it consists of a substitution for each free variable so that the formula becomes true. In the case of hierarchic and network databases, the answer need not be a relational table, but may be a hierarchic or network structure, respectively.

FIGURE 10.2.3
Constraints in Database Logic

(a) The constraints for the hierarchic database of Figure 10.1.3(a)

OFFICE:OFFICEADDRESS→TELEPHONE,MANAGER,AGENT
  A OFFICEADDRESS$_1$ A TELEPHONE$_1$ A TELEPHONE$_2$ A MANAGER$_1$ A MANAGER$_2$
  A AGENT$_1$ A AGENT$_2$
  (OFFICE(OFFICEADDRESS$_1$,TELEPHONE$_1$,MANAGER$_1$,AGENT$_1$)
  & OFFICE(OFFICEADDRESS$_1$,TELEPHONE$_2$,MANAGER$_2$,AGENT$_2$)
  → TELEPHONE$_1$ = TELEPHONE$_2$ & MANAGER$_1$ = MANAGER$_2$ & AGENT$_1$ = AGENT$_2$)

OFFICE-AGENT:OFFICEADDRESS,ANAME→ADDR,COMMISSION,CLIENT
  A OFFICEADDRESS$_1$ A TELEPHONE$_1$ A TELEPHONE$_2$ A MANAGER$_1$ A MANAGER$_2$
  A AGENT$_1$ A AGENT$_2$ A ANAME$_1$ A ADDR$_1$ A ADDR$_2$ A COMMISSION$_1$ A COMMISSION$_2$
  A CLIENT$_1$ A CLIENT$_2$
  (OFFICE-AGENT(OFFICEADDRESS$_1$, TELEPHONE$_1$, MANAGER$_1$,
      AGENT$_1$(ANAME$_1$,ADDR$_1$,COMMISSION$_1$,CLIENT$_1$))
  & OFFICE-AGENT(OFFICEADDRESS$_1$, TELEPHONE$_2$, MANAGER$_2$,
      AGENT$_2$(ANAME$_1$,ADDR$_2$,COMMISSION$_2$,CLIENT$_2$))
  → ADDR$_1$ = ADDR$_2$ & COMMISSION$_1$ = COMMISSION$_2$ & CLIENT$_1$ = CLIENT$_2$)

OFFICE-AGENT-CLIENT:OFFICEADDRESS,ANAME,CNAME→CADDR,POLICYTYPE,
                    POLICYNUMBER
  A OFFICEADDRESS$_1$ A TELEPHONE$_1$ A TELEPHONE$_2$ A MANAGER$_1$ A MANAGER$_2$
  A AGENT$_1$ A AGENT$_2$ A ANAME$_1$ A ADDR$_1$ A ADDR$_2$ A COMMISSION$_1$ A COMMISSION$_2$
  A CLIENT$_1$ A CLIENT$_2$ A CNAME$_1$ A CADDR$_1$ A CADDR$_2$ A POLICYTYPE$_1$ A POLICYTYPE$_2$
  A POLICYNUMBER$_1$ A POLICYNUMBER$_2$
  (OFFICE-AGENT-CLIENT(OFFICEADDRESS$_1$,TELEPHONE$_1$,MANAGER$_1$,AGENT$_1$
      (ANAME$_1$,ADDR$_1$,COMMISSION$_1$,CLIENT$_1$(CNAME$_1$,CADDR$_1$,POLICYTYPE$_1$,
      POLICYNUMBER$_1$)))
  & OFFICE-AGENT-CLIENT(OFFICEADDRESS$_1$,TELEPHONE$_2$,MANAGER$_2$,
      AGENT$_2$(ANAME$_1$,ADDR$_2$,COMMISSION$_2$,CLIENT$_2$(CNAME$_1$,CADDR$_2$,POLICYTYPE$_2$,
      POLICYNUMBER$_2$)))
  → CADDR$_1$ = CADDR$_2$ & POLICYTYPE$_1$ = POLICYTYPE$_2$ &
      POLICYNUMBER$_1$ = POLICYNUMBER$_2$)

(b) A global constraint for the network database of Figure 10.1.3(b)

EMPLOYEE:SSNO→NAME,ADDR,SALARY
  A EMPLOYEE$_1$ A EMPLOYEE$_2$ A SSNO$_1$ A NAME$_1$ A NAME$_2$ A ADDR$_1$ A ADDR$_2$
  A SALARY$_1$ A SALARY$_2$
  (EMPLOYEE$_1$(SSNO$_1$,NAME$_1$,ADDR$_1$,SALARY$_1$)
  & EMPLOYEE$_2$(SSNO$_1$,NAME$_2$,ADDR$_2$,SALARY$_2$)
  → NAME$_1$ = NAME$_2$ & ADDR$_1$ = ADDR$_2$ & SALARY$_1$ = SALARY$_2$)

(c) The constraint for the recursive network database of Figure 10.1.3(c)

PREREQ:CNO→CNAME,CREDITS,PREREQ
  A PREREQ$_1$ A PREREQ$_2$ A CNO$_1$ A CNAME$_1$ A CNAME$_2$ A CRED$_1$ A CRED$_2$ A PREREQ$_3$
  A PREREQ$_4$
  (PREREQ$_1$(CNO$_1$,CNAME$_1$,CRED$_1$,PREREQ$_3$)
  & PREREQ$_2$(CNO$_1$,CNAME$_2$,CRED$_2$,PREREQ$_4$)
  → CNAME$_1$ = CNAME$_2$ & CRED$_1$ = CRED$_2$ & PREREQ$_3$ = PREREQ$_4$)

FIGURE 10.2.4
Queries in Database Logic on the Hierarchic Insurance Company Example of Figure 10.1.1

(a) Print all the information for the office at 500 Maple St.

(*i*) GET (TELEPHONE$_1$,MANAGER$_1$,AGENT$_1$) :
       OFFICE(500 Maple St,TELEPHONE$_1$,MANAGER$_1$,AGENT$_1$)

(*ii*)

TELE PHONE	MANAGER	AGENT							
		ANAME	ADDR	COMM ISSION	CLIENT				
					CNAME	CADDR	POLICY TYPE	POLICY NUMBER	
235-7799	Robbins C	Baker T	805 Hills Rd	25000.00	Taylor B	44 Fifth Ave	T	LLM581 GFRDD41	
					West M	444 Second Ave	K	DGG498 HHBQW11	
		Lewis J	35 Fall Ln	43590.75	Davis D	55 Flower Dr	L	ABD660 DKUYT29	
					Johnson T	265 Pine Ave	K	FFT485 JDDRB75	
					Kramer B	2342 F St	L	FFR641 JJYHH83	
		Potter G	2673 Third Ave	37460.50	Falk R	33 Light Rd	K	AFF543 NNHMM43	
					Rogers D	730 Harold St	F	XHF113 GTRNN23	

(b) Print all the client names and their policynumbers.

(*i*) GET (CNAME$_1$,POLICYNUMBER$_1$) : E OFFICEADDRESS$_1$
       E TELEPHONE$_1$ E MANAGER$_1$ E AGENT$_1$ E ANAME$_1$
       E ADDR$_1$ E COMMISSION$_1$ E CLIENT$_1$ E CADDR$_1$
       E POLICYTYPE$_1$
       OFFICE-AGENT-CLIENT(OFFICEADDRESS$_1$,
         TELEPHONE$_1$,MANAGER$_1$,AGENT$_1$
         (ANAME$_1$,ADDR$_1$,COMMISSION$_1$,CLIENT$_1$
          (CNAME$_1$,CADDR$_1$,POLICYTYPE$_1$,POLICYNUMBER$_1$)))

(*ii*)

CNAME	POLICYNUMBER
Taylor B	LLM581GFRDD41
West M	DGG498HHBQW11
Davis D	ABD660DKUYT29
Johnson T	FFT485JDDRB75
Kramer B	FFR641JJYHH83
Falk R	AFF543NNHMM43
Rogers D	XHF113GTRNN23
Kennedy V	ABC556LFXBB31

(c) Print the name and office address of each agent who has a client with policytype T.

    (*i*) GET (ANAME$_1$,OFFICEADDRESS$_1$) !
            E TELEPHONE$_1$ E MANAGER$_1$ E AGENT$_1$ E ADDR$_1$
            E COMMISSION$_1$ E CLIENT$_1$ E CNAME$_1$ E CADDR$_1$
            E POLICYNUMBER$_1$
            OFFICE-AGENT-CLIENT(OFFICEADDRESS$_1$,
                TELEPHONE$_1$,MANAGER$_1$,
                AGENT$_1$(ANAME$_1$,ADDR$_1$,COMMISSION$_1$,CLIENT$_1$
                (CNAME$_1$,CADDR$_1$,T,POLICYNUMBER$_1$)))

    (*ii*)

ANAME	OFFICEADDRESS
Baker T	500 Maple St
Wayne A	1000 George Ave

      Figure 10.2.4 gives three queries on the hierarchic insurance example of Figure 10.1.1(a). In each case, the query is written first in database logic and the answer is shown on the database instance. Query (a) requests all the information for a specific office. This is a selection on the entire hierarchic table, so the result is also a hierarchic table. Query (b) asks for pairs of objects, each of which refers to an individual, so the answer is a relational table. We use the cluster predicate because we have to go down the whole hierarchy. Query (c) requests information about a parent node, AGENT, based on selection from a child node, CLIENT. Again, the answer is a relational table. In all three cases, we project on some of the attributes.

      Figure 10.2.5 gives one query each for the network databases of Figure 10.1.1(b) and (c). In query (a), we need to use two clusters because we are looking for information about employees based on both department and health plan names. We are basically dealing with the join of hierarchic tables here. For query (b), we obtain a subtable of a recursive network table which also forms a recursive network.

      Observe that database logic queries are generalizations of relational calculus queries. In a similar way, we could define database algebraic operations to generalize the relational algebraic operations. In fact, we have touched on some of these operations, such as selection, projection, and join, in our discussion of the queries above. We can similarly generalize a language like SQL to database logic. In this way, we can obtain various high-level query languages for hierarchic and network databases, such as the procedural database algebra and the nonprocedural database (calculus) logic. Because we previously considered a low-level language for the relational model in Section 4.5 (to embed it into a programming language), at this point we have both low-level and high-level database languages for all three major database models, as we demonstrate in Figure 10.2.6.

FIGURE 10.2.5
Queries in Database Logic on Network Databases

(a) Print the names and addresses of all employees who work in the Sales department and whose healthplan company is Blue Cross.

    (i) GET (NAME$_1$, ADDR$_1$) :
             E MANAGER$_1$ E LOCATION$_1$ E EMPLOYEE$_1$ E SSNO$_1$
             E SALARY$_1$ E EMPLOYEE$_2$ E ADDRESS$_1$ E TELNO$_1$
             (DEPARTMENT-EMPLOYEE(Sales,MANAGER$_1$,LOCATION$_1$,
                EMPLOYEE$_1$(SSNO$_1$,NAME$_1$,ADDR$_1$,SALARY$_1$))
             & HEALTHPLAN-EMPLOYEE(Blue Cross,ADDRESS$_1$,TELNO$_1$,
                EMPLOYEE$_2$(SSNO$_1$,NAME$_1$,ADDR$_1$,SALARY$_1$)))

    (ii)

NAME	ADDR
Jones T	139 Safe St

(b) Print all prerequisite information for COSC 338.

    (i) GET (PREREQ$_1$) : E PREREQ$_2$ E CNAME$_1$ E CRED$_1$
             PREREQ$_2$(COSC 338,CNAME$_1$,CRED$_1$,PREREQ$_1$)

    (ii)

CNO	CNAME	CRED	PREREQ		
			CNO	CNAME	CRED
COSC 280	ASSEMBLY LANGUAGE PROGRAMMING	3	COSC 236	STRUCTURED PROGRAMMING	3

FIGURE 10.2.6
Types of Database Languages for Various Database Models

high-level	relational calculus	database logic	database logic
low-level	embedded SQL	DL/I	NDL
	relational	**hierarchic**	**network**

10.3 External View Construction

In Section 1.2, where we discussed the three-level architecture for databases, we noted that while the conceptual database view describes the structure of the entire database, users generally interact only with portions of the database, called external views. We observed that there must be a mechanism to transform a query or an update from the external view to the conceptual view. In this section, we consider such transformations and show how to formalize them in logic. This demonstrates another way in which logic can be used for databases, in addition to providing a uniform language for expressing database schemas, constraints, and queries. In our examples, we deal with the case where both the conceptual and external views are relational, since in this case it suffices to use first-order logic. But our results can be applied to hierarchic and network databases also by using database logic.

Our first example uses the relational view of Figure 10.1.2 as the conceptual view. Usually an external view is obtained from the conceptual view by some algebraic operations such as projections, selections, and joins, often omitting some tables. An external view for this database appears in Figure 10.3.1. The external view DEPTINFO1 is obtained from the (conceptual) view COMPANY by omitting the table ITEM and by combining information from the EMPLOYEE and DEPARTMENT tables. We wish to obtain a table DEPTEMP for those employees whose salary is greater than $24,000.

Figure 10.3.2 defines a schema transformation which maps the external schema to the conceptual schema. Recall that there is a first-order language associated with every relational schema. A **schema transformation** *defines each predicate of the external view by a formula of the conceptual view.* In this case there is only one predicate, DEPTEMP, to be defined. The schema transformation indicates precisely how DEPTEMP is obtained from DEPARTMENT and EMPLOYEE. Let's call the languages for the external and conceptual schemas L_1 and L_2, respectively. Then, the definition for the transformation of each predicate of L_1 generates a transformation of every formula of L_1 to a formula of L_2. The new formula is obtained by the application of the appropriate transformation for each predicate where it appears in the first formula.

FIGURE 10.3.1
An External View

```
VIEW   DEPTINFO1
SCHEMA
   TABLES            ATTRIBUTES
     DEPTEMP           DNAME,ENAME,SALARY,LOCATION
   TYPES
     CHAR(2)           LOCATION
     CHAR(12)          DNAME
     CHAR(15)          ENAME
     INTEGER           SALARY
CONSTRAINTS
   DEPTEMP:DNAME->LOCATION
```

FIGURE 10.3.2
Schema Transformation

```
TRANSFORMATION   T
VIEW₁ : DEPTINFO1
VIEW₂ : COMPANY
  DEPTEMP(DNAME₁,ENAME₁,SALARY₁,LOCATION₁) ─────→
    E MANAGER₁ E SSNO₁
    ( DEPARTMENT(DNAME₁,LOCATION₁,MANAGER₁)
    & EMPLOYEE(SSNO₁,ENAME₁,DNAME₁,SALARY₁)
    & SALARY₁ > 24000)
```

Every schema transformation from the external schema to the conceptual schema has a dual property: it also defines a transformation of a database instance for the conceptual schema to a database instance for the external schema. Figure 10.3.3 diagrams these mappings. Then, by way of example, Figure 10.3.4 shows the instance of the external database schema obtained by the schema transformation of Figure 10.3.2 from the conceptual instance of Figure 4.1.1. We place rows in the tables defined by the external schema (in this case there is only one table, DEPTEMP) by applying the transformation formula to the conceptual instance. For example, we place <Sales,Jones B,24750,15> into the DEPTEMP table because in the conceptual instance there is a manager, L. Smith, and a social security number, 222-333-444, such that <Sales,15,Smith L> is in the DEPARTMENT table, <222333444,Jones B,Sales,24750> is in the EMPLOYEE table, and the salary, $24,750, is greater than $24,000.

We go back now to the first aspect of a schema transformation, the transformation of formulas from the language of the external view to the language of the conceptual view. Since each query is a formula in the relational calculus (or database logic for hierarchic and network databases), such a transformation can be used to convert a query from the external view to the conceptual view. An example appears in Figure 10.3.5. This query, given in part (a), asks for the name and salary of every employee in the Sales department (from the DEPTEMP table). We perform the transformation by substituting the formula from Figure 10.3.2 for DEPTEMP to obtain part (b) of Figure 10.3.5. We obtain the

FIGURE 10.3.3
The Mappings Associated with a Schema Transformation

```
                        transformation
External Schema  ─────────────────────────→  Conceptual Schema
                        transformation
External Instance  ←───────────────────────  Conceptual Instance
```

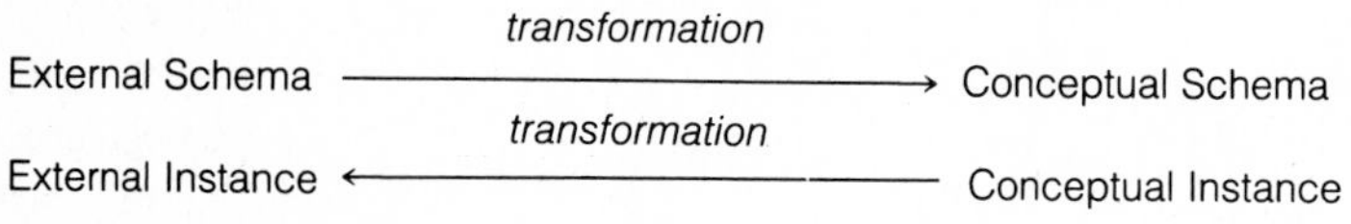

FIGURE 10.3.4
External Instance Obtained by the Transformation

DEPTEMP			
DNAME	ENAME	SALARY	LOCATION
Sales	Jones B	24750	15
Sales	Turner W	25005	15
DP	Cramer T	27790	29

FIGURE 10.3.5
Query Transformation

(a) Query in the external view

```
GET (ENAME₁,SALARY₁) : E LOCATION₁
      DEPTEMP(Sales,ENAME₁,SALARY₁,LOCATION₁)
```

(b) Transformed query

```
GET (ENAME₁,SALARY₁) : E LOCATION₁ E MANAGER₁ E SSNO₁
      ( DEPARTMENT(Sales,LOCATION₁,MANAGER₁)
      & EMPLOYEE(SSNO₁,ENAME₁,Sales,SALARY₁)
      & SALARY₁ > 24000 )
```

(c) Answer to the query

ENAME	SALARY
Jones B	24750
Turner W	25005

same answer in part (c) whether we evaluate the original query on the external instance of Figure 10.3.4 or we evaluate the transformed query on the original conceptual instance of Figure 4.1.1(b).

Recall that ordinarily the conceptual instance is the only one that really exists; the external instances are simply derived from it to serve the needs of users. Of course, a user can make a private copy of an external database—but then updates on the conceptual view are not reflected in the copy. This has become more of a problem recently as users have been downloading files to microcomputers for convenience and further processing. In any case, as far as a user is concerned, the external database is real and can be queried. These queries must, there-fore, be translated (automatically) to queries on the conceptual database.

We already have the mechanism to do this, because the schema transformation has to be defined first from the external view to the conceptual view. As we just saw, the schema transformation *automatically* yields the transformation for the queries. There is a possible problem with this method, however. We would like to be certain that the answer to a query on the external database is always the same as the answer to the transformed query on the conceptual database. If this is not the case, then the user working with an external view may get incorrect answers to a query. Our first theorem assures us that the query transformation method gives the right answers as long as the free variables represent atomic attributes—that is, attributes which are not also tables. We need this proviso because we cannot obtain a hierarchic or network table as an answer in a relational database. (This is not a restriction for the relational case.)

> **Theorem 10.3.1**   Let T be a schema transformation from
> view V_1 to view V_2. Suppose that I is an instance of V_2, and
> T[I] is the transformed instance. Let Q be a query in the
> language for V_1 whose free variables represent atomic attri-
> butes, and T[Q] the transformed query. Then the answer to
> Q on T[I] is identical to the answer to T[Q] on I.

Although the schema transformation assures the correctness of query transformations, there is an additional problem. It may be the case that the database instance obtained by the transformation from the concep-tual instance is not actually a legal external instance, because it does not satisfy the constraints of the external view. This problem does not appear in our example because the DEPTEMP table of Figure 10.3.4 satisfies the (single) external constraint of Figure 10.3.1. But the problem could arise as we now demonstrate. Figure 10.3.6 provides an alternative exter-nal view (for another user). This view differs from the one in Figure 10.3.1 only in its constraint. Since the two schemas are identical, the schema transformation remains the one shown in Figure 10.3.2. How-ever, now the external database obtained by the schema transformation, given in Figure 10.3.4, does not satisfy the constraint of this new external view. Hence, as far as the user is concerned, it is an illegal database.

We would like to protect users from this kind of problem (where the transformed instance is illegal) so that it cannot occur for them. This action should be taken when the schema transformation is defined. To do this, we make use of the fact that each constraint can be written in the appropriate language; thus, the schema transformation, besides

FIGURE 10.3.6
An Alternative External View

```
VIEW   DEPTINFO2
SCHEMA
  TABLES            ATTRIBUTES
    DEPTEMP         DNAME,ENAME,SALARY,LOCATION
  TYPES
    CHAR(2)         LOCATION
    CHAR(12)        DNAME
    CHAR(15)        ENAME
    INTEGER         SALARY
CONSTRAINTS
  DEPTEMP:DNAME->SALARY
```

automatically transforming queries, *also transforms constraints* from the external view to the conceptual view. Two examples of such transformations appear in Figure 10.3.7. (In some cases, subscript values are incremented to avoid confusion.) Recall now our discussion in Section 8.5 about implications of integrity constraints. Observe that the constraints of the conceptual view (see Figure 10.1.2) imply $T[E_1]$ but do not imply $T[E_2]$. Since in DEPARTMENT, DNAME functionally determines LOCATION, $T[E_1]$ must hold in every instance of the conceptual view. However, $T[E_2]$ need not hold; in particular, it is not true for the instance of Figure 4.1.1(b).

Let $E_1, \ldots, E_n$ be the constraints of the external view and C the set of constraints of the conceptual view. We say that a schema transformation, T, is a **view transformation,** if C implies $T[E_i]$ for each i. That is, a schema transformation is a view transformation *if the constraints of the conceptual view imply the transformed constraints of the external view.* We may think of this requirement as asserting that the conceptual view constraints are sufficiently strong for the external view constraints. (We cannot discuss implication directly between the constraints in the conceptual and external views since they are written in languages for different schemas.) In particular, the schema transformation from DEPTINFO1 to COMPANY is a view transformation, but the schema transformation from DEPTINFO2 to COMPANY is not. The next theorem shows the connections between constraints, transformations, and legal instances.

Theorem 10.3.2   A schema transformation T from view V_1 to view V_2 is a view transformation if and only if for every (legal) instance I of the conceptual view, T[I] is a(n) (legal) instance of the external view.

FIGURE 10.3.7
Constraint Transformations

(a) The constraint for view DEPTINFO1

    (*i*)   The original constraint (E_1)

        A DNAME$_1$ A ENAME$_1$ A ENAME$_2$ A SALARY$_1$ A SALARY$_2$ A LOCATION$_1$
        A LOCATION$_2$
        (DEPTEMP(DNAME$_1$,ENAME$_1$,SALARY$_1$,LOCATION$_1$)
        & DEPTEMP(DNAME$_1$,ENAME$_2$,SALARY$_2$,LOCATION$_2$)
        → LOCATION$_1$ = LOCATION$_2$)

    (*ii*)   The transformed constraint (T[E_1])

        A DNAME$_1$ A ENAME$_1$ A ENAME$_2$ A SALARY$_1$ A SALARY$_2$ A LOCATION$_1$ A LOCATION$_2$
        (E MANAGER$_1$ E SSNO$_1$
          (DEPARTMENT(DNAME$_1$,LOCATION$_1$,MANAGER$_1$)
          & EMPLOYEE(SSNO$_1$,ENAME$_1$,DNAME$_1$,SALARY$_1$)
          & SALARY$_1$ > 24000)
        & E MANAGER$_2$ E SSNO$_2$
          (DEPARTMENT(DNAME$_1$,LOCATION$_2$,MANAGER$_2$)
          & EMPLOYEE(SSNO$_2$,ENAME$_2$,DNAME$_1$,SALARY$_2$)
          & SALARY$_2$ > 24000)
        → LOCATION$_1$ = LOCATION$_2$)

(b) The constraint for view DEPTINFO2

    (*i*)   The original constraint (E_2)

        A DNAME$_1$ A ENAME$_1$ A ENAME$_2$ A SALARY$_1$ A SALARY$_2$ A LOCATION$_1$ A LOCATION$_2$
        (DEPTEMP(DNAME$_1$,ENAME$_1$,SALARY$_1$,LOCATION$_1$)
        & DEPTEMP(DNAME$_1$,ENAME$_2$,SALARY$_2$,LOCATION$_2$)
        → SALARY$_1$ = SALARY$_2$)

    (*ii*)   The transformed constraint (T[E_1])

        A DNAME$_1$ A ENAME$_1$ A ENAME$_2$ A SALARY$_1$ A SALARY$_2$ A LOCATION$_1$ A LOCATION$_2$
        (E MANAGER$_1$ E SSNO$_1$
          (DEPARTMENT(DNAME$_1$,LOCATION$_1$,MANAGER$_1$)
          & EMPLOYEE(SSNO$_1$,ENAME$_1$,DNAME$_1$,SALARY$_1$)
          & SALARY$_1$ > 24000)
        & E MANAGER$_2$ E SSNO$_2$
          (DEPARTMENT(DNAME$_1$,LOCATION$_2$,MANAGER$_2$)
          & EMPLOYEE(SSNO$_2$,ENAME$_2$,DNAME$_1$,SALARY$_2$)
          & SALARY$_2$ > 24000)
        → SALARY$_2$ = SALARY$_2$)

     Thus, according to this theorem, when we construct the external view and schema transformation for a user, we should check to make sure that the schema transformation is a view transformation. Because this process involves checking implications of formulas, it can be done by a theorem prover. (We have not discussed theorem proving in database logic. Although Theorem 8.4 does not generalize to database logic, it is possible to define deduction rules and thereby do theorem proving in it.) If the schema transformation is a view transformation, then we can be assured that every external instance (obtained from a conceptual instance) is legal for the user. Therefore, even if the conceptual view is updated, we can be assured that the user's database instance remains legal. Note that just checking a single instance is not sufficient. If the schema transformation is not a view transformation, then an external instance may happen to be legal—but once the conceptual instance is updated, the new external instance could still become illegal.

We have seen that given a properly constructed external view, where the transformation is a view transformation, the user always obtains a legal view, and the queries are automatically transformed correctly from the external view to the conceptual view. But a user may also wish to *update* an external view. These updates must also be transformed to the conceptual view. (Most updates to the conceptual view are probably performed this way.) However, for updates this transformation is not automatic from the schema transformation (which deals essentially with static objects). The updates must be simulated by separately written routines. Figure 10.3.8 shows examples of how to do this for two cases.

FIGURE 10.3.8
Update Simulation Routines

(a) An insertion simulator

```
SIM[INSERT(DEPTEMP)(d,e,s,l)] :
   Begin
      If  s > 24000
         Then
            Begin
               Search for d in the first column of DEPARTMENT;
               If d is not found
                  Then   INSERT(DEPARTMENT)(d,l,null);
               Search for <e,d> in the second and third
                  columns of EMPLOYEE;
               If <e,d> is not found
                  Then   INSERT(EMPLOYEE)(null,e,d,s)
            End
   End
```

(b) A deletion simulator

```
SIM[DELETE(DEPTEMP)(d,e,s,l)]:
   Begin
      DELETE(EMPLOYEE)(  ,e,d,s)
   End
```

Consider the insertion of a row into DEPTEMP. A routine for simulating this insertion for the view COMPANY is shown in part (a) of Figure 10.3.8. This simulator works as follows. First, it checks to make sure that the SALARY value is bigger than $24,000. Next, it searches the DEPARTMENT table for the DNAME value that is to be inserted. If the DNAME value is already there, then the simulator does nothing to the DEPARTMENT table; otherwise, it inserts a row with a null value for the unknown MANAGER value. Then, similarly, the simulator searches the EMPLOYEE table for the ENAME and DNAME values to be inserted. If they are already there, then it does nothing to the EMPLOYEE table; otherwise, it inserts a row with a null value for the SSNO column. We certainly cannot claim that this is the unique simulator for INSERT(DEPTEMP), as we can obtain different simulators by omitting one or both searches, for example.

In part (b), a deletion simulator for DEPTEMP is shown. This routine deletes (at least) one row from the EMPLOYEE table; it does not delete anything from the DEPARTMENT table. An alternative deletion simulator would delete the appropriate row from the DEPARTMENT table. In general, when the external view contains a table that is obtained from some conceptual tables by a join, there are usually several reasonable choices for update simulation routines. Most database systems at present do not allow users to write their own update simulators, but instead generate update simulators in some predetermined way based on the view definition. For this reason, users are generally not allowed to update a table, obtained by using the join operation, in their external view.

Let's consider what we may mean by a good update simulator. In Figure 10.3.9, the fundamental update simulation diagram, I represents an instance in the conceptual view. The corresponding instance in the external view, the one seen by the user, is T[I]. The user wishes to update T[I] to obtain the instance UPDATE(T[I]). Instead, what happens is that the update simulator constructs the new conceptual instance, SIM(UPDATE(I)). The new instance for the external view becomes T[SIM(UPDATE(I))]. We say that the simulator SIM(UPDATE) is **strongly correct** if T[SIM(UPDATE(I))] = UPDATE(T[I]) for every instance I. Unfortunately, it is not always possible to obtain a strongly correct simulator *because of possible side effects.* In particular, we could not even simulate the insertion of two new employees into the DEPTINFO table, since that would require the addition of two rows to the EMPLOYEE table with null values for SSNO. But this addition would violate the constraint EMPLOYEE:SSNO→ENAME,DNAME,SALARY. The side effect has to do with the SSNO value, which does not appear in the view DEPTINFO1. It is assumed, although this was not stated explicitly, that if a simulator yields an illegal (conceptual) database, it has no effect on the database.

FIGURE 10.3.9
The Update Simulation Diagram

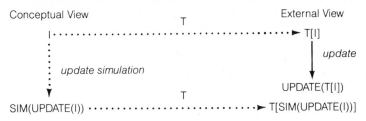

Although we may not always get strong correctness, we would like to be sure that if the simulator does something, the user obtains at least the required change in the (external) database. The required change is represented in logic by an atomic formula for insertion, by a negated atomic formula for deletion, and by a pair of atomic and negated atomic formulas for modification. We write the formula(s) as F[UPDATE]. For example, the required change for INSERT(DEPTEMP) (d,e,s,l) is the atomic formula DEPTEMP(d,e,s,l), which we can also write as F[INSERT(DEPTEMP)(d,e,s,l)]. We say that the simulator is **weakly correct** if, whenever the update simulation modifies the conceptual database instance, F[UPDATE] is true in T[SIM(UPDATE(I))]. To check that this definition holds, we must consider both the external and conceptual databases. This section ends by giving a sufficient condition for weak correctness that lets us check for it entirely in the conceptual database.

> **Theorem 10.3.3**   Suppose that whenever SIM(UPDATE(I))
> <> I, then T[F[UPDATE]] is true in SIM(UPDATE(I)). In such cases, the simulator is weakly correct.

By using this theorem, or the original definition, we can show that the simulator in part (b) of Figure 10.3.8 is weakly correct. (This simulator is also strongly correct. The insertion simulator can be made weakly correct by removing the searches in the DEPARTMENT and EMPLOYEE tables.)

10.4 Database Conversion

There are many cases where a database conversion is appropriate or necessary. We may want to use a new database system in place of the old one; perhaps we need to modify the schema and the constraints because of the changing user needs; or, maybe we wish to normalize a database with anomaly problems. In this section, we see how the notion of database transformation provides the framework for accomplishing such a conversion.

Before we start by discussing database normalization, consider the following observation. In our explanation of external view construction, it was quite clear that the transformation went in one direction only—from the external view to the conceptual view. This direction is appropriate, because an external view usually comprises only a portion of the conceptual view. However, in many cases we want transformations in both directions. For instance, in the case of database decomposition, we are also interested in being able to recapture the original database after normalization. We used the projection operation for decomposition and the join operation for going back to the original database. Thus, we had a *pair* of transformations, rather than just one.

Let's reconsider examples (a) and (b) from Figure 5.2.1, which are rewritten, using our notation for views from this chapter, in Figure 10.4.1. The two transformations appear in Figure 10.4.2. These are NORMALIZE, which maps the view NEWTASK to the view OLDTASK (this is like the transformation of an external view to a conceptual view), and the reverse transformation, DENORMALIZE. NORMALIZE represents the two projections, while DENORMALIZE represents the join. Recall that, in connection with normalization, we stressed the lossless join and dependency preserving properties. We would like to see what these concepts mean in the more general setting of two views with a pair of transformations between them.

We use the following setup: views V_1 and V_2 are given with the schema transformations $T_1: V_1 \rightarrow V_2$ and $T_2: V_2 \rightarrow V_1$. We assume that, in some sense, V_1 is the new view and V_2 is the old view. In our example, lossless join means that, given an instance I of the original view, if we apply NORMALIZE followed by DENORMALIZE, we get the original I back. We generalize this to say that $<T_1,T_2>$ on $<V_1,V_2>$ is **lossless** if for every instance I of V_2, $T_2[T_1[I]] = I$. Now recall the dependency preserving property. We used it earlier with functional dependency constraints to make sure that no such dependency on the original view is lost when we obtain the decomposed view. Therefore, in some sense, the constraints on both the external and conceptual views should be equally strong. We generalize this property and say that $<T_1,T_2>$ on $<V_1,V_2>$ is **constraint preserving** if both T_1 and T_2 are view interpretations.

To illustrate these notions, let's show that <NORMALIZE,DENORMALIZE> on <NEWTASK,OLDTASK> is both lossless and constraint preserving. The lossless property is an immediate consequence of the fact that the decomposition is lossless join. We must still show that both NORMALIZE and DENORMALIZE are view interpretations. In Figure 10.4.3, we write both the original and the transformed constraints. NORMALIZE is a view interpretation since the functional

FIGURE 10.4.1
Normalization of Views

(a) Original view

```
VIEW   OLDTASK
SCHEMA
   TABLES            ATTRIBUTES
      TASK              EMP,TASKID,TASKNAME
   TYPES
      CHAR(3)          TASKID
      CHAR(12)         TASKNAME
      CHAR(15)         EMP
CONSTRAINTS
   TASK:TASKID->TASKNAME
```

(b) Decomposed view

```
VIEW   NEWTASK
SCHEMA
   TABLES            ATTRIBUTES
      EMPTASKID         EMP,TASKID
      TASKINFO          TASKID,TASKNAME
   TYPES
      CHAR(3)          TASKID
      CHAR(12)         TASKNAME
      CHAR(15)         EMP
CONSTRAINTS
   TASKINFO:TASKID->TASKNAME
```

FIGURE 10.4.2
Schema Transformations

(a) From the decomposed view to the original view

```
TRANSFORMATION   NORMALIZE
VIEW₁ : NEWTASK
VIEW₂ : OLDTASK
   EMPTASKID(EMP₁,TASKID₁) ⟶
      E TASKNAME₁ TASK(EMP₁,TASKID₁,TASKNAME₁)
   TASKINFO(TASKID₁,TASKNAME₁) ⟶
      E EMP₁ TASK(EMP₁,TASKID₁,TASKNAME₁)
```

(b) From the original view to the decomposed view

```
TRANSFORMATION   DENORMALIZE
VIEW₁ : OLDTASK
VIEW₂ : NEWTASK
   TASK(EMP₁,TASKID₁,TASKNAME₁) ⟶
      EMPTASKID(EMP₁,TASKID₁) & TASKINFO(TASKID₁,TASKNAME₁)
```

FIGURE 10.4.3
Checking the Constraint Preserving Property

(a) The original constraint on NEWTASK

A TASKID$_1$ A TASKNAME$_1$ A TASKNAME$_2$
(TASKINFO(TASKID$_1$,TASKNAME$_1$) & TASKINFO(TASKID$_1$,TASKNAME$_2$)
$\rightarrow$ TASKNAME$_1$ = TASKNAME$_2$)

(b) The transformed constraint on OLDTASK

A TASKID$_1$ A TASKNAME$_1$ A TASKNAME$_2$
(E EMP$_1$ TASK(EMP$_1$,TASKID$_1$,TASKNAME$_1$)
& E EMP$_2$ TASK(EMP$_2$,TASKID$_1$,TASKNAME$_2$)
$\rightarrow$ TASKNAME$_1$ = TASKNAME$_2$)

(c) The original constraint on OLDTASK

A EMP$_1$ A EMP$_2$ A TASKID$_1$ A TASKNAME$_1$ A TASKNAME$_2$
(TASK(EMP$_1$,TASKID$_1$,TASKNAME$_1$) & TASK(EMP$_2$,TASKID$_1$,TASKNAME$_2$)
$\rightarrow$ TASKNAME$_1$ = TASKNAME$_2$)

(d) The transformed constraint on NEWTASK

A EMP$_1$ A EMP$_2$ A TASKID$_1$ A TASKNAME$_1$ A TASKNAME$_2$
(EMPTASKID(EMP$_1$, TASKID$_1$) & TASKINFO(TASKID$_1$,TASKNAME$_1$)
& EMPTASKID(EMP$_2$,TASKID$_1$) & TASKINFO(TASKID$_1$,TASKNAME$_2$)
$\rightarrow$ TASKNAME$_1$ = TASKNAME$_2$)

dependency on **TASKINFO** implies the transformed constraint of part (d). Similarly, **DENORMALIZE** is a view interpretation because the functional dependency on **TASK** implies (and in fact, is equivalent to) the transformed constraint of part (b).

In our next example, let's convert a hierarchic database view to a relational database view. The hierarchic view is the one given in Figure 10.1.3(a). The corresponding relational view, obtained according to the method outlined in Section 1.3, appears in Figure 10.4.4. We construct the schema transformation from the relational view to the hierarchic view in Figure 10.4.5. This transformation yields the relational database instance of Figure 10.4.6, corresponding to the hierarchic one of Figure 10.1.1(a). Figure 10.4.7 shows the transformed constraints of NEW-OFFICES in the language for OFFICES. Because these transformed constraints are implied by the constraints of the OFFICES view—see Figure 10.2.3(a)—we get a view interpretation.

Although the transformation MAKERELATIONAL allows us to obtain the relational database instance corresponding to a hierarchic instance, it does not help in converting programs on the hierarchic view

FIGURE 10.4.4
Relational View Corresponding to the Hierarchic View of Figure 10.1.3(a)

```
VIEW   NEWOFFICES
SCHEMA
   TABLES          ATTRIBUTES
      OFFICE          OFFICEADDRESS,TELEPHONE,MANAGER
      AGENT           OFFICEADDRESS,ANAME,ADDR,COMMISSION
      CLIENT          OFFICEADDRESS,ANAME,CNAME,CADDR,
                          POLICYTYPE,POLICYNUMBER

   TYPES
      CHAR(1)         POLICYTYPE
      CHAR(8)         TELEPHONE
      CHAR(13)        POLICYNUMBER
      CHAR(15)        MANAGER,ANAME,CNAME
      CHAR(20)        OFFICEADDRESS,ADDR,CADDR
      REAL            COMMISSION
CONSTRAINTS
   OFFICE:OFFICEADDRESS->TELEPHONE,MANAGER
   AGENT:OFFICEADDRESS,ANAME->ADDR,COMMISSION
   CLIENT:OFFICEADDRESS,ANAME,CNAME->CADDR,POLICYTYPE,
             POLICYNUMBER
```

FIGURE 10.4.5
Schema Transformation from the Relational View to the Hierarchic View

```
TRANSFORMATION   MAKERELATIONAL
VIEW₁ : NEWOFFICES
VIEW₂ : OFFICES
   OFFICE(OFFICEADDRESS₁,TELEPHONE₁,MANAGER₁) ⟶
     E AGENT₁ OFFICE(OFFICEADDRESS₁,TELEPHONE₁,MANAGER₁,AGENT₁)
   AGENT(OFFICEADDRESS₁,ANAME₁,ADDR₁,COMMISSION₁) ⟶
     E AGENT₁ E CLIENT₁ E TELEPHONE₁ E MANAGER₁
     OFFICE-AGENT(OFFICEADDRESS₁,TELEPHONE₁,MANAGER₁,AGENT₁(ANAME₁,
         ADDR₁,COMMISSION₁,CLIENT₁))
   CLIENT(OFFICEADDRESS₁,ANAME₁,CNAME₁,CADDR₁,POLICYTYPE₁,
         POLICYNUMBER₁) ⟶
     E AGENT₁ E CLIENT₁ E TELEPHONE₁ E MANAGER₁ E ADDR₁ E COMMISSION₁
     OFFICE-AGENT-CLIENT(OFFICEADDRESS₁,TELEPHONE₁,MANAGER₁,
         AGENT₁(ANAME₁,ADDR₁,COMMISSION₁,
         CLIENT₁(CNAME₁,CADDR₁,POLICYTYPE₁,
         POLICYNUMBER₁)))
```

to programs on the relational view. For that conversion we need the reverse transformation—presented in Figure 10.4.8. Only the transformation for the cluster predicate OFFICE-AGENT-CLIENT is given, since that determines the transformation of the other predicates as well. The transformation MAKEHIERARCHIC gives an automatic method for converting queries from the hierarchic database view OFFICES to the

FIGURE 10.4.6
Relational Instance Obtained by the Schema Transformation

OFFICE		
OFFICEADDRESS	TELEPHONE	MANAGER
500 Maple St 1000 George Ave	235-7799 777-5555	Robbins C Smith B

AGENT			
OFFICEADDRESS	ANAME	ADDR	COMMISSION
500 Maple St	Baker T	805 Hills Rd	25000.00
500 Maple St	Lewis J	35 Fall Ln	43590.75
500 Maple St	Potter G	2673 Third Ave	37460.50
1000 George Ave	Wayne A	260 First St	28050.70
1000 George Ave	Maple C	800 River St	15000.00

CLIENT					
OFFICE-ADDRESS	ANAME	CNAME	CADDR	POLICY TYPE	POLICY-NUMBER
500 Maple St	Baker T	Taylor B	44 Fifth Ave	T	LLM581-GFRDD41
500 Maple St	Baker T	West M	444 Second Ave	K	DGG498-HHBQW11
500 Maple St	Lewis J	Davis D	55 Flower Dr	L	ABD660-DKUYT29
500 Maple St	Lewis J	Johnson T	265 Pine Ave	K	FFT485-JDDRB75
500 Maple St	Lewis J	Kramer B	2342 F St	L	FFR641-JJYHH83
500 Maple St	Potter G	Falk R	33 Light Rd	K	AFF543-NNHMM43
500 Maple St	Potter G	Rogers D	730 Harold St	F	XHF113-GTRNN23
1000 George Ave	Wayne A	Kennedy V	89 Paul Ave	T	ABC556-LFXBB31

FIGURE 10.4.7
The Transformed Constraints of NEWOFFICES

OFFICE:OFFICEADDR→TELEPHONE,MANAGER   is transformed to
A OFFICEADDRESS$_1$, A TELEPHONE$_1$, A TELEPHONE$_2$ A MANAGER$_1$, A MANAGER$_2$
(E AGENT$_1$ OFFICE(OFFICEADDRESS$_1$,TELEPHONE$_1$,MANAGER$_1$,AGENT$_1$)
& E AGENT$_2$ OFFICE(OFFICEADDRESS$_1$,TELEPHONE$_2$,MANAGER$_2$,AGENT$_2$)
→ TELEPHONE$_1$ = TELEPHONE$_2$ & MANAGER$_1$ = MANAGER$_2$)

AGENT:OFFICEADDRESS,ANAME→ADDR,COMMISSION   is transformed to
A OFFICEADDRESS$_1$, A ANAME$_1$, A ADDR$_1$, A ADDR$_2$ A COMMISSION$_1$, A COMMISSION$_2$
(E AGENT$_1$ E CLIENT$_1$ E TELEPHONE$_1$ E MANAGER$_1$
   OFFICE-AGENT(OFFICEADDRESS$_1$,TELEPHONE$_1$,MANAGER$_1$,AGENT$_1$(ANAME$_1$,ADDR$_1$,
     COMMISSION$_1$,CLIENT$_1$))
& E AGENT$_2$ E CLIENT$_2$ E TELEPHONE$_2$ E MANAGER$_2$
   OFFICE-AGENT(OFFICEADDRESS$_1$,TELEPHONE$_2$,MANAGER$_2$,AGENT$_2$(ANAME$_1$,ADDR$_2$,
     COMMISSION$_2$,CLIENT$_2$))
→ ADDR$_1$ = ADDR$_2$ & COMMISSION$_1$ = COMMISSION$_2$)

CLIENT:OFFICEADDRESS,ANAME,CNAME→CADDR,POLICYTYPE,POLICYNUMBER
is transformed to
A OFFICEADDRESS$_1$, A ANAME$_1$, A CNAME$_1$, A CADDR$_1$, A CADDR$_2$ A POLICYTYPE$_1$,
A POLICYTYPE$_2$ A POLICYNUMBER$_1$, A POLICYNUMBER$_2$
(E AGENT$_1$ E CLIENT$_1$ E TELEPHONE$_1$ E MANAGER$_1$ E ADDR$_1$ E COMMISSION$_1$
   OFFICE-AGENT-CLIENT(OFFICEADDRESS$_1$,TELEPHONE$_1$,MANAGER$_1$,AGENT$_1$,
     (ANAME$_1$,ADDR$_1$,COMMISSION$_1$,CLIENT$_1$(CNAME$_1$,CADDR$_1$,POLICYTYPE$_1$,
     POLICYNUMBER$_1$)))
& E AGENT$_2$ E CLIENT$_2$ E TELEPHONE$_2$ E MANAGER$_2$ E ADDR$_2$ E COMMISSION$_2$
   OFFICE-AGENT-CLIENT(OFFICEADDRESS$_1$,TELEPHONE$_2$,MANAGER$_2$,
     AGENT$_2$(ANAME$_1$,ADDR$_2$,COMMISSION$_2$,CLIENT$_2$(CNAME$_1$,CADDR$_2$,POLICYTYPE$_2$,
     POLICYNUMBER$_2$)))
→ CADDR$_1$ = CADDR$_2$ & POLICYTYPE$_1$ = POLICYTYPE$_2$ &
  POLICYNUMBER$_1$ = POLICYNUMBER$_2$)

FIGURE 10.4.8
Schema Transformation from the Hierarchic View to the Relational View

TRANSFORMATION   MAKEHIERARCHIC
VIEW$_1$: OFFICES
VIEW$_2$: NEWOFFICES
OFFICE-AGENT-CLIENT(OFFICEADDRESS$_1$,TELEPHONE$_1$,MANAGER$_1$,AGENT$_1$(ANAME$_1$,
    ADDR$_1$,COMMISSION$_1$,CLIENT$_1$(CNAME$_1$,CADDR$_1$,POLICYTYPE$_1$,
    POLICYNUMBER$_1$)))
    ⟶
   OFFICE(OFFICEADDRESS$_1$,TELEPHONE$_1$,MANAGER$_1$)
  & AGENT(OFFICEADDRESS$_1$,ANAME$_1$,ADDR$_1$,COMMISSION$_1$)
  & CLIENT(OFFICEADDRESS$_1$,ANAME$_1$,CNAME$_1$,CADDR$_1$,POLICYTYPE$_1$,
  POLICYNUMBER$_1$)

FIGURE 10.4.9
Transformation of the Query in Figure 10.2.4(b) to the Relational View

```
GET (CNAME₁,POLICYNUMBER₁)  |  E OFFICEADDRESS₁ E TELEPHONE₁ E MANAGER₁
    E ANAME₁ E ADDR₁ E COMMISSION₁ E CADDR₁ E POLICYTYPE₁
    (˜OFFICE(OFFICEADDRESS₁,TELEPHONE₁,MANAGER₁)
    & AGENT(ANAME₁,ADDR₁,COMMISSION₁)
    & CLIENT(CNAME₁,CADDR₁,POLICYTYPE₁,POLICYNUMBER₁) )
```

FIGURE 10.4.10
A Hierarchic Update and Its Transformation to the Relational View

(a) The original update in the hierarchic view

```
INSERT (AGENT[1000 George Ave])
(Miller F,200 Harford Blvd,18260.75,-)
```

(b) The update simulator

```
SIM[INSERT(AGENT[oa])(an,ad,co,-)]:
   INSERT(AGENT)(oa,an,ad,co)
```

(c) The simulated update in the relational view

```
INSERT(AGENT)
(1000 George Ave,Miller F,200 Harford Blvd,18260.75)
```

relational database view NEWOFFICES. Figure 10.4.9 shows how the query of Figure 10.2.4(b) is transformed. (The tables AGENT and CLIENT drop out in the transformation, since they depend on the individual values OFFICEADDRESS and OFFICEADDRESS,ANAME, respectively.) Note that since the query of Figure 10.2.4(a) contains a predicate variable for AGENT, the answer is a hierarchic table. We cannot get the identical answer to any query in the relational view. Therefore, such a query has to be modified before transformation.

To transform programs from the hierarchic database view to the relational database view, we need to write update simulators. We have not yet discussed update commands in database logic, but the same commands, INSERT, DELETE, and MODIFY, which we gave for the relational calculus in Section 8.2, can be used. An example of an insertion of an agent (without clients) and its simulator appears in Figure 10.4.10. Note that when we insert into an AGENT table in the hierarchic view, we need to indicate which AGENT table it is by denoting a value for OFFICEADDRESS.

Because we now have the pair of transformations <MAKERELA-TIONAL,MAKEHIERARCHIC> on the pair of views <NEWOFF-ICES,OFFICES>, we may wonder if they satisfy the lossless and con-

FIGURE 10.4.11
The Transformed Constraints of OFFICES

OFFICE:OFFICEADDRESS→TELEPHONE,MANAGER,AGENT
is transformed to
A OFFICEADDRESS$_1$ A TELEPHONE$_1$ A TELEPHONE$_2$ A MANAGER$_1$ A MANAGER$_2$
(OFFICE(OFFICEADDRESS$_1$,TELEPHONE$_1$,MANAGER$_1$)
& OFFICE(OFFICEADDRESS$_1$,TELEPHONE$_2$,MANAGER$_2$)
→ TELEPHONE$_1$ = TELEPHONE$_2$ & MANAGER$_1$ = MANAGER$_2$)

OFFICE-AGENT:OFFICEADDRESS,ANAME→ADDR,COMMISSION,CLIENT
is transformed to
A OFFICEADDRESS$_1$ A TELEPHONE$_1$ A TELEPHONE$_2$ A MANAGER$_1$ A MANAGER$_2$ A ANAME$_1$
A ADDR$_1$ A ADDR$_2$ A COMMISSION$_1$ A COMMISSION$_2$
(OFFICE(OFFICEADDRESS$_1$,TELEPHONE$_1$,MANAGER$_1$)
& AGENT(OFFICEADDRESS$_1$,ANAME$_1$,ADDR$_1$,COMMISSION$_1$)
& OFFICE(OFFICEADDRESS$_1$,TELEPHONE$_2$,MANAGER$_2$)
& AGENT(OFFICEADDRESS$_1$,ANAME$_1$,ADDR$_2$,COMMISSION$_2$)
→ ADDR$_1$ = ADDR$_2$ & COMMISSION$_1$ = COMMISSION$_2$)

OFFICE-AGENT-CLIENT:OFFICEADDRESS,ANAME,CNAME→
CADDR,POLICYTYPE,POLICYNUMBER
is transformed to
A OFFICEADDRESS$_1$ A TELEPHONE$_1$ A TELEPHONE$_2$ A MANAGER$_1$ A MANAGER$_2$ A ANAME$_1$
A ADDR$_1$ A ADDR$_2$ A COMMISSION$_1$ A COMMISSION$_2$ A CNAME$_1$ A CADDR$_1$ A CADDR$_2$
A POLICYTYPE$_1$ A POLICYTYPE$_2$ A POLICYNUMBER$_1$ A POLICYNUMBER$_2$
(OFFICE(OFFICEADDRESS$_1$,TELEPHONE$_1$,MANAGER$_1$)
& AGENT(OFFICEADDRESS$_1$,ANAME$_1$,ADDR$_1$,COMMISSION$_1$)
& CLIENT(OFFICEADDRESS$_1$,ANAME$_1$,CNAME$_1$,CADDR$_1$,POLICYTYPE$_1$,POLICYNUMBER$_1$)
& OFFICE(OFFICEADDRESS$_1$,TELEPHONE$_2$,MANAGER$_2$)
& AGENT(OFFICEADDRESS$_1$,ANAME$_1$,ADDR$_2$,COMMISSION$_2$)
& CLIENT(OFFICEADDRESS$_1$,ANAME$_1$,CNAME$_1$,CADDR$_2$,POLICYTYPE$_2$,POLICYNUMBER$_2$)
→ CADDR$_1$ = CADDR$_2$ & POLICYTYPE$_1$ = POLICYTYPE$_2$ &
  POLICYNUMBER$_1$ = POLICYNUMBER$_2$)

straint preserving properties. As it turns out, the lossless property does not hold. In our example, if the database of Figure 10.1.1(a) is transformed by MAKERELATIONAL, and is then transformed back by MAKEHIERARCHIC, we lose the agent, C. Maple, in the process. (However, it is possible to change MAKEHIERARCHIC—by giving a separate definition for the cluster OFFICE-AGENT—to make the pair lossless.) For the constraint preserving property, since we already know that MAKERELATIONAL is a view interpretation, we next need to check that the transformation MAKEHIERARCHIC is a view transformation. The transformed constraints are shown in Figure 10.4.11. Because the transformed constraints are implied by the constraints of the NEW-OFFICES view, we obtain a view interpretation. Hence, <MAKERELA-TIONAL,MAKEHIERARCHIC> satisfies the constraint preserving property.

FIGURE 10.4.12
Simplification of a Transformed Query

(a) Original query on the view NEWOFFICES

```
GET (ANAME₁,OFFICEADDR₁,MANAGER₁) : E TELEPHONE₁
    E ADDR₁ E COMMISSION₁
    ( OFFICE(OFFICEADDR₁,TELEPHONE,MANAGER₁)
    & AGENT(OFFICEADDR₁,ANAME₁,ADDR₁,COMMISSION₁) )
```

(b) The transformed query on the view OFFICES

```
GET (ANAME₁,OFFICEADDR₁,MANAGER₁) : E TELEPHONE₁
    E ADDR₁ E COMMISSION₁
    ( E AGENT₁
    OFFICE(OFFICEADDR₁,TELEPHONE₁,MANAGER₁,AGENT₁)
    & E AGENT₂ E CLIENT₂ E TELEPHONE₂ E MANAGER₂
        OFFICE-AGENT(OFFICEADDR₁,TELEPHONE₂,MANAGER₂,
            AGENT₂(ANAME₁,ADDR₁,COMMISSION₁,CLIENT₂)) )
```

(c) The transformed query in prenex normal form

```
GET (ANAME₁,OFFICEADDR₁,MANAGER₁) : E TELEPHONE₁
    E ADDR₁ E COMMISSION₁
    ( E AGENT₁ E AGENT₂ E CLIENT₂ E TELEPHONE₂ E MANAGER₂
    ( OFFICE(OFFICEADDR₁,TELEPHONE₁,MANAGER₁,AGENT₁)
    & OFFICE-AGENT(OFFICEADDR₁,TELEPHONE₂,MANAGER₂,
        AGENT₂(ANAME₁,ADDR₁,COMMISSION₁,CLIENT₂)) )
```

(d) Applying a functional dependency to change the second conjunct

```
GET (ANAME₁,OFFICEADDR₁,MANAGER₁) :
    E TELEPHONE₁ E ADDR₁ E COMMISSION₁ E AGENT₁
    E CLIENT₂
    ( OFFICE(OFFICEADDR₁,TELEPHONE₁,MANAGER₁,AGENT₁)
    & OFFICE-AGENT(OFFICEADDR₁,TELEPHONE₁,MANAGER₁,
        AGENT₁(ANAME₁,ADDR₁,COMMISSION₁,CLIENT₂)) )
```

(e) Omitting the first conjunct by subsumption

```
GET (ANAME₁,OFFICEADDR₁,MANAGER₁) :
    E TELEPHONE₁ E ADDR₁ E COMMISSION₁ E AGENT₁
    E CLIENT₂
    OFFICE-AGENT(OFFICEADDR₁,TELEPHONE₁,MANAGER₁,
        AGENT₁(ANAME₁,ADDR₁,COMMISSION₁,CLIENT₂))
```

Section 8.2 discussed the *simplification* of relational calculus queries. Such simplification tends to be useful for queries written on the external view because the transformation process to the conceptual view often generates redundancies. Consider, for example, the schema transformation in Figure 10.4.5. Figure 10.4.12 shows a query for the NEWOFF-ICES view in part (a), and the transformed query to the OFFICES view in part (b). The query is transformed to prenex normal form by moving all the quantifiers to the front, as shown in part (c).

By the functional dependency OFFICE:OFFICEADDR→TELE-PHONE,MANAGER,AGENT, we can identify elements from the first and second conjunct, and thus modify the second conjunct to obtain the query in part (d) of Figure 10.4.12. At this point, we do not have identical conjuncts because the second conjunct is a cluster predicate. However, the first conjunct is really redundant, since the second conjunct is a cluster predicate which, in effect, includes the first one. We can, therefore, remove the first predicate to obtain the query shown in part (e). This example shows how the simplification method for relational database queries can be extended to a hierarchic database by the use of database logic.

In practice, if we are given a hierarchic or network database, database logic is not the language associated with it. To apply the methodology for database conversion presented here, transformations must be made from the given language to database logic and vice versa—as shown in Figure 10.4.13. The compiler or decompiler from or to database logic needs to be written only once for any language. Note that this method represents a solution to only a part of the database conversion problem; we have not considered the problems related to different hardware and operating systems.

FIGURE 10.4.13
Database Conversion

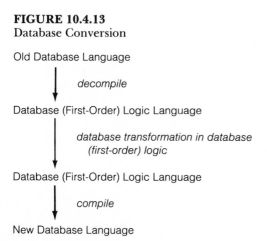

Old Database Language

decompile

Database (First-Order) Logic Language

database transformation in database (first-order) logic

Database (First-Order) Logic Language

compile

New Database Language

10.5 Exercises

10.1 Write a hierarchic view for the following:

    (a) The data structure diagram of Figure 3.5.2(a), with STORE-NO, DNAME, and SSNO the keys for STORE, DEPT, and EMPLOYEE, respectively.

    (b) The data structure diagram of Figure 3.5.2(b), with ONUMBER, SERIALNO, SSNO, NAME within ONUMBER and SSNO, and CASENO the keys for OFFICE, EQUIPMENT, LAWYER, CLIENT, and CASE, respectively.

    (c) The data structure diagram of Figure 3.5.2(c), with NAME, IDNO, NUMBER the keys for BRANCH, BORROWER, and OUTMATERIAL, respectively.

10.2 For each view in Exercise 10.1, give an instance in database logic.

10.3 Write a network view for the following:

    (a) The data structure diagram of Figure 2.5.2, omitting SYSTEM, with DNAME, SSNO, ACCTNO, and RECEIPTNO the keys for DEPARTMENT, EMPLOYEE, CUSTOMER, and SALE, respectively.

    (b) The data structure diagram of Figure 2.5.3, omitting SYSTEM, with ONUMBER, SERIALNO, SSNO, NAME within ONUMBER and SSNO, and CASENO the keys for OFFICE, EQUIPMENT, LAWYER, CLIENT, and CASE, respectively.

    (c) The data structure diagram of Figure 2.5.4, omitting SYSTEM, with NAME, NUMBER, IDNO, NUMBER, ESSNO, and SERIALNO the keys for BRANCH, IN_MATERIAL, BORROWER, OUT_MATERIAL, EMPLOYEE, and EQUIPMENT, respectively.

    (d) The data structure diagram of Figure 2.5.5, with TNAME, ESSNO, SERIALNO, RONUMBER, SERIALNO, and STOCKNO the keys for TEAM, EMPLOYEE, CUSTOMER, REPAIRORDER, EQUIPMENT, and PART, respectively.

    (e) The data structure diagram of Figure 10.5.1, with SERIALNO the key for MACHINE and IDNO the key for PART; in an instance for this diagram, a part A is below part B if part A is a component of part B.

10.4 For each view in Exercise 10.3, give an instance in database logic.

10.5 For each answer to part (a) of Exercise 10.1, (b) of 10.3, (c) of 10.1, and (d) of 10.3, write

    (*i*) The database language for the database logic representation.

    (*ii*) The constraints in database logic.

FIGURE 10.5.1
A Data Structure Diagram

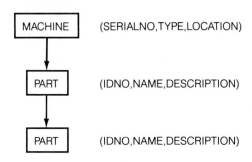

10.6 Represent each answer to part (a) of Exercise 10.2, (b) of 10.4, (c) of 10.2, and (d) of 10.4, as an interpretation.

10.7 Using your answer to part (b) of Exercise 10.1, express the following queries in database logic:

(a) Print the information about all lawyers (including clients and their cases) whose office number is 200.

(b) Print the serial number and cost of every computer in the office of the lawyer with social security number 123-12-3123.

(c) Print all the information about clients and their cases for every lawyer whose salary is greater than $50,000.

(d) Print the office number, social security number, and name of every lawyer who has at least one female client over the age of 64.

(e) Print the number for every office that has at least one lawyer whose salary is greater than $50,000.

10.8 Using your answer to part (a) of Exercise 10.3, express the following queries in database logic:

(a) Print all customer information including sales for the Furniture department.

(b) Print the name and salary of each employee in the Furniture department who made a sale for over $1000.

(c) For each sale over $500, print the date, the employee's social security number, and the customer's account number.

10.9 Using your answer to part (c) of Exercise 10.3, express the following queries in database logic:

(a) Print all information about the materials that are out with the borrower whose ID number is 266315.

(b) Print the name of every author whose material is available at the library branch on South Street.

(c) Print the names of all tasks of the employee S. Johnson at the Parkville branch which require a computer.

10.10 (a) Write a relational view in database logic for the TEAM, EMPLOYEE, CUSTOMER, and REPAIR_ORDER tables of Figure 4.6.5. Use TNAME, ESSNO, SERIALNO, and RO-NUMBER as the keys for TEAM, EMPLOYEE, CUSTOMER, and REPAIR_ORDER, respectively. Include any appropriate inclusion dependencies.

(b) Using your answer to item (a) as the conceptual view, write an external view with a single table that combines all customer and repair order information for cars with a year value greater than 82.

(c) Using your answers to items (a) and (b), write a schema transformation from the external view to the conceptual view.

(d) Show the external instance obtained by the transformation in item (c) on the database of Figure 4.6.5.

10.11 (a) For the external view of item (b) of Exercise 10.10, write a query to print for each customer the name, serial number, and date.

(b) Show the answer to the query in item (a), above, using the database of part (d) of Exercise 10.10.

(c) Use your answer to item (c) of Exercise 10.10 to transform the query in item (a), above, to a query on the conceptual view.

(d) Show the answer to the query in item (c), above, using the database of Figure 4.6.5.

10.12 (a) Transform the constraints for the external view of item (b) of Exercise 10.10 to the conceptual view using your answer to item (c) of the same exercise.

(b) Is the transformation of item (c) in Exercise 10.10 a view transformation? Why or why not?

10.13 (a) Write an insertion simulator for the schema transformation of item (c) of Exercise 10.10.

(b) Is your simulator given in item (a), above, strongly correct? Is it weakly correct? Explain.

(c) Write a deletion simulator for the schema transformation of item (c) in Exercise 10.10.

(d) Is your simulator given in item (c), above, strongly correct? Is it weakly correct? Explain.

10.14 (a) Write a view, NEWTASK, in database logic for the second decomposition of Figure 5.2.1(c).

(b) Write a pair of schema transformations between NEWTASK from item (a), above, and the view OLDTASK from Figure 10.4.1(a), where NORMALIZE: NEWTASK → OLDTASK, and DENORMALIZE: OLDTASK → NEWTASK.

(c) Use your answer to item (b) to transform the constraints on each view to the other view.

(d) Check the lossless and constraint preserving properties for <NORMALIZE,DENORMALIZE> and <DENORMALIZE, NORMALIZE> as defined in item (b), above.

10.15 Same as for Exercise 10.14, but for NEWTASK use the third decomposition of Figure 5.2.1(d).

10.16 (a) Write a hierarchic view for the portion of the data structure diagram of Figure 2.5.5 that contains TEAM, EMPLOYEE, CUSTOMER, and REPAIRORDER. Use TNAME, ESSNO, SERIALNO, and RONUMBER as the keys for TEAM, EMPLOYEE, CUSTOMER, and REPAIRORDER, respectively.

(b) Write a transformation, MAKEHIERARCHIC, from the view in item (a), above, to the view in item (a) of Exercise 10.10.

(c) Using your answer to item (b), show the hierarchic database instance obtained from Figure 4.6.5.

(d) Using your answer to item (b), transform the constraints from the view in item (a), above, to the view in item (a) of Exercise 10.10.

(e) Write a transformation, MAKERELATIONAL, from the view in item (a) of Exercise 10.10 to the view in item (a), above.

(f) Using your answer to item (e), transform the constraints from the view in item (a) of Exercise 10.10 to the view in item (a), above.

(g) Check the lossless and constraint preserving properties for <MAKERELATIONAL,MAKEHIERARCHIC>and<MAKE-HIERARCHIC,MAKERELATIONAL> defined in items (b) and (e), above.

10.17 (a) Write a query in database logic (the relational calculus) on the view in item (a) of Exercise 10.10 to print the serial number of every car handled by the Blue or Green team.

(b) Use your answer to item (e) of Exercise 10.16 to transform the query in item (a), above, to the view in item (a) of Exercise 10.16.

(c) Write a query in database logic on the view in item (a) of Exercise 10.16 to print the location of each team that had a repair order on May 3, 1987.

(d) Use your answer to item (b) of Exercise 10.16 to transform the query in item (c), above, to the view in item (a) of Exercise 10.10.

10.18 (a) Write an insertion simulator for the schema transformation in item (e) of Exercise 10.16 for inserting a customer into the database.

   (b) Is your simulator given in item (a) strongly correct? Is it weakly correct? Explain.

   (c) Write a deletion simulator for the schema transformation in item (e) of Exercise 10.16 for deleting an employee from the database.

   (d) Is your simulator given in item (c) strongly correct? Is it weakly correct? Explain.

   (e) Write a modification simulator for the schema transformation in item (b) of Exercise 10.16 for modifying the balance of a repair order.

   (f) Is your simulator given in item (e) strongly correct? Is it weakly correct? Explain.

10.6 Guide to Further Reading

[10.2] is the standard reference for the theory and applications of database logic. Database transformations, called interpretations there, are discussed in great detail. The notions of constraint preserving and lossless transformations are introduced in [10.1].

[10.1] Grant, J. "Constraint Preserving and Lossless Database Transformations." *Information Systems* 9 (1984), pp. 139–146.

[10.2] Jacobs, B. E. *Applied Database Logic.* Vol. 1. New York: Prentice-Hall, 1985.

Chapter *11*

Various Database
Topics

11.1 Null Values and Incomplete Information

In Section 4.3, which introduced SQL, we encountered the notion of null value. A **null value** is a special value which can be used to indicate that a particular value is unknown or inapplicable or nonexistent. In this section, we consider null values in more detail. We also consider some of the other aspects of incomplete information, such as the formalization of various types of incomplete information in logic. Since information is sometimes imprecise or fuzzy, we also investigate the incorporation of such fuzzy information in databases.

Let's start by considering the representation of null values in SQL. The basic idea of such a representation is that we can use a special value, written as NULL, for any attribute of a table, unless the table definition forbids us from doing so. For our example in this section, we use the schema definition of Figure 4.3.2(a); note that the NULL value is not allowed for DNAME and TASKNO in any table. Figure 11.1.1 shows a database instance for that schema which contains some null values. Two methods for inserting a row with a null value into a table are shown in Figure 11.1.2. Version (b) demonstrates that if columns are named in an INSERT statement, then a NULL value is automatically inserted for each unnamed column.

When we consider queries on tables containing null values, we need to understand how conditions are evaluated. SQL adopts a three-valued logic for this case with the truth values "true", "false", and "unknown". Every comparison with NULL is given the unknown truth value. The

FIGURE 11.1.1
A Database Instance with Null Values

DEPARTMENT		
DNAME	LOCATION	MANAGER
Engineering	12	Simon L
Sales	05	Johnson M
Word processing	03	Miller T
Service	10	NULL

TASK		
DNAME	TASKNO	TASKNAME
Engineering	1	micro
Engineering	2	math
Engineering	3	stat
Sales	4	big sale
Service	5	fixit
Word processing	6	letters

EMPLOYEE				
DNAME	SSNO	NAME	SALARY	ADDRESS
Engineering	111111111	Smith L	25000	NULL
Engineering	222222222	Rogers C	NULL	NULL
Sales	333333333	Bailey D	27600	261 Pine Ave
Sales	444444444	Rivers F	21070	55 Penn St
Sales	555555555	Smith L	31280	1750 Burke Ave
Word processing	666666666	Adams M	17285	NULL
Service	777777777	Davis D	NULL	1280 Boston Dr
Service	888888888	Wood J	22075	1280 Boston Dr

STATUS			
DNAME	SSNO	TASKNO	ST
Engineering	111111111	1	started
Engineering	111111111	2	completed
Engineering	222222222	3	completed
Engineering	222222222	1	NULL
Word processing	666666666	6	NULL
Sales	555555555	4	started
Service	777777777	5	midway

FIGURE 11.1.2
Inserting a Row with a Null Value

Insert the row <Sales,444444444,4,NULL> into the STATUS table.

(a) `INSERT`
`INTO STATUS`
`VALUES ('Sales','444444444',4,NULL);`

(b) `INSERT`
`INTO STATUS (DNAME,SSNO,TASKNO)`
`VALUES ('Sales,''444444444',4)`

FIGURE 11.1.3
Truth Tables for the Three-Valued Logic

(a) Negation

NOT

true	false
unknown	unknown
false	true

(b) Conjunction

AND	true	unknown	false
true	true	unknown	false
unknown	unknown	unknown	false
false	false	false	false

(c) Disjunction

OR	true	unknown	false
true	true	true	true
unknown	true	unknown	unknown
false	true	unknown	false

truth tables for the three truth values appear in Figure 11.1.3. We can justify these truth tables as follows. First of all, because they are identical to the standard truth tables if we restrict them to true and false, we only need to justify the entries involving the unknown truth value. Since the unknown truth value may be either true or false, we take its negation to be also unknown. In general, conjunction and disjunction with the unknown value yield the unknown value. However, the conjunction of a false value with any value is false, and the disjunction of a true value with any value is true. The tables reflect these properties of conjunction and disjunction. For an SQL query, a row is placed in the answer only if the condition, if any, evaluates to true.

Figure 11.1.4 displays five queries with their answers on the database of Figure 11.1.1. The answer to query (a) demonstrates that null values stay in a projection. The answer to query (b) shows that the condition must evaluate to true for a row to be in the result, as the comparison SALARY > 25000 takes on the truth value unknown whenever SALARY has the null value. Therefore, Rogers and Davis are not included in the answer, even though it is possible that one or both of them have salary above $25,000. Query (c) illustrates the ability of checking for null values by using the phrase IS NULL. The answer to query (d) shows that when a function is applied to a column which contains null values, the nulls are ignored. The last example indicates the weakness of the three-valued logic method: it does not always give all the answers. In particular, both Rogers and Davis should be included in the answer, since whatever their salaries are, they must be either greater than $25,000 or less than $30,000. However, this three-valued logic yields the unknown value for a disjunction of unknowns.

The use of null values is problematic when SQL is embedded in a programming language. Consider the example of parts (a) and (b) of Figure 4.5.4. SAL is a variable in a programming language; such a variable cannot be assigned a null value. But the EMPLOYEE table in Figure 11.1.1 contains the NULL value for the SALARY attribute for some rows. In embedded SQL applications, special provisions must be made for attributes for which null values are allowed.

From here on in this section, we will assume that a null value stands for a particular value which is unknown. In some cases, something is known about the value of an entry, even though the exact value is not known. For example, we may know that Davis's salary is $20,050 or $21,050, but not which value is correct. This kind of partial or incomplete information is not expressible with the types of tables used in SQL, but it can be expressed within the framework of first-order logic.

The proof-theoretic approach to databases, where we represent an instance as a set of formulas in first-order logic, was discussed in Section 9.1. This representation allows for the incorporation of incomplete information in databases. In part (a) of Figure 11.1.5, the EMPLOYEE table of Figure 11.1.1 is written as a set of formulas of first-order logic, the

FIGURE 11.1.4
SQL Queries for Tables with Null Values

(a) Print the name and salary of every employee in the EMPLOYEE table.

(*i*)
```
SELECT    NAME,SALARY
FROM      EMPLOYEE;
```

(*ii*)

NAME	SALARY
Smith L	25000
Rogers C	NULL
Bailey D	27600
Rivers F	21070
Smith L	31280
Adams M	17285
Davis D	NULL
Wood J	22075

(b) Print the department name, name, and salary for each employee whose salary is greater than $25,000.

(*i*)
```
SELECT    DNAME,NAME,SALARY
FROM      EMPLOYEE
WHERE     SALARY > 25000;
```

(*ii*)

DNAME	NAME	SALARY
Sales	Bailey D	27600
Sales	Smith L	31280

(c) Print the name and task name for every employee whose salary is unknown.

(*i*)
```
SELECT    NAME,TASKNAME
FROM      EMPLOYEE,STATUS,TASK
WHERE     SALARY IS NULL
    AND EMPLOYEE.SSNO  = STATUS.SSNO
    AND EMPLOYEE.DNAME = STATUS.DNAME
    AND EMPLOYEE.DNAME = TASK.DNAME
    AND STATUS.TASKNO  = TASK.TASKNO;
```

(*ii*)

NAME	TASKNAME
Rogers C	stat
Rogers C	micro
Davis D	fixit

(d) Print the lowest salary of an employee in the Service Department.

(*i*)
```
SELECT    MIN(SALARY)
FROM      EMPLOYEE
WHERE     DNAME = 'Service';
```

(*ii*)

SALARY
22075

(continued)

FIGURE 11.1.4 *(continued)*

(e) Print the social security number and name of each employee whose salary is either greater than $25,000 or less than $30,000.

(*i*)
```
SELECT   SSNO,NAME
FROM     EMPLOYEE
WHERE    SALARY > 25000
      OR SALARY < 30000;
```

(*ii*)

SSNO	NAME
111111111	Smith L
333333333	Bailey D
444444444	Rivers F
555555555	Smith L
666666666	Adams M
888888888	Wood J

FIGURE 11.1.5
The EMPLOYEE Table as a Set of Formulas in First-Order Logic

(a) Original form

E ADDRESS₁ EMPLOYEE(Engineering,111111111,Smith L,25000,ADDRESS₁)
E SALARY₁ E ADDRESS₂
  EMPLOYEE(Engineering,222222222,Rogers C,SALARY₁,ADDRESS₂)

EMPLOYEE(Sales,333333333,Bailey D,27600,261 Pine Ave)

EMPLOYEE(Sales,444444444,Rivers F,21070,55 Penn St)

EMPLOYEE(Sales,555555555,Smith L,31280,1750 Burke Ave)

E ADDRESS₃ EMPLOYEE(Word processing,666666666,Adams M,17285,ADDRESS₃)

EMPLOYEE(Service,777777777,Davis D,20050,1280 Boston Dr)
  ∨ EMPLOYEE(Service,777777777,Davis D,21050,1280 Boston Dr)

EMPLOYEE(Service,888888888,Wood J,22075,1280 Boston Dr)

(b) With Skolem constants

EMPLOYEE(Engineering,111111111,Smith L,25000,c − ADDRESS₁)

EMPLOYEE(Engineering,222222222,Rogers C,c − SALARY₁,c − ADDRESS₂)

EMPLOYEE(Sales,333333333,Bailey D,27600,261 Pine Ave)

EMPLOYEE(Sales,444444444,Rivers F,21070,55 Penn St)

EMPLOYEE(Sales,555555555,Smith L,31280,1750 Burke Ave)

EMPLOYEE(Word processing,666666666,Adams M,17285,c − ADDRESS₃)

EMPLOYEE(Service,777777777,Davis D,20050,1280 Boston Dr)
  ∨ EMPLOYEE(Service,777777777,Davis D,21050,1280 Boston Dr)

EMPLOYEE(Service,888888888,Wood J,22075,1280 Boston Dr)

salary of Davis having been changed to 20050 OR 21050 from NULL. An existential quantifier is used for a null value; because the address of Adams is unknown, we just say that there is an address for Adams. The statement about the salary of Davis is expressed by a disjunction. The two disjuncts represent the two possibilities for the salary value. Note, by the way, that the first-order logic formulas expressing incomplete information are not universal Horn and hence cannot be written in Prolog. When we discussed mechanical theorem proving in Section 8.4, we explained the elimination of existential quantifiers by Skolem functions and constants. We can eliminate the existential quantifiers here, also, by using Skolem constants—which we indicate by writing "c-" in front of the variable names in part (b) of Figure 11.1.5.

Figure 11.1.6 shows how this method can be used to answer queries. Recall first that a question must be negated before using resolution. In example (a) we can do the resolution with the substitution c-ADDRESS$_3$ for ADDRESS$_1$, indicating that the address of Adams is unknown. In the second example, when we ask for the social security number and salary of Davis, we get [] after two resolutions. In both cases the substitution for SSNO$_1$ is 777777777; therefore, the answer for social security number is 777777777. However, the substitutions for SALARY$_1$ are different: 20050 and 21050. This means that the answer for salary is 20050 OR 21050.

FIGURE 11.1.6
Answering Relational Calculus Queries in a Database with Incomplete Information

(a) What is the address of M. Adams?

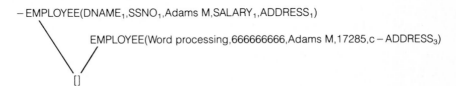

(b) What are the social security number and salary of D. Davis?

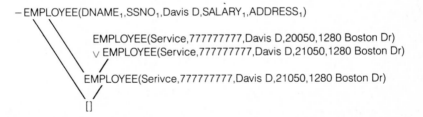

In Section 8.2, we discussed the Closed World Assumption (CWA) for relational databases. The principle of the CWA is that negative information is not stored in the database; the absence of a row in a table represents a negative fact. The CWA does not work in the presence of indefinite information. Using the database of Figure 11.1.5 and the CWA, we can conclude both −EMPLOYEE(Service,777777777,Davis D,20050,1280 Boston Dr) and −EMPLOYEE(Service,777777777,Davis D,21050,1280 Boston Dr). But these two formulas together with the database yield a contradiction. We must therefore generalize the CWA to the Generalized Closed World Assumption (GCWA) by claiming a negative fact *only* if its corresponding positive fact meets two conditions. That is, the corresponding positive fact can be neither (1) a disjunct in the database, nor (2) a fact that can be obtained by substituting some constant values for the Skolem constants in an atomic formula of the database (which may also be a disjunct). As in Section 9.1, if the incompleteness is present in a deductive database, then we have to modify the GCWA to deal with provability from the database.

We end this section by briefly discussing another aspect of incomplete information: situations where the information is imprecise or uncertain, as opposed to being precise but unknown. There is a framework, called **fuzzy logic,** which can be used to express such concepts. Figure 11.1.7 gives an example of a fuzzy database. There are four tables. Each table has a last column with the attribute FUZZY, whose domain is the set of real numbers between 0 and 1. The value 1 signifies definiteness or certainty, and the closer a value is to 1 the closer the corresponding statement is to true. Rows with the value 0 for FUZZY are known to be false and hence are not included.

For the AGEINFO table, we are certain about all the rows; hence, FUZZY has the value 1 for each row. Note how we express the fact that Linda likes Paul more than Charles by means of the FUZZY values in the LIKES table. The predicate "young" is a fuzzy predicate: it does not have a precise meaning. We can give it a meaning, as we do in the YOUNG table, by assigning values to different ages in some systematic way. The adverb "very" is fuzzy also; we give our meaning for it in the VERY table. But note that different people may come up with different fuzzy values for predicates such as "likes" and "young", as well as adverbs such as "very".

Now let's see how we can use a fuzzy database to answer queries. Figure 11.1.8 lists the rules for obtaining fuzzy values for the connectives and the quantifiers, as well as for a truth modifier. Truth modifiers include words like "very," "quite," "exceptionally," "extremely," "almost," "hardly," and "slightly." We will illustrate the rules in Figure 11.1.9 by writing three queries and their answers on the database of Figure 11.1.7. We write the queries in the relational calculus ignoring the FUZZY attribute. (The system should take care of the fuzzy values.) We use the rules for E, −,

FIGURE 11.1.7
A Fuzzy Database

AGEINFO		
NAME	AGE	FUZZY
Linda	25	1
Robert	28	1
Paul	40	1
Mary	32	1
Charles	30	1
Cathy	32	1

LIKES		
NAME1	NAME2	FUZZY
Linda	Paul	.8
Linda	Charles	.2
Robert	Mary	.5
Cathy	Charles	.7
Paul	Mary	.9
Mary	Paul	.8

YOUNG	
AGE	FUZZY
26	1
30	.8
34	.6
36	.4
39	.1

VERY	
VALUE	FUZZY
1	1
.9	.8
.8	.5
.7	.1

FIGURE 11.1.8
Rules for Fuzzy Logic

negation	$fuzzy(-P) = 1 - fuzzy(P)$
conjunction	$fuzzy(P_1 \& P_2) = min(fuzzy(P_1), fuzzy(P_2))$
disjunction	$fuzzy(P_1 \lor P_2) = max(fuzzy(P_1), fuzzy(P_2))$
existential quantifier	$fuzzy(ExP(x,y)) = max\{x \mid fuzzy(P(x,y))\}$
universal quantifier	$fuzzy(AxP(x,y)) = min\{x \mid fuzzy(P(x,y))\}$
truth modification	$fuzzy(modify(P(x))) = fuzzy(modify)(fuzzy(P(x)))$

and & in the first query. In particular, we obtain the row <Robert,.1>
as follows. First, we assume linear interpolation in the table YOUNG.
Thus, age 28 has the FUZZY value .9. Then we get <Robert,28,1> &
<28,.1> (as 1 − .9 = .1), which yields <Robert,28,.1>, and by the rule
for E we get <Robert,.1>. In query (b) we use truth modification to
obtain the VERY YOUNG table. Thus, for example, since Mary's age is
32, and 32 has the FUZZY value .7 for YOUNG, we obtain .1 as the
FUZZY value for VERY YOUNG.

FIGURE 11.1.9
Queries for a Fuzzy Database

(a) Print the names of those people who are not young.

   (i) GET (NAME$_1$)   :
           E AGE$_1$ (AGEINFO(NAME$_1$,AGE$_1$) & −YOUNG(AGE$_1$))

   (ii)

NAME	FUZZY
Robert	.1
Paul	1
Mary	.3
Charles	.2
Cathy	.3

(b) Print the names of those people who are very young.

   (i) GET NAME$_1$)   :
           E AGE$_1$ (AGEINFO(NAME$_1$,AGE$_1$) & VERY YOUNG(AGE$_1$))

   (ii)

NAME	FUZZY
Linda	1
Robert	.8
Mary	.1
Charles	.5
Cathy	.1

(c) Print the names of those people who like a young person.

   (i) GET (NAME$_1$)   : E NAME$_2$ E AGE$_1$
                  (AGEINFO(NAME$_2$,AGE$_1$) &
                  LIKES(NAME$_1$,NAME$_2$) & YOUNG(AGE$_1$))

   (ii)

NAME	FUZZY
Linda	.2
Robert	.5
Cathy	.7
Paul	.7

     In some cases, it is convenient to extend the language by adding a threshold value so that a row is listed in the answer *only* if its fuzzy value is at least as great as the threshold value. The idea is that only those rows are reasonable answers to the query. For instance, by applying this method with the threshold value .6, in query (b) we would list only the first two rows.

11.2 Time in Databases

Databases, just as other objects, exist in and change over time. We have already dealt with some aspects of time in Sections 6.3 and 6.4. In connection with database recovery, we touched on the use of a log, which is a record of the changes made by the transactions to the database. The notion of time is certainly involved there, as the log entries are ordered by time. Time also enters into the consideration of concurrent processing, where the problems are caused by the overlapping execution of several transactions. In particular, the timestamping method uses time explicitly. Actually, the notion of time was implicitly present even earlier in the book when we considered database updates.

We may think of a database instance as a snapshot of the database at some particular time. We update the database to reflect the present reality. For example, when an employee's salary changes, we update the database to reflect that fact. In many situations, it is important to keep the old values also. It may be useful, for example, in a database containing information about employees, to keep track of salaries as they change over time. It may be essential in a medical database to have various patient symptoms, medications, and test results available from the past, in addition to the present values. It is impossible to observe trends, such as for sales and profits, without having access to previous figures. The term **historical data** is often used to refer to data from the past. By the way, there is a similarity between the listing of historical data and the tracing of a program in a programming language, where the changing values of the variables are listed.

The question is how to represent historical data in a database. At the present time, most database systems do not provide any special mechanism for the user to represent historical data. However, various suggestions have been made to incorporate a historical aspect into databases. In this section, we look at some of these suggestions. Before doing so, note that we will consider "time" as the time a fact is entered into the database. It is assumed that the user need not have to explicitly enter a time value for a transaction; the system should do this automatically. Of course, if the database contains historical events with dates, then there is an explicit attribute for the time when an event took place. Another issue about time concerns effective dates. We do not consider this issue separately here; we will just assume that the effective date (of a salary change, for example) is the time that it is placed in the database.

In a relational database system, information is represented in the form of two-dimensional tables. It is natural to add time as a third dimension, so that a historical database becomes a three-dimensional entity. We indicate the historical database structure for the EMPLOYEE table of Figure 4.3.2(b) in Figure 11.2.1. To simplify matters, in the examples for this section we have only a single table in the database (with one excep-

FIGURE 11.2.1
Time as a Third Dimension

DNAME	SSNO	NAME	SALARY	ADDRESS
Engineering	111111111	Smith L	25000	1501 Roper St
Engineering	222222222	Rogers C	30000	2057 York Rd
Sales	333333333	Bailey D	27600	261 Pine Ave
Sales	444444444	Rivers F	21070	55 Penn St
Sales	555555555	Smith L	31280	1750 Burke Ave
Word processing	666666666	Adams M	17285	2121 Taylor St
Service	777777777	Davis D	20050	1280 Boston Dr
Service	888888888	Wood J	22075	1280 Boston Dr

(EMPLOYEE table; Time)

tion). However, our methods can be extended to the standard case in which there are several tables. In the two-dimensional picture, we can see only the present (last) instance of the table, because it covers the previous instances. Figure 11.2.2 shows three instances of the EMPLOYEE table at different times; numbers indicate the time values. We can see several different types of changes in each time interval. There are two changes from time 1 to time 2: there is a new employee, B. Mitchell, and D. Davis has a new address. Between time 2 and time 3, B. Mitchell has been replaced by J. Wood and everyone else's salary has been increased.

In using a historical database, like the EMPLOYEE tables with the TIME attribute, we would find it useful, at each point in time, to have information about all the individuals who have ever been in the database. Figure 11.2.3 (page 394) shows how to rewrite the historical instances and collapse the time dimension. In rewriting these instances, we find it is convenient to add another attribute, which we call EXISTS, to indicate whether the row for that employee exists *at that particular time* in the database. We are assuming that SSNO is the key, so at any time when an individual does not exist, we only list the key value. The other values are null values of the nonexistent type, rather than the unknown type that we emphasized in the previous section. It is not that we don't know Wood's salary at time 1; such a value just does not exist for this database. We call the version in Figure 11.2.3 a (two-dimensional) **time-completed** table. Note that using this time-completed version for the historical database requires extra work when information about a new employee is inserted: a row must be inserted for the new employee with an EXISTS value NO for every time value before the current one.

In Figure 11.2.4 (page 395), we apply the relational algebra to write some queries for the time-completed database of Figure 11.2.3. In three cases, we give two solutions since the queries, in English, may be interpreted differently. For query (a), the first solution yields even the social

FIGURE 11.2.2
Historical Instances of the EMPLOYEE Table

EMPLOYEE					
TIME	DNAME	SSNO	NAME	SALARY	ADDRESS
1	Engineering	111111111	Smith L	23100	1501 Roper St
1	Engineering	222222222	Rogers C	28200	2057 York Rd
1	Sales	333333333	Bailey D	26300	261 Pine Ave
1	Sales	444444444	Rivers F	20050	55 Penn St
1	Sales	555555555	Smith L	30000	1750 Burke Ave
1	Word processing	666666666	Adams M	17000	2121 Taylor St
1	Service	777777777	Davis D	20100	759 West Ave

EMPLOYEE					
TIME	DNAME	SSNO	NAME	SALARY	ADDRESS
2	Engineering	111111111	Smith L	23100	1501 Roper St
2	Engineering	222222222	Rogers C	28200	2057 York Rd
2	Sales	333333333	Bailey D	26300	261 Pine Ave
2	Sales	444444444	Rivers F	20050	55 Penn St
2	Sales	555555555	Smith L	30000	1750 Burke Ave
2	Word processing	666666666	Adams M	17000	2121 Taylor St
2	Service	777777777	Davis D	20100	1280 Boston Dr
2	Service	999999999	Mitchell B	23040	200 East Rd

EMPLOYEE					
TIME	DNAME	SSNO	NAME	SALARY	ADDRESS
3	Engineering	111111111	Smith L	25000	1501 Roper St
3	Engineering	222222222	Rogers C	30000	2057 York Rd
3	Sales	333333333	Bailey D	27600	261 Pine Ave
3	Sales	444444444	Rivers F	21070	55 Penn St
3	Sales	555555555	Smith L	31280	1750 Burke Ave
3	Word processing	666666666	Adams M	17285	2121 Taylor St
3	Service	777777777	Davis D	20050	1280 Boston Dr
3	Service	888888888	Wood J	22075	1280 Boston Dr

security numbers of former and later employees who are not working at that time; the second solution gives only those employees employed at time 2. Similarly, for query (b), the first solution finds *all* former and present employees, while the second solution finds only the present employees. In the two versions of query (c), the second one also includes the time value. For the last query, we assume that we also have the time-

FIGURE 11.2.3
The Time-Completed EMPLOYEE Table

			EMPLOYEE			
TIME	EXISTS	DNAME	SSNO	NAME	SALARY	ADDRESS
1	YES	Engineering	111111111	Smith L	23100	1501 Roper St
1	YES	Engineering	222222222	Rogers C	28200	2057 York Rd
1	YES	Sales	333333333	Bailey D	26300	261 Pine Ave
1	YES	Sales	444444444	Rivers F	20050	55 Penn St
1	YES	Sales	555555555	Smith L	30000	1750 Burke Ave
1	YES	Word processing	666666666	Adams M	17000	2121 Taylor St
1	YES	Service	777777777	Davis D	20100	759 West Ave
1	NO	NULL	888888888	NULL	NULL	NULL
1	NO	NULL	999999999	NULL	NULL	NULL
2	YES	Engineering	111111111	Smith L	23100	1501 Roper St
2	YES	Engineering	222222222	Rogers C	28200	2057 York Rd
2	YES	Sales	333333333	Bailey D	26300	261 Pine Ave
2	YES	Sales	444444444	Rivers F	20050	55 Penn St
2	YES	Sales	555555555	Smith L	30000	1750 Burke Ave
2	YES	Word processing	666666666	Adams M	17000	2121 Taylor St
2	YES	Service	777777777	Davis D	20100	1280 Boston Dr
2	NO	NULL	888888888	NULL	NULL	NULL
2	YES	Service	999999999	Mitchell B	23040	200 East Rd
3	YES	Engineering	111111111	Smith L	25000	1501 Roper St
3	YES	Engineering	222222222	Rogers C	30000	2057 York Rd
3	YES	Sales	333333333	Bailey D	27600	261 Pine Ave
3	YES	Sales	444444444	Rivers F	21070	55 Penn St
3	YES	Sales	555555555	Smith L	31280	1750 Burke Ave
3	YES	Word processing	666666666	Adams M	17285	2121 Taylor St
3	YES	Service	777777777	Davis D	20050	1280 Boston Dr
3	YES	Service	888888888	Wood J	22075	1280 Boston Dr
3	NO	NULL	999999999	NULL	NULL	NULL

completed table for DEPARTMENT. This statement works correctly even if Davis transfers to another department, because the time values must be equal in the join.

We would like to have a language in which we could express queries involving time in a nonprocedural way. For this purpose, we should be able to express time concepts such as the present, the past, a time interval, an overlap in time, before, after, start, and end. We would want to have these concepts built into the framework in which we manipulate the database. Our running example for this section has had only three time values, but in general, there may be many time values for a historical database. Each transaction which updates the database generates a new copy with its own timestamp. As we usually think of time in a continuous

FIGURE 11.2.4
The Relational Algebra on Time-Completed Tables

(a) Print all information about the employees at time 2.

    (*i*) `PRINT SELECT(EMPLOYEE: TIME = 2)`
    (*ii*) `PRINT SELECT(EMPLOYEE: TIME = 2 & EXISTS = 'YES')`

(b) Print the social security number of every employee.

    (*i*) `PRINT PROJECT(EMPLOYEE; SSNO)`
    (*ii*) `PRINT PROJECT(SELECT(EMPLOYEE: TIME = 3); SSNO)`

(c) Print all the salaries and addresses of D. Davis.

    (*i*) `PRINT PROJECT(SELECT(EMPLOYEE: NAME = 'Davis D');`
           `SALARY,ADDRESS)`
    (*ii*) `PRINT PROJECT(SELECT(EMPLOYEE: NAME = 'Davis D');`
           `TIME,SALARY,ADDRESS)`

(d) Print all the managers of D. Davis (assuming a DEPARTMENT table).

    `PRINT PROJECT(SELECT(JOIN(EMPLOYEE,DEPARTMENT):`
               `NAME = 'Davis D'); MANAGER)`

manner, of which the timestamps are specific values, we assume that the database does not change between consecutive time values. Thus, if t_1 and t_2 are consecutive time values, then we consider the database instance at any time t, where $t_1 \leq t < t_2$, to be the same as the instance at time t_1.

Figure 11.2.5 displays some queries involving time written in English and in a query language obtained from the relational calculus by augmenting it with symbols referring to time. For query (a), the TIME value must be the latest value in the database which does not come after January 17, 1986. If the database was updated on January 13, 1986, and again on January 20, 1986, then the database of January 17, 1986 is the same as the database of January 13, 1986. We express the query in two ways. For the second solution, @ is used to stand for such a time value. Thus, in this case @1-17-86 is 1-13-86. The word PRESENT is used in query (b) as a word for the latest (most recent) time value. Query (c) uses the predicate NEXT, which is considered true if the second value is the next time value in the database after the first value. In our running example, January 20, 1986 is the next time value after January 13, 1986. (We do not consider here the case of an employee who leaves and is later rehired with a lower salary.) The last query indicates a time interval by using $>=$, @, and $<=$.

Next we consider constraints that involve time. Usually these constraints are called **dynamic constraints,** because they *constrain the changes that updates can make to the database,* as opposed to **static constraints,** which *refer to an instance at a single time,* and which we studied in Chapter 5. Figure 11.2.6 gives two versions each for two dynamic constraints. The

FIGURE 11.2.5
Queries involving Time

(a) Print all information about employees for January 17, 1986.

    (*i*) GET (DNAME$_1$,SSNO$_1$,NAME$_1$,SALARY$_1$,ADDRESS$_1$) : E TIME$_1$
        (EMPLOYEE(TIME$_1$,YES,DNAME$_1$,SSNO$_1$,NAME$_1$,
            SALARY$_1$,ADDRESS$_1$)
        & TIME$_1$ <= 1-17-86
        & A TIME$_2$
          (E DNAME$_2$ E SSNO$_2$ E NAME$_2$ E SALARY$_2$
            E ADDRESS$_2$
          EMPLOYEE(TIME$_2$,YES,DNAME$_2$,
          SSNO$_2$,NAME$_2$,SALARY$_2$,ADDRESS$_2$)
          -> (TIME$_2$ <= TIME$_1$ $\lor$ TIME$_2$ > 1-17-86)))

    (*ii*) GET (DNAME$_1$,SSNO$_1$,NAME$_1$,SALARY$_1$,ADDRESS$_1$) :
        E TIME$_1$
        (EMPLOYEE(TIME$_1$,YES,DNAME$_1$,SSNO$_1$,NAME$_1$,
            SALARY$_1$,ADDRESS$_1$)
        & TIME$_1$ = @1-17-86)

(b) Print all present information about employees.

    GET (DNAME$_1$,SSNO$_1$,NAME$_1$,SALARY$_1$,ADDRESS$_1$) :
        EMPLOYEE(PRESENT,YES,DNAME$_1$,SSNO$_1$,NAME$_1$,
            SALARY$_1$,ADDRESS$_1$)

(c) Print the name of every employee who ever had a cut in salary.

    GET (NAME$_1$) : E TIME$_1$ E TIME$_2$ E DNAME$_1$ E DNAME$_2$
        E SSNO$_1$ E SALARY$_1$ E SALARY$_2$ E ADDRESS$_1$ E ADDRESS$_2$
        (EMPLOYEE(TIME$_1$,YES,DNAME$_1$,SSNO$_1$,NAME$_1$,SALARY$_1$,
            ADDRESS$_1$)
        & EMPLOYEE(TIME$_2$,YES,DNAME$_2$,SSNO$_1$,NAME$_1$,SALARY$_2$,
            ADDRESS$_2$)
        & NEXT(TIME$_1$,TIME$_2$)
        & SALARY$_1$ > SALARY$_2$)

(d) Print the name of every department for which D. Davis worked between June 6, 1983 and February 5, 1986.

    GET (DNAME$_1$) : E TIME$_1$ E SSNO$_1$ E SALARY$_1$ E ADDRESS$_1$
        (EMPLOYEE(TIME$_1$,YES,DNAME$_1$,SSNO$_1$,Davis D,SALARY$_1$,
            ADDRESS$_1$)
        & TIME$_1$ >= @6-6-83
        & TIME$_1$ <= 2-5-86)

FIGURE 11.2.6
Dynamic Constraints

(a) An employee's salary may not be decreased.

(*i*) A TIME$_1$ A TIME$_2$ A DNAME$_1$ A DNAME$_2$ A SSNO$_1$ A NAME$_1$
A NAME$_2$ A SALARY$_1$ A SALARY$_2$ A ADDRESS$_1$ A ADDRESS$_2$
(EMPLOYEE(TIME$_1$,YES,DNAME$_1$,SSNO$_1$,NAME$_1$,SALARY$_1$,
ADDRESS$_1$)
& EMPLOYEE(TIME$_2$,YES,DNAME$_2$,SSNO$_1$,NAME$_2$,SALARY$_2$,
ADDRESS$_2$)
& NEXT(TIME$_1$,TIME$_2$)
-> SALARY$_1$ <= SALARY$_2$)

(*ii*) A TIME$_1$ A TIME$_2$ A DNAME$_1$ A DNAME$_2$ A SSNO$_1$ A NAME$_1$
A NAME$_2$ A SALARY$_1$ A SALARY$_2$ A ADDRESS$_1$ A ADDRESS$_2$
(EMPLOYEE(TIME$_1$,YES,DNAME$_1$,SSNO$_1$,NAME$_1$,SALARY$_1$,
ADDRESS$_1$)
& EMPLOYEE(TIME$_2$,YES,DNAME$_2$,SSNO$_1$,NAME$_2$,SALARY$_2$,
ADDRESS$_2$)
& TIME$_1$ < TIME$_2$
-> SALARY$_1$ <= SALARY$_2$)

(b) After July 1, 1986 no one is allowed to transfer from the Sales department to the
Service department.

(*i*) A TIME$_1$ A TIME$_2$ A DNAME$_1$ A DNAME$_2$ A SSNO$_1$ A NAME$_1$
A NAME$_2$ A SALARY$_1$ A SALARY$_2$ A ADDRESS$_1$ A ADDRESS$_2$
(EMPLOYEE(TIME$_1$,YES,DNAME$_1$,SSNO$_1$,NAME$_1$,SALARY$_1$,
ADDRESS$_1$)
& EMPLOYEE(TIME$_2$,YES,DNAME$_2$,SSNO$_1$,NAME$_2$,SALARY$_2$,
ADDRESS$_2$)
& NEXT(TIME$_1$,TIME$_2$)
& TIME$_2$ >= 7-1-86
-> (-(DNAME$_1$ = Sales) $\vee$ -(DNAME$_2$ = Service)))

(*ii*) A TIME$_1$ A TIME$_2$ A DNAME$_1$ A DNAME$_2$ A SSNO$_1$ A NAME$_1$
A NAME$_2$ A SALARY$_1$ A SALARY$_2$ A ADDRESS$_1$ A ADDRESS$_2$
(EMPLOYEE(TIME$_1$,YES,DNAME$_1$,SSNO$_1$,NAME$_1$,SALARY$_1$,
ADDRESS$_1$)
& EMPLOYEE(TIME$_2$,YES,DNAME$_2$,SSNO$_1$,NAME$_2$,SALARY$_2$,
ADDRESS$_2$)
& TIME$_1$ < TIME$_2$
& TIME$_2$ >= 7-1-86
& (TIME$_1$ >=@ 7-1-86)
-> (-(DNAME$_1$ = Sales) $\vee$ -(DNAME$_2$ = Service)))

first version of constraint (a) allows a person to quit and later be rehired at a lower salary. That event is not allowed if the second version is maintained. For constraint (b), the first version deals only with direct transfers from the Sales department to the Service department. The second version also prohibits an indirect transfer from the Sales department to another department and eventually to the Service department. It is written in such a way that it does not apply to the portion of the historical database before July 1, 1986.

We have not yet considered the possibility that the database schema may also change over time. For the EMPLOYEE table, for instance, at some point we may not have had the DNAME attribute. Perhaps later we will want to add an attribute concerning vacation time or sick leave for each employee. If there is a data dictionary, then the schema is described there. This suggests that the data dictionary should also be a historical database, reflecting changes in the database schema, the users of the system, access authorizations, and the other information stored there.

We end this section by considering some aspects of physical representation that may be useful in the implementation of historical databases. We assume that the database is represented in some form based on the three-dimensional picture of Figure 11.2.1. We expect the present data to be the easiest to access. Indexing can be used over time to obtain any particular historical instance quickly. If there are pointers between consecutive instances over time, then the system can move quickly to the prior and next instance, especially if the index is a clustering index. Since consecutive instances tend to be very similar, and since it may take a great amount of space to store each instance completely, data compression can be used to indicate the differences between them. If the database is dynamic, with many updates, then it may be useful to store complete database instances at various time intervals with only the changes indicated at other times. These concepts are essentially the same as the backup copy and the log, which we discussed in Section 6.3.

11.3 Specialized and Expert Database Systems

So far in this book, we have been dealing with databases for commercial applications, traditional data processing. Our examples have been databases involving employees and tasks, bank transactions, and inventory information. Although such applications are important, there exist other types of databases with different properties and requirements. In this section, we consider some of these requirements for statistical, scientific, geographical, textual, and design databases. We also discuss expert database systems.

We start with **statistical databases.** These databases tend to be large, contain numerical data, and are used primarily for deriving statistical information. Examples include census data, environmental data, patient information, and tax returns. In most cases, the individual items of data and the individual records are not available to the public because of privacy laws. However, information such as the average medical deduction on tax returns in the income range $25,000–$50,000 for 1985, or the minimum and maximum time between heart attacks for men over age 50, may be available.

It is customary, in dealing with statistical databases, to divide the attributes for tables into two groups: category attributes and summary attributes. Figure 11.3.1 gives an example of a small portion of a relational database, partially filled in, to illustrate this distinction. The table shows the unemployment rate and the inflation rate from 1981 to 1985 for every state on a monthly basis. STATE, YEAR, and MONTH are the **category attributes:** they are the categories that we would use to look up some information; they also form the key for the table. UNEMP_RATE

FIGURE 11.3.1
Category and Summary Attributes

BUSINESS STATISTICS 1981–1985				
STATE	YEAR	MONTH	UNEMP_RATE	INFL_RATE
Alabama	1981	Jan	..	..
		.	.	.
		.	.	.
		Dec	..	..
	1982	Jan	..	..
		.	.	.
		.	.	.
		Dec	..	..
	1983	Jan	..	..
		.	.	.
		.	.	.
		Dec	..	..
	1984	Jan	..	..
		.	.	.
		.	.	.
		Dec	..	..
	1985	Jan	..	..
		.	.	.
		.	.	.
		Dec	..	..
Alaska	1981	Jan	..	..
.	.	.	.	.
.	.	.	.	.

and INFL_RATE are the **summary attributes:** they contain the mea-
sured data on which statistical analysis and summaries are performed.
Category attributes tend to have a small range, with the elements being
character strings or integers, while summary attributes often have a large
range of integers or real numbers. Statistical analysis may consist of taking a random sample or finding an average or variance or other statistical
function. In statistical databases, time is usually handled explicitly as a
category attribute. By the way, statistical tables often have a hierarchic
structure.

Statistical databases have some other features too. They tend to be
stable, with few, if any, deletions or modifications. Also, sometimes the
data values themselves are aggregates, such as averages. The large number of attributes, formats for values, codes, and abbreviations can make
the handling of such databases troublesome. For this reason, a data dictionary is particularly useful. In addition to the standard items, a data
dictionary here may include weighting factors, estimated errors, and
labels, as well as information such as who collected the data. Another
point about such databases is that users often want to have their views
not as virtual views, which do not really exist, but as actual views. The
latter make it easier to use the data for various kinds of statistical analysis
over a period of time. Since the data is stable, it is reasonable to create
actual views for users. Note that statistical databases often require the
capability to define and operate directly on vectors and matrices, and
that unlike for standard databases, users often need to store the results
of computations.

Now we return to the problem of security, discussed in a general
way in Section 6.1. Here we are concerned with statistical databases, but
these problems exist for any database from which users are allowed to
obtain statistical, rather than individual, information. To illustrate the
difficulties involved, consider the EMPLOYEE table of Figure 4.3.2(b)
as a (very small) representative of a situation where a user is allowed
statistical, but not individual, access to a table. In particular, a user is not
allowed to ask a query such as the one in part (a) of Figure 11.3.2, written
in SQL, to find the salary of M. Adams. But consider the version in part
(b), which asks for the average salary of employees in Word processing;
this seems like a reasonable request, yet it also identifies the same value,
and so represents a breach of security. The problem is that it may be
possible to identify an individual by a selection on other than the obvious
attributes, such as SSNO and NAME in this instance.

One suggested solution is for the database system to refuse answering a query which selects one or perhaps a small number of individuals.
But then, by using the SUM function, it is possible to obtain the same
result by first obtaining the sum of all the salaries, and from that subtracting the sum of the salaries of employees not in the Word processing
department. We give these two queries in part (c) of Figure 11.3.2. Thus,

FIGURE 11.3.2
Statistical Queries to Find an Individual Item

Find the salary of M. Adams.

```
(a)  SELECT   SALARY
     FROM     EMPLOYEE
     WHERE    NAME = 'Adams M';

(b)  SELECT   AVG(SALARY)
     FROM     EMPLOYEE
     WHERE    DNAME = 'Word processing';

(c)  SELECT   SUM(SALARY)
     FROM     EMPLOYEE;

     SELECT   SUM(SALARY)
     FROM     EMPLOYEE
     WHERE    DNAME <> 'Word processing';

(d)  SELECT   SUM(SALARY)
     FROM     EMPLOYEE
     WHERE    DNAME = 'Word processing' OR DNAME = 'Sales';

     SELECT   SUM(SALARY)
     FROM     EMPLOYEE
     WHERE    DNAME = 'Sales';
```

we see that it is also important to refuse answering queries that select almost all the individuals. This suggests a security measure of refusing to answer queries that refer to very few or very many individuals. Unfortunately, even that strategy is not necessarily enough to keep individual records secure. Suppose that the database system answers only queries for which the number of individuals is between 1/3 and 2/3 of all individuals, 3 and 5 in our example. Part (d) shows two queries from which we can again deduce the salary of Adams. The first query obtains the sum of the salaries of four employees, while the second obtains the sum of the salaries of the three we are not interested in. Again, subtraction yields the answer.

The problem in the last case was *overlap*. We had two queries which selected almost the same set of individuals. Thus, another strategy for maintaining security is to refuse answering a query whose selection criteria has a large overlap with a previous query. Unfortunately, not only is it difficult to determine the existence of such an overlap, it turns out that even identifying the overlap is not enough for complete security, although it can make obtaining individual information difficult. In fact, a statistical database can be compromised, unless such severe restrictions are placed on the allowable queries that the database becomes virtually useless for statistical purposes. To end our discussion about security, we consider two more possible safeguards. One idea is to interchange values, like the salary values, in such a way that overall accuracy is preserved for statistical queries but where individual answers may not be accurate. The other idea is to change individual values, say by adding to or subtracting from them, again in such a way that the overall accuracy of answers to reasonable statistical queries is not disturbed.

Now we turn to another specialized application, **scientific databases.** There is often a connection between scientific and statistical databases, as many scientific databases are analyzed statistically at various times. Multidimensionality is an important feature in scientific databases. Scientific databases often need to manipulate multidimensional matrices, objects which are quite different from the numbers and character strings of standard databases. Data compression is particularly important because of the sparsity of the matrices.

In many cases, the individual values in scientific databases are numbers obtained from experiments and observations. These numbers often obey scientific laws which are written in the form of equations. Such laws may be used as constraints on the database. For example, if we have two attributes, RADIUS and AREA for a circle, then the constraint is AREA = pi*RADIUS^2. This is very different from the kinds of constraints discussed in Chapter 5. Such a constraint also brings up the problems of accuracy and approximations with real numbers. Even in this case, the constraint may not be satisfied because of such problems. We may then choose a small threshold value, epsilon, so that a row is accepted if ABS(AREA − pi*RADIUS^2) < epsilon. Another problem involving accuracy occurs when two tables must be joined. The question is whether two rows should be joined only if the values for the common attributes are identical, or also if those values are very close to one another. Other problems in scientific databases include conversions between units and objects, and the changes of values in experiments over time.

Another specialized application concerns **geographical databases.** Suppose that we have pictorial and other information concerning a city and its surrounding area. We should be able to query the database for names and descriptions of objects as well as for distances between them. A natural object, such as a tree or a river, should be differentiated from a man-made object, such as a building or a bridge over a river. Information about such an object may include the width of a river and the ownership of a building. One important type of information concerns boundaries, as it is important to know the boundaries of objects such as an airport or a park.

It is difficult to indicate all of these spatial relationships between objects in a standard database system. Also, a user may want to be able to get pictures of various objects and to zoom in on areas of interest. Such a database should also be able to represent the position of objects in a three-dimensional coordinate system. Time is also of importance: a user may want to know when a particular picture was taken, as buildings get torn down and various changes take place over time. Other significant concepts include adjacency and containment. For instance, a particular building may belong to a university, while the adjacent building may contain government offices. The last item we mention involves the notion of distance, often in the sense of nearest, such as the nearest school or fire station to a house. All of these concepts must form an integrated whole for a spatial database system.

In the databases considered so far, we have dealt with single values, such as numbers or character strings for attributes, as well as vectors and matrices for statistical and scientific databases. In many cases, information is present in the form of text, such as law books for legal questions, a collection of articles in medical journals for the treatment of a disease, pamphlets for consumer use, and user guides to computer software. It is not convenient to represent **textual** information in the standard kinds of database systems, which often limit the size of text allowed in a field and, in general, do not deal with text in a flexible and efficient manner. Yet it is important to be able to extract specific information from large amounts of text.

Often text retrieval involves pattern matching. In a textual database concerning computers, for instance, we may ask for the references to a specific software package. Indexing on keywords is an important aid here, which allows the quick retrieval of references to a particular object. Sometimes indexing, by itself, is not sufficient, as in cases where the user does not know the proper keywords and uses more general terminology. Another problem with indexing is what to index; it is not always clear if a particular word should be made into a keyword. If we try to index too many words, then indexing itself may become a bottleneck. Sometimes keywords should be partially specified to take care of spelling differences as well as prefixes and suffixes.

There are several types of queries useful for textual databases. For example, a proximity query contains several keywords with a limit on the distances between them. Some queries require the application of Boolean operators AND, OR, NOT to keywords. Another useful kind of query is where two words must be in the same sentence. Some queries establish a threshold, where, for example, we may look for articles which contain at least m occurrences of a certain term. Note, by the way, that for textual databases, as for statistical databases, deletions and modifications are uncommon. Our final point about textual databases concerns the importance of synonyms.

Recently, databases have also been used with **design structures,** primarily in engineering. Designs usually go through many versions, and several people may work with the same design. Once again, time is an important factor, as old versions of designs must be preserved, tagged, and dated. Constraints involving designs may be very complex, dealing with the consistency or performance of the design and the designed object. Transactions tend to be quite long, as an individual may take a substantial amount of time in changing a design. For this reason, some of the recovery and concurrency mechanisms, created for databases whose applications involve many short transactions, need to be modified. In case of a system failure, most of the changes made to an old version should be recoverable, even if the transaction is not complete at the time of the crash. Another problem with such databases is the difficulty of identifying equivalent designs in terms of different representations.

So far in this section, we have dealt with databases containing some single type of object which is different from the standard formatted table so useful in data processing. In certain applications, such as office automation, it would be useful to have several different types of data: text, voice, image, and tabular data. Such databases are called **multimedia databases.** The problems in this case include the efficient storage of different types of data and the integration of different types of objects into a single coherent framework. Users need capabilities for entering different types of data and browsing through different types of data in a straightforward manner.

We end this section by considering **expert database systems,** a topic briefly discussed in Section 9.1 in conjunction with deductive databases. Expert database systems need to provide some important features, which are, at present, not available in standard database systems. One important aspect is the ability of such a system to deduce new facts. In Chapter 9, we discussed deductive databases that use a logic formalism for deduction. Expert knowledge is a collection of rules and principles which are used by (human) experts for solving problems. An expert system must be able to represent and use this kind of knowledge; an expert database system is one which combines the knowledge representation and reasoning capabilities of expert systems with the accessing, recovery, concurrency, and other aspects of large database systems.

The user interface is very important for expert systems. For example, a physician using a medical expert system may want to know the rationale for a particular diagnosis. The system must be able to display the appropriate rules, in a natural language format, that lead to a particular conclusion. Perhaps the physician is not aware of some connections between symptoms and illnesses, whose presence makes a particular recommendation reasonable. Clearly, the rules should not be contradictory, and they may have to deal with approximate and incomplete information. It should be possible to add new rules and to modify existing rules without much difficulty, as long as such changes do not introduce an inconsistency.

Traditionally, database systems and expert systems developed separately, with expert systems designed within the area of artificial intelligence on small databases. We discussed in Section 7.5 the Fifth Generation Computer Systems Project, whose aim is to construct knowledge information processing systems. An important aspect of such systems is the synthesis of database systems and expert systems. However, since the Fifth Generation Project is long-term, there have been several proposals to use an existing expert system and database system, and perhaps with some modifications, couple them into an expert database system. We indicate three proposed architectures in Figure 11.3.3.

Part (a) of Figure 11.3.3 shows the case of a separate database system and expert system. In this scenario, the user interfaces with the expert system which formulates queries for the database system. The common approach here is the tight coupling technique, where the database system contains the database that the expert system needs. If we identify Prolog with the rules for the expert system, the intensional database, we would have the extensional database not in Prolog, but managed by the database system. (However, some predicates may have both an extensional and an intensional part.) Thus, when data is needed from the extensional database, Prolog would access it through the database system. Requests to the database system may be batched for efficient access, rather than made one at a time. Additional work must be done to transform the search for a recursive predicate to a loop in database processing. Another possibility for the separate systems is loose coupling,

FIGURE 11.3.3
Architectures for Expert Database Systems

(a) Separate database and expert systems

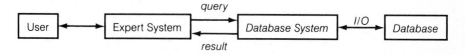

(b) Expert system within a database system

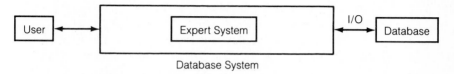

(c) Database system within an expert system

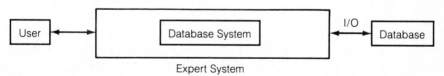

where an expert system is used to analyze data from the database system. In both cases, the expert system acts as a specialized frontend to the database system.

Part (b) of Figure 11.3.3 shows the diagram for an expert system embedded within a database system. Capabilities of expert systems, such as deduction, can be built into a database system using this approach. In particular, the view mechanism can be used to express nonrecursive intensional predicates. It is also possible for the expert system to have reasoning capabilities and to interact with users in natural language, but then the expert system becomes an integral part of the database system. The last version, shown in part (c), envisions the capabilities of a database system within an expert system. This is like placing database system features such as access methods for storage management, concurrency support, and recovery techniques within Prolog. At present, work is progressing along all of these lines for the development of expert database systems.

11.4 Database Uniformization

At the beginning of this book, in Section 1.1, we discussed the need for database systems. We saw that allowing files to be managed separately by programs led to many problems, including inconsistency, incompatibility, and inflexibility. We said that the answer to these problems is to use a database system for managing data in a uniform, consistent, and flexible manner. However, in some large organizations, various groups developed or purchased their own database systems. In some cases the merger of companies creates a situation where different but intersecting portions of a company's data are handled by several different database systems. The disadvantages of the use of several database systems on common or related data are similar to the problems with the older type of file management.

In this section we will sketch a portion of a solution to the problem of proliferating database systems, called database uniformization. The purpose of **database uniformization** is to merge the existing databases into one big database system. The original databases with their database systems become the sites of the new, uniform, distributed database system. Our discussion of the notion of a distributed database system (in Section 7.3) did not deal with the possibility that the database systems are based on different data models using different languages. We now consider the problems related to this heterogeneity of databases but not the standard problems of concurrency, security, and recovery—mentioned in Section 7.3 for the distributed case in general. Figure 11.4.1 shows an architecture for database uniformization.

FIGURE 11.4.1
Architecture for Database Uniformization

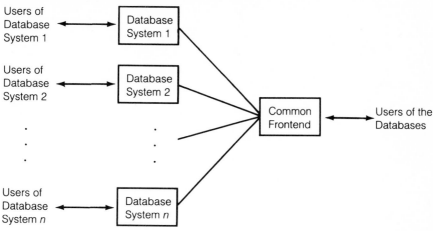

There are many different approaches to the database uniformization problem. For example, the ER model has been used for this purpose. Since database logic provides a uniform framework for relational, hierarchic, and network systems, it provides a convenient data model for database uniformization. By using the database logic approach, we can also use our discussion of database conversion, which is related to database uniformization, from Section 10.4.

The idea is to create a common frontend which allows each user to use the totality of all the databases as if they formed a single system. Users interact with the frontend by asking queries and updating information in the databases. The frontend must translate these commands to the commands of the individual sites in the formulation appropriate for each site. Each of the database systems continues to manage its own site, just as in the standard distributed case. Furthermore, present users of each specific database system can continue running their programs and doing their work using their system.

Some of the concepts involved in database uniformization can be illustrated with the following example. Assume that we have three views: the relational COMPANY view of Figure 10.1.2, the network EMPHEALTH view of Figure 10.1.3(b), and a hierarchic EMPTASK view, as shown in Figure 11.4.2. The first two views were discussed in Section 10.1. The EMPTASK view contains information about employees and their tasks; the last constraint globally identifies each TASKNAME value with its TASKID value. In our scenario, these three views already exist in a database logic system. In practice, a database logic system would

FIGURE 11.4.2
A Hierarchic View for Employees and Tasks

```
VIEW   EMPTASK
SCHEMA
   TABLES              ATTRIBUTES
      EMPLOYEE           ENAME,DNAME,TASK
      TASK               TASKID,TASKNAME,STATUS
   TYPES               ATTRIBUTES
      CHAR(2)            TASKID
      CHAR(10)           STATUS
      CHAR(12)           DNAME
      CHAR(15)           ENAME,TASKNAME
CONSTRAINTS
   EMPLOYEE:ENAME,DNAME->TASK
   EMPLOYEE-TASK:ENAME,DNAME,TASKID->STATUS
   TASK:TASKID->TASKNAME
```

have to be built first on top of the existing relational, hierarchic, and network systems, as pointed out at the end of Section 10.4. Also, the corresponding attributes from the different database systems need not have the same names, or even the same types. Thus, conversions between types may also have to be included in the uniformization process.

The view in Figure 11.4.3 may be considered as a preliminary conceptual view. It was obtained by simply taking the union of all the views. However, it is not really a good conceptual view, because it contains too much duplication. We would prefer to have a uniform global conceptual view with minimal duplication. There is not necessarily a single candidate for that; what we need to do is to *integrate* the three views. Figure 11.4.4 shows just such an integrated view. We decided to make this common conceptual view relational, and therefore based it on COMPANY. We added the ADDR attribute, however, from EMPHEALTH to EMPLOYEE, and also flattened the hierarchic EMPTASK view and the HEALTH-PLAN table—in the latter, omitting the non-key attributes which already exist in the EMPLOYEE table. Omitted as well was the DEPARTMENT-EMPLOYEE cluster, because its data already appears in the DEPART-MENT and EMPLOYEE tables. The constraints were taken from the original views with appropriate modifications to the changed tables.

Figure 11.4.5 diagrams the situation analogous to Figure 11.4.1, but using conceptual and external views. There may be several external views for each conceptual view. The union view is just the union of the individual views. In terms of the transformations presented in Section 10.3, the global conceptual view is an external view for the union view. Users may also have their own external views on the global conceptual view. (The arrows show the directions of the transformations.) A query

FIGURE 11.4.3
The Union of Views

```
VIEW   UNION
SCHEMA
  TABLES                        ATTRIBUTES
    COMPANY.DEPARTMENT            DNAME,LOCATION,MANAGER
    COMPANY.ITEM                  INAME,PRICE,VOLUME
    COMPANY.EMPLOYEE              SSNO,ENAME,DNAME,SALARY
    EMPTASK.EMPLOYEE              ENAME,DNAME,EMPTASK.TASK
    EMPTASK.TASK                  TASKID,TASKNAME,STATUS
    EMPHEALTH.DEPARTMENT          DNAME,MANAGER,LOCATION,
                                    EMPHEALTH.EMPLOYEE
    EMPHEALTH.HEALTHPLAN          COMPNAME,ADDRESS,TELNO,
                                    EMPHEALTH.EMPLOYEE
    EMPHEALTH.EMPLOYEE            SSNO,NAME,ADDR,SALARY
  TYPE                          ATTRIBUTES
    CHAR(2)                       LOCATION,TASKID
    CHAR(7)                       TELNO
    CHAR(9)                       SSNO
    CHAR(10)                      STATUS
    CHAR(12)                      DNAME,COMPNAME
    CHAR(15)                      MANAGER,ENAME,TASKNAME,NAME
    CHAR(20)                      INAME,ADDRESS,ADDR
    INTEGER                       VOLUME,SALARY
    REAL                          PRICE
CONSTRAINTS
  COMPANY.DEPARTMENT:DNAME->LOCATION,MANAGER
  COMPANY.ITEM:INAME->PRICE,VOLUME
  COMPANY.EMPLOYEE:SSNO->ENAME,DNAME,SALARY
  EMPTASK.EMPLOYEE:ENAME,DNAME->EMPTASK.TASK
  EMPTASK.EMPLOYEE-EMPTASK.TASK:
                NAME,DNAME,TASKID->STATUS
  EMPTASK.TASK:TASKID->TASKNAME
  EMPHEALTH.DEPARTMENT:DNAME->MANAGER,LOCATION,
                        EMPHEALTH.EMPLOYEE
  EMPHEALTH.HEALTHPLAN:COMPNAME->ADDRESS,TELNO,
                        EMPHEALTH.EMPLOYEE
  EMPHEALTH.EMPLOYEE:SSNO->NAME,ADDR,SALARY
```

posed by a user of a global external view must be transformed first to the global conceptual view and then to the union view.

The transformation from the global conceptual view to the union view in our example is shown in Figure 11.4.6. The DEPARTMENT table translates to a disjunction of the DEPARTMENT table in COMPANY and the DEPARTMENT table in EMPHEALTH. This means that the rows in the DEPARTMENT table for the global conceptual view are obtained by taking the union of the DEPARTMENT table in COMPANY with the DEPARTMENT table, omitting the EMPLOYEE subtable, in

FIGURE 11.4.4
The Integrated View

```
VIEW   ALLEMPINFO
SCHEMA
   TABLES           ATTRIBUTES
     DEPARTMENT     DNAME,LOCATION,MANAGER
     ITEM           INAME,PRICE,VOLUME
     EMPLOYEE       SSNO,ENAME,DNAME,ADDR,SALARY
     TASK           ENAME,DNAME,TASKID,TASKNAME,STATUS
     HEALTHPLAN     COMPNAME,ADDRESS,TELNO,SSNO
    TYPE                ATTRIBUTES
     CHAR(2)            LOCATION,TASKID
     CHAR(7)            TELNO
     CHAR(9)            SSNO
     CHAR(10)           STATUS
     CHAR(12)           DNAME,COMPNAME
     CHAR(15)           MANAGER,ENAME,TASKNAME
     CHAR(20)           INAME,ADDRESS,ADDR
     INTEGER            VOLUME,SALARY
     REAL               PRICE
CONSTRAINTS
   DEPARTMENT:DNAME->LOCATION,MANAGER
   ITEM:INAME->PRICE,VOLUME
   EMPLOYEE:SSNO->ENAME,DNAME,ADDR,SALARY
   TASK:ENAME,DNAME,TASKID->STATUS
   TASK:TASKID->TASKNAME
   HEALTHPLAN:COMPNAME->ADDRESS,TELNO
```

FIGURE 11.4.5
The Conceptual and External Views in Database Uniformization

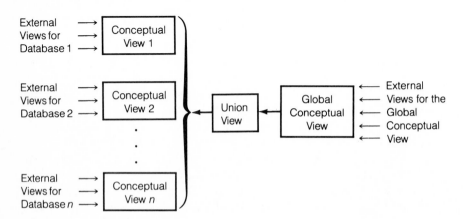

FIGURE 11.4.6
Transformation form the Global Conceptual View to the Union View

TRANSFORMATION   T

VIEW$_1$: ALLEMPINFO
VIEW$_2$: UNION

   DEPARTMENT(DNAME$_1$,LOCATION$_1$,MANAGER$_1$)
      COMPANY.DEPARTMENT(DNAME$_1$,LOCATION$_1$,MANAGER$_1$) $\longrightarrow$
    $\lor$ E EMPHEALTH.EMPLOYEE$_1$
      EMPHEALTH.DEPARTMENT(DNAME$_1$,MANAGER$_1$,LOCATION$_1$,
         EMPHEALTH.EMPLOYEE$_1$)

   ITEM(INAME$_1$,PRICE$_1$,VOLUME$_1$) $\longrightarrow$
     COMPANY.ITEM(INAME$_1$,PRICE$_1$,VOLUME$_1$)

   EMPLOYEE(SSNO$_1$,ENAME$_1$,DNAME$_1$, ADDR$_1$,SALARY$_1$) $\longrightarrow$
      COMPANY.EMPLOYEE(SSNO$_1$,ENAME$_1$,DNAME$_1$,SALARY$_1$)
      & ADDR$_1$ = NULL
    $\lor$ E MANAGER$_1$ E LOCATION$_1$ E EMPHEALTH.EMPLOYEE$_1$
      (EMPHEALTH.DEPARTMENT-EMPHEALTH.EMPLOYEE(DNAME$_1$,
        MANAGER$_1$,LOCATION$_1$,EMPHEALTH.EMPLOYEE$_1$
        (SSNO$_1$,NAME$_1$,ADDR$_1$,SALARY$_1$))
      & ENAME$_1$ = NAME$_1$)

   TASK(ENAME$_1$,DNAME$_1$,TASKID$_1$,TASKNAME$_1$,STATUS$_1$) $\longrightarrow$
    E EMPTASK.TASK$_1$
    EMPTASK.EMPLOYEE-EMPTASK.TASK(ENAME$_1$,DNAME$_1$,
      EMPTASK.TASK$_1$(TASKID$_1$,TASKNAME$_1$,STATUS$_1$))

   HEALTHPLAN(COMPNAME$_1$,ADDRESS$_1$,TELNO$_1$,SSNO$_1$) $\longrightarrow$
    E EMPHEALTH.EMPLOYEE$_1$ E NAME$_1$ E ADDR$_1$ E SALARY$_1$
    EMPHEALTH.HEALTHPLAN-EMPHEALTH.EMPLOYEE(COMPNAME$_1$,
      ADDRESS$_1$,TELNO$_1$,EMPHEALTH.EMPLOYEE$_1$
      (SSNO$_1$,NAME$_1$,ADDR$_1$,SALARY$_1$))

EMPHEALTH. In the case of a row of the EMPLOYEE table, which is obtained from the EMPLOYEE table of COMPANY, a NULL value is used for the nonexistent ADDR attribute.

In Section 10.3, we learned why schema transformations should also be view transformations. However, the transformation of Figure 11.4.6 is not a view transformation. We can see why this is so by considering the first constraint in ALLEMPINFO, since its transformation is not implied by the constraints in UNION. Both the constraint and its transformation appear in Figure 11.4.7. In the UNION view, separate functional dependencies in the DEPARTMENT tables of COMPANY and of EMPHEALTH uniquely identify LOCATION and MANAGER values based on a DNAME value. It is then possible to have the row <Service,125,Baker L> in the DEPARTMENT table of COMPANY and the row <Service,Baker L,255,EMPLOYEE[Service]> in the DEPART-

FIGURE 11.4.7
Constraint Transformation from ALLEMPINFO to UNION

(a) The constraint DEPARTMENT:DNAME→LOCATION,MANAGER

A DNAME$_1$ A LOCATION$_1$ A LOCATION$_2$ A MANAGER$_1$ A MANAGER$_2$
(DEPARTMENT(DNAME$_1$,LOCATION$_1$,MANAGER$_1$)
& DEPARTMENT(DNAME$_1$,LOCATION$_2$,MANAGER$_2$)
→ LOCATION$_1$ = LOCATION$_2$ & MANAGER$_1$ = MANAGER$_2$)

(b) The transformed constraint

A DNAME$_1$ A LOCATION$_1$ A LOCATION$_2$ A MANAGER$_1$ A MANAGER$_2$
((COMPANY.DEPARTMENT(DNAME$_1$,LOCATION$_1$,MANAGER$_1$)
   ∨ E EMPHEALTH.EMPLOYEE$_1$ EMPHEALTH.DEPARTMENT(DNAME$_1$,
       MANAGER$_1$,LOCATION$_1$,EMPHEALTH.EMPLOYEE$_1$))
& (COMPANY.DEPARTMENT(DNAME$_1$,LOCATION$_2$,MANAGER$_2$)
   ∨ E EMPHEALTH.EMPLOYEE$_2$ EMPHEALTH.DEPARTMENT(DNAME$_1$,
       MANAGER$_2$,LOCATION$_2$,EMPHEALTH.EMPLOYEE$_2$))
→ LOCATION$_1$ = LOCATION$_2$ & MANAGER$_1$ = MANAGER$_2$)

MENT table of EMPHEALTH, giving two different values for the location of the Service department. But there is a problem: the functional dependency in the ALLEMPINFO view is a global constraint whose meaning is *not* implied by the local constraints.

We can get around this problem in two ways. One method is to omit any global constraint not implied by separate local constraints. In this way, we can still keep a constraint, such as ITEM: INAME→PRICE,VOLUME, because all of its attributes come from a single view. The second method is to add constraints, such as the statement of Figure 11.4.7(b), to the UNION view. This statement represents a global integrity constraint, which cannot be obtained from the separate local integrity constraints. When such a constraint is not satisfied in the union, it means that there is an inconsistency in the union of the databases. This situation is analogous to the case where there were inconsistencies between files before a database system was introduced; with several database systems involving related data, it is possible to have inconsistencies between them. We can catch such inconsistencies during the uniformization process.

Let's consider queries next. A user would probably want to construct an external view for the global conceptual view, but we assume here that the external view is identical to the conceptual view. Consider Figure 11.4.8, which shows a query in part (a) and its transformed version in part (b). The execution of this query requires a search over two databases. The situation is similar to the case of a query in a distributed database system that requires data from several sites, except that now

FIGURE 11.4.8
Query Transformation from ALLEMPINFO to UNION

(a) Query: Find the names and addresses of all employees whose healthplan company is Blue Cross.

```
GET (ENAME₁,ADDR₁) ! E SSNO₁ E DNAME₁ E SALARY₁
    E ADDRESS₁ E TELNO₁
    ( EMPLOYEE(SSNO₁,ENAME₁,DNAME₁,ADDR₁,SALARY₁)
    & HEALTHPLAN(Blue Cross,ADDRESS₁,TELNO₁,SSNO₁)
```

(b) Transformed query

```
GET (ENAME₁,ADDR₁) ! E SSNO₁ E DNAME₁ E SALARY₁
    E ADDRESS₁ E TELNO₁
    ( ( COMPANY.EMPLOYEE(SSNO₁,ENAME₁,DNAME₁,SALARY₁)
        & ADDR₁ = NULL
      v E MANAGER₁ E LOCATION₁ E EMPHEALTH.EMPLOYEE₁
        ( EMPHEALTH.DEPARTMENT-EMPHEALTH.EMPLOYEE
          (DNAME₁,MANAGER₁,LOCATION₁,
          EMPHEALTH.EMPLOYEE₁(SSNO₁,NAME₁,ADDR₁,SALARY₁))
        & ENAME₁ = NAME₁ ) )
    & E EMPHEALTH.EMPLOYEE₂ E NAME₂ E ADDR₂ E SALARY₂
      EMPHEALTH.HEALTHPLAN-EMPHEALTH.EMPLOYEE
        (Blue Cross,ADDRESS₁,TELNO₁,EMPHEALTH.EMPLOYEE₂
        (SSNO₁,NAME₂,ADDR₂,SALARY₂)) )
```

the sites contain different database systems. As mentioned earlier, data conversions may also have to be performed when data exist in different formats.

Finally, we consider updates. A user's update on the global conceptual view (which may actually be a simulation of an update on a global external view) must be simulated on the underlying databases. In a case like an insertion into the DEPARTMENT table, we have several choices: we can insert only into the DEPARTMENT table for COMPANY, or for EMPHEALTH, or both. The proper choice may depend on the application.

11.5 Exercises

11.1 For the database in Figure 11.5.1, write the following queries in SQL and show the answer for each query:

(a) Print the serial number, type, and cost of every piece of equipment.

FIGURE 11.5.1
Tables with NULL Values

OFFICE	
ONUMBER	AREA
200	650
100	1010
305	470

EQUIPMENT			
SERIALNO	TYPE	COST	ONUMBER
AAXYZ12398	NULL	1789	NULL
XPVQR15296	Xerox Machine	1250	200
RHABC12350	Telephone	NULL	200

LAWYER						
ONUMBER	LSSNO	LNAME	ADDRESS	SALARY	STATUS	TELNO
200	123456789	Peters	86 Front Rd	NULL	Associate	555-6666
100	111223333	Williams	NULL	NULL	Partner	NULL
305	567123456	Murphy	2690 Valley Dr	48300	Associate	248-1000
200	444555666	Bingham	10 Leaf Pl	60000	NULL	258-2000

CLIENT						
ONUMBER	LSSNO	CNAME	ADDR	SEX	AGE	JNAME
200	123456789	Gibson	38 Park Ave	M	NULL	Steele
100	111223333	Jackson	1103 Candle St	F	NULL	Stone
100	111223333	French	29 Branch La	F	45	Burns
305	567123456	Ward	NULL	NULL	NULL	NULL
200	444555666	Johnson	NULL	M	24	Burns

(b) Print the serial number and type of every piece of equipment which is in an office whose area value is greater than 400.

(c) Print the social security number, name, address, and salary of every lawyer whose salary is greater than $50,000.

(d) Print the name of every lawyer who has a client whose age is unknown.

(e) Print the name and status of the lawyer with the youngest client.

(f) Print the name of every client whose age is less than 100.

11.2 (a) Write the four tables given in Figure 11.5.1 as formulas in first-order logic.

(b) Same as item (a), but make the following changes: In the first row of EQUIPMENT, the ONUMBER is 100 or 200 or 305. In the first row of LAWYER, the SALARY is between $20,000 and $30,000. In the CLIENT table, all AGE values are between 0 and 100 and the SEX value is "M" or "F".

11.3 For your answer to item (b) of Exercise 11.2, write the following relational calculus queries, and show how resolution can be used to answer them:

(a) What is the name of the lawyer with social security number 123-45-6789?

(b) What is the salary of the lawyer with social security number 123-45-6789?

(c) What are the sex and age of the client Ward?

(d) What types of equipment are in an office whose area is 650?

11.4 (a) Construct a fuzzy table for the modifier "extremely".

(b) Using the fuzzy database of Figure 11.1.7 and your answer to item (a), write the following queries in the relational calculus, and show the answer for each:

(i) Print the names of the extremely young people.

(ii) Print the names of those people who are liked by a very young person.

(iii) Print the names of those people who do not like an extremely young person.

(iv) Print the names of those people who either are very young or who like an extremely young person.

(v) Print the names of the extremely very young people.

11.5 Write the time-completed LAWYER and CLIENT tables for the historical instances given in Figure 11.5.2.

11.6 Using your answer to Exercise 11.5, write relational algebra queries and show the answer for each of the following:

(a) Print all information about lawyers at time 2.

(b) Print the name of every client and the judge associated with that client for the duration of the database.

(c) Print the time, social security number, name, address, and telephone number of every lawyer with salary greater than $40,000.

(d) Print the name of every lawyer and the time when that lawyer had a client who had a case where Burns was the judge.

(e) Print the office number, name, address, and status of every lawyer over time.

(f) Print the name of every lawyer who had an increase in salary each time.

FIGURE 11.5.2
Historical Instances of the LAWYER and CLIENT Tables

LAWYER							
TIME	ONUMBER	LSSNO	LNAME	ADDRESS	SALARY	STATUS	TELNO
1	200	123456789	Peters	86 Front Rd	25000	Associate	555-6666
1	100	111223333	Williams	104 Green St	91500	Partner	420-3000
1	305	567123456	Murphy	2690 Valley Dr	48300	Associate	248-1000
1	200	444555666	Bingham	10 Leaf Pl	60000	Associate	258-2000

LAWYER							
TIME	ONUMBER	LSSNO	LNAME	ADDRESS	SALARY	STATUS	TELNO
2	200	123456789	Peters	86 Front Rd	30000	Associate	555-6666
2	100	111223333	Williams	104 Green St	99000	Partner	420-3000
2	305	567123456	Murphy	2690 Valley Dr	48300	Associate	248-1000
2	100	444555666	Bingham	25 Mountain Pl	75000	Partner	425-3121
2	200	777889999	Silver	2000 North Dr	38000	Associate	258-2000

LAWYER							
TIME	ONUMBER	LSSNO	LNAME	ADDRESS	SALARY	STATUS	TELNO
3	200	123456789	Peters	86 Front Rd	30000	Associate	555-6666
3	305	567123456	Murphy	2690 Valley Dr	56000	Associate	248-1000
3	100	444555666	Bingham	25 Mountain Pl	75000	Partner	425-3121
3	200	777889999	Silver	66 River St	42500	Associate	397-2100
3	305	676788912	Jaffe	871 Maple Ave	31500	Associate	215-6913

CLIENT							
TIME	ONUMBER	LSSNO	CNAME	ADDR	SEX	AGE	JNAME
1	200	123456789	Gibson	38 Park Ave	M	27	Steele
1	100	111223333	Jackson	1103 Candle St	F	31	Stone
1	100	111223333	French	29 Branch La	F	45	Burns
1	305	567123456	Ward	613 Hart Rd	M	39	Steele
1	200	444555666	Johnson	77 Sunset St	M	24	Burns

CLIENT							
TIME	ONUMBER	LSSNO	CNAME	ADDR	SEX	AGE	JNAME
2	200	123456789	Gibson	38 Park Ave	M	28	Steele
2	100	111223333	Jackson	1103 Candle St	F	31	Stone
2	100	111223333	French	11 Colombus Dr	F	45	Burns
2	305	567123456	Ward	613 Hart Rd	M	40	Steele
2	100	444555666	Johnson	77 Sunset St	M	24	Burns
2	200	777889999	Parker	6010 First Ave	F	52	Steele

(continued)

CLIENT							
TIME	ONUMBER	LSSNO	CNAME	ADDR	SEX	AGE	JNAME
3	200	123456789	Gibson	38 Park Ave	M	28	Steele
3	305	567123456	Ward	613 Hart Rd	M	40	Steele
3	100	444555666	Jackson	1103 Candle St	F	32	Stone
3	100	444555666	Johnson	77 Sunshine Dr	M	24	Wayne
3	200	777889999	Parker	6010 First Ave	F	53	Steele
3	305	676788912	Taylor	401 L St	F	47	Wayne

11.7 Using your answer to Exercise 11.5, write relational calculus queries—using @, NEXT, and PRESENT, where appropriate—for the following:

(a) Print all information about lawyers for July 23, 1986.

(b) Print the name of every client and the judge associated with that client between May 1, 1986 and November 1, 1986.

(c) Print the social security number, name, address, and telephone number of every lawyer whose present salary is greater than $40,000.

(d) Print the name of every lawyer and the time when that lawyer had a client with a case before judge Burns.

(e) Print the office number, name, address, and status of every lawyer over time.

(f) Print the name of every lawyer who had an increase in salary each time.

11.8 Using your answer to Exercise 11.5, write dynamic constraints for the following:

(a) A lawyer's salary may not be decreased.

(b) A client's age may not be decreased.

(c) A client may not change lawyers.

(d) A client may change lawyers only if the lawyer leaves the firm.

11.9 This exercise refers to the database of Figure 4.6.2. All queries are to be written in SQL.

(a) Give three different methods to find Miller's salary.

(b) Give three different methods to find Taylor's salary.

(c) Give three different methods to find Ryan's salary.

11.10 (a) Write a relational view for the tables in Figure 4.6.4. Make reasonable assumptions for the constraints.

(b) Write a hierarchic view for the data structure diagram of Figure 3.5.2(c). Make reasonable assumptions for constraints.

(c) Write a network view for the portion of the data structure diagram of Figure 2.5.4 containing BRANCH, EMPLOYEE,

EQUIPMENT, and TASK. Make reasonable assumptions for constraints.

(d) Using your answers to items (a)–(c), write the union view.

(e) Using your answers to items (a)–(d), write an integrated view for the global conceptual view.

(f) Using your answers to items (d) and (e), write the transformation from the integrated view to the union view.

(g) Is the transformation in item (f) constraint preserving? Is it lossless? Explain.

11.6 Guide to Further Reading

Null values are discussed in Chapter 5 of [1.3] as well as in several chapters in [1.2] and [4.2]. [11.2] presents the theory, architecture, and language of the fuzzy relational database (FRDB) model. Statistical and scientific database issues are considered in [11.1] and in several other articles in the same issue.

[11.1] Shoshani, A., and H. K. T. Wong. "Statistical and Scientific Database Issues." *IEEE Transactions on Software Engineering* SE-11 (1985), pp. 1040–1047.

[11.2] Zemankova, M., and A. Kandel. "Implementing Imprecision in Information Systems." *Information Sciences* 37 (1985), pp. 107–141.

Chapter 12
Specific Database Systems

12.1 QBE

QBE stands for **Query-by-Example;** it is available both in a stand-alone version and as part of the IBM DB2 database system. The term QBE is used both for the system and the language; we deal with aspects of the language here. For DB2, QBE is an alternative to SQL. What distinguishes QBE from other database languages is its pictorial format, within which a user fills in blanks. These blanks are in skeleton tables for the tables of the database. Recently, some other database systems have also been developed which adopt a similar approach for user interaction with the database. QBE was developed by M. M. Zloof in the mid-1970s; however, not all the features proposed by Zloof were implemented.

Our examples use the database schema of Figure 4.3.2(a). Figure 12.1.1 gives the QBE versions of some of the queries in Figure 4.3.4. We (as users) obtain a table skeleton for the EMPLOYEE table by writing DRAW EMPLOYEE on the command line (not shown in the figure). Once QBE draws a table skeleton, we can start on the second line to fill in the blanks. (In the examples shown, the user's entries are shown in boldface.) We leave irrelevant columns empty and write "P." (Print) for the columns on which we want to project. In query (b) there is a selection on the SALARY attribute; such a selection condition may be placed in the table skeleton or in a separate box. Query (c) is the same as the previous one except that only one column is printed. The words UNQ, AO, and DO are used for eliminating duplicates and putting the answer in ascending or descending order, respectively, and are illustrated in the

FIGURE 12.1.1
QBE Queries

(a) Print the name and salary of every employee.

EMPLOYEE	DNAME	SSNO	NAME	SALARY	ADDRESS
			P.	P.	

(b) Print the department name, name, and salary for each employee whose salary is greater than $25,000.

EMPLOYEE	DNAME	SSNO	NAME	SALARY	ADDRESS
	P.		P.	P. >25000	

(c) Print all names of departments which have an employee whose salary is greater than $25,000.

EMPLOYEE	DNAME	SSNO	NAME	SALARY	ADDRESS
	P.			>25000	

(d) Print, without repetition, all names of departments which have an employee whose salary is greater than $25,000.

EMPLOYEE	DNAME	SSNO	NAME	SALARY	ADDRESS
	P.UNQ			>25000	

(e) Print the department name, name, and salary for each employee whose salary is greater than $25,000. Present the result in ascending order on salaries.

EMPLOYEE	DNAME	SSNO	NAME	SALARY	ADDRESS
	P.		P.	P.AO >25000	

last two queries. When sorting is done on more than one attribute, the numbers (1) and (2) after AO or DO (not illustrated here), are used to indicate the order in which the attributes are sorted.

The QBE versions of the queries of Figure 4.4.1 appear in Figure 12.1.2. *An element whose name starts with an underscore* is called an **example element**. The part after the underscore is arbitrary, but it is customary to write a sample value for the attribute. Thus, we use _SMITH as the example element for MANAGER, rather than _5, for example. Essentially, each example element is a variable name for a specific attribute. In those cases where attributes from more than one table need to be

FIGURE 12.1.2
QBE Queries Involving More Than One Table

(a) Combine and print all department and task information.

DEPARTMENT	DNAME	LOCATION	MANAGER
	_SALES	**_12**	**_SMITH**

TASK	DNAME	TASKNO	TASKNAME
	_SALES	**_5**	**_COMPUTER**

P.	**_SALES**	**_12**	**_SMITH**	**_5**	**_COMPUTER**

(b) Print the names of all employees in the Engineering department who have completed a task.

EMPLOYEE	DNAME	SSNO	NAME	SALARY	ADDRESS
	Engineering	**_123456789**	**P.**		

STATUS	DNAME	SSNO	TASKNO	ST
	Engineering	**_123456789**		**completed**

(c) Print the salary, task names, and manager of the employee whose social security number is 222-22-2222.

EMPLOYEE	DNAME	SSNO	NAME	SALARY	ADDRESS
	_SALES	**222222222**		**_30000**	

STATUS	DNAME	SSNO	TASKNO	ST
	_SALES	**222222222**	**_5**	

TASK	DNAME	TASKNO	TASKNAME
	_SALES	**_5**	**_COMPUTER**

(continued)

FIGURE 12.1.2 *(continued)*

DEPARTMENT	DNAME	LOCATION	MANAGER
	_SALES		_SMITH

P.	_30000	_COMPUTER	_SMITH

printed, QBE can be given a command to set up an additional unnamed table skeleton. This is done for queries (a) and (c), but not for query (b), in which the attribute of the result (NAME) occurs in one table.

The example elements in the unnamed result table skeleton indicate the types of elements that go into the result. The P. in the first column means that all the attribute values are to be printed for that table. Note that the example element _SALES in query (a) appears in both the DEPARTMENT and TASK table skeletons, as well as the result table skeleton. This pattern indicates a join on DNAME between DEPARTMENT and TASK. Query (b) involves selection on constants for DNAME and ST. Such a selection is indicated by placing the constant under the appropriate attribute. Constants may not begin with an underscore. The identical constant value for DNAME and the identical example element for SSNO indicate the join of the EMPLOYEE and STATUS tables. The last query involves joins on both the constant for SSNO as well as the example elements for DNAME and TASKNO.

In Figure 12.1.3, the queries from Figures 4.4.2 and 4.4.4(c) are written to illustrate additional concepts of QBE. Two versions for each query are given. To obtain the union of two selections on the EMPLOYEE table, the user writes a separate line for each. The other solution uses a CONDITIONS box which may contain any legal condition involving the attributes, constants, example elements, and built-in functions. The five standard built-in functions, CNT., AVG., SUM., MAX., and MIN., are available in QBE. The use of the function MAX is illustrated in the first solution for query (b). If UNQ. is added to a built-in function, then duplicates are eliminated in the calculation (as in SUM.UNQ.). The second version of query (b) uses negation in QBE. This version prints the name of the employee in the Service department for whom there does not exist an employee in the Service department with a higher salary.

Figure 12.1.4 illustrates QBE updates with those shown for SQL in Figure 4.5.2. Insertion, deletion, and modification are represented by

FIGURE 12.1.3
Additional QBE Queries

(a) Print the social security number and name of every employee who is either in the Sales department or Service department.

(*i*)

EMPLOYEE	DNAME	SSNO	NAME	SALARY	ADDRESS
	Sales	**P.**	**P.**		
	Service	**P.**	**P.**		

(*ii*)

EMPLOYEE	DNAME	SSNO	NAME	SALARY	ADDRESS
	_OFFICE	**P.**	**P.**		

CONDITIONS
_OFFICE = Sales OR _OFFICE = Service

(b) Print the name of the highest paid employee in the Service department.

(*i*)

EMPLOYEE	DNAME	SSNO	NAME	SALARY	ADDRESS
	Service		**P.**	**MAX.**	

(*ii*)

EMPLOYEE	DNAME	SSNO	NAME	SALARY	ADDRESS
	Service		**P.**	**_ 20000**	
¬	**Service**			**>_ 20000**	

the codes I., D., and U., respectively. Since insertion and deletion refer to whole rows, their codes are written in the first column under the table name. For insertion, the system places a NULL value in the table for the new row for any column that is left blank. Since modification usually refers to only specific columns, its code is not placed under the table name; instead, the new value for any attribute is placed after "U." The last update shows that we can request a repetition of an attribute in a table skeleton. The example element _20000 stands for the present salary; the second SALARY column indicates how the old value is modified.

We end our consideration of QBE with an illustration of how the QBE proposal allows the inclusion of a data dictionary that can be used to express integrity constraints and security authorizations. The idea is that everything should follow the QBE format of table skeletons. First, part (a) of Figure 12.1.5 shows how a new table may be added to the database in QBE. We start with an empty table skeleton, and we fill in the blanks even in the first row. The two I.'s refer to the insertion of the table and the insertion of the attributes. For each attribute, we have to indicate its domain, its data type, if it is part of a key, and if it is indexed.

FIGURE 12.1.4
QBE Updates

(a) Insert the row <Sales,444444444,4,completed> into the STATUS table.

STATUS	DNAME	SSNO	TASKNO	ST
I.	Sales	444444444	4	completed

(b) Delete the row from the EMPLOYEE table with social security number 111-11-1111.

EMPLOYEE	DNAME	SSNO	NAME	SALARY	ADDRESS
D.		111111111			

(c) Delete the rows from the STATUS table with social security number 111-11-1111.

STATUS	DNAME	SSNO	TASKNO	ST
D.		111111111		

(d) Modify the status of task 1 in the Engineering department for social security number 111-11-1111 to 'midway'.

STATUS	DNAME	SSNO	TASKNO	ST
	Engineering	111111111	1	U.midway

(e) Add $1000 to every employee's salary in the Service department.

EMPLOYEE	DNAME	SSNO	NAME	SALARY	SALARY	ADDRESS
	Service			_20000	U._20000 + 1000	

Part (b) of Figure 12.1.5 shows how to add the constraint that an employee's salary cannot be decreased. We start by requesting the EMPLOYEE table skeleton. The item in parentheses, U. here, refers to the fact that this is a constraint for database modification. The two I.'s in the second row refer to the insertion of the entry and the constraint. The I. in the third row indicates that the row contains the old values and is not part of the constraint. Part (c) shows how to obtain the list of constraints for the EMPLOYEE table. Authorization can also be granted using the QBE format as shown in parts (d) and (e) for two examples similar to the ones in Figure 6.1.6. Here, P. indicates a print (or read) authorization. The authorization does not apply to an attribute for which no entry is specified, like SALARY in the first case. When the authori-

FIGURE 12.1.5
The QBE Dictionary

(a) Add the EMPLOYEE table to the database schema.

I.EMPLOYEE.I.		DNAME	SSNO	NAME	SALARY	ADDRESS
DOMAIN	I.	DNAME	SSNO	NAME	SALARY	ADDRESS
TYPE	I.	CHAR(15)	CHAR(9)	CHAR(15)	INTEGER	CHAR(20)
KEY	I.	N	Y	N	N	N
INVERSION	I.	N	N	N	N	N

(b) For the EMPLOYEE table, insert the constraint that updates cannot decrease an employee's salary.

EMPLOYEE	DNAME	SSNO	NAME	SALARY	ADDRESS
I.CONSTR(U.).I.		_123456789		>_ 20000	
I.		_123456789		_ 20000	

(c) Find the constraints for the EMPLOYEE table.

EMPLOYEE	DNAME	SSNO	NAME	SALARY	ADDRESS
P.CONSTR.P.					

(d) Allow everyone to see the EMPLOYEE table except for salaries.

EMPLOYEE	DNAME	SSNO	NAME	SALARY	ADDRESS
I.AUTH(P.).I.	_Sales	_123456789	_Jones		_22 Oak St

(e) Allow Taylor to modify the SALARY attribute in the EMPLOYEE table for all employees in the Service department.

EMPLOYEE	DNAME	SSNO	NAME	SALARY	ADDRESS
I.AUTH(U.).Taylor I.	Service			_20000	

zation is for an individual, rather than for everyone, then the username must be given in the first column, as shown in the last example.

12.2 INGRES

INGRES is a database system marketed by Relational Technology Inc. It originated as a pioneering relational database system project at the University of California at Berkeley in the early 1970s. This product has been on the market commercially since 1981 in the VAX environment, and is available for various mainframes, minicomputers, and microcomputers. Over the years, various subsystems have been added to INGRES, including a data dictionary, a report writer, host language interfaces, forms management, graphics, and networking. We concentrate on the language **QUEL,** which is *the original basic data manipulation language for INGRES* (INGRES also supports SQL) and on **forms**, which is the common metaphor for the various INGRES subsystems. Section 8.2 touched on the two versions of the relational calculus, the domain calculus and the tuple calculus. We have been using the domain calculus so far; however, QUEL is based on the tuple calculus.

The queries written for QBE in Figure 12.1.1 are written in QUEL in Figure 12.2.1 for the same database schema. The QUEL queries are similar to SQL queries, but the variables are tuple variables, called range variables here. Although it is not always necessary to introduce

FIGUE 12.2.1
QUEL Queries

(a) Print the name and salary of every employee.

```
range of e is EMPLOYEE
retrieve (e.NAME, e.SALARY)
```

(b) Print the department name, name, and salary for each employee whose salary is greater than $25,000.

```
range of e is EMPLOYEE
retrieve (e.DNAME, e.NAME, e.SALARY) where
      e.SALARY > 25000
```

(c) Print all names of departments which have an employee whose salary is greater than $25,000.

```
range of e is EMPLOYEE
retrieve (e.DNAME) where e.SALARY > 25000
```

(d) Print, without repetition, all names of departments which have an employee whose salary is greater than $25,000.

```
range of e is EMPLOYEE
retrieve unique (e.DNAME) where e.SALARY > 25000
```

(e) Print the department name, name, and salary for each employee whose salary is greater than $25,000. Present the result in ascending order on salaries.

```
range of e is EMPLOYEE
retrieve (e.DNAME, e.NAME, e.SALARY) where
      e.SALARY > 25000 sort by SALARY:ascending
```

range variables for QUEL queries, it is common practice to do so. Each range variable stands for a row of a table. Queries are expressed by the **retrieve** statement. Projection is indicated by listing the attributes inside parentheses after the word "retrieve". Each attribute must be qualified by a table name or a range variable. As in SQL, selection is done by using a "where" clause. We can avoid repetition by using "unique", and place items in order by means of the "sort" clause. We specify the order by writing "ascending" or "descending"; if the answer is to be sorted on several attributes, then these attributes are listed in the sort clause separated by commas.

In Figure 12.2.2, the SQL queries from Figure 4.4.1 (done for QBE in Figure 12.1.2) are written in QUEL. Again, the QUEL queries are similar to the SQL queries, but we declare and use a range variable for each table. In Figure 12.2.3, some additional QUEL queries are shown. The first example shows a calculation in the query: a new attribute is

FIGURE 12.2.2
QUEL Queries Involving More Than One Table

(a) Combine and print all department and task information.

```
range of d is DEPARTMENT
range of t is TASK
retrieve (d.DNAME, d.LOCATION, d.MANAGER, t.TASKNO,
         t.TASKNAME) where d.DNAME = t.DNAME
```

(b) Print the names of all employees in the Engineering department who have completed a task.

```
range of e is EMPLOYEE
range of s is STATUS
retrieve (e.NAME) where e.DNAME = s.DNAME and
         e.DNAME = "Engineering" and
         s.ST = "completed" and
         e.SSNO = s.SSNO
```

(c) Print the salary, task names, and manager of the employee whose social security number is 222-22-2222.

```
range of e is EMPLOYEE
range of s is STATUS
range of t is TASK
range of d is DEPARTMENT
retrieve (e.SALARY, t.TASKNAME, d.MANAGER)
         where e.SSNO = "222222222" and d.NAME =
         e.DNAME and e.SSNO = s.SSNO
         and s.TASKNO = t.TASKNO
         and e.DNAME = s.DNAME
         and s.DNAME =t.DNAME
```

FIGURE 12.2.3
Additional QUEL Queries

(a) Print the names and new salaries of the employees in the Sales department if they are all given a 5% raise.

```
range of e is EMPLOYEE
retrieve (e.NAME, newsalary = e.SALARY * 1.05)
        where e.DNAME = "Sales"
```

(b) Same as at Figure 12.2.1(b), but put the result in a new table.

```
range of e is EMPLOYEE
retrieve into highsal (e.DNAME, e.NAME, e.SALARY)
        where e.SALARY > 25000
```

(c) Same as item (b), above, but create a view for the new table.

```
range of e is EMPLOYEE
define view bigsal (e.DNAME, e.NAME, e.SALARY)
        where e.SALARY > 25000
```

(d) Print the number of departments.

(*i*)
```
range of d is DEPARTMENT
  retrieve (departments = count(d.DNAME))
```

(*ii*)
```
range of e is EMPLOYEE
  retrieve (departments = countu(e.DNAME))
```

(e) Print the name of the highest paid employee in the Service department.

```
range of e is EMPLOYEE
retrieve (e.NAME) where e.DNAME = "Service" and
        e.SALARY = max(e.SALARY where
        e.DNAME = "Service")
```

introduced for which values are calculated from an attribute in the table. Example (b) illustrates the construction of a new table. This table is not a view: it is simply a new table, one that is not modified if EMPLOYEE is updated. A view is constructed in example (c). The last two examples show applications of built-in functions. The letter "u" at the end of the function name indicates that it does its computation on distinct values.

Figure 12.2.4 repeats the updates from Figures 4.5.2 and 12.1.4 in QUEL. QUEL uses the words "append", "delete", and "replace", respectively. For insertion, the values for the various attributes are indicated in parentheses after the table name. Typically, for deletion and modification, range variables and the "where" clause are used. Figure 12.2.5 demonstrates the creation of a table, an integrity constraint, and a granting of privileges. We show the use of "text" for character strings, and include the data type "money"; other data types are "i1", "i2", and "i4" for integers

FIGURE 12.2.4
QUEL Updates

(a) Insert the row <Sales,444444444,4,completed> into the STATUS table.

```
append to STATUS (DNAME = "Sales", SSNO =
           "444444444", TASKNO = 4, ST = "completed")
```

(b) Delete the row from the EMPLOYEE table with social security number 111-11-1111.

```
range of e is EMPLOYEE
delete e where e.SSNO = "111111111"
```

(c) Delete the rows from the STATUS table with social security number 111-11-1111.

```
range of s is STATUS
delete s where s.SSNO = "111111111"
```

(d) Modify the status of task 1 in the Engineering department for social security number 111-11-1111 to "midway".

```
range of s is STATUS
replace s (ST = "midway")
          where s.DNAME = "Engineering"
          and s.SSNO = "111111111" and s.TASKNO = 1
```

(e) Add $1000 to every employee's salary in the Service department.

```
range of e is EMPLOYEE
replace e (SALARY = e.SALARY + 1000)
          where e.DNAME = "Service"
```

FIGURE 12.2.5
Additional Aspects of QUEL

(a) Add the EMPLOYEE table to the database schema.

```
create EMPLOYEE (DNAME = text(15), SSNO = text(9),
          NAME = text(15), SALARY = money,
          ADDRESS = text(20))
```

(b) For the EMPLOYEE table, insert the constraint that SALARY values must be nonnegative.

```
range of e is EMPLOYEE
define integrity on e is e.SALARY >= 0
```

(c) Allow Taylor to modify the SALARY values of the EMPLOYEE table for all employees in the Service department at terminal tty5 for 9 a.m. to 5 p.m., Monday to Friday.

```
range of e is EMPLOYEE
define permit replace on e(SALARY) to taylor
          at tty5 from 9:00 to 17:00 on Mon to Fri
          where e.DNAME = "Service"
```

requiring the specific number of bytes, "f4" and "f8" for real numbers in a similar way, and "date". An integrity constraint can be specified by using a condition on a table. The granting of privileges has many options in QUEL; in our example, the type of privilege, namely "replace", as well as the attribute, the recipient of the privilege, computer terminal number and time and day restrictions, and a "where" clause are all specified.

INGRES is a forms-oriented database system. The rationale for using forms is that they are easy to use and provide a uniform visual tool for interfacing among different subsystems. In particular, the following menu-driven, forms-oriented subsystems are available: QBF (Query By Forms) for data manipulation with forms, VIFRED (Visual Forms Editor) for changing the appearance of forms, RBF (Report By Forms) for report writing by using forms, GBF (Graph By Forms) for drawing graphs using forms, and ABF (Applications By Forms) for writing application programs with forms. (In the near future, GBF will be replaced by a new graphics package called VIGRAPH.)

QBF allows retrievals and updates through the use of forms. The default form for the EMPLOYEE table is shown in part (a) of Figure 12.2.6. After writing the name of a table, like employee, the user is given menus to select the required operation. For a query, the menu item RETRIEVE is used. QBF then displays the form for EMPLOYEE. At this point, selections may be made by filling in the blanks in the form. By placing Sales after "DNAME:" we pick the selection condition DNAME = 'Sales'. In addition, the standard relational operations, $<, <=, >, >=, !=$, and $=$, can be used. Insertions are done by requesting the menu item APPEND and then filling in the blanks in the form. Deletions and modifications are performed by the menu item UPDATE, which involves a retrieval followed by an action.

In VIFRED, the default form shows underscore characters for each item, as shown for the EMPLOYEE table in part (b) of Figure 12.2.6. After "DNAME:" it places a "c" for character and then fifteen underscores for the fifteen possible characters in DNAME. The default form can be edited by shifting or deleting various items, adding blank lines and titles, and making other changes. RBF is a forms-oriented report writer and has the basic features discussed in Section 6.5. The default report for the EMPLOYEE table appears in part (c); the report contains a title, the date and time the report was run, standard column names, and a page number. In ABF, the user develops an application by filling in forms and using operations similar to the other INGRES forms-oriented subsystems.

We end our consideration of INGRES by briefly discussing programming languages and networking. The language QUEL can be embedded in the programming languages BASIC, C, COBOL, FORTRAN, and Pascal; embedded QUEL is called EQUEL. Recently, an interface to ADA from SQL, called ESQL/ADA, was announced for

FIGURE 12.2.6
Using Forms in INGRES

(a) Default form for the EMPLOYEE table in QBF

```
TABLE IS EMPLOYEE:

DNAME:                 SSNO:              NAME:

SALARY:           ADDRESS:
```

(b) Default form for the EMPLOYEE table in VIFRED

```
TABLE IS EMPLOYEE:

DNAME: c_____      SSNO: c_____

NAME: c_____       SALARY: i_____

ADDRESS: c_____

--------------------End-of-Form----------------------
```

(c) Default report for the EMPLOYEE table in RBF

```
     3-FEB-1986                                                9:15:17

                        Report on Table: EMPLOYEE
                        ------ -- ----- --------

     DNAME               SSNO        NAME      SALARY      ADDRESS
     -----               ----        ----      ------      -------

     Engineering         111111111   Smith L   25000       1501 Roper St
     Engineering         222222222   Rogers C  30000       2057 York Rd
     Sales               333333333   Bailey D  27600       261 Pine Ave
     Sales               444444444   Rivers F  21070       55 Penn St
     Sales               555555555   Smith L   31280       1750 Burke Ave
     Word processing     666666666   Adams M   17285       2121 Taylor St
     Service             777777777   Davis D   20050       1280 Boston Dr
     Service             888888888   Wood J    22075       1280 Boston Dr

                               -  1  -
```

INGRES. For networking, the latest announcement concerns INGRES/
STAR, which supplies distributed database management, including a global
data dictionary, over a network of computers using the INGRES system.

12.3 NOMAD2

Although some of the ideas for the fourth-generation programming
languages go back to the 1960s, these languages were first developed in
the mid-1970s and have become widely used since the early 1980s. Some
of them started as report generators or database query languages, and

have evolved into highly sophisticated systems. They generally feature an English-like nonprocedural language, which combines many of the capabilities of a database system as well as a standard high-level (third-generation) programming language. Fourth-generation programming languages usually also contain a graphics module, a subsystem for statistical analysis, a data dictionary, and features for specifying a screen setup. In this section, we briefly discuss some of the components of NOMAD2, a well-known fourth-generation programming language, released in 1980, and marketed by D&B Computing Services. NOMAD2 is an expanded and revised version of the original NOMAD, initially released in 1974, and is available for various IBM computers.

One interesting feature of NOMAD2 is that it allows both a relational and a hierarchic structure. We start by dealing with the relational aspects. Figure 12.3.1 shows how to write a database schema based on the DEPARTMENT, TASK, and STATUS tables of Figure 4.3.2(a). The name after SCHEMA, GSMITH, is a password. Each table is described in a MASTER declaration, and each attribute is called an ITEM. In the format portion, each "A" stands for a character and each "9" for a digit. The DEPARTMENT table has the key attribute DNAME; similarly, the TASK table has the key attribute TASKNO; and STATUS has the pair SSNO,S_TASKNO for its key. The tables are sorted on the key attribute(s).

For each item, we can specify a heading for printing purposes; if no heading is specified, then the item name is used. The placement of a colon inside a heading indicates a new line, so the heading for DNAME is placed on two lines. We make each ITEM unique in the schema to avoid having to qualify names. The STATUS table definition illustrates

FIGURE 12.3.1
A Relational Database Schema in NOMAD2

```
SCHEMA    GSMITH;
MASTER    DEPARTMENT  INSERT KEYED(DNAME);
  ITEM    DNAME    AS A15   HEADING 'DEPARTMENT:NAME';
  ITEM    LOCATION AS A2;
  ITEM    MANAGER  AS A15;
MASTER    TASK  INSERT KEYED(TASKNO);
  ITEM    T_DNAME  AS A15   HEADING 'DEPT NAME';
  ITEM    TASKNO   AS 999   HEADING 'TASK NUMBER';
  ITEM    TASKNAME AS A15   HEADING 'TASK NAME';
MASTER    STATUS   INSERT KEYED(SSNO,S_TASKNO);
  ITEM    SSNO     AS A9;
  ITEM    S_TASKNO AS 999   MEMBER'TASK'
            HEADING 'TASK:NUMBER';
  ITEM    ST       AS A10   HEADING 'TASK STATUS';
  DEFINE S_DNAME  AS EXTRACT'T_DNAME FROM TASK
            USING S_TASKNO';
```

two more concepts. S_TASKNO is defined as MEMBER 'TASK'; this represents an inclusion dependency (see Section 5.3), which states that each S_TASKNO value which is placed in the STATUS table must already be a TASKNO value (the key value) in the TASK table. The second point is that S_DNAME is a virtual item: it is defined as the corresponding T_DNAME value from the TASK table—using the S_TASKNO item for the key item, TASKNO, in TASK. Thus, S_DNAME values are not stored, but are obtained as needed. It is possible to write the definition this way because each task number belongs to (determines) a unique department. See Figure 12.3.2, which gives a database instance for this schema based on Figure 4.3.2(b). The S_DNAME attribute values are included because, to the user, it looks as if those values are stored in the STATUS table.

Figure 12.3.3 shows some queries for this database written in NOMAD2 and also shows the answers. The basic statement is the LIST

FIGURE 12.3.2
A Database Instance for the Schema of Figure 12.3.1

DEPARTMENT		
DNAME	LOCATION	MANAGER
ENGINEERING	12	SIMON L
SALES	05	JOHNSON M
SERVICE	10	WILLIAMS B

TASK		
T_DNAME	TASKNO	TASKNAME
ENGINEERING	1	MICRO
ENGINEERING	2	MATH
ENGINEERING	3	STAT
SALES	4	BIG SALE
WORD PROCESSING	6	LETTERS

STATUS			
SSNO	S_TASKNO	ST	S_DNAME
111111111	1	STARTED	ENGINEERING
111111111	2	COMPLETED	ENGINEERING
222222222	3	COMPLETED	ENGINEERING
222222222	1	MIDWAY	ENGINEERING
666666666	6	COMPLETED	WORD PROCESSING
555555555	4	STARTED	SALES

FIGURE 12.3.3
Queries in NOMAD2

(a) Print the manager names and names of all departments. Present the result in alphabetical order on manager names.

(*i*) `LIST  BY MANAGER  DNAME`

(*ii*)

```
                    DEPARTMENT
    MANAGER            NAME
    ----------      ----------
    JOHNSON M       SALES
    SIMON L         ENGINEERING
    WILLIAMS B      SERVICE
```

(b) Print the name of every task in the Engineering department.

(*i*) `LIST  TASKNAME  WHERE T_DNAME='ENGINEERING'`

(*ii*)
```
TASK NAME
---------
MICRO
MATH
STAT
```

(c) Print the department name, social security number, and task number for each completed task. Present the result in alphabetical order on department name and in descending order on social security number within department name. Give the column for social security numbers the heading "SOCIAL SECURITY NUMBER".

(*i*) `LIST  S_TASKNO  BY S_DNAME  BY SSNO DESC   -`
`      HEADING 'SS NUMBER'  WHERE ST='COMPLETED'`

(*ii*)
```
DEPT NAME              SS NUMBER     TASK NUMBER
---------------        ----------    -----------
ENGINEERING            222222222     03
                       111111111     02
WORD PROCESSING        666666666     06
```

statement. A "BY" in front of an attribute indicates that the items are to be ordered on that attribute. Thus, the answer to query (a) is ordered alphabetically on MANAGER; no ordering is specified in query (b), and in query (c) the answer is ordered on S_DNAME first, and then on SSNO within S_DNAME in descending order, as indicated by DESC. Note that the S_DNAME value ENGINEERING is not duplicated in the second row; this lack of duplication is in general what happens to repeated items sorted via BY. The WHERE clause is used to specify a retrieval condition. In interactive mode, a hyphen is placed at the end of a line if the statement is continued on the next line.

NOMAD2 has four statements for combining tables: MERGE, EXTRACT, SUBSET, and REJECT. All of these are variations on the join operation in the following sense. Let A and B represent the two tables and J the join of A and B for some attribute(s). Then MERGE is J U A U B, EXTRACT is J U A, SUBSET is J, and REJECT is A − J. Queries illustrating the use of these statements appear in Figure 12.3.4. In all cases, the attribute after BY is joined with the attribute after MATCHING. (By the way, MERGE implements an operation sometimes called the "outer join.")

Query (a) illustrates MERGE: even though the Service department has no tasks and the Word processing department has no location, they are included. There is also a title for this report. Query (b) shows EXTRACT ALL: the Service department is included, even though it has no tasks. We use EXTRACT ALL because EXTRACT would match only a single row from TASK for each department. Query (c) illustrates the true join; again we use ALL as for EXTRACT. (MERGE and REJECT do not use ALL.) Query (d) shows REJECT; that is, we reject all departments which have a matching department name in the TASK table, leaving only the Service department. The last example illustrates a combination of three tables and an IF clause. First, the join according to the SUBSET clause is performed as long as the result satisfies the IF condition. Then the EXTRACT operation is done.

Now we consider updates. A row may be inserted into a table by using either PROMPT or INSERT. In the case of PROMPT, the system prompts the user with each item name in a table, and the user can type in the values. How to use INSERT is shown in Figure 12.3.5(a). For deletions and updates, the appropriate rows must first be found; the LOCATE statement is usually employed for this purpose. Then a DELETE

FIGURE 12.3.4
Queries in NOMAD2 Involving Several Tables

(a) Print all the department names and their locations and task names, where available, with the title "ALL DEPARTMENTS".

(*i*)
```
LIST  BY DNAME  LOCATION -
    MERGE  MATCHING T_DNAME  TASKNAME -
    TITLE 'ALL DEPARTMENTS'
```

(*ii*)

```
                    ALL DEPARTMENTS

DEPARTMENT
    NAME              LOCATION         TASK NAME
----------------      --------         ---------
ENGINEERING           12               MICRO
                                       MATH
                                       STAT
SALES                 05               BIG SALE
SERVICE               10
WORD PROCESSING                        LETTERS
```

(continued)

FIGURE 12.3.4 *(continued)*

(b) Same as item (a), but only for departments which appear in the DEPARTMENT table and without the title.

(i) LIST BY DNAME   LOCATION -
      EXTRACT ALL   MATCHING T_DNAME   TASKNAME

(ii) DEPARTMENT

NAME	LOCATION	TASK NAME
ENGINEERING	12	MICRO
		MATH
		STAT
SALES	05	BIG SALE
SERVICE	10	

(c) Print the join of the DEPARTMENT and TASK tables with the title "THIS IS THE JOIN".

(i) LIST BY DNAME   LOCATION MANAGER -
      SUBSET ALL   MATCHING T_DNAME   TASKNO TASKNAME -
      TITLE 'THIS IS THE JOIN'

(ii)   THIS IS THE JOIN

DEPARTMENT NAME	LOCATION	MANAGER	TASK NUMBER	TASK NAME
ENGINEERING	12	SIMON L	01	MICRO
			02	MATH
			03	STAT
SALES	05	JOHNSON M	05	BIG SALE

(d) Print all department names, their locations, and managers, for those departments which do not appear in TASK, with the title "DEPARTMENTS WITHOUT TASKS".

(i) LIST BY DNAME   LOCATION MANAGER -
      REJECT MATCHING T_DNAME -
      TITLE 'DEPARTMENTS WITHOUT TASKS'

(ii)   DEPARTMENTS WITHOUT TASKS

DEPARTMENT NAME	LOCATION	MANAGER
SERVICE	10	WILLIAMS B

(e) For each department, except Engineering, which has a task, print the name and status of its task and the manager of the department.

(i) LIST BY T_DNAME   TASKNAME -
      SUBSET MATCHING S_DNAME   ST -
      IF DNAME NE 'ENGINEERING' -
      EXTRACT MATCHING DNAME   MANAGER

(ii)

DEPT NAME	TASK NAME	TASK STATUS	MANAGER
SALES	BIG SALE	STARTED	JOHNSON M
WORD PROCESSING	LETTERS	COMPLETED	

FIGURE 12.3.5
Updates in NOMAD2

(a) Insert the row <WORD PROCESSING,03,MILLER T> into the DEPARTMENT table.

```
INSERT DEPARTMENT  DNAME='WORD PROCESSING'
  LOCATION='03'  MANAGER='MILLER T'
```

(b) Delete the row for the Sales department from the DEPARTMENT table.

```
TOP   DEPARTMENT
LOCATE  DNAME='SALES'
DELETE  DEPARTMENT
```

(c) Delete the rows from the STATUS table with social security number 111-11-1111.

```
TOP   STATUS
DELETE   STATUS WHERE SSNO='111111111'
```

(d) Modify the status of task 1 for social security number 111-11-1111 to MIDWAY.

```
TOP   STATUS
LOCATE  SSNO='111111111' AND S_TASKNO=1
CHANGE  ST='MIDWAY'
```

(e) Modify the status of every task in the Engineering department to CANCELLED.

```
TOP STATUS
CHANGE  ST='CANCELLED'  WHERE S_DNAME='ENGINEERING'
```

(CHANGE) statement deletes (modifies) one or more records. Examples for deletion and modification appear in the rest of Figure 12.3.5. The TOP statement is used to make sure processing begins at the top of a table; otherwise, processing would start with the current (most recently accessed) row, and so the operation might be applied only to a portion of the table's contents.

As mentioned earlier, NOMAD2 also supports hierarchic processing. Figure 12.3.6 shows how an EMPLOYEE table, considered to be a child of the DEPARTMENT table, would be described in the SCHEMA. The special data type NAME is used here for handling names; the numerical SALARY item is to be printed with a dollar sign in front. Each row in the DEPARTMENT table is associated with a set of rows in the EMPLOYEE table. Thus, for example, when employees are inserted for the Engineering department, the DEPARTMENT table must be positioned at the Engineering department. A LIST statement can now be used to print items involving both of these two tables in a hierarchic manner; there is no need for any of the join statements. NOMAD2 allows any number of hierarchic levels, so that, for example, EMPLOYEE can also be a parent node for another SEGMENT table. Thus, NOMAD2 combines features of a relational and a hierarchic database system.

FIGURE 12.3.6
Representation of a Child Node in a Hierarchy

```
SEGMENT  EMPLOYEE   PARENT=DEPARTMENT   INSERT KEYED(E_SSNO);
   ITEM  E_SSNO     AS A9      HEADING 'SSNO';
   ITEM  E_NAME     AS NAME    HEADING 'EMPNAME';
   ITEM  SALARY     AS $999999;
   ITEM  ADDRESS    AS A20;
```

In this very brief survey of NOMAD2, we did not even touch on many interesting features of the language. In particular, NOMAD2 contains a data dictionary, a large number of functions (including ones for statistical analysis), many other powerful report-writing capabilities, branching and looping constructs, screen-formatting commands, extensive graphics, locking commands for concurrent use, as well as interfaces with programming languages like COBOL, FORTRAN, PL/I, and Assembler. Recently, EZNomad, a screen-driven version of NOMAD2, was introduced, as were interfaces with several major database systems and a menu-driven data dictionary.

12.4 dBASE III PLUS

Since 1980, many database systems have been written and marketed for microcomputers. These systems, for all practical purposes, do not have the storage capabilities of database systems on mainframes and minicomputers, and typically they have few, if any, features for security, integrity, recovery, or concurrency. However, they do have components that make them easy to use for people who are not computer professionals, and their cost is minuscule in comparison to the database systems on larger computers.

One of the most popular database systems for IBM and compatible microcomputers is marketed by Ashton-Tate and is called dBASE III PLUS. dBASE III PLUS has its origin in dBASE II, a database system written for 8-bit microcomputers in 1980. dBASE II was later implemented for IBM and compatible microcomputers; then it was expanded, revised, and released in 1984 under the name dBASE III. We deal with the latest version, dBASE III PLUS, which was released in 1986. However, most of our discussion of dBASE III PLUS is applicable to dBASE III also, since the core dBASE language is the same for both; dBASE is a combination of a database language and a programming language. At the end of the section, some of the new capabilities which are present only in dBASE III PLUS will be indicated.

We will use the database schema from Figure 4.3.2(a) for our example. It should be noted that dBASE uses a dot as the prompt in interactive

FIGURE 12.4.1
dBASE Queries

(a) Print the name and salary of every employee.

```
LIST NAME, SALARY
```

(b) Print the department name, name, and salary for each employee whose salary is greater than $25,000.

```
LIST DNAME, NAME, SALARY FOR SALARY > 25000
```

(c) Print the department name, name, and salary for each employee whose salary is greater than $25,000. Present the result in ascending order on salaries.

(*i*)
```
SORT TO SALORDER ON SALARY
USE SALORDER
LIST DNAME, NAME, SALARY FOR SALARY > 25000
```

(*ii*)
```
INDEX ON SALARY TO SALIND
USE EMPLOYEE INDEX SALIND
LIST DNAME, NAME, SALARY FOR SALARY > 25000
```

mode, so that the user writes statements after the dot. We start by creating the schema. Each table is created separately by a CREATE statement, which consists of CREATE followed by the name of the table. Then the user is prompted for writing the attributes, called field names, and their data types. dBASE allows the data types C for character, M for memo, N for numeric, L for logical, and D for date. The width of each character and numeric variable must also be indicated. (The memo data type is used for long character strings.) After a table is created, the user is prompted to place data in the table, but is not required to do so.

Let's assume now that the DEPT, TASK, EMPLOYEE, and STATUS tables have already been created and exist with data as in Figure 4.3.2(b). (We abbreviate DEPARTMENT to DEPT because of the dBASE limitation of file [table] names to eight characters.) Figure 12.4.1 shows statements written in dBASE for some of the queries in Figure 12.1.1. We assume that the EMPLOYEE file has previously been opened by the USE EMPLOYEE statement. These examples use the LIST verb to see the results on the screen. With the LIST statement, a projection is performed by listing the projected attributes, separated by commas; a selection is obtained by writing a condition after FOR. Two solutions are shown for listing items in order in part (c). In the first case, we sort the table on SALARY to obtain a new table, SALORDER. In the second version, we create an indexing on SALARY and then use the table in the indexed order. In most cases, indexing is preferred over sorting because it is much faster.

FIGURE 12.4.2
dBASE Queries Involving More Than One Table

(a) Combine and print all department and task information.

```
SELECT 2
USE TASK
SELECT 1
USE DEPT
JOIN WITH TASK TO DEPTTASK FOR DNAME = TASK->DNAME;
   FIELDS DNAME, LOCATION, MANAGER, TASK->TASKNO,;
   TASK->TASKNAME
SELECT 3
USE DEPTTASK
LIST
```

(b) Print the names of all employees in the Engineering department who have completed a task.

```
SELECT 1
USE STATUS
SELECT 2
USE EMPLOYEE
COPY TO ENG FIELDS SSNO, NAME FOR DNAME = 'Engineering'
SELECT 3
USE ENG
JOIN WITH STATUS TO RESULT;
   FOR STATUS->ST = 'Completed' .AND.;
   SSNO = STATUS->SSNO;
   FIELDS NAME
SELECT 4
USE RESULT
LIST
```

Figure 12.4.2 shows the first two queries, involving two tables each, written from Figure 12.1.2. In dBASE, two tables cannot be active at the same time in one area. Ten areas are available, and an area is selected by using the SELECT statement. In example (a), the TASK table is opened in area 2 and the DEPT table in area 1. Then a new table, DEPTTASK, is created by performing the join. Attributes from a table in another area must be prefixed using the area number or table name followed by an arrow. The semicolon is used to indicate the continuation of the statement on the next line; otherwise, each line represents a statement. In example (b), first a subtable is obtained by projecting on SSNO and NAME and selecting on the condition DNAME = 'Engineering'. This table is joined with the STATUS table while the selection involving the condition on the ST value is being done. We can see that dBASE retrieval is based on the relational algebra.

We next consider updates and moving around in the database. Insertion is achieved by using either APPEND or INSERT. In both cases, the user is prompted to add values for the attributes in the most recently accessed table. APPEND places the new row at the end, while INSERT places the new row at the current row location (thereby moving all records up by one location). In dBASE, each row is identified by a number, which is displayed along with the row. In particular, we can request to see the fifth row by writing LIST RECORD 5, and the next three rows by writing LIST NEXT 3.

The DELETE command marks the current row for deletion. Alternately, we can write a DELETE to mark one or more rows based on a condition for deletion, as shown in part (a) of Figure 12.4.3. The PACK command is used to carry out the actual deletion of the marked records. Two examples of REPLACE, which modifies the current or selected rows, appear in parts (b) and (c). Then, in part (d), the user checks to see the salaries of the employees in the Sales department if they obtain a 5% raise.

A structured programming language is also included with dBASE. For this reason, variables, called memory variables, are available for value assignment. Branching is accomplished by the IF . . . ELSE . . . ENDIF

FIGURE 12.4.3
dBASE Updates

(a) Delete the rows from the STATUS table with social security number 111-11-1111.

```
USE STATUS
DELETE FOR SSNO = '111111111'
PACK
```

(b) Modify the status of task 1 in the Engineering department for social security number 111-11-1111 to 'midway'.

```
USE STATUS
REPLACE ST WITH 'midway' FOR DNAME = 'Engineering';
   .AND. SSNO = '111111111' .AND. TASKNO = 1
```

(c) Add $1000 to everyone's salary in the Service department.

```
USE EMPLOYEE
REPLACE SALARY WITH SALARY + 1000 for DNAME = 'Service'
```

(d) Print the names and new salaries of the employees in the Sales department if they are all given a 5% raise.

```
USE EMPLOYEE
LIST NAME, SALARY * 1.05 FOR DNAME = 'Sales'
```

and the DO CASE . . . ENDCASE statements. Loops are set up by DO WHILE . . . ENDDO. Procedures are written in a command file; to execute a procedure, write DO followed by the file name. A procedure may call other procedures, with parameters, much like in a standard programming language. The RETURN statement is used to return control to the calling procedure.

Included in dBASE are the standard functions AVERAGE, COUNT, and SUM, as well as various other mathematical and character string manipulations functions. Also, dBASE contains an interactive report writer. Margins, line spacing, and page width can be set, and subtotals and headers requested. A data dictionary is available by using commands such as DIR for the names of the tables, DISPLAY MEMORY for displaying the (memory) variables, DISPLAY STATUS for showing information about the currently active tables, and DISPLAY STRUCTURE for showing the structure of the table in use. There are also many commands for setting system parameters, such as SET PRINT ON to send output to the printer and SET DEFAULT TO . . . to set the default disk drive.

We end our discussion by briefly describing some of the features available in dBASE III PLUS, but not in dBASE III. Applications Generator is a menu-driven program which can be used to create dBASE programs and to design reports. Screen Painter is a menu-driven program for creating screens. Several new commands and functions add programming capabilities to the dBASE language. Additional types of files are also available. A view file represents a programming environment: it may contain fields, files, and relationships between files. A catalog file can be used to group related files, such as views, indexes, reports, and queries, which pertain to some application.

dBASE III PLUS can be used in a local-area network environment. Within such a network, users may share files, programs, and I/O devices, such as printers. The language, dBASE ADMINISTRATOR, is an extension of dBASE; it contains concurrency control and security commands and additional utilities. Concurrency control is achieved by locking. Security is established through the optional PROTECT program: it provides for passwords, file and field access, and data encryption.

12.5 Lotus 1-2-3

Since its introduction in 1983, Lotus 1-2-3 has become one of the most popular business software packages for IBM and compatible microcomputers. 1-2-3 is a system that is based on the spreadsheet model, but—unlike many other spreadsheet packages—also contains database and graphics capabilities. 1-2-3's user assistance features, via menus and prompts, have been an important factor in its popularity. In this section, we consider the relationship between spreadsheets and databases primarily via 1-2-3. We do not discuss 1-2-3's graphics aspects.

A **spreadsheet,** called **worksheet** in 1-2-3, is a table, like a table in a database. For a spreadsheet, however, the elements in a column are not required to have the same data type. A spreadsheet example appears in Figure 12.5.1. The rows are numbered starting at 1, and each column is labeled by a letter combination, starting with "A". A spreadsheet in 1-2-3 (Release 2) may have up to 8192 rows and 256 columns. Except for small spreadsheets, at any time only a portion of the spreadsheet can be seen on the screen; in our examples, we show all the nonblank entries. Note that column A contains a character string, "Year", in rows 1 and 8, numbers in rows 3, 4, 5, 6, 9, and 10, and is blank for the other rows. In rows 3−6 there are certain numerical relationships between columns: E is C + D, F is B − E, and H is a percentage of F based on G.

Each row-column location is called a **cell.** Commands exist to move a cell at a time and to get to a cell by its location. The width of a cell may be changed, and the display format within a cell may be modified. The advantage of a spreadsheet system is its flexibility of allowing any type of element in a cell and its provision for the automatic calculation of formulas. The value for the cell E3 is obtained as C3 + D3, which is the sum of the values of the two numbers immediately to the left of the cell. We may store this formula in the cell as + C3 + D3 (we start with + to avoid confusion with a label), but 1-2-3 presents the *value* of the formula to the user. Since E4, E5, and E6 are obtained in the same way, the same formula can be copied to be used there. For E3, 1-2-3 interprets C3 and D3 in the formula as addresses relative to cell E3, so for E4 the same formula is interpreted as C4 + D4. With such formulas in the cells, 1-2-3 automatically recalculates the values if a cell in a formula is changed. Thus, if C3 is changed, that change is reflected in E3 and any other cells dependent on C3, possibly indirectly, such as by depending on E3.

A **range** is a rectangular area in the spreadsheet. It is represented by the positions of its highest left and lowest right cells. In particular, B3..H6 is a range which represents the numerical values concerning

FIGURE 12.5.1
A Spreadsheet

	A	B	C	D	E	F	G	H ...
1	Year	Sales	Salaries	Other	Total	Gross	Tax	Net
2				Expenses	Expenses	Profit		Profit
3	1982	107500	38150	42336	80486	27014	25%	20260.5
4	1983	82675	39414	43005	82419	256	25%	192
5	1984	102454	32100	48575	80675	21779	25%	16334.25
6	1985	133516	48320	57849	106169	27347	25%	20510.25
7								
8	Year	Item	Cost					
9	1985	Computers	13262.50					
10	1985	Supplies	2611.30					
.								
.								
.								

profit calculation. A8..C10 is another range; this one contains labels as well as numerical information. 1-2-3 allows the manipulation of a whole range by moving it, erasing it, copying it, and storing it. Some functions work on entire ranges; for example, @SUM(B3..C6) calculates the sum of all the items in the range. A range can be named and also easily changed. Every cell, by itself, can also be treated as a range.

Now let's consider the database capabilities of 1-2-3. It is easy to construct a table in a spreadsheet, because the spreadsheet has a tabular format. In fact, we can store a whole database in a spreadsheet, where each table is a range, if the database is not larger than the spreadsheet. The first row of each such range contains the attributes, and the rest of the rows contain the rows of the table. Within this framework, it is easy to add a column to a table and to update a table. For example, a row of the table can be deleted by making it a range and deleting its values from the spreadsheet.

The Data Query command is used for projection and selection. This command involves three ranges: the input range, the criterion range, and the output range. The input range contains the original table. The output range is used for projection: we place the projected attributes there. The criterion range contains the selection criterion. Figure 12.5.2 illustrates a use of the Data Query command.

In Figure 12.5.2(a), the input range is A3..D10 (based on the EMPLOYEE table in Figure 4.3.2(b)), the first criterion range is F2..G3, another criterion range is F8..F10, one output range is A13..C13, and the other output range is F12..G12. In the case of an equality comparison, the actual value is placed under the attribute; for other comparisons, the location of the first value in the table is indicated. For the first criterion, D4 contains the first Salary value in the table. Thus, the first selection criterion is the condition Dname = 'Sales' AND Salary > 25000. The second selection criterion is the condition Dname = 'Service' OR Dname = 'Engineering', as a disjunction is indicated by separate rows. Figure 12.5.2(b) shows the result of applying the Data Query command twice, once for each criterion. 1-2-3 enters the result in the spreadsheet below the attributes in the output range.

The example in Figure 12.5.3(a) illustrates another possibility for a criterion. Here the criterion range is G1..H2. The condition E2>C2 selects those rows for which Profit85 is greater than Profit83. The other condition, C2>C1, compares values between two rows: it selects those rows whose Profit83 value is greater than the previous row's Profit83 value. This condition is automatically satisfied for the first row, since a label, like Profit83, is assigned the numerical value 0. The criterion is a conjunction of these two conditions. We show the result in Figure 12.5.3(b). The logical operators, #NOT#, #AND#, and #OR#, may also be used for writing compound conditions.

So far we have dealt with the Extract operation for the Data Query command. The Unique operation is like Extract, but it eliminates dupli-

FIGURE 12.5.2
Queries in 1-2-3

(a) Before

```
|-------------------------------------------------------------------------
|          A          B          C          D    E    F             G
|    |---------------------------------------------------------------------
| 1|                Employee   Table
| 2|                                                  Dname         Salary
| 3|Dname          Ssno       Name       Salary       Sales         +D4>25000
| 4|Engineering    111111111  Smith L    25000
| 5|Engineering    222222222  Rogers C   30000
| 6|Sales          333333333  Bailey D   27600
| 7|Sales          444444444  Rivers F   21070
| 8|Sales          555555555  Smith L    31280       Dname
| 9|Service        777777777  Davis D    20050       Service
|10|Service        888888888  Wood J     22075       Engineering
|11|
|12|                                                  Ssno          Name
|13|Ssno           Name       Salary
```

(b) After

```
|-------------------------------------------------------------------------
|          A          B          C          D    E    F             G
|    |---------------------------------------------------------------------
| 1|                Employee   Table
| 2|                                                  Dname         Salary
| 3|Dname          Ssno       Name       Salary       Sales         +D4>25000
| 4|Engineering    111111111  Smith L    25000
| 5|Engineering    222222222  Rogers C   30000
| 6|Sales          333333333  Bailey D   27600
| 7|Sales          444444444  Rivers F   21070
| 8|Sales          555555555  Smith L    31280       Dname
| 9|Service        777777777  Davis D    20050       Service
|10|Service        888888888  Wood J     22075       Engineering
|11|
|12|                                                  Ssno          Name
|13|Ssno           Name       Salary                  111111111     Smith L
|14|333333333      Bailey D   27600                   222222222     Rogers C
|15|555555555      Smith L    31280                   777777777     Davis D
|16|                                                  888888888     Wood J
```

cate answers. The Delete operation removes the selected rows from the table. Finally, the Find operation can be used to go through all the rows of the table which satisfy the criterion, one at a time. 1-2-3 also has various statistical functions to calculate the variance and standard deviation, in addition to the usual count, maximum, minimum, sum, and average for selected rows. The Data Sort command is used to sort a table on one or two columns in either ascending or descending order.

We can see that 1-2-3 provides the usual database functions for a single table. However, 1-2-3 and the other spreadsheet systems do not have a join operation to combine information in tables. Let's see how the join could be added to tables stored in a spreadsheet. If both tables were stored in the same spreadsheet, as in Figure 12.5.4, then we would need two input ranges, a criterion range and an output range. In our example, the input ranges are A2..C5 and A9..C14, the criterion range is E1..E2 (the label is immaterial), and the output range is A16..E16. We could

FIGURE 12.5.3
Another Query in 1-2-3

(a) Before

```
|------------------------------------------------------------------------------
|        A         B         C         D         E      F      G         H
|    |-------------------------------------------------------------------------
| 1 |Region  Profit82  Profit83  Profit84  Profit85         Profit83  Profit85
| 2 |1        105460     87500    106580    134750           C2>C1     E2>C2
| 3 |2         44570     56000     58590     75000
| 4 |3         66390     61580     84000     82350
| 5 |4        126000    134000     97500    131550
| 6 |5        133500    146000    151535    175050
| 7 |
| 8 |         Region    Profit83  Profit85
```

(b) After

```
|------------------------------------------------------------------------------
|        A         B         C         D         E      F      G         H
|    |-------------------------------------------------------------------------
| 1 |Region  Profit82  Profit83  Profit84  Profit85         Profit83  Profit85
| 2 |1        105460     87500    106580    134750           C2>C1     E2>C2
| 3 |2         44570     56000     58590     75000
| 4 |3         66390     61580     84000     82350
| 5 |4        126000    134000     97500    131550
| 6 |5        133500    146000    151535    175050
| 7 |
| 8 |         Region    Profit83  Profit85
| 9 |         1          87500    134750
|10 |         3          61580     82350
|11 |         5         146000    175050
```

specify projections in the output range and selections in the criterion range. If the two tables were not in the same spreadsheet, then we would have to combine the two spreadsheets first; in fact, 1-2-3 has a File Combine command to do just that.

Additionally, both the union and subtraction operations could be implemented within the spreadsheet framework, thereby yielding all the operations of the relational algebra. In particular, the union operation (without checking for repetition) could be performed by just moving a range and using File Combine, if necessary. Note that for all database operations, including selection, it is possible that the original table and the result together do not fit into a spreadsheet. But this problem is more likely to occur for binary operations on large tables.

Another approach for combining databases and spreadsheets is to have connections between a database system and a spreadsheet system. In Chapters 4 and 6, we discussed some aspects of the ORACLE relational database system which uses SQL. ORACLE offers the SQL*Calc spreadsheet system, which is very similar to 1-2-3. But SQL*Calc allows a user to enter an SQL command into a cell, just as if it were a formula. Such an SQL command must refer to a database in ORACLE. In this way, a user can obtain data from a database, then manipulate it in spreadsheet mode, and use the calculations in the spreadsheet to update the database.

FIGURE 12.5.4
Hypothetical Join Operation in a Spreadsheet

(a) Before

```
| ------------------------------------------------------------------------
|            A              B              C          D          E
|   | ----------------------------------------------------------------------
| 1|                   Department Table                          Location
| 2|Dname              Location        Manager                   +A3=+A10
| 3|Engineering        12              Simon L
| 4|Sales              5               Johnson M
| 5|Service            10              Williams B
| 6|
| 7|
| 8|                   Task Table
| 9|Dname              Taskno          Taskname
|10|Engineering        1               micro
|11|Engineering        2               math
|12|Engineering        3               stat
|13|Sales              4               big sale
|14|Service            5               fixit
|15|
|16|Department.Dname Location          Manager    Taskno    Taskname
```

(b) After

```
| ------------------------------------------------------------------------
|            A              B              C          D          E
|   | ----------------------------------------------------------------------
| 1|                   Department Table                          Location
| 2|Dname              Location        Manager                   +A3=+A10
| 3|Engineering        12              Simon L
| 4|Sales              5               Johnson M
| 5|Service            10              Williams B
| 6|
| 7|
| 8|                   Task Table
| 9|Dname              Taskno          Taskname
|10|Engineering        1               micro
|11|Engineering        2               math
|12|Engineering        3               stat
|13|Sales              4               big sale
|14|Service            5               fixit
|15|
|16|Department.Dname Location          Manager    Taskno    Taskname
|17|Engineering        12              Simon L    1         micro
|18|Engineering        12              Simon L    2         math
|19|Engineering        12              Simon L    3         stat
|20|Sales              5               Johnson M  4         big sale
|21|Service            10              Williams B 5         fixit
```

Most spreadsheet systems available at this time run on microcomputers and contain few, if any, database operations. Spreadsheet systems also tend to be limited by the maximum size of the spreadsheet. The size must be limited because the active spreadsheet is stored in memory during processing. (This problem is increasingly alleviated by the availability of extra memory.) On the other hand, active tables for database systems need not be stored in memory; thus, dBASE III PLUS, for instance, allows up to one billion rows per table with up to 128 attributes. However, the great flexibility inherent in the spreadsheet model, using formulas based on entry locations, allows for automatic calculations that are not so easily implemented in a database system.

As we saw earlier, all the database operations could be performed within the spreadsheet framework. But databases can be stored more efficiently in a database system, because the database system can take advantage of the table definitions in the schema for storage and during database processing. The great flexibility inherent in the spreadsheet model becomes a disadvantage in dealing with large databases. Also, it would probably be more difficult to implement integrity constraints and security features in a spreadsheet system than in a database system. At present, spreadsheet systems do not or only minimally deal with these topics or with other concerns such as concurrency.

12.6 Some Other Database Systems

In the first eleven chapters of this book, we stressed concepts rather than specific systems. However, we did discuss some aspects of certain database and related systems such as IMS, DB2, ORACLE, Prolog, micro-PROLOG, IDM, Intellect, and Delta. In the first five sections of this chapter, we briefly considered some features of five additional systems: QBE, INGRES, NOMAD2, dBASE III, and Lotus 1-2-3. In this section we discuss even more briefly the database oriented products of four software companies: Computer Corporation of America (CCA), Information Builders, Micro-rim, and Software AG. At the end of the section, we indicate some of the recent trends in database products and expected future developments.

CCA's database system, MODEL 204, runs on IBM mainframes. CCA, like many other database system vendors, actually provides a family of products integrated with MODEL 204. For example, PC/204 is used to send data between a MODEL 204 database and an IBM or compatible PC for spreadsheet processing with a program like Lotus 1-2-3, in both directions. PC/204 is a menu-driven system which, among other things, guides the user to specify and format data from the database into a spreadsheet.

CCA also markets WORKSHOP/204, which is an integrated set of programs used for application development. Some of the component programs in WORKSHOP/204 are DEVELOPER, USER LANGUAGE, PAINTER, and DICTIONARY. DEVELOPER is a menu-driven application generator. USER LANGUAGE is a fourth-generation programming language that can be used for both batch and interactive processing, and which allows the user to perform database creation and maintenance on-line. PAINTER is a screen formatting program for USER LANGUAGE. DICTIONARY is the data dictionary which contains descriptions of the data and the users. In particular, USER LANGUAGE programs are directly documented in DICTIONARY. There are actually two dictionaries: a dictionary for each file and a data dictionary, DICTIONARY/204, for the entire system. The latter contains entities which may include files, fields, programs, reports, forms, and personnel.

The more recently introduced PC/WORKSHOP is an extension of the WORKSHOP/204 environment; it allows users to write applications on the PC in USER LANGUAGE. Additionally, CCA provides an integrated set of programs, called the Intelligent Information Center, which includes some of the products we already mentioned, and a communications package, PROD/NET.

The database structure in the MODEL 204 DBMS is closely related to the relational model. There are no pointers between files; the connections are by value only. An index may be created on any field of the file. Most index updates are deferred so as not to slow down database processing too much. Fields have variable lengths and data type declarations are optional. Several data compression techniques, such as not storing nulls and leading or trailing blanks, are used. A file may be organized in entry order, or by hashing, or by sorting. If the entry order is used, then each new record is placed in the next available location. Hashing on the key field allows for very efficient retrieval. Sorting on a key field allows the efficient retrieval of records in order. MODEL 204 lets the user modify the file structures by adding new fields and changing indexes dynamically.

USER LANGUAGE is the data manipulation language for MODEL 204. Selection is performed by the FIND ALL RECORDS WHICH (FD) statement. Indexed access to records is obtained by the FOR EACH VALUE (FRV) statement, usually in association with a range of values. A join between two files is set up manually by the nested loops method: an FD statement in one file is issued and a FOR EACH RECORD IN (the first file) statement is used to set up the nested loop for the second file. USER LANGUAGE contains a SORT statement for sorting records on any number of fields. It also contains report-writing capabilities, including facilities for page breaks, titles, headings, footings, and other types of formatting. USER LANGUAGE contains the standard built-in functions; additional mathematical functions are available in MATH PACK. A PROMPT statement can be used to write application programs that set up a screen and prompt the user of a program. The update statements are STORE, ADD, DELETE, and CHANGE.

Thus, USER LANGUAGE is a fourth-generation procedural language, as it contains the standard looping and branching constructs as well as database query and report-writing capabilities. However, host language interfaces to FORTRAN, COBOL, PL/I, and Assembler language are also available. MODEL 204 procedures are programs which can be stored for later use. Additionally, MODEL 204 contains various recovery, security, and performance monitoring utilities. Recently, two new programs have been announced: TEXT/204 and PICTURE/204 can store and retrieve documents and images, respectively.

Next we consider FOCUS, a fourth-generation language, introduced in 1975 and marketed by Information Builders. FOCUS is available for IBM mainframes, DEC minicomputers, and, as PC/FOCUS, for various microcomputers. FOCUS has interfaces to several database and file systems, including ISAM, IMS, ADABAS, and SQL/DS, so that it can be used as a query language and report writer not only for files set up specifically for FOCUS, but also for files existing under other systems. FOCUS interfaces with FORTRAN, COBOL, and Pascal through procedure calls. A package for statistical analysis, which prompts the user for parameters, is included in FOCUS. A graphics subsystem is available to plot graphs such as bar charts, pie charts, line charts, and scatter diagrams. A spreadsheet called FOCCALC, which is integrated with FOCUS, is also available. An interesting feature of FOCUS is the LET statement, which allows the user to substitute one word for another word or phrase; this way, the language can be restructured for foreign languages or specialized terminology.

FOCUS has features that allow its files to be designed in a relational, hierarchic, or network manner. A hierarchic structure is obtained by defining a segment (file) type to have a parent. However, the hierarchy need not be traversed by starting at the root; it is possible to define a view so that any segment may be a starting point. For such a view, the rest of the hierarchy is modified by placing the entry segment at the top and transforming its parent to be its child, possibly in a recursive manner. Virtual files may be set up by using cross-referenced segments. For this purpose, the actual files must be indexed so that the cross-referencing can use the index values. By cross-referencing, it is possible to set up a network structure.

FOCUS contains the join operation for manipulating a database in a relational manner; however, the join can also be applied to segments within a hierarchy. There are two commands for the join, JOIN and MATCH. We consider only MATCH here because of its interesting options and because JOIN requires that one of the files be indexed. The options deal with the handling of matching and nonmatching records. As in Section 12.3, we write J for the join, A for the first file including elements not matched in the second, and B for the second file including elements not matched in the first. With the operation applied on the matching attribute, the options, with the corresponding sets, are as follows: OLD-NOT-NEW is $A - J$, NEW-NOT-OLD is $B - J$, OLD-NOR-NEW is $(A - J) \cup (B - J)$, OLD-AND-NEW is J, OLD is $A \cup J$, NEW is $B \cup J$, and OLD-OR-NEW is $J \cup A \cup B$.

FOCUS also contains various report-writing capabilities. Four verbs generate detail lines: PRINT, used for regular printing, LIST, used for printing with each row numbered, COUNT, and SUM. Projection is performed by listing the attributes (fieldnames); selection is done using an IF clause. Facilities exist for grouping objects, working with expressions, and obtaining various row and column totals and subtotals. Printing commands are available for starting a new page, skipping lines, underlining, and writing column headings, among others.

We end our discussion of FOCUS with a few additional concepts and features. For updates, the records are usually found by matching certain attribute values. The PROMPT and VALIDATE commands are available for prompting a user and validating the reply. By using the phrase ON MATCH REJECT, it is possible to enforce a key constraint. It is also possible to combine related files before updates by making them the children of a SYSTEM file. The Dialogue Manager allows a person to enter values of variables during the running of a program. FIDEL (Focus Interactive Data Entry Language) is a screen manager which facilitates setting up forms. Recently, FOCUS VISION, an image storage and retrieval system, was announced to be used as an additional package to PC/FOCUS.

Next we consider the microcomputer database system R:base 5000, which is marketed by Microrim, Inc. The older versions were called R:base 4000 and R:base 6000. R:base 5000 runs on IBM PC and compatible microcomputers. R:base 5000 is a single-user system; however, R:base 5000 Multi-User is available for local-area networks; it contains additional security and locking features also. Recently, a new version, R:base System V, was announced. This new version can be used for local-area networks, and it has various improvements over the previous versions, including faster sorting and better form creation.

R:base 5000 contains a menu-driven application development system, called Application Express. The Application Express system can be used to define tables, columns, menus, simple data entry screens, and simple reports. For more complex applications, the R:base 5000 commands must be used. The system contains relational database operations called SELECT, INTERSECT, UNION, PROJECT, APPEND, JOIN, and SUBTRACT, which, among them, include all the operations of the relational algebra. However, the names are not used in the same way as we defined them in Section 4.2 for the relational algebra. For example, INTERSECT is more like a join than an intersection, and SELECT can be used both for selection and projection. JOIN can be used with various comparisons as a theta-join. UNION takes the join and adds rows for nonmatching rows, while SUBTRACT retains only the nonmatching rows. Database updates are performed by ENTER, EDIT, and CHANGE.

FORMS is a command used for setting up a form; REPORTS is the command for creating a report format. Both of these commands work with menus and prompts. Data validation is provided by the RULES command, which allows the user to state a rule, such as AGE>12, that all AGE values must satisfy when entered into the appropriate table. The standard built-in functions may be accessed by using COMPUTE. Indexing may also be performed for fast access. R:base 5000 contains a built-in programming language also, including the IF and WHILE statements. The PROMPT statement can be used within a program to prompt the user of the program.

Besides the usual built-in operations like GREATER THAN, attribute selection criteria include EXISTS, FAILS, and CONTAINS, the last of which is used for character string matching. An interactive HELP command and a Data Dictionary, which contains the structure of the database, are also available. The EXPAND and REMOVE COLUMN commands can be used to change the structure of a table. The data types are DATE, TIME, DOLLAR, INTEGER, REAL, and TEXT. The SET POINTER command positions a pointer to a particular row in a table. The pointer can be moved to the next row by means of the NEXT command.

Separate enhancements to R:base 5000 include CLOUT, a natural language interface, and a host language interface to FORTRAN and Pascal. CLOUT contains a built-in vocabulary of commonly used words and phrases in database queries. The user can add new words and phrases to the vocabulary interactively. The system also tries to correct spelling errors automatically.

The last software firm we consider is Software AG of North America. Here we briefly summarize some aspects of its ADABAS database system, which runs on IBM mainframes and VAX minicomputers. The data model for ADABAS allows no pointers between records; in that sense, it is closely related to the relational model. However, a file may have a hierarchic structure as multiple-valued fields are allowed. The optional data compression algorithm removes leading zeros and trailing blanks, and compresses null values to a single character. Each record has a unique logical address, called internal sequence number, which is mapped by an address converter to a physical address. Indexing is used heavily in ADABAS, both on fields and on portions and combinations of fields. Hashing is another method used for data storage and access. External views are available and called userviews.

ADABAS includes the usual types of utilities for loading, recovery, auditing, and tuning. A locking mechanism is used for concurrency control; there are security features at the file, field, and value levels. Several languages are associated with ADABAS: ADASCRIPT+, ADACOM, ADAMINT, and NATURAL. ADASCRIPT+ is an end-user language for writing queries and updates, and for generating reports. ADACOM is a batch report generator. ADAMINT is the data manipulation language which can be embedded within host language statements in Assembler, COBOL, FORTRAN, and PL/I to ADABAS. Recently, AdaSQL was announced; this system will translate SQL commands to ADABAS. Both ADASCRIPT+ and ADACOM (and NATURAL, which we discuss next) can be used to interface with an interactive Data Dictionary.

NATURAL is a fourth-generation language that can be used with ADABAS and some file systems. As such, it can be used as a query language and report writer; features for the latter include line and page control, breaks, titles, tab and spacing, underlining, duplicate suppression, and default formats. As a programming language, it does computations, has built-in functions, does sorting, has variables, and contains branching, looping, and subroutine call statements. Additional features include validity checks, facilities for setting up menus, and a MAP command for screen generation. The compiler is interactive and catches syntax errors during program writing. Super Natural is a menu-driven version of NATURAL.

As we consider the various database and related systems on the market, several trends are evident. Many mainframe and minicomputer database vendors have developed several related products including the database system and a fourth-generation language. Database design tools are beginning to appear. Much effort has gone into making database systems easier to use; that is one reason for the strength of the relational model. Some software firms have either rewritten their database packages to make them relational or have provided a relational frontend. SQL has become the primary language for mainframe and minicomputer relational database systems. However, several hierarchic and network systems are very efficient and will continue to be used.

Since the beginning of the 1980s, microcomputers have proliferated, with increasing capabilities and more powerful software. Database systems on microcomputers have become quite sophisticated; as they are becoming multi-user oriented, transaction and concurrency processing as well as security features are being added. Microcomputer-based software has increased the popularity of menus and interactive help facilities. Distributed database systems at all hardware levels are becoming important.

The recent emergence of artificial intelligence as an important aspect of databases will have far-reaching consequences. Natural language query interfaces are becoming popular. The combination of (1) the reasoning and flexibility involved in artificial intelligence–based systems with (2) the accessing methods and other features of database systems for handling large volumes of data—as exemplified in the emerging expert database systems—provides a powerful capability. The Fifth Generation and related projects are trying to make the promise of a truly intelligent computer system, with vast amounts of information interconnected over a global network, into reality.

12.7 Exercises

12.1 Write QBE queries and updates for Exercise 4.2.

12.2 Write QBE queries and updates for Exercise 4.3.

12.3 Write QBE queries and updates for Exercise 4.4.

12.4 Write QBE queries and updates for Exercise 4.5.

12.5 Write QBE queries and updates for Exercise 4.6.

12.6 Write QUEL queries and updates for Exercise 4.3.

12.7 Write QUEL queries and updates for Exercise 4.4.

12.8 Write QUEL queries and updates for Exercise 4.5.

12.9 Write QUEL queries and updates for Exercise 4.6.

12.10 Write a NOMAD2 database schema for the database of Figure 4.6.2.

12.11 Using your answer to Exercise 12.10, write NOMAD2 queries and updates for Exercise 4.3.

12.12 Write dBASE queries and updates for Exercise 4.4.

12.13 Write dBASE queries and updates for Exercise 4.5.

12.14 Write dBASE queries and updates for Exercise 4.6.

12.8 Guide to Further Reading

QBE is discussed in [1.1] Chapter 11, [1.2] Chapter 14, [1.3] Chapters 2 and 4, [1.4] Chapters 6 and 10, and [4.2] Chapter 15. The QUEL language is presented in [1.4] Chapter 8 and the whole INGRES system is described in [12.4]. The standard reference for NOMAD2 is [12.2], for dBASE III PLUS is [12.1], and for Lotus 1-2-3 is [12.3]. In general, the reference manuals are the standard guides for all systems. User groups for these popular systems are another source of information.

[12.1] Ashton-Tate. *Learning and Using dBASE III PLUS*. Ashton-Tate, 1985.

[12.2] D&B Computing Services. *NOMAD2 Reference Manual*. D&B Computing Services, 1983.

[12.3] *Lotus 1-2-3 User's Manual*. Cambridge, Mass.: Lotus Development Corp., 1983.

[12.4] Relational Technology Inc. *Introduction to INGRES*. Berkeley, Calif.: Relational Technology Inc., 1984.

Index